# A MEASURE
# OF GREATNESS

PUBLICATION OF THIS WORK
WAS ASSISTED BY A GENEROUS
DONATION FROM BHP

# A MEASURE OF GREATNESS

## THE ORIGINS OF THE AUSTRALIAN IRON AND STEEL INDUSTRY

E. M. Johnston-Liik
George Liik
R. G. Ward

MELBOURNE UNIVERSITY PRESS

Melbourne University Press
PO Box 278, Carlton South, Victoria 3053, Australia

First published 1998

Text © Edith Mary Johnston-Liik, George Liik, Robert George Ward 1998
Design and typography © Melbourne University Press 1998

This book is copyright. Apart from any use permitted under the *Copyright Act 1968* and subsequent amendments, no part may be reproduced, stored in a retrieval system or transmitted by any means or process whatsoever without the prior written permission of the publisher.

Designed by Lauren Statham, Alice Graphics
Typeset by Syarikat Seng Teik Sdn. Bhd., Malaysia in 10.5pt/13.5pt Plantin Light
Printed in Australia by McPherson's Printing Group

National Library of Australia Cataloguing-in-Publication entry

Johnston-Liik, E. M. (Edith Mary).
 A measure of greatness: the origins of the Australian iron and steel industry.
 Bibliography.
 Includes index.
 ISBN 0 522 84721 8.
 1. Steel industry and trade—Australia—History. I. Ward, Robert George. II. Liik, George. III. Title.
338.476691420994

For Niina Liik
and in memory of Ann Ward

# FOREWORD

TODAY AUSTRALIA has an iron and steel industry which is internationally recognised as one of the most efficient in the world. This has not always been so. The first Australian blast furnace was only operated to produce pig-iron in 1863, some 500 years after pig-iron was first produced in Europe.

Australia thus began its iron and steel-making industry in competition with a well-established industry overseas, with enormous problems arising from the lack of skilled workers and experienced management, from the absence of good road and rail communications, and sometimes with the opposition of governments.

It is a credit to the pioneers of the industry that they persevered and progressively overcame the often unique difficulties of working in a new land. At least twelve blast furnaces were built and failed in the last century, and it was not until Charles Hoskins took over the bankrupt iron and steelworks at Lithgow in 1908 that a viable industry emerged. This was followed by the opening of the Broken Hill Proprietary Company's steelworks at Newcastle in 1915, which quickly proved that a properly funded and well-managed steelworks could be profitable.

BHP was fortunate in having two outstanding managers in Guillaume Delprat, who recognised the superiority of the South Australian iron ore deposits and orchestrated the early development of the Newcastle steelworks, and Essington Lewis, who carefully steered and consolidated the company's steel-making activities following World War I and gave BHP the financial strength to absorb the Australian Iron and Steel Company's steel operations at Port Kembla in 1935.

## FOREWORD

This merger of AIS with BHP allowed the development of a single co-ordinated industry which served Australia well during its period of relative isolation during World War II. Since then BHP has continued to expand its steel-making activities and has also used its financial strength to develop other resource-based industries. I am proud to have played a role in this growth of a national industry.

This story is well worth retelling, not simply as the record of the growth of an industry, but as an account of the way in which technology and the attitudes of management, unions and governments have changed over the years.

Although BHP has been envied by many, it is the habit of some Australians to be suspicious of the actions of large companies. Perhaps this book will help to instil in Australians a little more pride in companies such as BHP which have grown from modest beginnings and can now compete successfully with large companies overseas.

>Sir Ian McLennan
>Past Chairman
>The Broken Hill Proprietary Company Limited

# CONTENTS

| | |
|---|---|
| Foreword by Sir Ian McLennan | *vii* |
| Acknowledgements | *xv* |
| Conversions | *xvii* |
| INTRODUCTION | *1* |
| 1 BLUE SKY | *4* |
| 2 THE INTERNATIONAL IRON RUSH AND AUSTRALIAN REALITIES | *26* |
| 3 AN AMERICAN ENTREPRENEUR AT LITHGOW | *54* |
| 4 A PYRRHIC VICTORY | *69* |
| 5 TOWARDS A SOCIAL CONTRACT | *90* |
| 6 PROMETHEUS BOUND | *110* |
| 7 NATIONALISATION OR PRIVATE ENTERPRISE? | *129* |
| 8 INTERSTATE AND INTERNATIONAL | *152* |
| 9 THE NEWCASTLE STEELWORKS | *183* |
| 10 MANAGEMENT AND LABOUR | *209* |
| 11 A NEW WORLD | *227* |
| 12 CRISIS AND SURVIVAL | *254* |
| 13 THE AUSTRALIAN IRON AND STEEL COMPANY | *280* |
| 14 A NATIONAL INDUSTRY | *304* |
| Notes | *325* |
| Bibliography | *344* |
| Index | *350* |

# ILLUSTRATIONS

Unless otherwise indicated, illustrations and their references numbers are from BHP Archives, Melbourne.

| | |
|---|---:|
| Significant locations in the early development of the Australian iron and steel industry | *xviii* |
| Commemorative casting from the opening of the Fitz Roy Iron Works<br>Courtesy B.T. Loton, Chairman, BHP Co. Ltd | 8 |
| Ironmaking centres on the Sydney coal basin | 10 |
| Enoch Hughes<br>*Australasian Ironmonger*, 1893, vol. 12, no. 8 | 13 |
| Steam-driven helve hammer in use at the Fitz Roy Iron Works<br>*Illustrated Sydney News*, 18 February 1869 | 20 |
| Rolling mills at the Fitz Roy Iron Works<br>*Illustrated Sydney News*, 18 February 1869 | 21 |
| Fitz Roy Ironworks in its heyday<br>Courtesy Wingecaribee Shire Council; BHP Archives MTG 2 | 23 |
| Ruins of the Fitz Roy Iron Works<br>MTG 4 | 23 |
| The British and Tasmanian Charcoal Iron Company's blast furnace plant during construction<br>Courtesy Queen Victoria Museum and Art Gallery, Launceston, Tasmania | 40 |
| Official opening of the British and Tasmanian Charcoal Iron Company blast furnace<br>*Illustrated Australian News*, 10 July 1876 | 41 |
| British and Tasmanian Charcoal Iron Company's blast furnace plant<br>*Illustrated Australian News*, 10 July 1876 | 43 |
| Remains of the Ilfracombe Iron Company blast furnace near Beaconsfield, Tasmania<br>*BHP Review*, Spring 1969, vol. 45 | 44 |

ILLUSTRATIONS

The Derwent Iron Company blast furnace 45
*Australasian Sketcher*, 10 May 1879

Official opening of the trial blast furnace at Lal Lal 48
*Illustrated Australian News*, 28 November 1878

Ironstone quarry, Lal Lal 49
Annual Report of the Secretary for Mines (Victoria), 1910; courtesy Forests Commission Victoria

Lal Lal blast furnace 50
Annual Report of the Secretary for Mines (Victoria), 1910; courtesy Forests Commission Victoria

Ruins of the Lal Lal blast furnace 51
Annual Report of the Secretary for Mines (Victoria), 1910; courtesy Forests Commission Victoria

James Rutherford 55
Courtesy Mitchell Library, State Library of New South Wales, P1/R

Eskbank ironworks blast furnace 63
Courtesy La Trobe Picture Collection, State Library of Victoria, H 15317

William Sandford 70
*Australasian*, 25 May 1907

Eskbank Iron and Steelworks 74
R. I. Jack and A. Cremin, *Australia's Age of Iron*, Oxford University Press, 1994

Official opening of the William Sandford & Co. Ltd. blast furnace, Lithgow 81
*Australian Hardware and Machinery*, 1 June 1907

Banner of the New South Wales branch of the Federated Ironworkers' Association of Australia 105
Courtesy Sydney branch of the Federated Ironworkers' Association of Australia

Charles Henry Hoskins 116
Hoskins Black Book, PM 1320; BHP Archives P800

The 27-inch reversing mill at Eskbank 118
LG 79

Charles Hoskins on the morning after the riot 136
Cecil Hoskins, *The Hoskins Saga*, 1968; courtesy Mr Donald G. Hoskins

The blast furnace plant at Lithgow 145
Hoskins Black Book, BHP Archives PM 1320, LG 29

Charging ingots into a coal-fired reheating furnace at Eskbank 148
LG 53

Teeming steel from an 80-ton ladle into two-ton ingot moulds, Eskbank 149
Hoskins Black Book, BHP Archives PM 1320

Manual quarrying operations at the initial Iron Knob quarry 158
IK 178

Guillaume Daniel Delprat 161
P 191

John Darling 165
P 175

David Baker 167
P 24

## ILLUSTRATIONS

| | |
|---|---|
| Opening the blast furnace taphole, BHP Newcastle steelworks<br>N 1911 | *188* |
| Frontispiece from *Souvenir of Opening the Newcastle Steel Works*<br>N 2035 | *190* |
| Tour of inspection after the official opening of the BHP Newcastle steelworks<br>N 953 | *191* |
| Ingots being stripped from their moulds, BHP Newcastle steelworks<br>N 1248 | *194* |
| Leslie Bradford<br>P 88 | *197* |
| Bloom being rolled from an ingot in the bloom mill, BHP Newcastle steelworks<br>N 726 | *200* |
| Workers returning to Newcastle from the steelworks<br>*Souvenir of Opening the Newcastle Steel Works;* N 2034 | *215* |
| Mill operators controlling the bloom mill at BHP Newcastle steelworks, 1920<br>N 1958 | *225* |
| Essington Lewis<br>Photograph by Athol Shmith; BHP Archives P 393 | *228* |
| Harold Gordon Darling<br>P 166 | *237* |
| Ingots being teemed at BHP Newcastle steelworks<br>N 1700 | *255* |
| The 3-high plate mill, BHP Newcastle steelworks<br>N 812 | *260* |
| Scrap being delivered by a works locomotive for charging to open-hearth furnaces, BHP Newcastle steelworks<br>N 972 | *264* |
| The BHP ship *Iron Warrior* at the Newcastle steelworks wharf<br>Photograph by Frank Hurley; N 1563 | *267* |
| Charging molten blast furnace iron into an open-hearth furnace<br>Photograph by Frank Hurley; N 968 | *270* |
| Aerial view of the BHP Newcastle steelworks<br>N 1887 | *278* |
| Arthur Sidney Hoskins<br>Cecil Hoskins, *The Hoskins Saga*, 1968; courtesy Mr Donald G. Hoskins | *281* |
| Cecil Harold Hoskins<br>P 303 | *282* |
| The steam locomotive 'Eskbank', AIS steelworks<br>PK 0206 | *286* |
| The *Iron Warrior* unloads the first ore to be delivered at the AIS steelworks jetty, Port Kembla<br>PK 2199 | *287* |
| AIS steelworks, Port Kembla, No. 1 blast furnace plant under construction<br>PK 0267 | *288* |

ILLUSTRATIONS

| | |
|---|---|
| Cast-iron pipes being made in the spun pipe plant at AIS steelworks, Port Kembla<br>PK 1088 | *289* |
| Pig mill at AIS steelworks, Port Kembla<br>PK 1102 | *291* |
| The AIS 40-inch bloom mill, Port Kembla<br>PK 1981 | *295* |
| The 36-inch structural mill at AIS steelworks, Port Kembla<br>PK 1723 | *296* |
| Inside the cast house of No. 1 blast furnace, AIS steelworks, Port Kembla<br>PK 0781 | *299* |
| The 10/13-inch merchant mill, AIS steelworks, Port Kembla<br>PK 1951 | *301* |
| Electric shovel loading blasted iron ore in the Middleback Ranges<br>IM 106 | *305* |
| Reheating furnaces and roll stands in the sheet mill at AIS steelworks, Port Kembla<br>PK 1020 | *309* |
| The 3-high Lewis mill at the sheet mill, AIS steelworks, Port Kembla<br>PK 1097 | *310* |
| The first coke being pushed from the by-product recovery coke ovens at AIS steelworks, Port Kembla<br>PK 0401 | *319* |
| Construction work on the No. 2 blast furnace, AIS steelworks, Port Kembla<br>PK 0047 | *319* |
| The AIS steelworks, Port Kembla<br>Photograph by Arthur Cratchley; 1669/3 | *323* |

# ACKNOWLEDGEMENTS

IN THE COURSE OF WRITING this book we have received advice, encouragement, and information from many people in the steel industry and the academic world. It is only possible to acknowledge a small fraction of these people and to give general thanks to the unnamed majority.

From the outset we received great support and encouragement from senior people at BHP. Sir James McNeill, then Chairman, gave us access to the company's archives which proved invaluable. This enabled the book to include previously unpublished material, both written and photographic, which helped to make it particularly authoritative in matters affecting BHP. We also benefited greatly from talks with various BHP chairmen, notably Sir Ian McLennan, Sir Colin Syme and Brian Loton. Bob Ward acknowledges a particular debt to Sir Ian, who passed to him an enthusiasm for the steel industry which has enlightened his life.

Many other BHP officers have made valuable inputs and helped form our understanding of the ethos of the steel-making part of the company. Particular among them have been Bill Burgess, Gus Parish, Bob Coulton, John Norgard, John Sullivan and Jack Anderton. We are also grateful to Donald Hoskins, who gave us his perspective of the steel industry pre-World War II, and of the role of the Hoskins family.

In academia we have also received much encouragement and assistance. Professor Geoffrey Blainey of the University of Melbourne generously gave the venture his blessing in an area which could be considered his own, and Professor Ian Jack of the University of Sydney gave us valuable background on the Lithgow blast furnaces. We would also like to

## ACKNOWLEDGEMENTS

thank Professor Jim Piper and the Research Unit of Macquarie University for their encouragement, Cora Duim and Linda Paoloni for their assistance in typing various drafts of the manuscript, and Professor Frank Clarke for many interesting discussions on how the industry impinged on the general development of Australian history.

Narelle Crux and Helen Smith, successive BHP corporate archivists, and the staff of BHP Archives have been most welcoming of our activities, and especial thanks are due to Alana Birchall and Ayala Deasey whose work respectively in organising the illustrations and collecting the references was heroic. Invaluable help was given by Dr J. J. Johnson and Damian Cash whose work as research assistants did much to provide the foundations of this book.

The publication of this book would not have been possible without generous financial assistance from BHP for which we gratefully thank both John Prescott and Peter Laver.

# CONVERSIONS

Contemporary units of measurement have been used to retain the historic reality of nineteenth- and early twentieth-century costs, weights and distances.

| | |
|---|---|
| 1 inch | 2.54 centimetres |
| 1 foot (12 inches) | 30.5 centimetres |
| 1 yard (3 feet) | 0.91 metres |
| 1 mile | 1.61 kilometres |
| 1 acre | 0.405 hectares |
| 1 pound | 0.45 kilograms |
| 1 hundredweight (112 pounds) | 50.8 kilograms |
| 1 ton (2240 pounds) | 1.02 tonnes |

### CURRENCY

On 14 February 1966 Australian currency changed from pounds, shillings and pence (£, s, d) to dollars and cents at the rate of £1 = $2.00. Twelve pence made up one shilling; twenty shillings made up one pound.

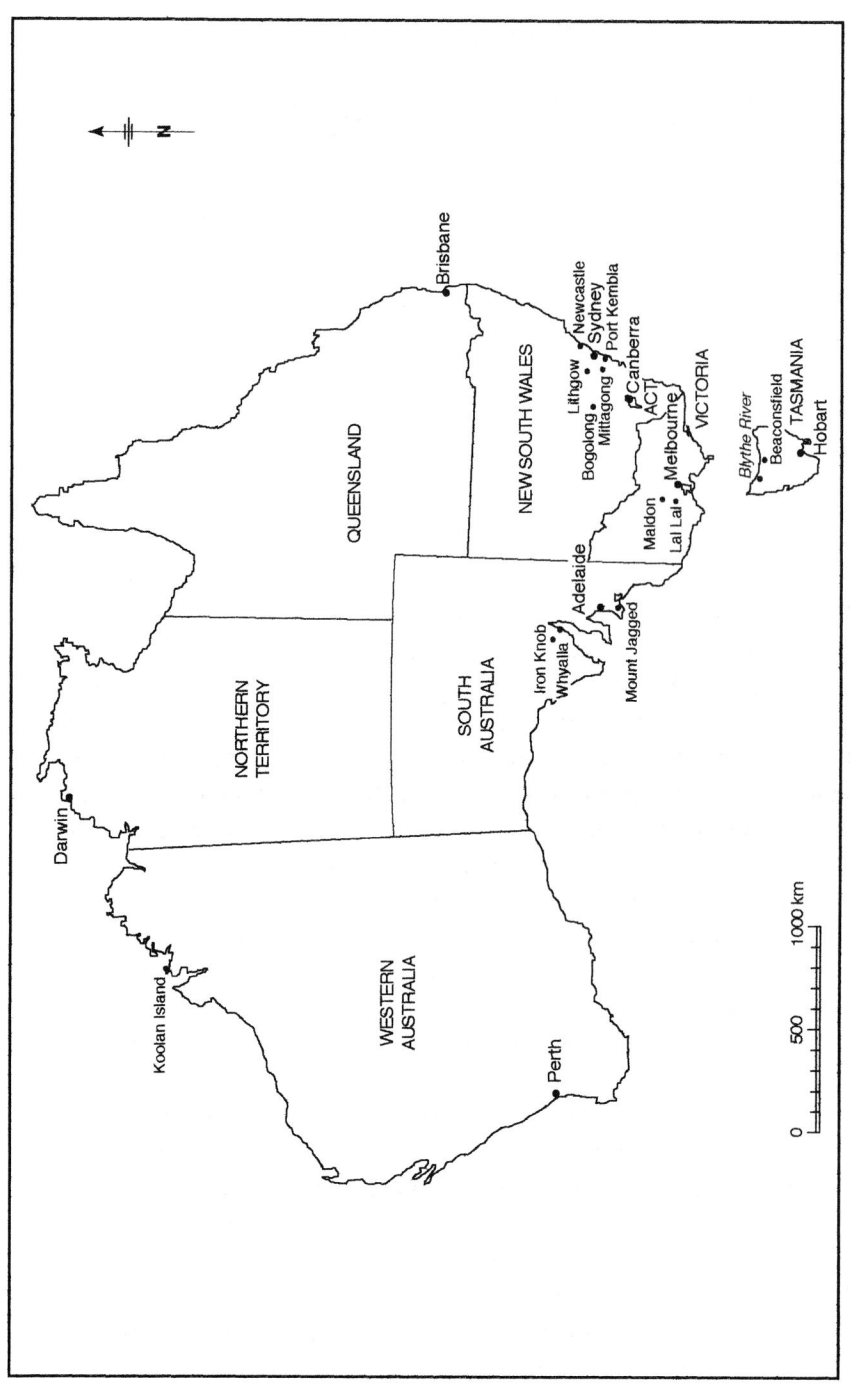

Significant Australian iron and steel industry locations.

# INTRODUCTION

FROM THE TAPPING of the early blast furnaces to the relentless flow of solid steel from the computer-controlled continuous caster, the production of iron and steel has been an awe-inspiring drama unmatched by any other industrial activity. The early iron-makers of the industrial revolution required enormous reserves of physical strength for their arduous and often dangerous work. This combined with the uncertainty of human control over the pyrotechnics of molten metal gave the early industrial manufacture of iron its reputation as a heroic industry. More significantly, the manufacture of iron and steel is a team industry, with all this implies in human relationships. It was no accident that the iron and steel industry bred the pioneers of modern management, who focused attention on the organisation of human, as well as the acquisition of material capital. Therein lay the sources of the infant Australian industry's strengths and weaknesses in a democratically orientated society as yet unsure of its priorities and goals.

Securing a viable iron and steel industry has been a prominent ambition in the economic programme of many developing nations, especially in the second half of the twentieth century. Their leaders often saw the industry as a measure of economic independence and national prestige. But its premature establishment has frequently proved a severe drain on inadequately developed national resources and unsophisticated internal markets. In the heady political atmosphere of the nineteenth century many Australian entrepreneurs shared this desire for self-sufficiency and also suffered its disappointments. It was their vision of first colonial and then commonwealth independence that sustained more than half a century of uncertain starts and short-lived hopes.

Few major industries exist in isolation from global commercial realities, and the remote Australian iron and steel industry was no exception to this rule. Thus, while local colour has understandably dominated descriptive accounts in the past, their use for analytical historians and economists has been often limited by leisurely antiquarian methodologies. Above all local determinants need to be set against a galaxy of international influences the importance of which has been steadily enhanced with the perspective of time.

The first tentative attempts were made to create a native industry based on local resources in the late 1840s, when the entire population of the six Australian colonies was well under half a million. Nearly seventy years later in 1915, when BHP's Newcastle works came into production, the Commonwealth of Australia's population, approximately 5 000 000, was still too small to provide a cost-effective home market. Fortunately, it was an increasingly urbanised population with urban requirements for transport, piped water and gas; moreover, the rural sector made traditional demands for the agricultural machinery essential for productive farming added to which was the exceptional demand for wire-fencing in the long battle against the rabbit and the dingo. Most significant of all was the need for an infrastructure for the newly federated states and here the demand for railway lines provided an elastic and seemingly inexhaustible market. But all of this was given a new meaning by World War I, which gave the infant industry protection and its subsequent dynamic.

Mistakes in the selection of technology and industrial location were made regularly by expatriate ironmakers whose ideas had been conditioned by their English experience. Overdue emphasis was frequently placed on locating blast furnaces close to deposits of iron ore with little regard to the availability of water, fuel and limestone, or of convenient transport and access to markets capable of absorbing their products. These errors of location were often compounded by problems associated with inadequate capital resources and operational or managerial skills. Some enterprises were bedevilled by intractable impurities in the iron ore which rendered the iron unusable. But, although the nineteenth-century ironmakers made almost every conceivable error in their rush to create an industry, they did provide a foundation on which a viable Australian steel industry could be developed in the twentieth century.

The imperial connection itself played a multiplicity of roles. Early developments in the Australian iron industry were influenced not only by the material and political requirements of the individual colonies, but also by the state of the industry in Great Britain and the demands of Britain's overseas markets, both imperial and world-wide. But the isolation of the Australian continent also ensured that the development of an iron and steel industry would, in the first instance, be dependent upon the requirements of the home market. This complication brought it into conflict with currently accepted commercial beliefs and established trade patterns, for iron had been a staple export of the mother country, which in return imported primary products and minerals. Somewhat perversely this trade regime had for a while coexisted with the dogma of the Victorian age: free trade. In the colonies the contradiction could not be ignored for long, however, for a new capital- and labour-intensive industry required protection, both in view of the high cost of labour and the need for a 'catching-up' period to establish the requisite skills and experience. The early Australian ironmasters had already been hampered by distance and isolation in their attempts to 'catch-up' when the important technological advances of the 1850s abroad exacerbated their disadvantages. To make things worse the discovery of gold and other minerals in the early 1850s temporarily depleted the already slender workforce. Nevertheless, the long-term benefits of the gold rush soon followed, bringing greatly increased local capital and attracting a future labour force for many ironworkers who came to join the gold rush later returned to their old trade.

However, the problems which remained were deep-seated. At every point of crisis the way in which such problems were tackled reflected the tensions produced by the twin fundamentals of imperial decline and global industrial readjustment. These included the capital intensity of the industry, the high cost of labour and the often confrontational relationship between labour and management. At the same time commercial fine-tuning to meet supply and demand was difficult for the home market was restricted and subject to dumping, while the export market was volatile and distance inevitably made planning of any kind extremely complicated if not hazardous.

# 1
## BLUE SKY

IN THE HARSH COMMERCIAL world of the nineteenth century the viability of *primary* iron production became increasingly dependent upon economies of scale and corresponding markets. The ill-fated attempts to establish iron and steel industries in South Australia, New South Wales, Tasmania and Victoria reflected these general preconditions. In most cases the failure of the early industries was so rapid and so absolute that it left little archaeological or even documentary evidence. Thus it is uncertain exactly how many attempts at establishing an iron-smelting business utilising local raw materials were made during the last century, but it seems quite likely that there were at least a dozen scattered through the eastern and southern colonies. It is probable that the earliest attempts were made in South Australia, where private interest and official support combined to encourage the development of the colony's resources.

London, the centre of imperial finance, saw many publications designed to interest prospective investors in colonial ventures. Among these was a book by Francis Dutton called *South Australia and its Mines*, published in 1846. It extolled the purity of South Australian iron ores, samples of which on testing had produced excellent iron. Dutton commented that, although the colony lacked coal, there were abundant supplies of wood and 'the iron produced from wood smelting is the best of all'.[1] Two years later G. B. Wilkinson's *South Australia: its Advantages and Resources* was published. He reported that in 1847 a blacksmith at Mount Barker 'had produced metal of an excellent quality' from local ores, concluding that 'if only we had cheap and plentiful labour the iron ores of the colony would be a source of inexhaustible wealth'.[2]

In September 1847 the *South Australian Gazette and Colonial Register* had announced that 'smelting works' had been erected near Cox's Creek, in the vicinity of the modern town of Hahndorf.[3] Little was heard of this enterprise until April 1849 when, after a government report on the great abundance of iron ore in the region, a prospectus was issued for the Forest Iron Smelting and Steam Sawing Company, which was to take over the timber sawing and iron smelting previously carried on in Cox's Creek 'for some time'. The prospectus stated that twenty-five people were employed and the 'smiths have commenced working by night as well as by day'. This suggests there might have been a blast furnace as that would have required shift work, although it is more probable that the works produced wrought iron direct from iron ore in some form of hearth furnace. The plant listed included a 60-horsepower steam engine, an extensive assortment of sawmill equipment, engineers' and blacksmiths' tools and implements, and timber carriages and bullocks.[4]

The Board of the new company was impressive. All were men of substance with common mercantile, mining and banking interests in the colony. Many directors were members of the Legislative Council, including Alexander Lang Elder, John Hart, John Baker and William Younghusband. The capital of the company stated as £10 000 in £5 shares and a deposit of ten shillings was required for each share option. The company's objectives were 'to saw timber for building and other purposes, and to manufacture various descriptions of iron and steel'.[5] Obviously they did not succeed in their iron-smelting operation as nothing more is known about the company.

The government of South Australia was aware of the market link between railways and a local iron and steel industry. Although the railway age did not materialise until the 1860s, a decade earlier the Legislative Council had formed a Select Committee to investigate the expediency of establishing a general system of railways throughout the colony.[6] The Select Committee included Hart, Baker and Elder, all directors, or former directors, of the Forest Iron Smelting and Steam Sawing Company. In 1851 the Legislative Council received a petition asking that they request the Lieutenant-Governor to offer a premium of £500 for the first five tons of good quality pig-iron to be made in South Australia. The petition for the £500 bonus originated with George Hamilton, who the Select Committee called as an expert witness. He was stated to be experienced in public works in England and in the British iron industry. Sir Henry Fox Young, the Lieutenant-Governor, accepted the recommendation of the Legislative Council that a premium 'be paid to the person who before the 1st July next, shall produce 5 tons of the best sample iron, manufactured from ore found in the Province, of a quality equal to the best imported iron made at a cost not exceeding the cost of the best imported iron of a similar quality'. The £500, claimable from 31 March 1852, was added to the 1852 estimates. A commission was appointed to decide upon the expected claims, but, in the event, the £500 remained unclaimed.[7]

The best documented of the early attempts to produce iron were those made at Mittagong in New South Wales. Here persistent efforts were made to smelt iron on a commercial basis between 1848 and 1876. Thereafter plans for resurrecting the ironworks continued for a further thirty-four years. The works at Mittagong provide a microcosm of the technological history of the iron industry. Between 1848 and 1870 three companies, with confusingly similar names, worked successively on the site. The first, the Fitz Roy Ironworks, was formed in 1848. This company had three name changes. Reorganised in 1851 it was renamed the Fitz Roy Iron Mining Company. Then, in 1854, a private bill passed by the New South Wales legislature incorporated it as the Fitz Roy Iron and Coal Mining Company. This first enterprise was finally dissolved in 1857. The second, the Fitz Roy Iron Company 1857–65, was incorporated in 1860 as the Fitzroy Iron Works Company and reincorporated in 1865 as the Fitz Roy Iron Works Ltd, and was finally wound up in 1870. However, in the promising conditions of the early 1870s the third group, an English consortium—the Fitzroy Bessemer Steel, Hematite, Iron and Coal Co. Ltd. made a final attempt to prove the industrial profitability of the site.[8] Parts of the plant, mainly the rolling mills, were in use during the 1880s and an abortive attempt was made to recommence smelting in 1889 by Mr W. Brazenall, a local entrepreneur. The viability of the site was again under consideration in the 1890s.[9] Nothing came of this project.

The existence of iron deposits in the Mittagong area had been known since 1833. In 1848 a consortium of Sydney business men, John Neale, Thomas Holmes, Thomas Tipple Smith and William Tipple Smith, bought 300 acres of land in the vicinity with the intention of establishing an ironworks.[10] They erected a Catalan hearth. Catalan hearths, a form of bloomery, had existed for about a thousand years in southern Europe. They were a traditional preindustrial method of making iron and took their name from the province of Catalonia in north-eastern Spain. Their capacity was small and each charge produced a lump (or loupe) of crude iron weighing up to 350 pounds. No details of this Mittagong furnace are known to exist. It was almost certainly constructed of masonry and iron plates to a European design. The hearth would typically have occupied the corner of a workshop and in appearance it would have resembled a blacksmith's forge-fire, although it would have been deeper, with an open top of about perhaps thirty inches square and an internal depth of perhaps twenty-four inches. Under ideal circumstances furnaces of this kind were known to produce up to half a ton of iron a day.

The temperature of the hearth was vitally important to the success of the operation; this was controlled by blowing a blast of air into the bed of hot charcoal through a single tuyère which passed through the wall of the furnace. This was connected to blowing equipment operated by a steam-driven beam engine outside the workshop. The ore and charcoal were moved around inside the furnace in a hot zone created by the air blast until the iron ore was reduced and the particles of iron were brought together in a spongy lump. This was then hammered to expel liquid slag and to produce a bloom of crude wrought iron. The labour of working the furnace would have been very heavy and particularly arduous in the Australian summer. However, at Mittagong this thousand-year-old technology was used to smelt iron ore until 1864 when a conventional, if already antiquated, blast furnace was blown in.[11]

Technically, the Fitz Roy Ironworks were initially successful; they produced iron of a reasonable quality. They were named after the then Governor of New South Wales, Sir Charles FitzRoy, whose subsequent visit to the site in March 1850 was celebrated by the casting of fifty presentation models of a lion *restant*, the heraldic animal on the FitzRoy family crest. These were cast from from imported pig-iron remelted in a cupola furnace in the works foundry. Cupolas resembled small blast furnaces. Their introduction, in 1794, is attributed to the famous English ironmaster, John Wilkinson. Remelting iron in them produced a more uniform metal and hence better castings.[12] The cupola furnaces at Mittagong resembled stumpy, round chimneys encased in iron plates, perhaps twelve feet high and less than three feet in diameter. Charge materials were fed into the top and a blast of air provided by a small steam-driven engine was blown in near the bottom. This use of an air blast in the Mittagong Catalan hearth and cupola furnaces may have given rise to the incorrect assumption that the first blast furnace in Australia was in operation at Mittagong in 1848.

Iron casting of a lion restant made to commemorate the opening of the Fitz Roy Iron Works by Governor Sir Charles FitzRoy in 1850. Fifty of these souvenirs were presented to guests at the official opening.

The governor's visit reflected and encouraged public interest in the new venture.[13] This was further enhanced when, in the same year, the Fitz Roy works provided the iron for the ceremonial spade used to turn the first sod in the Sydney to Parramatta railway. It was at this time that the Fitz Roy Iron Mining Company was established by deed of settlement. Floated with a capital of £8000 in £5 shares, its shareholders included all of the original syndicate except J. T. Neale and represented both the business and pastoral interests in New South Wales.[14]

Mittagong, like Lithgow, Newcastle and Port Kembla, is on the exposed rim of the New South Wales coalfield. It was ultimately intended to use this coal, but the first smeltings were almost certainly made with charcoal from the abundant local timber. After the Fitz Roy Iron Mining Company was established the directors appointed a Mr Morgan from the Newcastle Coal and Copper Smelting Company to prepare a feasibility study on the commercial potential of the site. The report was favourable, but Morgan drew the directors' attention to a potential fuel problem, emphasising the need to discover a suitable supply of coking coal.[15]

Fuel subsequently proved a serious problem for all of the companies on the site. Not all types of coal provide a coke of sufficient strength to carry the 'burden' of ore and flux when a blast furnace is charged. Thus, although there was coal in the neighbourhood, there was no deposit of suitable coking coal sufficiently near to provide a cheap supply of fuel. Furthermore, the ratio of coal to ore remained high throughout the life of the Fitz Roy ironworks as, despite the innovations made by each successive company, the technology remained antiquated by world standards. In modern terminology, the plant never came close to achieving 'world best practice'.

The local ore deposits which drew the investors to the site in the first place also had problems. At first this was not realised as a government official, J. H. Thomas, twice, in 1855 and 1859, reported favourably on the potential of the venture. He estimated an iron content of 64 per cent averaged over eight assays of the ore. From these assays he concluded that 'the superior richness of this ore, equal at least to any of the most valuable of those of Sweden or North America, would most assuredly secure for it an extensive demand in England for conversion into the finest steel'.[16] Unfortunately, the ore proved to be limonite ($FeCO_3$) and the deposits relatively shallow with an average metallic content of less than 50 per cent, whereas the American and Swedish deposits to which he compared it were of the much more valuable hematite ($Fe_2O_3$) variety.

During the first decade deficiencies in ore proved a less immediate problem than either deficiencies in fuel or management. The small plant initially produced at least 100 blooms until the tilt hammer, used to force out the molten slag from the crude iron made in the Catalan hearth, broke in 1852. This brought smelting to an end. The company then sent its ore to P. N. Russell's foundry in Sydney for treatment.[17] Before this misfortune a number of articles made from Fitz Roy iron had attracted public interest but this enthusiasm had not extended to actual investment.[18]

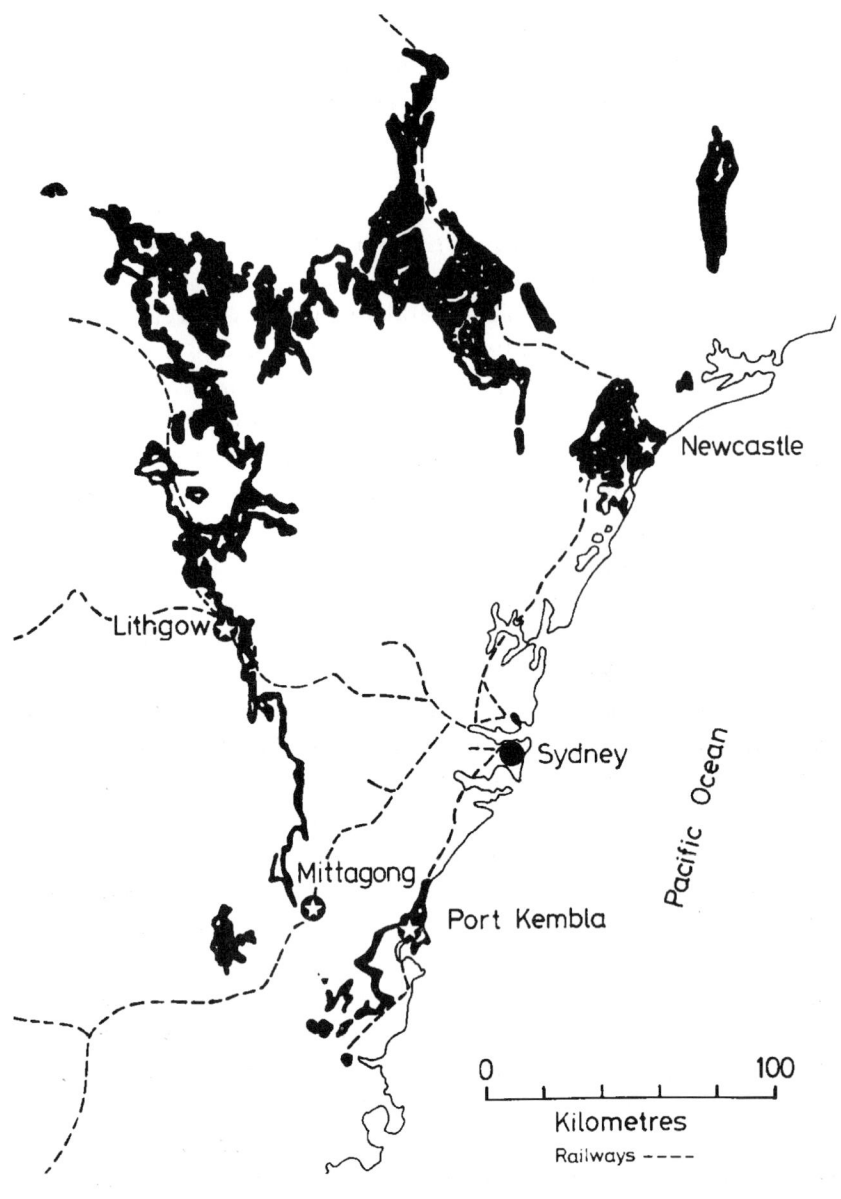

Ironmaking centres on the rim of the Sydney coal basin. Coal outcrops in black.

After the company's incorporation in 1854 the chairman, F. J. Rothery, could only retain corporate liquidity by raising loans totalling £9500. These were secured by a mortgage on the company's property.[19] New plant was ordered to enable the company to attract government contracts for rails. The directors saw a dual advantage in the rapidly expanding railroad. The manufacture of rails would provide a market for their product; the railways would, by providing cheap and easy transport, make other markets available.

By now it was clear that the siting of heavy industry in the bush, remote from its potential markets, was a serious mistake. Goods had to be transported seventy-five miles by bullock carts to and from Sydney over the Hume Highway, then a mountainous dirt track. Presumably memories of the traditional British and European siting of such industries influenced the early Australian entrepreneurs. The choice of similar sites in Britain had usually been influenced by the availability of wood for charcoal, and water to provide power for the machinery; by the end of the eighteenth century canals provided easy transportation. There may have been an unjustified belief in the speedy expansion of the railways and an over-confidence that they would provide a panacea for all problems in communications. Nevertheless, it is probable that that a deeper error of principle underlay the colonists' efforts. The New South Wales businessmen decided that the *proximity* of iron ore to the works was the essential factor in the establishment of the industry. This misconception was to have long and painful consequences for the relocation of an industry once established was not only expensive but socially disruptive.

By April 1856 it was clear that not only was the financial basis of the Fitz Roy Iron and Coal Mining Company inadequate but that it also had managerial problems.[20] Rolling machinery intended for the manufacture of rails had been ordered from England and shipped in January 1856.[21] By June the shareholders were sufficiently concerned to form a committee 'to determine on the best method of removing the machinery from Sydney to the works and of proceeding with the works of the company'. A further investigation into the books and accounts of the company resulted in the directors being charged with mismanagement. The charges involved such activities as illegal meetings, irregularities in the Board minutes and the transaction of business, the bribing of journalists to write favourable reports to attract overseas capital, the purchase of a 'useless' team of bullocks from Mr Holmes (a director) and 'worthless' machinery from Mr Povey (the manager). An assortment of other alleged misdemeanours included misleading the New South Wales Legislative Council on the state of the company's affairs, and the inexplicable 'disappearance' of a load of iron *en route* to Sydney.[22]

The chairman, F. J. Rothery, resigned from the Board shortly after the enquiry began, and before the report was presented. He attempted to foreclose his mortgage on the company's property and was only restrained from this by an *ex parte* injunction brought by one of his former colleagues on the Board.[23] All business at the site stopped and in the ensuing acrimony the shareholders could not even agree to wind up the company. Eventually, early in the following year, 1857, another shareholder, H. W. Johnson, persuaded some of his remaining colleagues to reconstruct the company. The rolling equipment ordered by the previous Board was then installed but, after a trial run in July 1858, lack of capital kept the works idle during the ensuing year.[24]

In 1859 circumstances looked more optimistic. The company received promises of financial support from a group of leading businessmen, including William Terrey, Thomas Chalder and Joseph Cartwright Rossiter. Further encouragement came when the New South Wales government ordered an inspection to ascertain 'the capacity of the works for extensive operations . . . especially as regards the sale of railway bars'. The directors fervently hoped for 'the extension of railway communications which will enable iron to be more cheaply smelted than at present',[25] for British iron could still be imported into Sydney more cheaply than it could be manufactured locally.

By 1859 the Fitz Roy Iron Company's works had become a complex iron smelting and manufacturing centre. Its machinery included a puddling furnace, a 5-ton tilt hammer and there were squeezers to consolidate the white hot balls of reduced iron from the puddling furnace and to press out as much as possible of the entrapped liquid slag. There was a complete set of merchant, railway bar and boiler-plate rollers, driven by a 40-horsepower engine, to roll the blooms into marketable wrought-iron sections after they left the squeezers and tilt hammer. The works also included a Chilean mill for grinding fire clay for brick-making, kilns for firing bricks and lime, and a brass foundry. Although the works were still without a blast furnace, there were two cupola furnaces which could be used to remelt imported pig-iron together with unusable iron from the Catalan hearth.[26]

On 10 August 1858 the *Sydney Morning Herald* had announced that smelting trials of local ore had produced sixteen hundredweight of iron, but this was almost certainly made in a cupola furnace. The same report referred to blast furnace machinery then *en route* from England which included a 100-horsepower blowing engine and boilers. This equipment, from William Fairbairn and Sons of Manchester, had still not arrived at the end of 1859 and there is no evidence that it was utilised until the well-documented 1864 blast furnace was blown in. Nevertheless, by colonial standards, the Fitz Roy works were a significant industrial operation. Despite their unsuitable location, they were comparable in size with many works utilising imported iron, brass and copper then existing in Sydney, Melbourne, Brisbane and Adelaide.

The reconstructed Fitz Roy Iron Company Ltd was finally floated in December 1859, but it failed to attract sufficient public support to make the works operative. However, three years later, the arrival of the Great Southern Railway again revived interest in the possibility of manufacturing iron from local resources, for the track was built of iron imported from Great Britain. A further New South Wales government inspection was then carried out by a Mr Moody. He made an enthusiastic report and the works were leased to a Melbourne businessman, B. W. Lattin. Lattin agreed to make the necessary improvements in return for shares in the company.[27]

Enoch Hughes, 1831–1893, a pioneer of the Australian iron industry. His career included management at the Victorian Iron Rolling Mills (Melbourne), the Fitz Roy Iron Works (Mittagong), the City Iron Works (Sydney) and the Eskbank works (Lithgow).

The ironworks at Mittagong now reached the zenith of its chequered career. In 1863 Lattin appointed a comparatively recent migrant from England, Enoch Hughes of the Victorian Iron Rolling Mills, Melbourne, to manage the works. Born about 1831 at Dudley in Staffordshire, Enoch Hughes was to play a prominent role in the erection of early Australian blast furnaces. His father has been variously described as a farmer and a brick manufacturer. These changes of occupation were common in early nineteenth-century England. Hughes arrived in Australia on 1 January 1858 having previously 'served upwards of twenty years with two of the principal firms in Staffordshire, viz BBH Bloomfield Iron Works; Mr Tipton and G. Jones, of the Chillington and Springvale Iron Works, near Wolverhampton, whose service I left for Australia'.[28] He and a Mr Marks imported the machinery for the Victorian Iron Rolling Mills. The opening of the rolling mills in July 1860 caused considerable public interest and the *Argus* duly emphasised their significance both because 'these are the first mills of the kind which have been opened on this side of the line [equator], and, as an earnest of the development in these colonies of that manufacturing excellence so peculiarly the attribute of the mother country'.[29] The works were acclaimed as the first to roll iron in Australia, but this is incorrect. They were definitely preceded by the earlier Fitz Roy Ironworks. A few years later the mills were sold as a going concern to Messrs Cairns and Amos.

Both of the firms that Hughes had worked for in England operated blast furnaces and the area he came from specialised in sheet-rolling. Hughes was both energetic and optimistic. Shortly after his arrival at Mittagong he declared that he could successfully compete with the English iron exporters and the New South Wales government decided to place a contract with the Fitzroy Iron Works for 50 tons of rails per week for eight months and 120 tons thereafter.[30]

By July 1863 the refurbished works were working to capacity; there were 'about 70 men employed upon the various works which comprise the coalmines, the quarries, and the firebricks. A tramway of two and a half miles connects the works with the coal mines . . . a blast furnace and engine house are in the course of erection the masonry of which is of a very substantial character'.[31] Trams (carts on rails) were used to move goods short distances to and within the works. They were usually drawn by horses or pushed by humans.

The Mittagong blast furnace was a massive structure of dressed Hawkesbury sandstone. It had a heavy square base surmounted by a round shaft strengthened with iron hoops and lined with fire-bricks.

Overall the shaft was 46 feet high and 13 feet 8 inches at its maximum internal diameter. It was open at the top where it was charged with iron ore, limestone and fuel—either coal, coke or charcoal. Barrows carrying the charge were pushed along a tramway across a bridge joining the furnace top to the adjacent hillside. Here the charge materials were stored and measured into barrows as required by the furnacemen.[32] The ruins of a similar layout can be seen at Lal Lal near Ballarat in Victoria.

Contemporary blast furnace production depended largely on the rate at which air could be blown into the bottom of the furnace. At Mittagong the blowing machinery consisted of two horizontal steam engines each rated at 25 horsepower. The piston of each engine was directly coupled to the piston of a large, cast-iron blowing-cylinder 4 feet in diameter with a stroke of 3 feet 4 inches. The action was smoothed by coupling the pistons to a large flywheel. Steam provided the energy for early industrial enterprises and large engines were also in use in flour mills, engineering works and for pumping water from gold mines. The Mittagong blowing engine was one of the larger pieces of machinery in Australia at this time. The air blast, with a pressure of $4^1/_2$ pounds per square inch was connected to three tuyères. These were located in three of the four arches in the square base of the furnace. The fourth arch gave access to the forepart of the furnace hearth where, following nineteenth-century practice, the iron would be tapped between two and four times a day.[33]

Enoch Hughes supervised the building of both the Mittagong blast furnace and later the very similar first blast furnace at Lithgow. In 1872 he publicly claimed to be 'the pioneer and erector of the whole of our colonial ironworks' on the strength of his part in erecting the Victorian Rolling Mills in Melbourne and the City Iron Works in Sydney in addition to the Fitz Roy blast furnace. If only by his own set values, Hughes was probably correct. At the time Hughes left England about 125 blast furnaces were operating within twelve miles of his birthplace, the Staffordshire town of Dudley where the industry had been so long established that the area was known as the Black Country. Many features typical of furnaces in this area are recognisable in the Fitz Roy furnace. In his account of the generic Black Country furnace Dufrénoy, in *Voyage Métalurgique en Angleterre*, published in Paris in 1837, gives an illustration of a cold blast furnace with a massive square base surrounded with a slightly tapering round stack that looks remarkably similar to photographs of the Mittagong furnace.[34] The Stanton Ironworks near Nottingham had also started a three-furnace plant in 1846 using blast furnaces almost identical with those at Mittagong.

Unfortunately, Hughes had left England in 1847 at a time when, after many years of stagnation, a great revolution in blast furnace design was underway. The significance of these changes was apparently not appreciated by Hughes. In 1829 J. B. Neilson, of the Clyde Ironworks, Glasgow, had invented a way of heating the air blown into the blast furnace by blowing it through an iron stove fuelled with coal. Shortly afterwards another Scot, John Condie, introduced a method of water-cooling the tuyères. This allowed an increase in the temperature of the blast. Neilson's invention was almost immediately recognised. It trebled the production of pig-iron from the same amount of fuel. As early as 1835 hot blast furnaces were common in Britain. Surprisingly, although the utilisation of hot gas from the furnace had been successfully achieved at the Schopfheim ironworks in Germany in 1832, the further savings resulting from the recovery of blast furnace gas did not become customary in England until after 1850 when George Parry of the Ebbw Vale ironworks in Monmouthshire introduced the bell-and-hopper method of closing the furnace top, a device which is still frequently used today.

All of these inventions and improvements required increasing and continuous capital expenditure if competition was to be forestalled and profits to be maximised. They were also labour-intensive. Increased industrialisation brought far-reaching changes in the organisation of labour and an alteration in the role of the craftsmen as techniques changed and the expanded ironworks required larger numbers of unskilled and semi-skilled workers—a situation which intensified with the advent of steel. The early Australian ironworkers were British migrants many of whom had been most acutely affected by the nature and rapidity of these changes; they brought with them the British traditions of labour and unionism under which they had previously worked.

By the time the Mittagong blast furnace was blown in hot blast had been adopted in the majority of Black Country furnaces and the idea of using top gas for heating boilers and blast stoves was becoming accepted. In furnace construction the heavy masonry or brick construction was being replaced by a light cylindrical 'cupola type' brick stack encased in a wrought iron shell supported by iron columns, allowing easy access to the tuyères and the hearth at the bottom of the furnace. None of these refinements was initially incorporated in the Mittagong furnace, which was essentially out of date before it was blown in on 30 July 1864.[35]

Even before the furnace was blown in the directors began to encounter the financial problems which had plagued their predecessors. In

February 1864 the company borrowed £6000 against a mortgage on its property. By mid 1864 £38 000 had been expended and a further £1550 was recommended to build puddling furnaces.[36] The blast furnace was barely blown in when, in August 1864, Lattin, who had financed most of these improvements in return for shares in the company, surrendered his leases and in the following October severed any active connection with the company. The parting was apparently an acrimonious one as Hughes, who was Lattin's manager, subsequently wrote of the Fitz Roy blast furnace works that 'I had the honour to erect but never to work, a circumstance which is best known to the shareholders'.[37]

Lattin later went bankrupt and it is possible that the directors, who were shrewd men, may have realised the limitations of Hughes's experience in view of the rapidly changing technology of the industry. The furnace, which appears to have operated satisfactorily and made a considerable, if unknown, quantity of acceptable iron, was blown out about the time that Lattin left. Its cold blast and open top would have ensured that the fuel consumption of this first Australian blast furnace was uneconomically high.

In October 1864 the company brought out from England J. K. Hampshire, formerly manager of the Whittington Iron Works near Chesterfield in Derbyshire, to manage and modernise the works. Hampshire converted the furnace to hot blast by installing a pipe stove in which the air blast passed through cast-iron pipes heated by a coal fire before going into the furnace through the water-cooled tuyères.[38] The improved furnace was blown in on 2 May 1865. At the start of the campaign, or production run, the output was quite creditable for a furnace of this type, fuelled by a mixture of coke and coal. In a period of thirty-six weeks from 30 June 1865 smelting averaged 66.5 tons of pig-iron per week.* In one week, 92 tons of iron were smelted. However, as the campaign continued, the furnace became increasingly blocked by accretions or 'scaffolds' on the walls. Production dropped and the furnace, having produced just under 3000 tons of iron, was blown out in April 1866. Improvements in the blast furnace were limited by the size and nature of its original construction.

Early in 1865 some of the iron already made was remelted in Fitz Roy cupola furnaces and on 25 February 1865 the governor, Sir John Young, witnessed the casting of the first of the 54 two-and-a-half-ton cylinders

---

* Pig-iron took its name from the shape of the castings made when the molten iron from the furnace was run into sand moulds, the castings fancifully being considered to resemble a sow with piglets.

required for the Gundagai railway bridge. Thirty-eight years later, J. P. Franki, who had been assistant manager at Mittagong in 1865, told the 1903 Royal Commission on bonuses that 'we then made magnificent iron'.

May and June 1865 marked the peak of iron production at Mittagong. Early in June the *Sydney Morning Herald* described them as follows: 'the works at present erected form a kind of irregular quadrangle; of which the blacksmith's shop and pattern shed form the west side, the air heating apparatus forms the east side, the engine house and the boilers the south, and the hot blast furnace, cupola and moulding-shop form the north side'. On 21 June 1865 the Fitzroy Iron Works Bill incorporated the company with a nominal capital of £60 000 in £5 shares.[39] The ironworks employees had previously lived in slab and bark houses around the works. More assured, the company now viewed the future with optimism and plans were made for an established and properly laid out town. Land was assigned for a Methodist church and 132 plots of land were sold at prices between £70 and £125 each.[40]

Nevertheless, the size and limitations of the blast furnace and other machinery, combined with the high cost of labour in New South Wales, ensured that the Fitz Roy ironworks could not produce iron at less than £5 17s 6d per ton. This compared unfavourably with the price of imported pig-iron then selling on the Sydney market for £5 per ton.[41] Consequently, despite their achievements, on 21 April 1866 the Mittagong works were once again forced to close. It was later admitted in an interview between the directors and Colonial Secretary Parkes that part of the reason for this closure was a lack of confidence between the Board and the manager.[42] It was now obvious that without direct or indirect protection Fitz Roy iron could not compete on the open Sydney market. In May 1867 the company petitioned the governor of New South Wales for support in the form of guaranteeing the interest for a £50 000 debenture issue. The Governor, Sir John Young, refused to commit himself. However, he agreed to lay the petition before the Executive Council, pointing out that it would have to come before New South Wales's 'free trade' parliament.[43]

The Fitz Roy delegation consisted of E. Vickery, J. Frazer, S. Zollner, J. Keep, B. Fredrichs, F. Lasseter, H. C. Burnell, J. J. Moore and the company secretary, J. W. Watkins. Most of these men were involved in various branches of secondary iron manufacture in Sydney. They stressed the importance of the iron industry to the colony. It would generate employment and create new industries; furthermore, government had a direct interest in the cheap production of rails; and finally their security, the works itself, was excellent.[44]

In fact the petition brought the company into direct conflict not only with the free trade convictions of the New South Wales politicians but also with sections of the colony's business community. When the Fitz Roy deputation met the Premier, James Martin, he assured them of his private sympathy, while stating that parliament would be very cautious before it embarked upon so novel a scheme. Indeed members might wonder why the proprietors, wealthy men, could not guarantee the loan themselves. The Colonial Secretary, Henry Parkes, likewise expressed his sympathy. He felt that with proper management the venture would ultimately succeed, but, he pointed out, the management record of the company was far from satisfactory. He also felt that their request would 'rather clash with the principles of free trade which the gentlemen of the delegation were professing'. It was his opinion that 'the less that government interfered with the operations of the people the better'.[45]

The petition was opposed as an 'audacious and impolitic request', which, if granted, would amount to 'the creation of a most unjust, pernicious and damaging monopoly'. The opposing deputation, J. Lippmann, B. Mountcastle and P. R. Holdsworth, opposed the means as much as the ends. They were not anti-protectionist as such, for instance Mountcastle thought that 100 per cent duty on imported iron would be the solution. Holdsworth argued that a tariff was the correct answer, but Lippmann, a Sydney hat manufacturer, protested that it would be unjust to favour iron-making above other colonial enterprises also needing support.

The tariff solution was unlikely to appeal to the Fitz Roy delegation in view of their additional iron-working activities which depended on obtaining pig-iron as cheaply as possible. But the idea of a government guaranteed debenture was another matter. This solution aroused considerable public debate, including discussion in successive issues of the *Sydney Morning Herald* in June 1867. An editorial published on 4 June declared that 'no loan ought to be guaranteed excepting for purely state purposes'. At the same time it suggested that an exception might be made for the industry along the lines of support sometimes given to the farmers when the crops failed.

The quality of the product was not in debate. Fitz Roy iron was endorsed by the large foundry, P. N. Russell & Co. Vickery used girders manufactured from Fitz Roy iron in his Pitt Street building, Vickery's

Chambers, only demolished in the 1930s. Undaunted by set-backs, the directors now leased the merchant and rolling mills to Enoch Hughes. Hughes converted the large stocks of pig-iron into bar and merchant iron. Meanwhile the directors started to explore the market possibilities including the export market to post-gold-rush California.[46]

In order to modify the blast furnace section of the works, the directors attempted to raise more capital from the shareholders. At the same time they appointed a Welsh mining engineer, Thomas Levick, as manager. Levick did not enjoy good health and he remained only eighteen months in Australia. During this time he recognised the inefficiency of fuel utilisation in the plant and its contribution to high production costs. Quite simply, the primitive open-top design of the blast furnace allowed potentially valuable gas to escape and burn at the furnace's charging hole. This, it was observed, 'belches forth from its summit blue sulphurous flame'. Levick closed the top with a bell-and-hopper arrangement similar to that introduced by Parry in 1850 at the Ebbw Vale Iron Company in Levick's native Wales.[47]

By the 1860s the bell-and-hopper arrangement was common in Britain. The bell was an iron cone suspended from its apex, and in its raised

Steam-driven helve hammer in use at the Fitz Roy Iron Works, c. 1869. Iron balls from the puddling furnaces are being hammered into rough blooms.

position it made a seal against a fixed circular iron hopper so that the valuable fuel gas could not escape. This gas passed from the space underneath the bell through a hole in the side of the shaft into a 'downcomer' outside the furnace leading to a gas main which distributed the gas to the hot blast stoves and the steam-raising boilers. The furnace charge of ore, flux or fuel was dumped on the bell and the top gas only escaped when the bell was lowered to drop the charge into the furnace. Despite this expensive refurbishment it was still cheaper to import pig-iron from England where a number of furnaces, for example, the large ones in the Cleveland area, had production rates approaching 100 tons per day.

Meanwhile, Enoch Hughes found that his tenancy of the merchant and rolling mills was uneconomic. He resigned his lease in 1868. Hughes lacked capital, and in the opinion of the *Sydney Morning Herald*, 'had not the full amount of practical knowledge requisite for making the work profitable'. Given Hughes's background and experience in both England and Australia it appears more likely that the economic dice were loaded against him. There were more conveniently situated rolling mills in Sydney and Melbourne. Moreover, Hughes's successors, Bladen &

Rolling mills at the Fitz Roy Iron Works, *c.* 1869. Roughly forged blooms from the hammer are being rolled to sizes required by the wrought iron market.

Co., were equally unsuccessful and likewise relinquished their lease; some idea of the scope of their enterprise can be gauged by the fact that they employed twenty-two men as puddlers, drivers, assistants and labourers. Work on the site then ceased and in November 1869 the Fitz Roy Iron Works Ltd. was dissolved. On 10 January the company's property was auctioned by Richardson and Wrench for the 'mere pittance' of £10 000. It was purchased by John Frazer, one of the shareholders in the defunct company.[48]

The 1870s brought an indian summer to the Fitz Roy ironworks. In 1873 the Fitzroy Bessemer Steel, Hematite, Iron and Coal Co. Ltd. was incorporated in England with a capital of £200 000 in £10 shares. Its Australian subscribers included a number of shareholders who had been prominent in the former company; for instance, John Keep, John Frazer, J. L. Montefiore, Ebenezer Vickery and Simon Zollner.[49] The Board of directors hoped that Bessemer's name would inspire public confidence and financial investment. It is uncertain whether Sir Henry Bessemer actually authorised the company to use his name, although it is unlikely that a company registered in England would have done so without his consent. Certainly he was at this time searching for ores suitable for the steel-making process that bears his name.

Before the late 1850s the commercial production of steel had been limited in quantity and specialised in production. Various methods of hardening and toughening iron had been tried throughout the centuries. In each case the quantity produced was small, its utility limited and its quality often unpredictable. Sheffield in England was the unchallenged leader of the steel trade. Its reputation was largely built on the process invented in 1740 by a Doncaster clockmaker, Benjamin Huntsman. Accurate clocks were vitally important for navigation. In searching for a reliable metal for their manufacture Huntsman discovered the crucible method of making steel. Wrought iron and other materials are melted in a clay crucible in a coke furnace at a high temperature for about five hours. The crucible is then withdrawn from the furnace and the steel cast into moulds. This was a long and a delicate process producing only about 100 pounds of steel in each crucible, and suitable clay for the crucibles was not universally available. This was the situation when, suddenly, in the mid 1850s the manufacture of steel on a large commercial scale became possible with the parallel inventions of Bessemer, Siemens and their English, American, and European contemporaries.

In 1855 Henry Bessemer (1813–98) patented a process which made a new product, mild steel. It was based on the use of air blown through

# 1 BLUE SKY

Fitz Roy Ironworks in its heyday, early 1870s. The blast furnace at centre left is fed by a trestle bridge from a materials shed on the neighbouring hillside. Wrought iron was made in puddling furnaces in the building at centre front, boilers and the blowing engine are located in the buildings at the rear, and pigs and castings were made in the building at left. A heap for calcining ore before use in the blast furnace is visible in the right foreground.

Ruins of the Fitz Roy Iron Works prior to demolition in 1927. Remnants of the trestle bridge and the downcomer (vertical) pipe, which removed gas from the top of the blast furnace to fire the boilers, are visible.

molten blast furnace iron in a 'converter'; this decarburised the iron more effectively and less laboriously than puddling. Moreover, Bessemer's method produced several tons of steel very quickly—in minutes instead of hours. But his early trials ran into considerable difficulties as his method only worked successfully with iron ore that had a low phosphorus content. Furthermore the steel was often brittle with numerous blow-holes.

Some of Bessemer's problems were solved by Robert Mushet (1811–91). Mushet discovered that the addition of spiegel, an alloy of manganese and iron, could be used for the dual purpose of removing the brittleness from the steel and preventing gas bubbles from forming in the ingots. Mushet went on experimenting and produced a variety of alloy steels for tools, in particular tungsten and manganese steels. To make useable steel, phosphorus, which is found in many varieties of iron ore, has to removed in the steel-making process, otherwise it will make the steel brittle. Phosphorus limited Bessemer's choice of ores, and led to his world-wide search for suitable ores and possibly the attachment of his name to the Australian company. The phosphorus problem remained intractable until, in 1879, Sydney Gilchrist Thomas (1850–85) and his cousin Percy Gilchrist succeeded in holding the phosphorus in the slag by using a converter lined with dolomite.

At Mittagong the new company failed to anticipate the short-lived nature of the unusual market demand for iron in the 1870s. Expecting that this demand would continue they spent some £22 536 in refurbishing the works. Their improvements included another pipe stove to increase the temperature of the blast. But, by the time the furnace was once again blown in February 1876 the market had already peaked. Import prices had fallen sharply and the small and antiquated furnace was, despite all attempts to improve it, uneconomical. In addition the furnace had barely been blown in when a shortage of water compelled it to be blown out in March 1876. Smelting was resumed in June and continued until 16 March 1877. Production rates as high as 120 tons per week were claimed for this last campaign, during which the blast furnace produced 3273 tons of pig-iron and the puddling furnaces made 52 tons of merchant iron.[50]

After it was blown out in 1877 the blast furnace stood unused for a further half century; although, in November 1889, the *Australasian Ironmonger* reported that a Mr W. Brazenall 'had erected a blast furnace at Mittagong, and is producing from the crude ore found in the vicinity fine samples of pig iron'.[51] It would seem more probable that Brazenall used the existing furnace but nothing further is known of this venture. Rolling continued for a time. During the 1880s the rolling mills were renovated and leased to Larkin, Hunter and Henshaw. Larkin, who took over from his associates, rolled the rails for the tramway linking the Joadja Creek Shale mine with the main railway but at the completion of the contract the works were once again idle.

In 1884 John Frazer sold out to the Mittagong Land Co. Ltd, and William Sandford, afterwards of Lithgow, leased the mills to make sheet iron and reroll rails under contract to the New South Wales government. After six months he too resigned his lease and began his famous association with the Eskbank works and Lithgow. Despite occasional rumours that the ironworks would be reopened they remained closed. The blast furnace stood unused for half a century before its demolition in 1927. The site which had once provided homes and a livelihood for a community of 600 to 700 people returned to the bush.[52]

# 2

# THE INTERNATIONAL IRON RUSH AND AUSTRALIAN REALITIES

DESPITE ITS ISOLATION Australia has always been affected by international conditions. An early example of this was the world-wide investment boom and slump of the early and mid 1870s. The first industrial revolution reached its climax in Britain in the 1870s. In Australia this decade marked the peak of entrepreneurial activity in the iron-smelting industry before Federation. This sudden and concentrated activity was a direct reaction to economic conditions in Europe and North America. A sharply accelerated demand for pig- and wrought iron resulted in an sudden and unforeseen shortage, leading to an abrupt escalation in the price of iron world-wide.[1]

The failure of the iron supply to meet demand marked a watershed in the history of industrialisation. The causes and consequences of this abrupt and complex phenomenon were sufficiently conflicting to ensure that certain aspects of it remained continuing subjects of debate. This is particularly the case with arguments centring around finance, banking and rates of interest, as well as the international applicability of the gold standard in relation to the amount of gold available and the technological investment required to service increasing industrialisation. Other long-term arguments involved questions of internal and external capital investment, freight rates, technical education and its application, the inflexibility of long-established traditions in labour and management and the outdated location of plant.

Professor Sidney Pollard, reviewing this international iron shortage and economic turning-point, concludes that:

> above all, it was the progress of technology, at the heart of industrialisation, which both enabled and compelled the state to take on ever increasing functions . . . the state everywhere shed its reluctance to intervene in the economy. Among its most important new spheres of action was the attempted steerage and control over industry, and in particular, economic growth and the process of industrialisation itself.[2]

As early as 1875 the Welsh ironmaster William Menelaus of Dowlais commented that:

> Governments have encouraged the growth of gigantic industries devoted to the manufacture of iron and steel; and anyone who has had the privilege of seeing the vast works of Creusot [France] and Essen [Germany] would, I think admit that no government, however wise or strong, would lightly venture on a policy which would interfere with the prosperity of such establishments.

In some respects the Australian colonies could adjust to this type of government surveillance and participation fairly easily for government had always reserved the right to intervene directly in certain areas of the economy: for example, in granting land rights and contracts for public works such as the railways. The new question was how, or precisely to what extent, government should participate in the development of industry. The diverse attitudes of the Australian colonies over protection, bonuses and free trade mirrored a world-wide ambivalence on the subject, and this accounted for the shaky start of the second phase of industrialiation.

Here, the flaws in Britain's industrial revolution began to count. Had Britain been prepared to meet the surge in pig-iron prices with real depth in its capacity, it is conceivable that colonial smelting would have been delayed indefinitely, as colonial iron trades would have continued to look overseas for supplies of iron and steel. But it was in fact Britain whose position became threatened, and for reasons usually quite unconnected with raw colonial efforts at smelting. In the event, the changing pecking order of the international giants provided Australia's opportunity, a point so important that it needs some explanation.

Britain, as the first industrial nation, had enormous and immediate advantages, particularly as its political framework had proved sufficiently flexible for immense social and environmental changes to occur without destroying national stability. Nevertheless, much of its success had been based on individual entrepreneurship and technique. Training was practical rather than scientific. The British manager had received his training on the shop-floor rather than in the university. Consequently many British ironmasters underestimated the formal scientific education so highly valued and respected on the Continent. By the second half of the nineteenth century, when Britain's industrial supremacy was increasingly under challenge, the defects of Britain's educational system were becoming apparent. The extent to which British manufactures were falling behind was highlighted by the exhibits of British manufacturers at the Paris Universal Exposition of 1867. Their inadequacies on this occasion aroused national consternation and parliament reacted to public opinion by appointing a Select Committee on Scientific Instruction.

Conservative British ironmasters were reluctant to admit the challenge to their former supremacy or to concede that scientific metallurgy had much to offer the practical needs of the industry. Even the Cleveland ironmaster Isaac Lothian Bell, who actually had a scientific training, did not hesitate to tell the British Association in 1867, the same year as the Paris Exposition, that 'with regard to the application of science the ironmasters in other countries, as here, can only lament how little chemistry has been able to effect in the blast-furnace or puddling process'. Not surprisingly the French metallurgist, Professor Samson Jordan found Bell's approach 'not calculated to advance the reputation of English ironmasters as progressive men'![3]

Six years later Bell, in his 1873 presidential address to the Iron and Steel Institute, was more cautious stating that:

> the cultivation of metallurgical science has been much more industriously pursued abroad than has hitherto been the case in this country . . . we should have to arrange alongside our brilliant successes a list of our costly failures . . . had we as a nation been a little more systematic in our methods of study, it is possible that some of the fruitless attempts at improvement made by ourselves might have been avoided.[4]

Although the British ironmasters remained divided on the merits of scientific education, they recognised the need for the dissemination of knowledge within the trade. In January 1869 they established the Iron and Steel Institute. John Jones, who was appointed secretary to the Institute, was well aware of the problem as a few years before, in 1866, he had founded the *Iron and Coal Trades Review*. The nineteenth-century Australian ironmasters followed the British rather than the European views on the merits of formal scientific training, a tendency only remedied by of hard experience.

British industry, in the late 1860s and early 1870s, was suddenly confronted by a sharply increased demand for wrought iron from its potential industrial rivals. Not understanding the transient nature of this demand, the British industrialists expanded an already outmoded technology to meet it. Furthermore, the British ironmasters as a whole failed to realise the potential of steel over wrought iron. They relied on the relatively low investment required to expand wrought iron manufacture, increasing their puddling furnaces rather than installing Bessemer converters or open-hearth furnaces. This was unavoidable in certain areas, for instance, in Middlesbrough, where phosphorus was present in the local ores, which at that time meant that these could not be used to make steel. Subsequently, British ironmasters were naturally reluctant to scrap new plant which, although cheaper than the new technology, still represented a very large capital investment. Meanwhile circumstances delayed expansion of capacity by American and European competitors sufficiently long to allow them to adopt the new basic steel-making technologies that could remove phosphorus from pig-iron: both the United States and Europe, in particular Germany, had to confront and solve severe political problems between 1865 and 1871.

In the United States the unresolved problems in the nature of the federal union erupted into civil war between the states in 1860. At this time 60 per cent of US pig-iron came from the 125 blast furnaces in Pennsylvania and the remainder largely from Ohio, New York, New Jersey and Maryland. Under 56 tons of the annual total of 919 770 tons was produced in the southern states of Kentucky and Tennessee. Technical reasons connected with the clay used in making crucibles had prevented the establishment of a crucible steel industry, such as existed in England. In 1860 the annual production of blister steel—from thirteen small works in Pittsburgh—was under 12 000 tons.[5] National expansion and the political and social tension between state and federal governments, which preceded the war, further complicated already existing uncertainties over the role of government in industry. Indeed the war may have acted as a stabilising influence by dictating the pace and direction of metallurgical science and technology through the development of armaments that foreshadowed the rapid advances in weaponry in the later nineteenth century.

In the initial post-war period, reconstruction and expansion in the United States made immense demands on the industry. These were met largely by the *ad hoc* arrangements of entrepreneurs and, as the home industry was unable to meet their demands, pig- and wrought iron were imported from Britain. However, during the 1870s, US production of pig-iron alone increased 231 per cent; by 1880 there were 681 blast furnaces, and iron was being manufactured in twenty-five states. Between 1860 and 1880 output rose from 919 770 to 4 295 414 tons. A conflict over patents and the war had delayed the introduction of Bessemer steel—the first Bessemer plant did not come into operation in the United States until 1864. Nevertheless, by 1870 the annual output of steel was 42 000 tons and a decade later, 1 203 173 tons.[6] The war had only temporarily retarded the large-scale industrial development. Between 1865 and 1870, 3000 miles of rail were laid each year. In these immediate post-war years there was a sudden demand for pig-iron which the home producers could not satisfy. This created an initially large but short-lived demand for the importation of British pig-iron.

In Europe similar conditions occurred a few years later as the movements for German and Italian unification retarded the industrial development of much of Europe during the 1850s and 1860s. The success of the 'blood and iron' policy of the Prussian Chancellor, Count Otto von Bismarck, highlighted the work of the German steelmaster, Alfred Krupp (1812–87). Krupp's Essen works became known as the 'arsenal of the Reich'—a reputation renewed in 1914 and again in 1939. Alfred Krupp had operated his father's ironworks since he inherited them at the age of fourteen. He combined considerable scientific interest and metallurgical skill with commercial acumen. Although the Essen works were never principally an armaments factory, Krupp manufactured guns to test and improve the metals produced in the research laboratory he established in 1863. European unrest culminated in the Franco-Prussian war of 1870, in which France was overwhelmingly defeated. The French Empire of Napoleon III collapsed. Under the terms of the Treaty of Frankfurt, France was forced to cede Alsace-Lorraine with its valuable coal and iron deposits. These enabled Germany to develop the industrial potential of the Ruhr and, in particular, a massive iron and steel industry to sustain the might of the new German Empire.

Britain's foremost industrial rival in the manufacture of iron and steel had been France. But the politically insecure Napoleon III had been distracted by his European and foreign policies, including a high profile in the Middle East. This included his encouragement for the building of the

Suez Canal, completed in 1869 by the French engineer and former diplomat Ferdinand, Vicomte de Lesseps. The British government regarded this project with their traditional suspicion of French motives but they were to be the ultimate beneficiaries as in 1875 the British Prime Minister, Benjamin Disraeli, persuaded his government to acquire a controlling interest in the Suez Canal Company. The Canal greatly reduced the distance and therefore the time and cost of travel between Britain and Australia.

The new route depended upon, and was created by, the new marine technology. The viability of the reduced distance depended upon the power of steam rather than wind. Continuing improvements in shipbuilding and design led to a fall in freight rates. For instance, in January 1873 freight rates on pig-iron from Glasgow to Melbourne were £1 per ton but by May 1882 they had fallen to 17s 6d.[7] The phasing out of sailing ships came gradually. Although by the 1870s the tonnage of *new* steamships on the British Register exceeded that of new sailing ships, the *overall* tonnage of steamships did not exceed that of sail until the mid 1880s.

In Britain some of the the more far-sighted ironmasters realised, as the iron boom came to a sudden end, exactly what had happened. Among them was William Menelaus, who in his 1875 presidential address to the Iron and Steel Institute warned that:

> we have but little demand from Europe and we seem to have lost our American market entirely. With our free-trade notions we all believe that our neighbours in Europe and our friends in the United States are pursuing a mistaken policy; that they had better confine themselves to the charming Arcadian occupations of growing 'corn and wine', and let England continue to drudge in the grimy business of iron and steel making . . . I confess that on this point I am far from hopeful. If it were merely a trade question we might expect that bye-and-bye the example of England might be followed as a matter of self-interest, but it is needless to say that in powerful countries the home production of iron and steel means more than giving employment to a portion of the population. In certain contingencies it renders a nation independent of foreign supplies at times when such dependence would cripple the most powerful nation in the world . . . We must I think frankly accept the position in which we are placed, and prepare to seek new markets for our produce in countries which, even if they had the will, have not yet the power to impose restrictions on our trade.

Hitherto importing iron and manufactured goods and exporting wool had created a mutually satisfactory balance of trade between Britain and Australia. The Australian market was still comparatively small and divided among the individual colonies. These conditions had encouraged the development of secondary rather than primary iron manufacture reflected in the numerous small- to medium-sized ironworks, whose operations were based on processing imported iron for the domestic market. *The Official Record of the Sydney Intercolonial Exhibition of 1870* listed exhibits from fifty-seven iron and tin works, fifty-nine iron, brass and copper foundries, and forty-eight machinist engineers. The individual requirements of these works were more suited to purchasing small parcels of imported pig-iron, steel or wrought iron than to absorbing the potentially larger, less reliable and more expensive local product.

These considerations had important bearings on Australian perceptions of the structure of the iron industry as a whole. The abnormal fluctuation in the world prices for pig-iron in the early 1870s led to a premature attempt to restructure the whole chain of iron manufacture, from resource to the final products. Nevertheless, the ironworking, or factory, stages of the industry were not only its colonial focus; they were also the source of much of its business and labour politics, which ran through noted conduits like trade unions and parliaments. Any new iron-making component would obviously have to share an industry with politically seasoned labour activists from the ironworking sector. In view of its contemporary and subsequent significance for labour relations and markets the structure and organisation of the nineteenth-century ironworking industry needs to be described in some detail. The following examples in Sydney alone demonstrate the depth to which the factory sectors' roots had struck into the colonial political economy.

The oldest foundry in Sydney was Dawson's, established in 1833 by Captain Richard Dawson, who had retired from seafaring to embark on a commercial career as a marine blacksmith. The works were situated in Lower George Street, near Circular Quay, on a $1^1/_2$-acre site. By 1868 the site had become cramped as the firm had profited 'from the great extension of the iron trade within the last few years'. It had three cupola furnaces and the *Sydney Morning Herald* reported that 'the business of this establishment lies mainly in casting for the trade generally and chiefly in the marine branch; though a very considerable amount of general engineering work has recently been undertaken'. The firm employed seventy men and five boys. The foundry's consumption of pig-iron for castings averaged about ten tons per week.[8]

At the time of the 1870 Sydney Exhibition one of the most up-to-date works was the City Iron Works at Johnston's Bay, erected, or more possibly 'modernised', for Alexander Brown by Enoch Hughes some time after Hughes left Mittagong in 1864. In 1870 the *Illustrated Sydney News* featured the works in an article. This included a vivid description of rolling and the very heavy manual work involved, adding: 'some idea of the intense heat of the operation may be formed when we say that the men have their legs and thighs bound around with many folds of sheepskin leather in addition to stout leather aprons'. About forty men and boys were employed in the works at this time. At the Exhibition the City Iron Works displayed iron bars, tyres, rails and angles. They were awarded a silver medal for 'the introduction of new manufactures of iron into the colony especially plates and railway tyres'.[9]

Another firm, Joseph Mather's engineering works, employed seventy to a hundred men; they specialised in marine engineering but they also undertook general civil and agricultural work. A slightly smaller establishment, Chapman Brothers' George Street works, 'originally started as agricultural implement makers . . . within the last few years, however, they have gradually got into the general engineering and boilermaking trades'. They employed on average fifty men and about twelve boys using $10^1/_2$ tons of pig- and $6^1/_2$ tons of malleable iron per month. By 1870 most firms, whatever their origins, had a broad-based mixture of marine, domestic, agricultural and general manufactures. Few Australian ironworks were highly specialised. While this prevented economies of scale, it allowed them to balance fluctuations in demand from the different market sectors.

One specialised operation was Zollner's galvanised iron factory in Dixon Street. This was the same Simon Zollner who had been a leading shareholder in the Fitz Roy Ironworks and a prominent spokesman in the 1867 deputation to the New South Wales government asking for assistance. He was also to be a shareholder in the 1873 Fitzroy Bessemer Steel, Hematite, Iron and Coal Co. Ltd. In 1868 the *Sydney Morning Herald* declared that his was 'the only factory where the process of galvanising iron is carried on in the colonies'. Zollner's speciality was tubs and buckets for which there was a large market, and it was claimed that he could 'outstrip foreign competition in such articles'.[10] At this time galvanised receptacles were replacing wooden tubs in the coal-mines as well as in the more familiar agrarian and domestic spheres.

A very much larger enterprise was that of P. N. Russell & Co., situated on a four-acre site with extensive wharfage on Darling Harbour.

Russell's establishment included two cupola furnaces and twenty-five forges, 14-feet heavy plate rollers and plant for making various types of machinery. The works were steam-powered and the equipment included a Nasmyth hammer and a Hawthorne hammer and also a Cook's riveting machine for boilermaking. They manufactured agricultural machinery, such as wool presses and sheep-washing plant, sugar crushing and boiling equipment; materials for construction work (including girders for the Anthony Hordern building and the Sydney GPO), cylinders for the Gundagai and Maitland bridges, rolling stock for the New South Wales railways. They even built two gunboats for the New Zealand government. The works required on average about ninety tons of pig-iron a month and at this period few Australian ironworks, apart from those engaged in rolling rails, would have required a larger supply of raw materials.

Russell's works employed 250 men and boys in such occupations as engineers, fitters, moulders, boilermakers, shipwrights, millwrights, brass founders and finishers, carpenters, blacksmiths and their apprentices. The total work-force, including those working outside at deliveries and similar services, was about 300. Interestingly, in view of the later opposition to this practice in the 1917 strike, timekeeping was 'by means of tickets, so that no matter how large the number of hands required, a complete record of the time is obtained'. Wages varied from 1s to 1s 6d per hour for the men and 2d to 7d for the boys. These wages, which in 1868 were 'general throughout the trade', had been agreed following a general strike of the iron trades in 1859, when 'the parties ultimately came to an understanding by a little giving way on each side and since that time . . . a far better understanding has existed between men and masters'.[11]

In fact, between 1856 and 1861 a series of ironworkers' strikes were centred on Russell's works. They were part of a general industrial movement for improved pay and conditions, including an eight-hour day. Two early, though short-lived, trade unions, the Australian Iron Trades Protective Association and the Friendly Trade Society of Iron Moulders emerged from these disputes. In this they followed the British tradition in which unionism moved from skilled to unskilled labour: they were craft unions. They re-emerged in 1872 after the formation, in 1871, of the Sydney Trades and Labour Council. In general, wages were good and employment relatively constant. In their anxiety to make the most of favourable economic opportunities the ironmasters conceded to many of the employees' demands, including one for two meal breaks in an eight-hour day. This proved unworkable. On 31 December 1873 the employers, who had united in the Iron Trades Employers Association, posted notices that on and after 2 January 1874 hours of work would be from 8.15 a.m. to 5.15 p.m. with an hour for lunch. The ironworkers complained, not only about the alteration in their conditions but also that they, or their representatives, had not been consulted by the employers. The ensuing strike, despite the attempted mediation of former Chief Justice, Sir Alfred Stephen, lasted until 2 March when it was resolved by a compromise—two meal breaks in summer and one in winter.[12]

From their inception governments played a major part in the economic development of first colonial and then federated Australia. Business and society in all the colonies were accustomed to look to government for support. The expansion of road and rail communications brought much-sought government contracts to the private ironworks. Furthermore, the colonial governments were often directly involved: for instance, the New South Wales government had two railway works, one at Redfern for the southern and western lines and the other at Honeysuckle Point for the northern line. At these works there was 'a very fine collection of the best and most powerful engineering machinery'. In all they employed 207 men and boys 'of which 63 men are directly connected with the iron trade'. Equipment at the Redfern works included 'a very large and powerful Nasmyth's steam hammer. The weight of the hammer itself is 45 cwt. and it falls with a force of about 6 tons at each stroke'. There was also a 15-hundredweight Nasmyth hammer in the smiths' shops and cranes operated between the hammers and the furnace. Since 1866 the engineer in charge, Mr Thomas, had instituted piece-work, and in a subsequent report he pointed out that 'the 204 miles of line opened in 1867 have been worked for £1,000 *less* than the 144 miles in 1865'. Traditionally much of the iron trade operated on a piece-work or contract basis and the newspaper reporter continued, 'this system of piecework having been found to answer so well, it is intended to extend it as far as possible in every direction'.[13] Nevertheless, the nature as well as the method of piece-work ensured its unpopularity with the unions.

The majority of Australian ironworkers were British by birth or descent and their attitudes to industrial organisation were modelled on the British experience. The first industrial revolution, a completely new and unpredicted phenomenon, began to make its impact on British society at the end of the eighteenth century. Australian unionism developed from the British trade unionism that emerged from that first phase of the industrial revolution. Both were distinctly different from the unionism that emerged in continental Europe towards the end of the century and after the beginning of the mass industrialisation of unskilled labour. The British and Australian unions evolved out of the preindustrial craft system. Workers in the iron industry were used to a hierarchical industrial structure in which the capital and plant were provided by the ironmaster. He contracted the work to the various craftsmen, puddlers, furnacemen, rollers and other skilled workers and paid them on a sliding scale related to the fluctuating price of pig-iron on the local market. The craftsmen-contractors then paid their hands. There was no national standard and local customs and traditions remained a dominant consideration.

Prosperity had encouraged labour unrest in Britain during the 1860s when there had been widespread, but local and individual rather than national, strikes and lock-outs. Then in 1869, encouraged by the growing concern over the consequences of these industrial disturbances, the manufacturing iron trades in the north of England established a Board of Conciliation and Arbitration. This imaginative move was largely due to the combined work of its first chairman, a Quaker ironmaster, David Dale, and the labour leader John Kane, its first secretary. In 1871 their example was followed by the ironmakers of Staffordshire and Worcestershire but with more limited success as, since the Black Country firms were smaller and more numerous, agreement was more difficult to achieve.[14]

Unionism in nineteenth-century Britain had three phases: from 1800 to 1824, when trade unions or combinations were illegal; from 1825 to 1875, when many trade union activities were of doubtful or precarious legality, for example, those of the Tolpuddle Martyrs in 1834, while the 1867 decision in *Hornby v. Close* declared that trade unions acted in restraint of trade and were therefore illegal; and after 1875, when Disraeli's conservative government, expanding the restricted legislation of Gladstone's liberal government in 1871, gave trade unions full recognition, legal status and rights. From 1871 the Trade Union Congress met annually 'to promote cooperation in respect of general questions affecting labour and to watch over its interests in Parliament'. Politically, the workers had been enfranchised by the Derby–Disraeli Reform Act of 1867, which gave virtual manhood suffrage in the towns. Labour organisation, however, remained craft-oriented, concerned with local rather than national conditions. These traditions were already entrenched when Robert Knight, the secretary of the boilermakers' union, began in the 1880s to encourage systematic collective bargaining as a substitute for craft regulation and *ad hoc* conferences.[15] Meanwhile many British ironworkers were encouraged to emigrate to the rapidly developing Australian colonies, expecting a better life in a land where wages were high and skills at a premium.

By the 1870s the Australian iron manufacturers were enjoying a thriving market based both on the normal demands of a rapidly growing society and, particularly in Victoria, on the extraordinary demands produced by the desire for conspicuous consumption created by the gold rushes. These market conditions were abruptly shaken by the sudden rise in the price of the pig-iron, which the Australian colonies, in common with most of the world, imported solely from Britain. The late 1860s and early 1870s saw the high-water mark of Britain's international industrial supremacy, for, although Britain continued to develop, it was at a slower rate than its European and North American rivals. However, towards the end of the 1860s—and before this relative decline became apparent—international political and industrial issues interacted to produce a sudden boom at the beginning of the 1870s. This was followed by a sharp recession in the middle of the decade.

Australian manufacturers, with their comparatively small businesses, did not carrying large stocks of iron and they were caught by these unforeseen market conditions. For example, the average price of pig-iron in Victoria was £4 10s in 1870. Then between June and August 1872 the price of imported British pig-iron rose from £6 15s to £11, falling back to £9 in 1873.[16] Similar escalations occurred in all the Australian colonies. The Australian entrepreneurs did not recognise the temporary nature of this phenomenon. But they did recollect that cheap imported iron had largely contributed to the failure of the Fitz Roy works. They thought that the time had come when a local supply of iron could be economically secured. It was a simplistic assessment of complex international conditions.

The complex causation did not occur to the Australian businessmen any more than it did to most of their British suppliers. They simply saw a scarcity and a potential market which could be filled by import substitution. Melbourne, whose businessmen were the principal participants in this endeavour, was approaching the height of its nineteenth-century confidence. By the early 1870s the Melbourne ironmasters were demanding more British iron than could be supplied. They were acutely affected by its sudden scarcity and erratically escalating cost. Post-gold-rush Victoria had capital to invest, but its mineral resources other than gold were slender. Victorian attention soon focused on a new mining frontier across the Bass Strait. For in 1871 discoveries of tin at Mount Bischoff had led to a Tasmanian minerals boom. This revived interest in Tasmania's potential iron resources. These had been known as early as 1805[17] when Lieutenant-Governor Patterson had sent samples of Tasmanian iron ore to Governor King in Sydney.

Exuberant Victorian optimism along with intercolonial reciprocity characterised the Tasmanian venture into iron-making. This was clearly expressed in late 1873 when S. H. Wintle wrote in the *Mercury* that 'this island of Tasmania ought to become one of the largest iron producing countries in the world . . . even our Victorian neighbours begin to entertain the belief that their gold resources will eventually sink into comparative insignificance before the development of Tasmanian iron'.[18]

Early in May 1872 William Leonard argued that Tasmania's unused and easily accessible resources of iron ore were a 'disgrace, shame and sin'.[19] Leonard, who was manager of the Hotham Ironworks in Victoria, came from a long-established family of Virginian ironworkers. He represented another feature of the 1870s, namely, the appearance of the American-Australian connection in the industry. Leonard's comments did not go unnoticed. In September 1872 the Tasmanian Charcoal Iron Company was registered in Victoria. By January 1874 the company had fifty-one shareholders of whom forty-four were Victorians.

On 6 December 1872 the Governor of Tasmania, Charles du Cane, laid the foundation stone of an experimental furnace at the recently named settlement of Leonardsburgh about seven miles west from the present-day town of Beaconsfield in northern Tasmania, expressing in public the hope that the new town would one day eclipse Pittsburgh. In private he was less optimistic as, in a despatch to the Secretary of State, du Cane remarked that the amount of capital required was very large and the market uncertain.

Nevertheless, the confidence of the investors was reflected in the size of the enterprise. The paid-up capital of the company was £80 000. The directors showed a praiseworthy encouragement of local scientific expertise and a willingness to experiment with new technology in the shape of a furnace invented by a Melbourne physician, Dr William Harrison. This furnace was reputed to be similar but larger than an ordinary reverberatory furnace, and it incorporated a retort for generating hydrogen gas. This was expected to assist the reduction of the ore and result in an 'enormous economy of heat'. Towards the end of February 1873 Harrison's furnace was ready and two trial runs were made in March and April.

These produced a substantial quantity of iron which Harrison claimed was of excellent quality—'like steel'. A Sheffield cutler in Melbourne was

## 2 THE IRON RUSH AND AUSTRALIAN REALITIES

reported to have made a number of high-tensile tools from it. Unfortunately, in the process the chimney stack of the furnace had been badly cracked. The optimistic inventor tried to argue that this was wonderful news. Indeed evidence of 'how splendidly intense the furnace works'. The directors were not impressed. They had realised the risks of relying solely upon Dr Harrison's invention[20] and enquiries overseas had already resulted in the appointment of Robert Scott, formerly manager of the important Coltness Ironworks in Scotland, to investigate and to report upon the company's operations.

Scott arrived at the time Harrison's furnace was encountering difficulties. His report encouraged the directors to adhere to well-tried British methods. They resolved upon the erection of a massive ironworks, designed to accommodate four blast furnaces of British design, a Bessemer steel plant, and rolling mills. The need for increased capital was obvious. With this in mind the company was renamed the British and Tasmanian Charcoal Iron Company Ltd. (BTCIC) in the hope of attracting British investment. Its nominal capital was expanded to £250 000. Andrew Barclay & Sons of Kilmarnock, Scotland, not far from the Coltness Ironworks, successfully tendered for the plant. This was to be sited at the base of Redbill Point near the present-day town of Ilfraville on the West Arm of the Tamar River in northern Tasmania, about ten miles north of Beaconsfield.

On 13 March 1875 1350 tons of machinery arrived on the barque *Cape Finisterre* accompanied by ten skilled tradesmen. They erected the plant in a little over a year.[21] The furnace was built on a freestone and concrete base. Upon this Scotch fire-bricks were erected and the whole structure was encased in wrought iron. Externally the furnace presented a uniform diameter but internally its configuration was similar to the chimney of a kerosene lamp; for the first ten feet from the hearth, the internal diameter was about six feet and for the next twenty-five feet it gradually widened out to its largest internal diameter of fifteen feet from which it gradually diminished to a top diameter of nine feet. The complex internal form demanded great accuracy in fitting the fire-bricks to preserve the desired profile.

A photograph of this plant under construction is dominated by the blast furnace stack and charging lift, and a large horizontal reservoir or 'regulator' to even out pulsations in the blast. Pipe stoves for heating the blast are visible to each side of the blast furnace, and the 250-horsepower steam-driven blowing engine is just visible behind the large vertical pipe on the right which carries the blast from the blowing engine to the

The British and Tasmanian Charcoal Iron Company's blast furnace plant during construction. The absences of a complete chimney and an engine-house suggest this sole surviving photograph of the plant dates from 1875. The blast furnace stands behind the horizontal blast regulator tube and the steam-driven elevator.

regulator. Curiously the blowing engine was a beam engine of the 'grasshopper' type in which the beam was pivoted not at middle but at the end, an arrangement which was inherently out of balance and consequently rarely used for large engines.

The blast furnace was outwardly a cylindrical tower, 65 feet high with a diameter of 23 feet surmounted by a squat chimney or 'tunnel head' which extended the total height of the furnace to about 75 feet. The tunnel head had four filling-holes through which the furnace was charged with ore, fuel or limestone. Access to the feeding-holes was provided by a gangway with an iron railing. To facilitate the charging of the furnace, materials were transported to the gangway or platform surrounding the tunnel head by a double steam elevator. The pulleys appear to have been at least 75 feet above the ground. A double shaft was used so that one cage could be loaded at the bottom whilst another was being emptied at the top. The cages each held a hand barrow that could be pushed by one man.

This blast furnace was of the 'Scottish type', so named after the furnaces erected at Dundyvan in the early 1830s. These used cast-iron pillars to support the stack, giving free access to the lower part of the furnace. The BTCIC furnace was, in fact, very similar to the furnace built at Russell's Hall, Staffordshire about 1860. It is described in the volume on 'Iron and Steel' in Percy's classic *Metallurgy*. Both furnaces were open topped. Pictures of the BTCIC furnace show no evidence of a downcomer, although by the 1870s the fuel economy of the closed top was internationally recognised, as was the importance of utilising the hot gases. This omission is particularly strange in view of the directors' concern over the cost of fuel. Since 1850 closed-top furnaces had become increasingly customary in Great Britain. In New South Wales eight years before, in 1868, Thomas Levick had closed the top of the Fitz Roy Ironworks' blast furnace at Mittagong.

Despite its name the BTCIC used coke made from Bulli coal freighted from New South Wales. This highlighted the problem of fuel. Not even the most stringent economies could reduce its cost below £1 5s a ton.[22] A railway carried the coal from the company's deep-water jetty south along Redbill Point to the works. An extension of this line to the southwest of the works led to the iron ore quarries about five miles away. At the northern end of the company's enclosure, adjoining the furnace and pig-beds, stood a tall chimney stack, 100 feet high and 14 feet wide at its base, to dispose of the smoke from the steam boilers and the waste gases conveyed to it by underground flues. There were about forty coke ovens, charcoal kilns and a clay mill. South of the works a group of some thirty cottages comprised the town of Port Lempriere.

Official opening of the British and Tasmanian Charcoal Iron Company blast furnace by Governor Weld, 1876. The blast furnace (centre) is flanked by two hot-blast stoves. Pig-beds awaiting liquid iron from the furnace are in the foreground (left).

This was a massive enterprise. The BTCIC furnace was indisputably the largest in nineteenth-century Australia. Its design conformed approximately to that of British furnaces of the same period. But it had some outdated characteristics, in particular its open top and to a lesser extent the selection of a beam engine to produce the blast. These had been largely superseded in Great Britain by direct-acting steam engines, similar to those in use at Mittagong ten years previously.

The furnace was blown in on 25 May 1876 and a few days later it had produced 'a very good cast'. It was then operated on reduced blast pending its inauguration, on 17 June 1876, by Governor du Cane's successor, Governor Weld. Most of the distinguished visitors attending the inauguration were greatly impressed. Weld, however, shared his predecessor's reservations. In his inaugural address he recalled Hudibras's warning about 'the perils that environ the man that meddles with cold iron'.[23] His fears were justified as unfortunately the iron ore contained, in varying amounts, chromium and sulphur. This made the metal too hard to be workable. Confronted with an unsaleable product, the directors made every effort to solve this metallurgical problem. A large sample was sent to England for analysis and 'experiments were made by the very best authorities and under the most skilled supervision' but to no avail.[24]

As a metallurgical phenomenon the iron aroused considerable interest. On 15 March 1877 a paper on Tasmanian chrome iron was read to the Chemical Society meeting in London. A few months later R. F. Mushet, the distinguished metallurgist who had played a key role in solving the difficulties that surrounded the early experiments of the Bessemer process, assured T. C. Just that it was 'a very valuable iron for mixing with other brands for puddling into bar-iron required to possess great tensile strength and hardness'. However, not even this recommendation encouraged either British or Australian ironmasters to purchase the new Tasmanian iron, particularly as in trials the presence of 2–6 per cent of chrome in the pig-iron was found to retard the puddling process. Certainly the directors sought the best advice and many of these trials were carried out in various Sheffield works, including Bessemer's own works.[25]

In their extensive attempts to overcome the problem, the company employed an analytical chemist who stayed at the works and carefully monitored the input and output of the furnace. The limestone flux was adjusted, the treatment of the ore was varied, even hand-picked, but the directors' scientific approach was to no avail. The problem arose entirely from the composition of the ore and it remained intractable. The furnace operated impeccably, producing between twelve and fourteen tons of iron thrice daily. In all, the works produced over 6000 tons of pig-iron before the furnace was finally blown out in August 1877. The directors accepted defeat reluctantly. T. C. Just, a leading exponent of the venture, expressed regret that there was not enough capital left to transport ore to the works from other Tasmanian deposits, in particular from Penguin and Blythe River, reflecting his realization of the significance of a deep-water site for transport.[26]

The shareholders in Melbourne met on 16 May 1878. They decided that they had no financial alternative to dissolving the company. However, on the same day a new company, the Purchase Company Ltd., was established with a capital of £80 000 to purchase the mine, plant and property of the BTCIC. The original company had spent some £90 000 on the enterprise which, according to T. C. Just, was sold for £38 000. The new company hoped to continue experimenting with the local ores. They exported some 4000 tons of pig-iron to Victoria and to Britain, where it sold at the current market price. But they failed to resolve the

British and Tasmanian Charcoal Iron Company's blast furnace plant, 1876. Burning gases at the furnace top indicate that the blast furnace is operating. The 250-horsepower beam engine for providing the blast is housed in the building at centre, from which blast is conveyed to the hot-blast stoves and furnace through the conspicuous horizontal tubular regulator.

problems that defeated their predecessors. In September 1882 the Purchase Company was also dissolved. The breaking up of the plant probably followed quickly upon the dissolution of the company. Today no evidence of this spectacular venture remains except for piles of slag and fire-bricks half-buried in the sand at Redbill Point. In 1891 the water-tanks along the Main Line railway in northern Tasmania were reputed to have been constructed from the shell of the BTCIC blast furnace.

By comparison the three other Tasmanian ventures, the Ilfracombe, Derwent and Tamar blast furnaces, were small and employed outmoded technology. However, they had the advantage that, apart from the blowing engines, they could be constructed from local materials and utilise local skills. Their economic viability depended upon the continuing high cost of imported iron; they had failed commercially before the larger BTCIC furnace was even blown in. These furnaces had a production rate of less than five tons a day, or about one-eighth of the BTCIC and, so long as the price of iron remained high, this smaller output, requiring a simpler marketing infrastructure, was possibly suited to the fragmented nature of the contemporary iron manufacturing trade. These furnaces differed from that of the BTCIC not only in size—they were all less than

Remains of the Ilfracombe Iron Company blast furnace near Beaconsfield, Tasmania, *c.* 1969. The iron furnace shell has been sheared off at tuyère level by a falling tree.

45 feet high—but also in using charcoal as fuel. This was understandable because there no local coking coal while there was abundant wood available. Moreover, smelting a ton of ore required a considerably lesser weight of charcoal than coke, largely because of the absence of ash-producing minerals in the charcoal. The blast required for a charcoal furnace was less than that required for a coke-fired furnace of the same capacity, and a charcoal furnace also required considerably less limestone flux.

Of the five Tasmanian blast furnaces the only significant remains today are those of the Ilfracombe Iron Company's furnace, three miles south-west of Beaconsfield, close to the iron ore deposits at Peaked Hill. A 14-foot square masonry foundation remains which had supported a brick-lined furnace encased in a 10-foot diameter iron shell about 45 feet high. Like the other two small Tasmanian furnaces, this had no provision for heating the blast or collecting gas from the furnace top. The company was registered in Victoria in January 1873 with a paid-up capital of £42 000. A small quantity of iron was produced during trials in November 1873. Overall the performance was disappointing, probably due to a

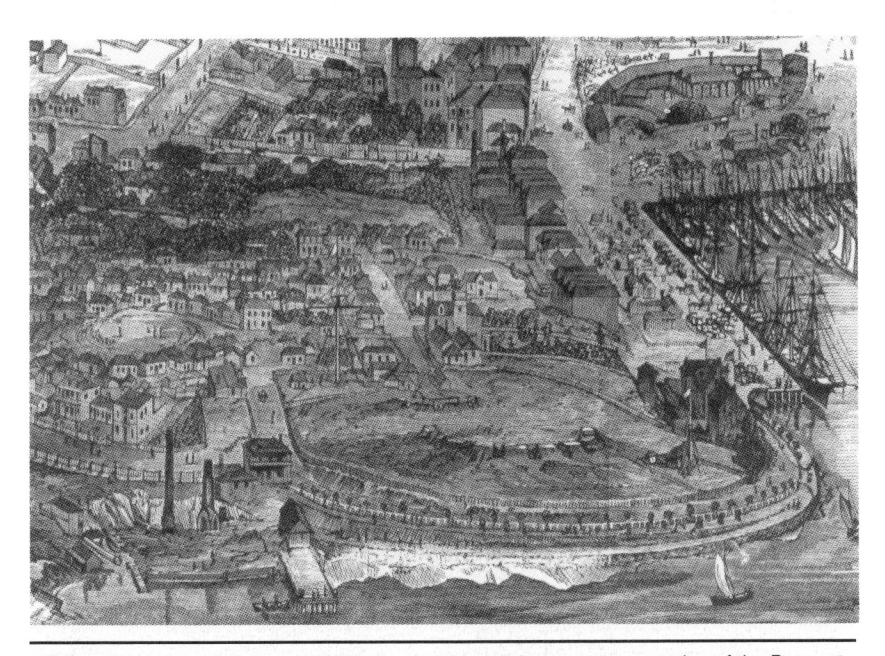

'Balloon's-eye' view of Hobart, 1879, showing the only known representation of the Derwent Iron Company blast furnace. The by-then derelict furnace and chimney are at wharf level on a natural terrace towards the left corner. The battery in Princes Park is in the right foreground, with Salamanca Place on the right.

combination of poor design and lack of experience by the operators. By mid 1874 the venture was abandoned and the assets of the company were in the hands of the sheriff.[27]

At the same time as the Ilfracombe Iron Company was building its plant in northern Tasmania, the Derwent Iron Works had contracted with Ripon Shield for the construction of a small blast furnace on Battery Point in Hobart. Unlike any other Australian blast furnace this one was built in the heart of a major town. The iron ore was brought thirty-five miles by water from Forcett and near Sorell Causeway to a wharf on Battery Point.[28] This venture is of particular interest because its siting showed a recognition of the importance of both access to markets and being accessible by sea.

The Hobart furnace consisted of a 12-foot square base housing the hearth and boshes of the furnace, surmounted by a round, brick-built stack reinforced by iron hoops, giving the furnace a total height to the filling-hole of 33 feet. Blowing in took place in July 1874 with little success. Trials continued under the supervision of one of the proprietors, Christie Beaudarick, until smooth operation was finally achieved on 7 November when a good cast of 28 hundredweight of pig-iron was made. This was later made into iron castings including a bell (the classical test for iron quality) at a local foundry. Thereafter the furnace was only operated spasmodically, probably due to difficulties in obtaining raw materials. It appears to have been blown out for the last time in mid 1875, about twelve months after its initial blowing in.[29] Its total production was claimed to have been over 100 tons of pig-iron. Although the technological problems of furnace operation appear to have been overcome, a small furnace producing perhaps two tons of iron per day could not hope to compete with the rapidly falling prices of imported iron. Also, the idea of importing *all* raw materials was perhaps too novel to attract adequate financial support.

The fourth company enticed by the Tasmanian resources and the market conditions of the early 1870s was the Tamar Hematite Iron Company. This company built two blast furnaces at Scotchman's Point on the Tamar Middle Arm, about a mile and a quarter east of Beaconsfield, not far from the Ilfracombe Iron Company's site. The company was managed by A. Swift, who had previously managed an English ironworks. In addition to the main blast furnace there was a small, experimental blast furnace designed to test the ore and to determine the optimum proportions of raw materials to be used in charging the main furnace.

Success was achieved with the small furnace in December 1874. After this the main furnace was lit on 31 December. The first tap was made successfully on 2 January 1875. This furnace also operated well, producing four–five tons per day when in full blast. This was a creditable performance for a cold-blast charcoal iron furnace blown by only a 16–20 horsepower engine. The furnace was finally blown out some months later in July 1875. During these months it produced 500–600 tons of pig-iron, a third of which was apparently exported to England! The pig-iron was regarded as superior to best Scottish iron and was used without difficulty in foundries at Launceston and Melbourne. Despite this success, the falling prices of pig-iron and the untimely death of the company's enterprising manager, A. Swift, prevented any revival of its activities.[30]

The Tamar Hematite Iron Company's furnace was the most successful of these low-technology Tasmanian blast furnaces. Quite clearly it failed for economic, and possibly managerial, rather than technological reasons. Considerable secrecy surrounded the construction of both of its furnaces. Fragmentary comments suggest that the main furnace was similar to the furnace which had been constructed a year earlier for the Derwent Iron Works at Battery Point in Hobart. Both furnaces were built by Ripon Shield. Nothing is known of the design of the smaller experimental furnace except that it utilised blast from the same blowing cylinders as were later used for the blast to the main furnace.[31] The main Tamar furnace, with a base of 20 square feet and a height of 40 feet, was larger than the Derwent furnace but its old-fashioned construction is typified by the use of a single block of sandstone weighing fourteen tons to form the bottom of the hearth.

A significant aspect of the four Tasmanian ventures is that they were almost exclusively Victorian both in their enterprise and finance. These iron-making ventures never received the support of the pastoralist-dominated Tasmanian Legislative Council. Indeed the *Cornwall Chronicle* declared that the Council 'prefer a population of sheep to an industrious mining population'.[32] The earlier influx of miners had proved socially disruptive in this dominantly agrarian society and Donald Cameron, MLC, in a debate on an appropriation for a road into the tin-mining districts, declared that Victoria was an undesirable illustration of the perils of a mining population.

The Tasmanian government refused tariff protection to the new industry. Foreign iron imported into the colony remained free of duty throughout the decade, while coal, which the BTCIC imported from New South Wales, was subjected to an intercolonial duty of one shilling per ton. Even if the Tasmanian government had desired and supported the iron industry, it is doubtful if any of these attempts could have had long-term success. It was still not clearly understood that the availability of cheap coking coal was more important than adequate supplies of ore in creating a viable iron industry.

Apart from the various Tasmanian ventures, Victorian entrepreneurs financed at least three blast furnaces in Victoria during this period. The most important Victorian iron-smelting venture was at Lal Lal, near the famed goldmining town of Ballarat. After the gold rushes Ballarat remained a centre of industry with many foundries producing mining equipment and railway locomotives in addition to the usual agricultural and domestic necessities. The Victorian government, through the Department of Mines, gave active encouragement to the Ballarat businessmen even to the extent of promising a government bonus for exploiting the local deposits of limonite ($FeCO_3$).

Official opening of the trial blast furnace at Lal Lal, 1878. The furnace is made from an old boiler shell, placed on end and lined with fire-bricks. The arrangement of the taphole shows that this was an 'open-forepart' design, as were presumably all nineteenth-century Australian furnaces. The furnace is about to be tapped into the pig-bed in the foreground. Previously cast pigs are piled at right.

2 THE IRON RUSH AND AUSTRALIAN REALITIES

Ironstone quarry, Lal Lal, 1882. Ironstone was mined by typical pick-and-shovel methods, and moved to the nearby furnace in small, four-wheeled tubs, which ran on wooden rails.

A small Ballarat company, the Lal Lal Iron Company, was formed in 1873. The following year they obtained leases to iron ore deposits near Lal Lal, not far from Ballarat. An experimental blast furnace, twenty-eight feet high, was constructed using a boiler shell stood on its end as its casing. The local woods provided an ample supply of charcoal, but limestone had to be brought from Geelong and this was expensive. The blast furnace was first tapped on 19 October 1875. In four campaigns, before it was dismantled in 1880, it produced over 350 tons of pig-iron. This was well received by Ballarat iron foundries. The small furnace had proved that good iron could be made from local iron ore. Encouraged by these results, the proprietors embarked on a more ambitious undertaking. They decided to build a larger furnace on the same site with a capacity of $7^1/_2$ tons per day.[33]

In 1880 a new blast furnace was built at Lal Lal. Its ruins can still be seen today and, although the bush has grown around it, it remains a fine example of early nineteenth-century technology. It was built by Christie Beaudarick, previously of the Derwent Iron Works in Tasmania. The furnace shaft was 46 feet high with an internal diameter of 10 feet at the bosh. Built of locally quarried sandstone, it was lined with imported firebricks. These are still clearly impressed with a 'Stourbridge' stamp, indicative of their English origin. Externally the furnace was typical of many English blast furnaces of the early nineteenth century as seen in the illustration; it had four arches at hearth level, accommodating the three tuyères and the taphole. Charcoal, limestone, and coal and coke, the proportions judged according to the type of iron required, were wheeled in barrows across the timber bridge to the top of the stack. Here they were discharged through openings in the sheet iron 'tunnel head'. The tunnel head increased the height of the structure by ten feet. As with all blast furnaces, it required extensive supporting equipment. This included a 50-horsepower beam-action steam engine and blowing cylinders, two Cornish boilers and a tramway system delivering feed materials to the furnace.

The second furnace was blown in on 26 March 1881. After producing almost 2300 tons of pig-iron in four campaigns, it was blown out for the last time in July 1884. The company found it impossible to sell pig-iron at £5 17s 4d, when the price of imported iron was £4 10s. Even at

Lal Lal blast furnace, 1882. The furnace followed the early nineteenth-century practice of being built with a heavy masonry stack against a hillside. Charge materials were assembled in the large store (right) and wheeled in barrows across the bridge to the furnace top. The blowing engine was located under double-pitched roof beyond the bridge, and the cold blast was led to three tuyères in arches at the bottom of the furnace. Molten iron and slag were tapped in the fourth arch (facing downhill), and the iron was cast into pigs or shaped castings in the long, low casting shed behind the furnace.

## 2 THE IRON RUSH AND AUSTRALIAN REALITIES

Ruins of the Lal Lal blast furnace, photographed in 1908 and showing the furnace largely as it remains today. The dressed outer stonework has been stolen, exposing the rubble infilling and, at the top, the brick furnace lining.

the time it was commissioned, in 1880, the price of imported pig-iron had dropped dramatically. By 1884, when the enterprise was abandoned, the company was in severe financial difficulties. Realising that the manufacture of pig-iron was no longer commercially viable, the company had attempted to diversify by making iron castings at its Lal Lal foundry. However, the Ballarat foundries construed this as a threat to their prosperity and boycotted the local product. The company was finally wound up in 1889.[34]

In addition to these larger enterprises a number of small blast furnaces were constructed through the country especially during the 1870s. These include the Victorian Iron Company's blast furnace at Limestone Gully near Maldon which does not appear to have ever been blown in.[35] Experiments in smelting ore taken from the proposed furnace site were made in Melbourne, probably in a foundry cupola, which produced a good grey iron. This encouraged the Victorian Iron Company to build the first Victorian blast furnace in 1873 at Limestone Gully.[36] The blast furnace was almost completed when the contractor renounced the contract and, as the company could not raise sufficient fresh capital to renew the operation, the project was abandoned. Similarly, the Bogolong Iron Mining Company erected a blast furnace near Yass in New South Wales. This blast furnace had a short life as, although its first smelting in 1874 produced satisfactory iron, it burnt away the locally produced fire-bricks and the furnace was never repaired.[37] The crude stonework of this primitive furnace still stands to this day, with an overall height of only twenty feet.[38] This furnace shows an almost perfect resemblance to an American furnace of 1836 reproduced in Hoskins's *Black Book*.

South Australia also participated in the iron-smelting fervour of the 1870s. The government offered a bonus of £2000 to the ironmaster who produced the first 500 tons of pig-iron in the colony. Early in 1874 a group of Adelaide businessmen formed the South Australian Iron and Steel Company with a capital of £3000. The company acquired leases on the iron ore deposits at Mount Jagged, about twelve miles from Port Victor. Encouraged by the government bonus, they erected a blast furnace near the Hindmarsh Falls. From contemporary reports it seems probable that the internal configuration was copied from diagrams of charcoal blast furnaces at Vordernberg in Austria. These had been published five years previously in H. Bauerman's *Treatise on the Metallurgy of Iron*. It was very small, about thirty feet high and six feet across the boshes. The stack was built of English fire-bricks sheathed with iron plates, carried on a pentagonal base of common red bricks lined with fire-bricks. The plant included a 20-horsepower blowing engine. The blast furnace was allegedly capable of an output of about 7$^1/_2$ tons of pig-iron per day. It is doubtful if it ever exceeded half this figure. The furnace was in blast intermittently between July and November 1874, but every few days it became obstructed. Then it had to be allowed to cool in order to clear it; consequently only about forty tons of pig-iron were ever produced.[39]

Altered economic conditions also ensured the failure of this enterprise, as well as a lack of skilled iron-makers. The management engaged two furnacemen who had never operated a primitive cold blast charcoal furnace. Local verdicts varied in assigning the failure to their 'inexperience' or 'intoxication'. Given the condition of the furnace, the furnacemen could also have been affected by carbon monoxide poisoning. In any case, after repeated failures the management sacked all the staff and closed the works. The incompetence of the furnacemen was conclusively demonstrated by the company's manager, an Adelaide broker. He acquired a copy of Bauerman's book and, following its instructions, proceeded to operate the blast furnace. Within three days he had made more pig-iron than the furnacemen during a similar period.[40] However, by now the furnace had been so badly damaged that most of the blast was escaping through the cracks in the masonry, for 'it cracked and opened in every direction around the bottom'. Furthermore, public interest had flagged and, with only £109 in the bank, the company accepted defeat.

Most of these enthusiastic failures highlighted specific elements in a many-faceted and capital-intensive undertaking. The Tasmanian failures led to an increasing understanding of the relatively greater importance of the local availability of good coking-coal than iron ore. This ensured that for the next half century all new ironworks would be established on the outcropping rim of the Sydney coal basin. Despite the unsympathetic attitude of the New South Wales government, potential ironmasters were encouraged by the market provided by the rapidly growing colonial population. The expanding railways offered a solution to the serious freight problems, apparent at both Mittagong and in Tasmania. Despite its failures, this period of growth was to establish the iron and steel industry's potential as an important basis for the economic development of Australia.

# 3

# AN AMERICAN ENTREPRENEUR AT LITHGOW

IN THE SAME YEAR as the Fitz Roy Iron Works company was dissolved, 1869, the railway moving westward from Sydney crossed the Blue Mountains and arrived in the Lithgow valley. The western descent was an impressive engineering feat involving the construction of the spectacular Zig-Zag railway. In the course of this work extensive deposits of coal had been discovered. To Charles Lyne, the effect on the Lithgow valley was like 'the wonderful results which followed the rubbing of the lamp whose virtues are told in Eastern story' for:

> Capital and enterprise saw their opportunity and immediately seized it. The appearance of coal seams led to the opening of coal mines; rich deposits of iron ore brought about the speedy establishment of ironworks; beds of clay, highly valuable for bricks and pottery, prompted the construction of brick and pottery works; the existence of a copper mine not many miles distant along the railway suggested the erection of copper-smelting works; good timber on the mountains pointed to the fitting up of steam sawmills; and the salubrity of the climate, as well as the general suitableness of the place for the purpose, showed the late Mr T. S. Mort the advantage of making the district a great meat emporium for the supply of the metropolis, and, if necessary, the markets of England . . . The sounds of industry are to be heard on every hand, and its signs are never absent, for night and day the fires of the furnaces are to be seen, and frequently the numerous chimneys, the straight columns of smoke, and

the haze hanging about, have much of the appearance of a manufacturing town in England.[1]

Almost overnight Lithgow became a boom town, absorbing the small rural villages around it and bringing to them a very different population. In 1939 Thomas Reid, who had been a schoolboy at Lithgow in 1882, recollected the early Lithgow ironworkers as 'rough, big-hearted men' drawn from the English, Welsh and Scottish iron- and steelworks. Their chief diversions were quoit playing, beer drinking and bare-knuckle fighting. Many of them could play a musical instrument and their lighter entertainments included singing and step-dancing.[2]

The principal pioneer in the establishment of the Eskbank works at Lithgow was James Rutherford. From his dictated autobiography,[3] published in the weeks before and after his death in 1911, Rutherford emerges as an optimistic, flamboyant and generous person. A shrewd, energetic and decisive businessman, he was not adverse to 'a good big row' if things were not as 'shipshape' as he expected. As a young American he had intended to prospect for gold in California but was deflected to Australia instead. After many adventures and a colourful career as a horse-trader, he discovered his real gifts as an organiser and an entrepreneur.

James Rutherford, entrepreneur and creator of the Eskbank ironworks, 1874. He remained a part-owner of the iron works until selling out to William Sandford in 1892.

In 1861 Rutherford was one of a group of businessmen who purchased the famous Victorian coaching enterprise, Cobb & Co. This consortium reorganised the coaching service in Victoria and then extended it to New South Wales, where they established their headquarters at Bathurst. Bathurst was an ideal location for the coaching business, for, although a wealthy pastoral and from time to time a gold-rush centre, it had no rail communication until the 1870s. Rutherford took up residence here and for the rest of his long life—he lived to be eighty-four—he was actively and generously involved in the affairs of the municipality.

After the railway crossed the Blue Mountains changes in methods of transport on the western plains were obviously imminent. The close connection of the iron industry with the expanding railways and the availability of raw materials in the vicinity of nearby Lithgow probably alerted Rutherford to the entrepreneurial opportunity to establish an ironworks there. In 1874 Rutherford met Dan Williams, a Canadian railway contractor engaged in adding a second track to the railway line to Lithgow and they

> agreed to spend £10,000 to open up the resources of the country for the benefit of posterity . . . then others joined us . . . a start was made with so many £500 shares, and calls were made as required. There were quite a number of shareholders but they dropped out one by one through inability to pay up, and eventually Williams and I found that we had 50 shares.

The company was floated in 1874 with shares offered at £500. Rutherford and Williams were joined by local pastoralists, including Thomas Brown, the lessor of the works site and the supplier of its coal. London business interests were represented by Thomas Denny. Rutherford and Williams were the major shareholders: eventually Rutherford held thirty-five and Williams twenty-nine shares. Among the most influential shareholders was the New South Wales politician John Sutherland, MLA for Paddington.[4]

Unlike most of the early iron smelters Rutherford had previously no known connection with the iron industry in any of its forms. He appears to have regarded it solely as an entrepreneurial opportunity. Williams, much more cautious than Rutherford, knew something about the iron business. For expert knowledge Rutherford was, and remained, entirely dependent upon others. Recollecting their plans many years later Rutherford was reputed to have said: 'when Williams and I entered into

## 3 AN AMERICAN ENTREPRENEUR

this venture, we did not expect [it] to result in failure, but we knew that we would encounter any amount of difficulties'.

In the early 1870s Rutherford met Enoch Hughes. Hughes is a figure of considerable importance in the early development of the Australian iron industry. Unfortunately much of our knowledge of Hughes's career is conjectural, but from the information available he appears to have been a man of energy and enthusiasm, possessed of considerable powers of persuasion. He was responsible for the erection of the blast furnaces at Mittagong in 1864 and Lithgow in 1875, and was also probably responsible for their design. After leaving the Fitz Roy works he refurbished the City Iron Works in Sydney for Alexander Brown.[5] Brown had previously been associated with the Australian Agricultural Company, which, despite its name, was one of the major coal-mining companies in the Newcastle area. Hughes then worked for the Enmore Patent Pressed Brick Works in New South Wales. Hughes's Newcastle connection may have provoked a letter which he wrote to the *Sydney Morning Herald*. He wrote:

> Fitzroy will remain idle, as I find it would pay better to send the iron ore to Newcastle to smelt it than to smelt it at the present place on account of the cost of coals and carriage to Sydney. At the time I erected the Fitzroy I was not aware of the existence of such a place as Newcastle, or I should at once have given up all hopes of ever making iron at Fitzroy to compete with any one that may commence at Newcastle . . . the facilities at Newcastle are such that cannot be surpassed both for coals and iron ore.[6]

The letter includes estimates for a blast furnace with a capacity of 120 tons per week and the wages bill for a staff of sixteen. Finally, he stated that he had detailed plans available for inspection by any interested party.

Hughes obviously remained fascinated with the idea of building blast furnaces, but for some reason, possibly financial, he abandoned the idea of Newcastle. In 1874 he was exploring the possibilities of the Lithgow area. Rutherford states that 'having met the late Enoch Hughes, who professed to be an iron expert, we secured through him a lease of 100 acres for a period of 50 years'. This was the Eskbank site.

Unfortunately, Hughes's technical knowledge does not appear to have advanced from the time of his arrival in Victoria in 1858. Thus in an industry with a rapidly changing technology his knowledge was a diminishing asset. The Eskbank blast furnace, which was blown in towards the end of 1875, showed no significant development from the improved

Fitzroy furnace of 1864. Technologically it was outdated even before it was blown in. The records available are not particularly informative but its similarity with the contemporary Fitzroy furnace is obvious from the table.

**Blast furnaces erected by Enoch Hughes**

| Specifications | Fitzroy (1864–77) | Eskbank (1875–82) | Onehunga (1890) |
| --- | --- | --- | --- |
| Height to filling-hole (feet) | 46 | 45 | 45 |
| Maximum diameter at boshes (feet) | 13.7 | 12 | 11 |
| Construction | masonry | masonry | masonry |
| Number of tuyères | 3 | 3 | ? |
| Production (tons per day) | 17 | 15 | 14–17 |
| Blowing engine (hp) | 50 | 78 | 40 |
| Blast | hot (from 1865) | hot | hot |
| Top | closed, single bell (from 1868) | closed, single bell | ? |

At this time some furnaces, for instance in the Cleveland area in England, had production rates approaching 100 tons per day.

However, despite his imperfections, Hughes was indisputably one of the few experienced ironmasters in the Australian colonies. It is perhaps a tribute to his practical skills that, despite its primitive design, the Eskbank furnace operated comparatively smoothly, if unprofitably, for nearly seven years, from 1875 to 1882. The output for these years had a total value of £119 451; it comprised:

- pig-iron (8844 tons)
- bars and rails (8323 tons)
- castings (1237 tons)
- bolts and nuts (51.5 tons)

Thus the furnace amply demonstrated the feasibility of making iron in the Lithgow district.

The foundation stone of the Esbank blast furnace was laid on 1 January 1875 by the Hon. John Sutherland MLA, Minister for Public Works in the Parkes 1872–75 administration, and a shareholder in the company. The furnace came into production towards the end of the same

## 3 AN AMERICAN ENTREPRENEUR

year.[7] Sutherland, a former Lord Mayor of Sydney, was born in Scotland. He had a particular interest in technical education and he was a vice-president of the Sydney Mechanics School of Arts. A builder by trade, his ministerial portfolio included the New South Wales railways. These linked the new ironworks with their Sydney market. Unlike some of his ministerial colleagues he was not a doctrinaire protectionist. He was anxious to encourage local industry, in particular the iron industry, as he felt that it would provide a foundation for other colonial enterprises.

During much of 1875 Rutherford was absent in America. He had been anxious to register the company as one of limited liability, but, for registration, the shareholders had to apply within a year of the company's formation. They also had to be unanimous, and prepared to meet the costs. Unfortunately these criteria were not met. On his return Rutherford found that the company was heavily in debt. Moreover, the blast furnace had not been blown in, although it was blown in shortly after. In view of Rutherford's other business commitments, and despite his own, Sutherland became managing director of the new enterprise with an annual salary of £750.

Sutherland was primarily a New South Wales politician. Not surprisingly he proved an unsuccessful managing director of a new ironworks nearly a hundred miles from Sydney, the normal centre of his activities. He had heavy political commitments and faced an investigation by the Elections and Qualifications committee. He was cleared but, in February 1880, he felt it incumbent upon him to resign his seat. Even apart from the government contract to reroll rails held by his firm, he was managing director of an unlimited liability company that, by 1880, was approximately £100 000 in debt. He was re-elected an MLA the following November, this time for Redfern.

By the late 1870s Rutherford was concerned at the cost of coal for the ironworks. It was 6s 6d per ton laden. He made a verbal agreement with the Eskbank company to purchase from Thomas Brown 860 acres of coal lands lying 'on either side of the railway lines for a distance of two or three miles together with his five shares in the industry'. The purchase price was £45 000. To meet it Rutherford borrowed from another of his enterprises, Cobb & Co., which had money lying in the bank at 4 per cent interest. This was to be repaid in six months at 8 per cent interest. However, the shareholders refused to honour the verbal agreement, so Rutherford sold the ironworks coal at 5s per ton laden and made a profit.

The purchase was a shrewd move. Belatedly realising this, the company gave him a promissory note for the money he was owed; 'then to make things all right I sold the note and passed it over to a friend to cash, and the company had to pay up or go to the wall'! At this time he was notified by the Commercial Bank of Sydney that the company was overdrawn to the extent of £75 000. In addition it had other liabilities amounting to £25 000. At this point Rutherford realised that if he was to recover his losses and the company's liabilities, he would have to manage the ironworks himself. The other shareholders gradually withdrew from the unprofitable venture. This left Williams and Rutherford responsible for both the works and its very substantial debts. Williams's health was declining, and he returned to North America where, a few years later, he died.

Meanwhile, in 1881, Enoch Hughes left Lithgow. A few years later, probably about 1888, he went to the Onehunga Ironworks Company near Auckland. Here his career appears to have followed a similar sequence of events to his careers in Mittagong and Lithgow. The *Australasian Ironmonger* enthusiastically reported that:

> surprise is manifested by everybody who pays a visit to Mr Hughes, the present manager. The works are now nearly completed, and in a few weeks will be ready to turn out all kinds of bar iron from 3/8 rounds to 8 × 3/4; also sheet iron of the most general sizes . . . a plant for galvanising iron now in transit from England, with the men who are experienced in rolling sheets, will soon be attached . . . The machinery consists of one 80 h.p., two 50 h.p. and one 12 h.p. engines, two rolling mills with a host of rolls for all sizes of bars, a complete set of sheet rolls, 2 steam hammers, 2 shearing machines, one cut off circular saw and 4 furnaces . . . The motive power is produced from four boilers all attached, so that . . . every machine can be put in motion at the same time. Attached to the mill is a foundry and a fitting shop . . . Fire bricks are also being made of very superior quality . . . Attention is now being given by the company to blast furnaces, with the prospect of ultimately shutting out imported pigs. About 50 men are at present employed. The capacity of the works when completed will be about 300 tons weekly.[8]

The article contains laudatory remarks about the layout of the works, commenting that 'the smoothness with which the machinery runs is very noticeable'.

Nevertheless, the venture obviously had had problems as, when the new sheet mill was started on 13 August 1889, it was reported that 'the spirit of doubt has almost totally disappeared, and confidence in the success of the (thus far ill-fated) venture at Onehunga is triumphant' as:

> everything works well, but it is found that the steam boiler is not sufficient to work all three mills together. They are now putting in a large boiler 60 h.p., with a certificate up to 110 lbs. per inch. The blast furnace which is now up 15ft., will have a total height when finished of 45 ft.[9]

Obviously it was to be another clone of the Mittagong and Eskbank blast furnaces. Professional rollers had been recently imported from America and 'the first sheets rolled (very thin) were torn in pieces by the crowd to be attached to watch chains, &c.' The Onehunga brass band enlivened the celebrations. Brass bands were a traditional contribution to early industrial celebrations.

The furnace came on blast early in July 1890.[10] Then, about November 1890, there was an accident 'by which part of the sheet-roll machinery has been smashed' and it was expected to be repaired within 'a few weeks'. Otherwise business was reported to be good. However, a month later the *Australasian Ironmonger* reported that 'Mr Enoch Hughes sues the Onehunga Ironworks Co. for £500 damages for terminating his engagement without notice. Case to stand over till the next session'.[11] Probably Hughes lost his case as he returned to Melbourne in September 1892 where, on 11 April 1893, he died. On his death certificate he is described as a foreman. He appears never to have found a satisfactory career in the country of his adoption. He was, like so many of his contemporaries, the victim of a rapidly changing technology. In spite of this, he deserves an honoured place in the roll of early Australian ironmakers.

Until his departure in 1881, the day-to-day management of the Eskbank ironworks was in the hands of Enoch Hughes, and Sutherland exercised an overall supervison. However, in 1882, shortly after Hughes left, Sutherland resigned as managing director. He remained well disposed towards the enterprise for, although his direct association with the Eskbank ironworks was short, its effects were enduring. Until 1920 iron products from the Eskbank works enjoyed particularly favourable rail freight charges. This hidden bonus is indicative of the pragmatism of the ostensibly free-trade governments of New South Wales, which were often torn between their doctrinaire principles and a more basic desire to encourage local industries. Although Sutherland's pragmatism occasionally presented problems for his ministerial colleagues,[12] this partially concealed bonus proved an essential feature in the survival of the works during its early years. The alteration of freight rates in 1920 made the already contemplated move of the Hoskins iron and steelmaking operations to Port Kembla an economic necessity. In 1903 the Royal Commission for Bonuses was told that the freight rates shown in the table had with 'slight variations' been granted to the Eskbank Iron Company since 1880. The railways offered various contract prices because, their officials informed the Commissioners, 'we recognise that the profit is not made upon the carriage of a particular commodity, so much as on the traffic incidental to its production. We do not like to lose profit'. The contract of Rutherford's successor, Sandford's, had the proviso that 'the iron shall be treated at his works at Lithgow'.[13]

**Freight rates for manufactured iron**

|  | When consigned | When forwarded by other consignors |  |
| --- | --- | --- | --- |
| Miles from Eskbank | In lots of 2 tons and over | 5 tons (per ton) | Smaller quantities |
| 50 | 6s 0d | 18s 9d | 22s 11d |
| 96 | 8s 0d* 10s 6d† | 34s 10d | 43s 0d |
| 100 | 10s 10d | 36s 3d | 44s 9d |
| 150 | 18s 8d | 52s 0d | 64s 5d |
| 200 | 21s 5d | 66s 0d | 81s 11d |
| 250 | 21s 5d | 76s 6d | 95s 1d |
| 300 | 24s 2d | 87s 0d | 108s 2d |
| 350 | 26s 11d | 97s 6d | 121s 4d |
| 400 | 29s 8d | 108s 0d | 134s 5d |
| 450 | 32s 5d | 118s 6d | 147s 7d |
| 500 | 35s 2d | 129s 0d | 160s 8d |

*To Sydney for export in 8-ton trucks
†For home use.

A number of causes probably contributed to the unprofitability of the first Eskbank blast furnace. Firstly, the changed international market conditions of the later 1870s affected Eskbank along with the other colonial ironworks. By the latter part of the decade wrought and pig-iron could still be imported from Britain more cheaply than they could be produced in the Australian colonies, despite the favourable freight rates Sutherland had arranged for the journey between Sydney and Lithgow. Secondly, the Eskbank ironworks, like the other contemporary colonial smelting operations, suffered from outdated technology. Difficulties more

Eskbank ironworks blast furnace, blown-in in 1875, demolished 1884. A technically outdated sandstone furnace. The barrow at the top of the incline is about to be discharged into the furnace.

specific to Lithgow were the inexperienced management, local attitudes and labour problems.

Between 1876 and 1882 Rutherford and his associates added to the blast furnace a foundry for making iron castings, six puddling furnaces for converting pig-iron into wrought iron, an 18-inch rolling mill with a 100-horsepower steam engine capable of rolling rails, a Nasmyth steam hammer, and two mill furnaces for reheating partially finished wrought iron. The closed-top blast furnace was 55 feet high to the top of the tunnel head and charge materials were brought up an incline for delivery into the filling-hole at the top of the stack. There were two hot-blast stoves and the blast to the three tuyères was driven by a 78-horsepower engine.[14] The furnace was capable of producing 100 tons of grey iron or 115 tons of white iron per week.

Both Sutherland and Rutherford lacked a basic knowledge of the industry and, given their other interests, could only provide part-time management. Rutherford's American background and attitudes were probably a disadvantage in a xenophobic commercial community. Certainly he felt, with some justice, that his product had been unfairly boycotted by the Sydney iron manufacturers' cartel, the Hardware Association, to whom he had offered very liberal terms; the trade price was £14 per ton and Rutherford asked £10 per ton to be paid only when they actually sold the iron. The Hardware Association considered the offer and rejected it; at the same time they offered to relieve Rutherford of the plant! Rutherford refused and attempted unsuccessfully to sell direct to blacksmiths, engineers and other iron users.

Some years afterwards Rutherford alleged that John Keep, chairman of the Sydney Hardware Association and a former shareholder in the Fitzroy Bessemer Steel, Hematite, Iron and Coal Co. Ltd. had told him that, 'we will have nothing to do with your iron and will oppose you by all means in our power'. Relations between Rutherford and his market, the Sydney iron founders, were far from cordial. John Keep & Sons were among those who had had long associations with Mittagong. It is possible that their influence ensured that Rutherford was frozen out of the Sydney market.[15] In fact this was another version of the problem that had confronted the Lal Lal Iron Company in Victoria in their relations with the Ballarat ironworking companies. It highlighted the need either to undersell imported iron decisively or to establish a link between the ironmakers and the iron users.

The blast furnace was finally blown out in 1882 when, it is alleged, Rutherford, exasperated with its unprofitability, blew up the furnace's foundations with two dray-loads of blasting powder thus removing the temptation of ever blowing it in again. Whether this actually happened or there was an accident of some sort it is impossible to state decisively. However in 1904 the story was recollected by O. C. Beale, President of the Sydney Chamber of Commerce. It was printed in the November issue of *Australasian Hardware and Machinery* only to be queried by W. J. Keep in the December issue. Keep suggested that dynamite might have been over-enthusiastically used to clear out the 'bear' of solidified iron found in the hearth of blown-out furnaces, which, at that time, was generally removed by blasting. In 1906 William Thornley, then general manager at Eskbank, told the Royal Commission on Customs and Excise Tariffs that 'the blast furnace was abandoned, and taken down about eighteen years ago'. Rutherford, in his dictated autobiography, neither confirmed nor denied the story. It would have been in keeping with Rutherford's extrovert personality to have turned an accidental disaster into an intentional design. Certainly this story became a part of Lithgow folklore and it reappears in *The Hoskins Saga*.[16]

After the blast furnace ceased operations in 1882 the foundry and rolling equipment continued in operation and, until a new blast furnace was blown in twenty-five years later, the Eskbank works were solely a centre of iron rolling, casting and forging. Rutherford was naturally anxious to run the works as economically and efficiently as possible to restore them to solvency. The works had been managed on the contractual basis traditional in the British iron industry.[17] Rutherford with his American background probably failed to understand the delicate relationship this involved, while the men may have hoped to benefit from his relative ignorance of both the industry itself and its traditions. From the start Rutherford and William Miller, the head roller and workers' spokesman, were antagonistic.

Miller's quarrel with Rutherford erupted in 1882 when the latter tried to adjust the puddlers' wages. These were the key to the wage structure and traditionally operated on a sliding scale geared to the market price of pig-iron. According to Rutherford he was confronted by a combination of the workers led by Miller who, knowing that there was plenty of work and assuming that Rutherford could not afford any delays, refused to accept any lowering of wages. Rutherford responded by a lock-out stating: 'I had a clause in the agreement that I could stop the works any time without giving the men any notice'. At the same time he arranged a six-month extension on his government contract with the New South Wales railways.

A meeting was then arranged between Rutherford and the workers, led by Miller. This started in deadlock and ended in a reluctant compromise. However, the meeting was barely over when the men heard that the Superintendent of Roads had received a letter from William Lyne, the Minister for Public Works, instructing him to offer the men work on the roads near Lithgow. The men were 'jubilant' at the news and the strike was on again. Rutherford recalled that 'at the end of six months they came crawling back again and I afterwards carried on without further trouble'.[18] He attributed their return to the hard labour of road works in the heat, but, as they were ironworkers, it appears more probable that their contract was completed.

Nearly sixty years later, Thomas Reid, who was a schoolboy at the time, claimed that Rutherford leased the works to a workers' co-operative between 1882 and 1886.[19] However, Rutherford gives no indication of operating any form of worker participation other than the traditional contract system. Similarly Miller, the reputed leader of this co-operative, when he was examined by the Royal Commission for Bonuses for Manufactures in 1902, made no mention of a co-operative at Lithgow, although he discussed workers' conditions, wages and the contract system.[20] At that time he had just retired after fifty years in the iron industry, twenty-six of them in Australia. In his evidence he stated that before coming to Australia he had worked in England and Scotland. The idea of a worker's co-operative was not unknown in the iron industry in Britain. It had its origins in the trade union philosophies of Robert Owen. Drinkfield Ironworks at Darlington in the north of England was set up with a nominal capital of £100 000 to be run on a co-operative basis but this venture collapsed in 1868.[21] Possibly Reid heard this enterprise discussed.

The contract system allowed, at least superficially, a high degree of worker independence and Reid recollected occasions when the workers would throw a brick into the air to decide whether to work that day. If it fell they declared a holiday! But, as payment was by piece-work, no production meant no wages, although it is possible that, given Rutherford's ignorance of the industry, the workers claimed more freedom than was usual within the traditional contract system. Certainly the situation was unsatisfactory, as the work-force fell by over 70 per cent between 1882 and 1886.

As a roller, Miller represented the aristocracy of labour among the ironworkers. He was their natural leader. Rutherford would have contracted the work to him, and Miller would have paid those who worked under him. Miller was born at Coatbridge, Scotland in 1835, where he served his apprenticeship in one of the local ironworks and was a head roller at the age of thirty. Miller then worked 'the only' reversing mill operating in Scotland at that time. After moving around to gain experience, he arrived in Australia in the 1870s. He was working as a roller at Mittagong in 1876. In 1878 he moved to Lithgow where Sutherland, another Scot, was managing the ironworks. This may have been significant as labour relations degenerated after Rutherford took over the management. Rutherford was abroad in 1885–86. During this period, in March 1886, the New South Wales government divided their contract for rolling rails between the Fitz Roy ironworks, then leased by William Sandford, and the Eskbank ironworks, where Miller was working under contract to Rutherford.

Sandford and Miller signed for their respective ironworks. Shortly afterwards Miller left Lithgow to take up the contract for rolling all the rod and bar iron at the Onehunga ironworks in New Zealand, where Enoch Hughes was manager and about to build his third and last blast furnace.[22] Sandford moved to Lithgow to take up the management of the Eskbank ironworks. On May 1887 both rail contracts were assigned to Eskbank and a bond for them was given by Rutherford and others on behalf of the company.

After five years in New Zealand, Miller returned to Lithgow in 1890. He was more fortunate than Enoch Hughes as, on his return, he settled down at Lithgow and in 1894 when the plate, sheet iron and steel rolling mill was opened the *Sydney Morning Herald* declared that 'Mr W. Miller a really practical ironworker, is now manager of the works. Nearly the whole of the works is carried out by contractors and paid on tonnage of good finished iron'. Miller retired in 1902 and visited England and the United States. However, his retirement proved to be only temporary and in the special article produced by the *Lithgow Mercury* to commemorate the opening of the blast furnace in 1907 there is both a brief biography of him and a photograph taken with the other heads of departments. He obviously settled down under Sandford and he was still working at the age of seventy-two.[23]

Many years later Rutherford described Sandford's arrival at Lithgow in 1886 'in quest of some waste plant . . . he eventually took a lease of the ironworks from me. I leased them to him on a royalty. Mr Sandford went to work there at a nominal salary £5 per week, and a standing share of the profits'.[24]

This arrangement was made about 1890 when Rutherford was anxious to sell the works. As Sandford had no capital the transfer took place in two stages. In 1890 Williams's executor was paid a deposit of £12 000, with Rutherford standing surety for £7000. The original asking price was £70 000 but Rutherford states that three years later in 1893—a year of financial crisis—Sandford paid him £30 000 advanced by the Commercial Bank and that, declared Rutherford 'was the end of my association with the ironworks'.

Rutherford's account of the transfer of the ironworks is occasionally ambiguous, and certainly over-simplified. Possibly this was not entirely due to his age and distance from the events. The eventual settlement appears to have been made as the result of the law suit brought by Sandford against Rutherford in the Equity Court of New South Wales on 22 and 23 March 1891. Sandford asked the court to declare that:

a partnership existed between himself and the defendant in reference to the re-rolling of iron rails for the government; and that the defendant might be ordered to pay £7,500 into the bank account, and restrained from appropriating such sum to his own use; that £4,000 of that sum might be applied in discharge of the plaintiff's liability for new machinery.

The case was settled out of court. Rutherford paid £3250 into a bank account (which appears to have been the account for the business), less the amount of Sandford's legal costs. These Rutherford undertook to advance with an interest of 7 per cent on the £3250. Sandford was to be entitled to the 'entire benefit of the Government contract to sell 10,000 tons of rails so far as such rails are worked up at the Eskbank works'. If the rails were sold without being worked up, the profit on resale was to be divided between them and the rails were not to be sold at under £4 10s per ton without Rutherford's consent. Rutherford and Sandford were declared not to be partners and, if Sandford had discharged his indebtedness within twelve months, Rutherford agreed 'not to re-enter for any breach of contract already committed'.[25]

Many years later Rutherford stated his reasons for selling. 'I could not put up with the men and other work demanded my attention.' In his old age he was gratified that he was '"the Father of the Iron Industry in Australia" and Mr Sandford himself has described me as such'.[26] Nevertheless, he probably found Eskbank among the least satisfactory of his many business enterprises. James Rutherford was not so much an ironmaster as an entrepreneur in search of opportunities. His real interests lay not in the industrial town of Lithgow, the site of the ironworks, but in the thriving pastoral community in and around Bathurst, the headquarters of Cobb & Co. To the developing civic life of Bathurst he made a lasting contribution.

# 4

# A PYRRHIC VICTORY

WILLIAM SANDFORD, who has arguably the strongest claim to being the father of the modern Australian iron and steel industry, was born in 1841 at Torrington, Devonshire. He was educated at a commercial college, with a view to a career in banking. However, he disliked banking and joined the London to Bristol section of the Great Western Railway. This appears to have aroused his interest in the manufacture of iron and steel as he became secretary to the Ashton Gate Iron Rolling Mills. Afterwards he joined the firm of John Lysaght, which produced puddled iron in the black country and then galvanised it in their Bristol plant.

John Lysaght, the founder of the firm, invented a technique of making wire netting, which he patented, along with a steam power drive for looms. Lysaght was interested in Australia and convinced of its commercial potential, a belief encouraged by the reaction of the primary producers to the increasing rabbit and dingo menace. In 1883 John Lysaght sent Sandford with his eldest son to establish the first wire netting factory in Australia. Lysaght and his brother chose a site on the Parramatta River at Chiswick in Sydney. Once the works were established, Sandford tried to interest his employers in starting a local iron- and steelworks. He failed. As he had little, or no, capital, he leased the ironworks first at Mittagong and then at Lithgow.[1]

During his years at Eskbank, Sandford's chronic shortage of capital led to inefficiencies and *ad hoc* arrangements in the operation and

William Sandford, proprietor of the Fitzroy Iron Works, 1886–1892, and of the Eskbank Iron and Steelworks, 1892–1907, at the official opening of the Lithgow No. 1 blast furnace, 13 May 1907.

lay-out of the plant, much of which became increasingly obsolete. Between the blowing out of the blast furnace in 1882 and the completion of Sandford's purchase of the works in 1893, Rutherford had installed a foundry comprising two cupolas and an overhead crane. But, during these years, new and capital-intensive technology was being rapidly developed in ironworks overseas, particularly in Germany and America. Seldom free from financial difficulties, Sandford was overwhelmed by them in the end.

William Miller, in his evidence before the 1903 Royal Commission on bonuses, highlighted the problem of antiquated plant 'a mill that will turn out 20 tons here would produce 60 tons in England' adding that 'at Eskbank, the work is done by sheer weight of bone and muscle'.[2] Traditionally iron- and steelworkers had been respected for their physical toughness. Nevertheless, the conditions under which the Eskbank workers laboured appear to have been both more strenuous and less productive than those of their contemporaries in Europe or America.

Thomas Reid recollected that, when the blast furnace was still operating, one of the busiest groups of workers was the slaggers. The low-grade local ore produced a considerable volume of slag, which was tapped into a round ring on a horse-drawn, flat-topped truck and hauled to the dump. Breaking the recently cast and still very hot iron pigs from the 'sow' was another particularly tough job. This was done by men wielding iron bars and wearing wooden clogs to protect their feet from the heat.[3]

The labour problems which had created such difficulties for Rutherford, remained. However, Sandford's English background combined with his knowledge of the iron industry and managerial skills to make them less crucial. In any case, the depression of the early 1890s meant that both the ironmaster and his workers were fighting for survival. The root of the problem, of course, lay in the obsolescence of the works combined with the high expectations of the immigrant workers. At the same time, the industry, operating in a free trade economy, was still linked to the cost of imported British iron.

The wages sought were, by any standard, too high. This was so, not only in comparison with English metalworkers but even in comparison with contemporary American workers, who with the most modern technology and government support were paid, on average, three shillings more per day than their English counterparts. In 1902 William Miller told the Royal Commission on bonuses that American rates would satisfy the men but then, he agreed, 'we could not compete in the open market'. He pointed out that many of the men were migrants and 'the men would not come out here to work unless they could do better than at home'. Furthermore, the cost of living was higher in Australia than in England or Scotland, the source of the imported iron that was underselling the local product.

More than half of the men employed at Eskbank in the 1890s were working under the contract system: 'their wages rise in rotation towards the roller, the heater's pay being next to that of the roller', and Miller, the head roller and workers' leader, told the commissioners, 'when I was rolling at Eskbank up to last March I had 17 men under me'. In 1903 William Thornley, the general manager of the Eskbank ironworks stated that 'it is very difficult to say what proportion of the wages would remain in the contractors' hands, because we do not know what the contractors pay. We have no control over the wages'.[4]

In 1903 there were about 350 men employed at the ironworks and a half to one-third of these were contract workers mainly employed in the rolling mills. As the technology changed, the traditional organisation of labour under the contract system broke down, resulting in an increasing lack of uniformity in labour management. Various parts of the works operated under contractual piece-work arrangements with groups of workers, while in other areas there was an hourly, daily or weekly wage.

Work was erratic. Although a twelve-hour shift was possible it appears to have been rare, particularly when the supply of old iron rails for rerolling declined during the 1890s. On being questioned on how many hours were normally worked, Herbert Bladon, an iron roller, told the Royal Commission on Bonuses that 'we commence work at a quarter to six, and we are often done by 3 o'clock or 3.30 in the afternoon'. On being further questioned he stated that although the aggregate working period could be from ten to ten and a half hours this included time off for breakfast and dinner, leaving a fraction over eight hours. He added 'we do not work continuously for even that period, because we have only two furnaces going, and we have spells in between for "smoke-ho's!"'. William Thornley, Sandford's manager, told the same Royal Commission that the sheet mill workers had refused to accept the offer of an eight-hour day unless it meant no reduction in wages and, he commented, 'they all belong to the one society'.[5] This was the Eskbank Ironworkers' Association of Mill and Forge Workers, a craft union. The various methods of work and the uncertain viability of the industry ensured that there was no workable union structure at Eskbank until the twentieth century.

The original plant installed at Eskbank by Rutherford and his associates had included an 18-inch mill with two stands of rolls—one for roughing and one for finishing. The mill was 'driven by an 80 hp. engine with a 20 ton fly-wheel, which was cast on the works from ores of the colony when the blast furnace was running'. It was fed by two heating furnaces, a ball furnace and six puddling furnaces. Each puddling furnace produced four balls of iron in one heat and there were eight heats in the ten- to twelve-hour shift. The balls were taken on bogies from the puddling furnaces to the Nasmyth hammer, where they were forged to approximately six-inch square blooms weighing about one to two hundredweight; from the forge these blooms went to the rolling mills where they were rolled into 'muck' bars some ten to fifteen feet long and about three to six inches wide by an inch thick, and finally cut into various lengths, piled and then rerolled into finished sections.[6] The inconvenient layout of the works resulted in considerable unnecessary heat loss during these sequential processes.

The Eskbank works manufactured ferrous goods for a variety of purposes. This was the period when worn-out wrought iron rails were being replaced by steel but, although scrap was cheap, uncertain demand precluded economies of scale and the machinery had to be frequently re-set for different jobs. This slowed production and increased costs. Sandford added to the plant a guide mill 'for rolling small sizes of bar and shoeing iron'.

In 1891, a protectionist ministry came into office in New South Wales. The outlook changed. Sandford, envisaging future support, started to make major improvements in the plant. In 1893 the first sheet mill in Australia was officially opened by the New South Wales Secretary for Public Works, William Lyne, who rolled the first sheet.[7] Sandford had introduced the sheet mill partly because of a £2 duty imposed on imported galvanised iron some years before. However, no sooner had the mill been installed than in 1894 the anti-protectionist ministry of George Reid took office and abolished the tariff. The New South Wales government had reverted to their opposition to *overt* protection. A corrugating and galvanising plant was also added at this time. By 1894 Sandford calculated that he had spent £15 000 in upgrading the plant, £96 866 in wages and £14 956 on freight.

A description of the works in 1898 notes that 'the whole of the raw material now being used in these works consists of scrap iron and old railway rails . . . principally from New South Wales; also partly-manufactured new imported bars, which are used as a mixture' and that 'the present output of the works which includes all kinds of bars and sections of iron, black and galvanised sheets, railway spikes and castings, is about 5,000 tons *per annum*'. The steam power for the works was supplied by ten large boilers; there were thirteen small and large engines and three steam hammers. The works were 'connected by a branch siding from Eskbank railway station, by which the raw material is brought in at one side and the finished goods taken away at the other'.

In 1898 Rutherford's 18-inch mill was only operating three days in the week, producing bars up to twelve inches wide and a variety of large sizes of angles, tees and channels. However, the reporter noted that 'Mr Sandford is now putting down a very large new engine for the guide mill for rolling the greater variety of sizes of iron and wire rods, also new rolls for rolling copper refined at the local smelting works into rods, sheets and plates. Part of the machinery is now on the ground for another sheet mill'.[8]

From 1886 to 1906 Sandford rolled scrap iron and, later, imported steel blooms. From 1900 these were augmented by the small amount of steel manufactured at the works. Expansion into the production of iron and steel was a matter of necessity as well as of choice for in 1902 Sandford admitted to the Royal Commission on bonuses that:

> when I started the works there were immense quantities of raw material available in the shape of scrap iron. The Railway Commissioners in New South Wales had thousands of tons of it, and I have seen some of it sold as low as 5s. per ton. The advantage of having the coal at Lithgow, and of being able to take the scrap iron available there is what induced me to establish the ironworks there.[9]

Originally he had been able to make mutually advantageous contracts with the New South Wales government to have the scrap delivered at Eskbank. By the end of the 1890s the supply of scrap iron in New South Wales had dried up. Sandford was then forced to purchase it not only from the other Australian colonies but even from New Zealand, as 'on account of steel taking the place of iron there is very little scrap to be had'. From 1899 to 1902 he estimated that he had imported 15 000 tons from Victoria through the ports of Newcastle and Sydney and then by train to Lithgow. His last freight contract with the New South Wales railways had been at £4 16 6 per ton.[10] Apart from any other consideration, lack of scrap made it imperative for Sandford to embark first on steelmaking and finally on the construction of a blast furnace to make pig-iron. Ultimately, this dilemma reduced him to an insolvency that was unavoidable without substantial public or private support. Sandford has

Eskbank Iron and Steelworks, 1905—an industrial complex manufacturing a range of cast iron, wrought iron and steel products

been widely acclaimed as Australia's first steel manufacturer. This is incorrect, but his steel-making and ironworking enterprises, products of scrap and determination, were harbingers of something far greater: an integrated iron and steel industry.

One of Sandford's most important additions to the Eskbank plant before the installation of the blast furnace in 1907 was a small, $4^1/_2$-ton Siemens–Martin furnace for the manufacture of steel. This plant was erected according to plans supplied by Frederick Siemens & Co. of London and was opened in 1900. It was of the 'new form' design invented by Dr Harvey.[11] It was intended to be remarkably fuel efficient, but these claims were not borne out in practice. The melters had great difficulty in achieving sufficiently high temperatures for successful steelmaking. To install the furnace Sandford engaged J. B. Jones. Jones began his career at the Dowlais Iron Works in Wales and had subsequently been employed by Dr Harvey to install steel furnaces at the Ebbw Vale Iron, Coal and Steel Company.[12]

There were many contenders for the title of Australia's first steel-maker. Sandford is often suggested, although it was not an honour which he himself claimed. There is considerable evidence to indicate that steel was being made in Victorian foundries more than a decade before Sandford made his first steel at Lithgow, and by at least three different processes. However, these earlier manufacturers went bankrupt in the depressed industrial conditions of the 1890s and the subsequent attribution to Sandford is possibly due to the survival and continuity of the Eskbank works.

Melbourne, like Sydney, had numerous iron foundries. Some of these were large enterprises developed to meet the requirements of the rapidly expanding city. The real pioneer in Australian steel-making was probably Langlands Foundry which, in the 1880s, was the largest in Melbourne with a capital of £100 000. In February 1887 Langlands announced in the *Australasian Trade Review* that they had 'recently completed arrangements for the importation of a steelmaking plant on the Bessemer process'. A month later the *Australasian Ironmonger*, the leading trade journal, congratulated the company on being the 'first to introduce steel-making plant into the colony'. The plant, which was manufactured in Sheffield by A. Davey & Co., included more than one converter.[13]

Langlands announced the arrival of the new plant at the Company's half-yearly meeting on 11 August 1887. The following November the plant was producing castings of up to two tons and manufacturing five-foot spur wheels, and the company declared that they 'found that the demand for cast steel was continually increasing'. Between March 1889 and February 1892 the company's letterhead declared that it was the sole agent for the 'Alfred Davey, Bessemer-Steel Process' and that it specialised in the 'manufacture of Bessemer and Crucible Cast Steel'.[14] This advertisement ceased after 1892 and it is probable that Langlands stopped making steel at this time. During the 1890s Langlands was confronted with increasing financial difficulties and in 1897 the company went into liquidation.[15]

At about the same time as Langlands began to manufacture Bessemer steel, the Victorian Steel Foundry Company Ltd, a small company founded in 1886 with a capital of £5000, pioneered the production of crucible steel castings in the Australian colonies. Its crucibles had a capacity of one hundredweight. This was typical of the process. By 1888 a growing demand for steel encouraged them to increase their plant. The foundry was in Victoria Street, Carlton, and the company's products included drills, cranks, wheels and hammers. The records of the company stop in October 1888. Nothing further is known about it.[16] Crucible steel was later manufactured not only by Langlands but also by the Sheffield Steel Works in Brunswick. In 1891 the Sheffield Steel Works specialised in making steel bells for fire brigades.[17]

In August 1889 John Heskett & Co. of South Melbourne started the manufacture of steel by the Siemens–Martin open-hearth process. Unlike Sandford's largely imported open-hearth furnace, this plant was almost entirely of colonial manufacture. Initially it produced about a ton of steel a day and in October 1889 it was reported that the company was employed on a contract to supply the Harbour Trust with bucket-back links, the first to have been made of steel in Australia, and the contract had been obtained in competition with British tenders. The raw materials used in this process were scrap files and hematite pig-iron. The company also made castings for government cranes. John Heskett had formerly been manager of the famous Middlesbrough steelworks, Bolckow, Vaughan & Co. Ltd, where Thomas and Gilchrist had conducted the final experiments for the Thomas Basic Process. In 1889 the *Australasian Ironmonger* credited Heskett with being the first to introduce steel-making by open-hearth process into 'these colonies'. The journal did not make this claim for William Sandford's venture some eleven years later.[18]

The installation at Eskbank of the small Siemens–Martin furnace in 1900 was followed by two more in 1902 and 1906. Despite this increased capacity Sandford still could not produce steel at competitive prices. It continued to be cheaper for the Australian manufacturer to import steel. Sandford blamed this situation on the high cost of labour, claiming that his weekly wages bill of £1000 was too high for him to compete with British and foreign iron and steel. In an attempt to offset foreign competition and to compensate for a lack of tariffs, wages in various sections of the Eskbank works were reduced by between 5 and 15 per cent.[19] Subsequent increases were to be subjected to a sliding scale based on the net selling price of iron, galvanised iron and steel.

Despite the special rates, rail freight charges remained a problem; for example, in 1902 they amounted to £10 000. By 1900 Sandford's dilemma was acute: he did not have the resources to modernise the Eskbank works, but unless he embarked on large-scale manufacture of iron and steel, he could not survive. On 5 July 1901, with a view to increasing the operating capital, the company went public: William Sandford Ltd was floated with a capital of £70 000 in 70 000 £1 shares, 55 000 of which were held by Sandford and his family.

Sandford was advised by Enoch James, who had been sent to the United States as a commissioner of the British Iron Trades Association to report on American industrial conditions and competition. James, both going to and coming from the United States, visited Lithgow, inspecting the works and investigating the available resources. His report was enthusiastic. He advocated the purchase of a blast furnace from Davey Brothers, Sheffield, estimating that iron could be made at Lithgow for 35s per ton. Sandford agreed, placed the order and expended £20 000 in the expectation that the anticipated government support would attract the necessary British capital.[20] Many manufacturers, including Sandford, had hoped that Federation would bring a national industrial policy providing assistance to the country's developing industry in the form of protective tariffs or bonus incentives.

In the event, the question of supporting the iron industry with either bonuses or tariffs provoked a long, drawn-out debate that lasted for most of the first decade after Federation. A further complication was the Labor Party's official adherence to a policy of nationalisation, thereby creating an uncertainty that discouraged foreign investment. At this time Sandford actually tried to persuade the New South Wales government to take over the works on condition that they would retain him as manager. However, the New South Wales government, now a consensus coalition under the premiership of the protectionist John See, was reluctant to embark on either establishing or acquiring a state ironworks. See was reflecting coalition opinion when he declared in July 1902 that it was better for 'such works to be undertaken by private enterprise'.[21]

The Eskbank works were not without potential rivals as in the quarter of a century from 1880 to 1905 there were a number of aborted schemes for establishing iron- and steelworks. As the majority were predicated on government assistance, they did not materialise. Among them were the ambitious schemes of William Jamieson's Blythe River Iron Mines Co. Ltd.; the Australasian Iron and Steel Co. Ltd; the Federal Iron Company, involving Christie Beaudarick, formerly associated with the Derwent and Lal Lal furnaces; the Victorian Iron Mines Syndicate; the Steel Syndicate of New South Wales, in which Dr Harrison of BTCIC fame participated; the Illawarra Syndicate, supported by Joseph Mitchell and the Iron, Steel and Metals Manufacturing Company Ltd of South Melbourne. The last-named company used the Moore–Heskett direct reduction process. This is the only known example of the direct process for the reduction of iron ore to iron ever to operate in Australia.[22]

Shortly after Federation, Sandford, in the expectation of a federal tariff, opened a second and more efficient sheet and corrugating mill. However, by 1904 when the Royal Commission on Bonuses for Manufactures finally met, both of the Eskbank sheet mills were a liability. To achieve profitability Sandford then decided that his only option was to offset the lack of tariffs with New South Wales government contracts. In 1903 Sandford already held certain state government railway contracts, including one for dog-spikes. This had required the installation of a special plant.

In 1905 the New South Wales government invited tenders from persons willing to establish the iron and steel manufacture in the state geared to meet the requirements of the government. Sandford made the only tender. It was accepted and, on 25 October 1905, a seven-year contract was signed for goods to be supplied from 1 January 1907. It was on the strength of this contract that Sandford commissioned a blast furnace. After extensive enquiries in Britain and the United States, the design selected was by J. H. Harrison of Middlesbrough. This new furnace was of contemporary British design and size. It had a nominal capacity of 1000 tons per week, or approximately ten times the output of the Rutherford furnace.[23]

William Sandford's son, John, who represented the firm in Britain, and William Thornley were largely responsible both for selecting the technology and appointing the men to operate it. They negotiated the contract with Harrison and engaged P. G. Pennymore, the blast furnace manager of Blaenavon Co. Ltd in Wales, to erect and manage the new blast furnace at Eskbank.[24] Pennymore arrived at Lithgow early in 1906 and brought three experienced foremen with him. In addition John Sandford and William Thornley appointed F. H. Wigham, then manager of the steelworks and rolling mills at George Cradock & Co., Wakefield, as steelworks manager at Eskbank, and E. Penzer, works manager of J. & W. Marshall's works at Smethwick near Birmingham, as manager of the Eskbank rolling mills. Thus all the major production departments were in the hands of British experts. From their records they were an able group of men of whom Sandford was justly proud.[25] Nevertheless, the selection of a British blast furnace is surprising, for American technology was pre-eminent at that time. The decision may have been influenced by the imperial connection and the need to attract capital, as well as by the British background of both Sandford and his general manager, William Thornley.

The furnace was typical of those in the Cleveland district of England in the late nineteenth century. Seventy-five feet high and nineteen feet in diameter internally at its widest point, it was massive in relation to all previous Australian blast furnaces. Rutherford's earlier stone-built furnace, built at nearby Eskbank and demolished in 1882, had dimensions of fifty-five and twelve feet respectively. The Sandford furnace had a steel-cased stack supported on ten cast iron columns each weighing seven tons, and was closed at the top by a single bell-and-hopper. Today all that remain are the furnace hearth and some ruins, including those of the turbine room and the engine house which had contained the blowing apparatus. It is a sad memorial to a brave enterprise.

Built on a site about a mile and a quarter from the existing ironworks, the blast furnace was intended to be the first unit of a new integrated iron- and steel-making complex planned to include four blast furnaces. The new location was attractive both on account of its proximity to the main Sydney–Lithgow railway and because there was space for expansion. However, in the short term it increased Sandford's operating inefficiencies as cold pig-iron had to be transported from the pig-beds to the steel-making furnaces in the existing ironworks. The thermally efficient practice would have been to transfer the hot liquid metal directly from the blast furnace to the steel-making furnaces. This logistical problem undoubtedly contributed to the ultimate financial failure of the plant.

The furnace was charged by hand; barrows carrying approximately ten hundredweight of coke or limestone, or fourteen and a half hundredweight of ore, were filled from wooden bins at ground level and then hoisted, by steam-driven elevator, 75 feet to the charging platform from which they were tipped manually on to the bell. This labour-intensive method of charging the furnace required thirty-two men per shift, and the practice persisted until 1928 when iron manufacture at Lithgow ceased.[26] At the time when the furnace was installed mechanical charging systems had been in use for nearly a quarter of a century. They were first used in 1883 on the record-breaking Lucy furnace of the Carnegie Steel Corporation in Pittsburgh. By 1907 they were operating on a number of overseas furnaces. But, significantly, they were not used in Britain until 1905 when they were introduced into the Frodingham Ironworks at Scunthorpe, too late to affect the design of the Eskbank furnace. Mechanical charging was not adopted in Australia until 1915 when an American-style furnace was blown in at the Broken Hill Proprietary Company's Newcastle steelworks.

The blast was initially provided by a vertical Davy steam-driven blowing-engine. This was supplied by Davy Brothers, Sheffield, and produced a blast of 15 000 cubic feet per minute at 8 pounds per square inch. Apparently it proved inadequate as shortly after the furnace was commissioned a Parsons turbine of 20 000 cubic feet capacity and an output pressure of 12 pounds per square inch was installed. The air blast passed from the blowing engines to three Cowper stoves—conspicuous in most photographs of the plant—each 22 feet in diameter and 74 feet high. These raised the the blast temperature to 600–800°F (315–425°C) and were the first regenerative stoves to be used for blast heating in Australia. Previously where a hot blast was used it was heated in pipe stoves. In these the air was conducted through cast-iron pipes arranged in an oven which was heated either by blast furnace gas or by coal. The life of these pipes was short and their replacement expensive, while the leakage of the blast often prevented the satisfactory operation of the furnace.

The leakage problem had been overcome by Cowper who, in 1857, invented a stove that used the regenerative principle advocated by William Siemens and later used in the Siemens–Martin steel-making furnace. Cowper stoves contained a honeycomb of refactory brickwork which alternately was heated by burning blast furnace gas and used to heat the blast. A continuous supply of hot blast required several stoves, as some had to be heating up—'on gas'—while others were 'on blast'. Sandford's original three stoves were increased to four in 1912.

Another significant technical difference from most earlier Australian furnaces was the use of a closed hearth. The 'closed forehearth' or 'closed hearth' was patented in England by F. Luhrmann of Osnabrück in Prussia in 1867 and, although simple and effective, it was slow to replace the 'open forepart' until the use of higher blast pressures made it essential. In the closed hearth the furnaceman had no access to the bottom of the furnace. Liquid iron was removed from the hearth through a taphole which was plugged with clay between taps. Most previous Australian furnaces had an 'open forepart', allowing the furnaceman to clear blockages in the hearth by the use of various bars and hooks worked through an arch at the bottom of the furnace. This severely interrupted the production of iron because the blast had to be stopped during the clearing-out process.

A blast furnace of the size built by Sandford had a voracious appetite for raw materials. When working at full capacity it required each week a total of at least 3000 tons of coke, ore and limestone. In its early years the furnace was operated less intensely as the demand for iron was limited. Nevertheless, even this required much more ore than could be obtained from the small deposits of varying quality used by Rutherford. To meet this Sandford opened a new quarry at Carcoar, ninety-six miles by rail west of Lithgow. This produced medium grade ore containing about

Official opening of the William Sandford & Co. Ltd. blast furnace, Lithgow, 1907. From left to right are the engine-house, boilers, blast furnace and stoves, and the steam-driven elevator. Visitors seen in the foreground are standing dangerously close to the pig-beds, awaiting the flow of molten iron.

56 per cent iron. It was to provide a million tons of ore before it became exhausted in 1923. Coke was purchased locally from Oakey Park Colliery. Its quality was marginal and its quantity often inadequate. This led to the undesirable operating practice of charging raw coal mixed with coke directly to the furnace. Later Oakey Park supplies were to be supplemented by higher-grade coke purchased from the Illawarra and Newcastle regions. Limestone was obtained from the Commonwealth Portland Cement Company at Portland, New South Wales.

The official opening ceremony on Monday, 13 May 1907, was performed by the Premier of New South Wales, Joseph Carruthers, in the presence of 'a cheerful, expectant, and influential group of Sydney citizens also State and Federal politicians and other public men' who were brought to Lithgow from Sydney by special train. In honour of the occasion the works were festooned with bunting bearing such slogans as 'Welcome to Ferropolis' and 'Bravo Sandford', while the band struck up 'appropriate selections'—including the 'Village Blacksmith'. A banquet followed and was concluded with a great number of enthusiastic imperial and patriotic speeches. In his speech the premier adopted a strong states' rights approach, supporting state encouragement, but against federal protection. He declared: 'we do not want any interference here from the Federal Government . . . we do not want them coddling up other industries in South Australia and Tasmania. We do not want the taxpayers of New South Wales taxed . . . to bring into existence . . . some other industry'.[27] Federation was still a very new and only half-accepted concept.

In his reply Sandford emphasised three issues. He stressed the economic importance of the venture: 'I consider that the country that can make the cheapest steel has the other countries at its feet as far as manufacturing in most of its branches are concerned'. Secondly, he stressed the importance of the industry in relation to national defence declaring that 'pig-iron was the base of defensive materials'. Developing this theme he looked forward to 'the time when we in Australia will be able to make all our own steel, not only our requirements in time of peace, but in time of war'. Thirdly, he emphasised his methods of management and the direct interest in the works of many of the 800 workers, some of whom had bought shares when the company had become public.

> From mining the iron ore to the finished article, the business was controlled by one board of directors and general manager, from one office. The directors were all heads of departments. A large number of the men were

interested in the progress of the works, in the shape of holders of fully paid up shares, freehold land and houses. The men have their council with president and secretary. Every six months the sales books were audited by a chartered accountant, the men paying half the cost and the firm the other half. If it were found that the average selling price was 5s ton higher than for the previous six months, wages were advanced for the next six months 2 per cent. and so on. The same thing applied when prices went down. The firm embraced all the works, colliery and freehold estate, so that its scheme was complete. He mentioned this to show how they had managed to exist during past years.[28]

This system was possibly a hybrid derived partly from the method of workers' supervision customary in the coal industry and partly from the sliding scale contract linked to the selling price of iron, traditional in the British iron industry. It worked. The relationship between labour and management was comparatively tranquil during Sandford's years at Lithgow.

Despite the outward success of the glittering opening, William Sandford was a deeply worried man. In his speech he also commented that while 'the Premier had referred to the possibilities of expansion of this industry . . . if the works were stopped to-morrow, some thousands of breadwinners in all the various walks of life in connection with the town would be immediately affected and their incomes reduced'.

From 1903 to 1907 Sandford had tried unsuccessfully to make the works financially viable. In 1902 the works made a profit of £2750. A similar profit was made in 1903, but in 1904 there was a loss. The brighter aspect encouraged by profits of £3005 and £6041 in 1905 and 1906 respectively was offset by a loss in 1907, the final year of the company's operation. The new blast furnace and its ancillaries had cost £100 000, some £30 000 more than the original estimate. It had been financed by a further overdraft of £63 500 from the Commercial Banking Company of Sydney, bringing the company's total overdraft to £131 000. The company was clearly over-committed. To acquire the working capital to operate the new plant, Sandford offered 100 000 £1 shares on the open market. The float was unsuccessful as only 18 599 shares were taken up.[29]

Moreover, despite the enthusiasm which accompanied the blowing in of the blast furnace, there was an immediate problem in finding a market for the quantity of pig-iron that it produced. This was probably exacerbated by a conservative opposition to the native product.

However, another of William Sandford's sons, Roy, took over the marketing side of the business and proved an exceptionally successful salesman. In under three weeks in August 1907 he sold 3750 tons of pig-iron in Melbourne. He attributed this success to the fact that the Melbourne manufacturers 'were believers in protection and the establishment of local enterprise' as well as to his knowledge of chemistry and experience in iron-making. This enabled him to demonstrate the quality of his product by running 'casts in the foundrymen's own cupola using more and different scrap with our iron than they had been able to use with No. 1 imported Garthsherrie'.[30]

In New South Wales from May 1907 G. & C. Hoskins had used Lithgow pig-iron in its Ultimo pipe works and, knowing the product, Charles Hoskins later applied for 10 000 shares in William Sandford Ltd's new issues but 'on condition that his auditors could examine our books beforehand'. After perusing the books Hoskins withdrew his offer. Sandford attributed his withdrawal to 'the need of a bonus'.[31] The bonus question had been under consideration since Federation, but the issue had proved so complex that the bonus was not granted until the passing of the *Manufacturers Encouragement Act* in December 1908—a year after Charles Hoskins had become the owner of the Eskbank ironworks.

G. & C. Hoskins Ltd was the largest single customer of William Sandford Ltd. The company purchased the pig-iron for its extensive cast-iron pipe production. George and Charles Hoskins were clever and ingenious engineers as well as astute and entrepreneurial businessmen with a strong and enduring family loyalty, continued over two generations of Hoskins brothers. This made them a formidable team, and possibly ensured their survival. From 1888 the company held a contract from the Sydney Metropolitan Water Board to supply the pipes that carried the main Sydney water supply. They acquired this contract when the original contractor, Wilmot & Morgan, failed to seal the lead joints in the pipes. Charles Hoskins observed the failure and, when Wilmot & Morgan surrendered the contract, he tendered for it to the Metropolitan Water Board. On being awarded the contract, the Hoskins brothers satisfactorily sealed the pipes by wrapping the joints with kerosene-soaked ropes. These, when ignited, generated sufficient heat to melt the lead solder. Other contracts, including laying the duplicate main, followed.[32] The firm was admirably suited to supply the demands of a rapidly growing urban society requiring pipes for gas as well as water.

# 4 A PYRRHIC VICTORY

In 1892 the Sydney Metropolitan Water, Sewage and Drainage Board split its contract between Pope & Mather, who were to make 4- and 6-inch pipes and fittings, and G. & C. Hoskins, who were to make over 6- and up to 12-inch pipes. These contracts were for five years renewable and from 1892 no cast-iron pipes were imported into New South Wales. On the failure of Pope & Mather in 1904, G. & C. Hoskins became the Metropolitan Water, Sewage and Drainage Board's sole suppliers of cast-iron pipes and fittings. Their sales of cast-iron pipes were not confined to Sydney or even to the country towns of New South Wales. They also fulfilled a number of interstate contracts. The largest of these came in 1898 when they, and Mephan Ferguson of Melbourne, contracted for £1 025 124 with the government of Western Australia to lay the pipes to bring water to the Western Australian goldfields. This contract was successfully completed on 4 August 1904 amid general acclaim. When on 14 May 1907 Charles and George Hoskins attended the official blowing in of the new blast furnace of their prospective supplier of pig-iron, William Sandford Ltd, they were a leading and solidly established New South Wales firm with two plants situated in Ultimo and manufacturing iron pipes and machinery.

Within six months of the spectacular opening ceremony at Eskbank it was clear that Sandford had failed to raise the capital he needed to sustain his expanded works. He turned to the Liberal government of New South Wales for assistance. The government had four choices: to turn a deaf ear and to let the works close; to nationalise them, which was against its policy; to support Sandford; or to find a buyer with sufficient capital to develop the enterprise. Confronted with this problem the administration appointed a committee composed of W. H. Forrest, G. E. Brodie and E. M. de Burgh to investigate the overall position of the works. They reported that:

> The most valuable iron is now produced without difficulty, and compares favourably with the best products of the world. Demands in the open market and repeated orders show that the pig iron is giving satisfaction. The tests made of steel and iron produced in the works from the pig are satisfactory ... That such results have been obtained since the blast furnace started ... show that the expectations of this most important industry have been more than realised.

The *Australasian Hardware and Machinery* concluded that 'what these investigators felt the company needed was money to augment the plant already in position'. The precise financial position of the company as estimated by the specially appointed accountant, Albert Borchard, is shown in the balance sheet.

**Balance sheet**

*Assets*

| | £ |
|---|---|
| Blast furnace plant and site of 56 acres | 100 000 |
| Ironworks plant and site of 20 acres | 77 000 |
| Freehold farm site of 400 acres | 49 000 |
| Colliery | 20 000 |
| Carcoar and Cadia iron ore leaseholds | 5 000 |
| Debtors, including the government and deposits on contracts | 35 000 |
| Stocks of raw and manufactured materials | 45 000 |
| Sundries | 3 000 |
| **Total Assets** | **324 000** |

*Liabilities*

| | £ |
|---|---|
| Bank | 131 000 |
| Other creditors (including W. Sandford, £4000). | 32 000 |
| **Total Liabilities** | **163 000** |
| **BALANCE** | **161 000** |

On 3 December C. G. Wade, who had succeeded J. H. Carruthers as premier in October 1907, placed before the legislature a proposal to rescue William Sandford Ltd from its insolvency and to provide it with sufficient capital to allow it to continue operation. The premier explained that 'The company was really suffering from two defects—its capital and its plant were alike inadequate. Owing to undercapitalisation it was living from hand to mouth. Liquid assets were needed to carry on smoothly, and additional steel furnaces to increase the output and secure bigger profits'. He then proposed a loan of £70 000 at 4 per cent interest, £25 000 to be advanced immediately as working capital and the balance to be applied to the erection of new plant. The bank was to continue the company's present loan with its ceiling of £135 000 to run

for ten years at 4 per cent instead of the present 5 per cent interest. The government was to have first claim on the company for £25 000 and for the remainder to rank *pari passu* with the bank.[33]

The proposal met with considerable opposition. The leader of the opposition, the Labor politician J. S. T. McGowen, moved as an amendment 'that the state take over as a going concern the business of the company known as William Sandford Ltd. at a valuation based on the present value of the business on the open market, and work the industry as a state concern'. The majority were unwilling to go to this extreme. Nevertheless, they insisted 'that the state loan should take priority of any security held by the bank'. The premier, seeing that the numbers were against him, agreed to this modification. But the Commercial Banking Company of Sydney refused to concede the government first mortgage and foreclosed.[34]

On 9 December the citizens of Lithgow, aware of the social consequences of the loss of approximately 1000 jobs which over the last nine months had brought in an income of £69 000, sent a deputation to the premier. They received his assurance that 'everything possible would be done to secure a settlement of the difficulty. Although the government was at the end of its present resources, he was not without hope of some acceptable scheme being formulated'. At this point the Eskbank ironworks closed down, except for the blast furnace as this 'would cost £500 to start again'. The workers reacted by holding a meeting to express their sympathy for and loyalty to Sandford at this difficult time.

On 19 December it was announced that G. & C. Hoskins Ltd would take over the works as a going concern and 'one of the first acts of the new proprietors was to send the season's greetings to the employees at Lithgow, accompanied by a cheque for £100 to relieve any temporary pressure'. The money was sent to the Commercial Bank and the men out of work were asked to appoint a committee of three to arrange for its distribution.

Many years later Sir Cecil Hoskins recalled that:

Although they [Hoskins] had not been directly interested in production work at Lithgow prior to Sandford's financial failure, they were in point of fact quite interested in any plant which could produce pig iron . . . It was almost a natural corollary, when the Commercial Banking Company of Sydney Limited foreclosed on William Sandford Ltd and when the implications of this were appreciated by the New South Wales Government, that an approach should be made to the firm of G. & C. Hoskins Limited to see whether they would be interested in carrying on the infant iron and steel industry ... After negotiations it was announced that G. & C. Hoskins would stand in the position of William Sandford Ltd. as owners of the Eskbank Ironworks.

Hoskins took over the overdrafts of £45 000 on the old ironworks and £93 000 on the new blast furnace. They agreed to pay £14 700 to shareholders in the form of 4 per cent interminable bonds. In addition the Hoskins firm made an *ex gratia* gift of £50 000 to be paid in five equal parts to William Sandford 'in recognition of the work he had done in pioneering the iron and steel industry at Lithgow'.

As the Metropolitan Water Board's contractor for pipes and a large consumer of pig-iron in their manufacture, G. & C. Hoskins was obviously high on the list of entrepreneurs with sufficient capital to take over such an undertaking if it was to remain in private hands. However, embarking on such an enterprise could easily strain the resources of even a medium to large private company and the Hoskins brothers were very well aware of this fact. Sir Cecil Hoskins recollected that, despite the heavy debts which they had incurred:

> they knew that they had to modernise the Lithgow plant and spend a considerable amount of capital on this modernisation. They could not, indeed they dared not, relax their pipe making or their engineering interests because these represented in very truth their capital life-blood, and it was these that had made possible their new ownership of the Lithgow Ironworks.

Many years afterwards William Sandford's son Roy wrote that his father had told the *Sydney Morning Herald*:

> I am accepting the offer of Messrs. G. and C. Hoskins as a matter of necessity ... My feelings are the reverse of satisfactory because I attempted TO DO WHAT HAS NEVER BEEN DONE IN ANY COUNTRY IN THE WORLD—ESTABLISH THE IRON INDUSTRY WITHOUT DUTIES OR A BONUS—AND I HAVE FAILED.[35]

Roy Sandford also admitted that his father had said 'I have every confidence in Messrs. G. and C. Hoskins, and I believe that the burden of iron production is on shoulders well fitted to bear it'. William Sandford retired to live at Eastwood in Sydney where, in 1932, he died in his ninety-second year. He remained a highly respected figure in the iron and steel world. His son declared that he had refused a knighthood because of his sense of failure.[36]

At the conclusion of Sandford's evidence to the New South Wales Royal Commission on the Iron and Steel Industry in 1911, Commissioner Paul, whose *Report* was generally unfavourable to those involved in the industry, gave some indication of Sandford's standing among his contemporaries when he commented that 'in meeting you it has afforded me the utmost pleasure to come into contact with one whose name will be handed down in history as one of the great pioneers of the iron and steel industry in Australia, and whose name today is almost synonymous with that of iron'.[37] William Sandford's career had proved that an iron and steel industry in Australia required more than determination and unsupported entrepreneurship. His successors were not only to have greater financial backing from their other enterprises but also firm support from the state, as politicians, and their electors, began to comprehend both the nature and complexity of the industry and its centrality to the development of industrial independence and national defence.

# 5

# TOWARDS A SOCIAL CONTRACT

AUSTRALIAN ATTITUDES TO LABOUR have often appeared incomprehensible to other countries and they have sometimes been blamed for the country's failure to achieve its industrial potential. Of course symptoms can be misread as easily as causation can be distorted, so it is useful to remember some basic facts. Australian society, in its non-Aboriginal manifestation, is palpably new. This is not merely to restate what every textbook tells: that the first settlements occurred barely two hundred years ago. Rather, Australia's newness is a newness of spirit that comes from viewing the past at best as but a part of collective wisdom rather than an icon. The essence of the difference is speed of change. Little more than a few generations separate today's immigrant protagonists from a canvas that was totally devoid of them and their precursors from the British Isles. Yet in this blur of time lies the story of a nation's identity and, in an even briefer moment in it, the foundations of its industry and industrial relations. More precisely, the period 1890–1914, when circumstances obliged Australians to declare for themselves a social contract, also laid the basis of heavy industry, notably iron and steel, and its modern management. Undoubtedly analogous coincidences occurred elsewhere, but rarely in such stark relief and with such speed. An understanding of these years is therefore crucial to a comprehension of much that followed.

The migrant population of nineteenth-century Australia was remarkably homogeneous, being mainly from the United Kingdom. From the end of the gold rush in the 1850s until after the great depression in the 1930s, emigration to Australia was slight. Occasionally, as in the decades 1891–1900 and 1921–30, more people were actually leaving than settling in the country.[1] In 1900, at the time of Federation, 77 per cent of the 3 771 000 white Australians were native-born.[2] The society they dreamt of drew its basic philosophy from their British origins, but isolation had provided added dimensions. Some of these pressures were new, or environmental; others were extensions of divisions within British society itself, social, sectarian and even ethnic, which intensified the need for mechanisms of social equipoise[3].

It was clear by the time of the Hoskins take-over at Lithgow that the iron and steel industry was becoming part of Australian politics. Increasingly it was being seen as an 'issue' in a society which contained many unresolved contradictions. This was because Australia's early Europeans bore the stamp of the first industrial nation. Their conflicts over industrialisation, its aims and social costs, were an important part of the settlers' cultural inheritance. However, unlike in Britain, labour was at a premium in Australia and the power of the ballot box gave further weight to its position in the industrial equation. It is therefore important to stop and look at both the realities and the aspirations of labour at the point where the new iron industry, potentially a massive employer of labour, was about to take off.

Australian capital and labour at least shared a faith in governments, albeit for different reasons. Both schools confidently took wealth creation as a given constant, the maintenance of which it was the duty of a government to guarantee. Only the unread or the artful could pretend to be true believers in *laissez-faire*. The actual state of Australian industrialisation was, paradoxically, always many degrees behind its industrial politics and culture. Infused with Victorian optimism, and regardless of the practicalities, the idea had become established that all Australians were entitled to a better life. Socialist theories let the less materially fortunate members of society feel that they had a *moral* claim to a greater share of any economic surplus. A society was envisaged in which altruism balanced need and the spirit of egalitarianism placated the tyranny of envy. Unfortunately the road to the Celestial City was beset by the mundane realities of economics as well as the frailties of human nature.

This was the society into which the iron-making industry was poised to make its crucial leap. It brought with it its own anachronism, the predating of the iron-making industry by the ironworking industry, whose labour structures were already firmly established. But these industries were of comparatively small or moderate dimensions. In contrast the iron-making industry was a large, and potentially massive, employer of labour. As such it was inevitable that it would challenge already established political ways. This alone would bring it into conflict with essentially conservative labour forces.

Australian nationalism developed slowly. But in the depressed 1890s, as Professor J. M. Ward observed, 'a new recognition, occurring among men of all parties, that governments would inevitably become more active in controlling social and economic affairs'. He analysed the desire for Federation as follows: 'the upsurge of interest in federation arose principally from the hope that problems such as trade recession, the alarming contraction of Australian credit abroad, the collapse of the property market and the turmoil in the banking system would be alleviated by Federal action'.[4]

The decade preceding Federation had seen the severest economic depression Australia had known. Although the depression was world-wide, this did little to cushion the shock to the confidence of the Australian colonies. In addition, the banking crisis of 1889 and the recurring crises of the early 1890s emphasised the colonies' dependence upon overseas capital. The depression had been particularly acute in the rural sector, traditionally the strength of the economy, where it was exacerbated by a long drought. This delayed the start of recovery until 1905.

Consequently, debates on Federation took place against a background of depression and the emergence of labour as a political force. The Australian Labor Party, which emerged in the late nineteenth century, was a mixture of pragmatic ambitions and doctrinaire aspirations. From the beginning the movement had an in-built dichotomy. The strongest element was the Anglo-Australian strand whose dynamic was the expanded trade union movement of the late nineteenth century. Its essential concerns were with pay, conditions and a more equal division of the real or perceived economic surplus. It combined the aspirations of the migrant and the nationalism of the native-born. Most importantly, it sought to operate within the existing legal and political framework. In *Civilising Capitalism* Bede Nairn writes that not only was capitalism fundamental to all the Australian colonies but:

> Labour men knew enough history, especially nineteenth century European history, to realise the dangers of theories of social reconstruction that sought to improve the lot of the working man by promising freedom

through the abolition of the social foundations and institutions that, to British peoples made freedom possible. Labour was open to cosmopolitan schemes for improvement, but it fitted them into the acceptable democratic routine.

Many of the early Labor politicians eschewed doctrinaire socialism, fearing that it was allied to anarchy. Instead they stuck firmly to what they considered to be a pragmatic approach to reform. Similarly, the majority of labour voters were cautious and conservative, especially when it came to foreign ideas propagated by revolutionaries 'who wished to sacrifice some people in order to perfect others'.[5] Furthermore, the elitist element in socialism ran counter to the Australian belief in egalitarianism.

Nevertheless, the arrival of the Labor Party undoubtedly 'injected powerful class and social elements into politics'. The movement also had strong theoretical undercurrents with their origins in European and North American radicalism. The political party was always under pressure from the more militant opinion in the movement. This ginger group found its extreme expression, apart from anarchism, in the *Communist Manifesto* in which German intellectual Karl Marx advanced the theory that:

> the history of all hitherto existing society is the history of class struggles . . . that each time ended, either in a revolutionary reconstitution of society at large, or in the common ruin of the contending classes . . . society as a whole is more and more splitting into two great hostile camps, into two great classes directly facing each other: Bourgeoisie and Proletariat . . . in short the Communists everywhere support every revolutionary movement against the existing social and political order of things . . . They openly declare that their ends can be attained only by the forcible overthrow of all existing social conditions.

However, material progress brought modifications in social and political philosophy. Society became healthier, wealthier and better educated. Industrialisation had created the surplus wealth that was largely responsible for these changes. More individuals became directly affected by, and therefore interested in, government. Moreover, the labour-intensive new technology brought with it the hope of full employment and the concept of the 'right to work'—a phenomenon unknown in preindustrial societies, dominated by the seasonal nature of agrarian employment.

It is significant that both in Britain and Australia the union movement itself spread unimpeded from the skilled to the unskilled and that the enfranchisement of the workers *preceded* the establishment of a political Labor party. The right to political expression was, therefore, never in contention. The union provided the training ground for politics, although the demands of union and parliamentary politics often proved surprisingly different. Prominent among nineteenth-century politicians from union backgrounds were Richard Sleath, J. H. Cann, W. J. Ferguson, and Josiah Thomas from Broken Hill, as well as W. G. Spence of the Australian Workers' Union. All of these men sat in the New South Wales legislature in the late 1890s, while Cann and Thomas went on to distinguished careers in state and federal parliaments respectively.[6] In 1912 Cann, as Treasurer of New South Wales, was to play an important role in the negotiations leading to the the Newcastle Iron and Steel Bill.

The organisation of large, unskilled unions in the late nineteenth century increasingly emphasised class consciousness and favoured the adoption of philosophical panaceas, especially in times of economic uncertainty. These unions became confrontational as owners and managers felt beleaguered by a combination of adverse economic conditions and a hostile work-force, both of which usually went together. For instance, as early as 1886, the association of mine managers at Broken Hill was formed as a counterweight to the already established unions.[7] In 1890 the BHP Board minuted the opinion of its American general manager, W. H. Patton, 'on the labour question, which he regarded the chief source of future trouble'.[8] It was felt that under circumstances of hypothetical normality, such as did not yet exist in Australia, common interest, common sense and a complex class system would keep the evolutionary and revolutionary wings of labour safely apart.

A wide variety of socialist ideas found credence in the Australian society of the late nineteenth and early twentieth centuries. Collectivist views, particularly those from Britain and the United States, found a ready acceptance, being identified with native ideas of egalitarianism and mateship. One of the most enthusiastic advocates of these ideas was the Queensland journalist William Lane. He was particularly attracted to the philosophy of the American Edward Bellamy. Lane was born in England but before arriving in Australia he had worked in Canada and the United States. A Utopian socialist, he advocated not only the views of Bellamy but also those of other socialists including Charles Kingsley, Laurence Gronlund, Henry George and Sydney Webb. Lane inspired one of the more bizarre manifestations of these beliefs when, in 1893, he attempted, at the height of the depression, to establish a socialist Utopia in Paraguay.[9] Here, it soon became apparent that intellectual agreement on socialist views did not necessarily lead to smooth communal living and, although the 'New Australia' venture lasted eleven years, Lane himself returned home in 1899. The idea was not unique as about the same time the sister of the German philosopher Nietzsche was founding 'New Germany', a rather different Paraguayan Utopia.

The 1890s depression inevitably hit unskilled workers most severely, a phenomenon that was to recur in subsequent depressions. It has been estimated that 25 to 33 per cent of the work-force was unemployed by 1893.[10] Many unions went bankrupt and many firms, including Langlands, the earliest Australian steel-maker, collapsed. Among the metal unions severely affected was the Amalgamated Society of Iron-workers' Assistants of Victoria. From 1894 to 1899 they, in common with many of their brethren, were unable to pay affiliation dues to the Melbourne Trades Hall Council. In New South Wales the Iron Trades Union followed the fate of its predecessor, the Iron Trades Protective Association and, along with many other early unions, vanished. In the early decades of the union movement, economic fluctuations and limited resources made the continuity of individual unions unstable.[11]

During the 1890s Australia's gross national product fell by over a quarter and it did not regain its 1891 level until 1906.[12] However, the hope of creating a social Utopia in Australia survived the economic disaster of the 1890s and the search for political answers to economic problems continued. Businesses and trade unions were gradually rebuilt by wary and cautious employers and employees. Unions sought greater security in numbers. The union movement encouraged amalgamations between similar unions in the belief that such amalgamations would not only increase the union's bargaining power but also lead to uniformity of pay and conditions throughout a particular occupation. To this end, amalgamations were easier to achieve between unskilled unions. Craft unions were naturally anxious to ensure that the recognition of their skills was not lost, particularly if amalgamation placed their members in a minority.

The craft origins of the union movement ensured that its structure would remain hierarchical and diverse. It also encouraged a strict demarcation of function between unions. Inevitably this created problems as changing technology demoted old and gave rise to new skills. Management, on the other hand, was conscious of the differing economic circumstances of various industries employing similar or related skills. Thus it was anxious to ensure a link between the unions and specific industries that would account for individual conditions.

Three major strikes outside the rising iron industry highlighted the social unrest focused by the impact of the depression in the early 1890s: the maritime strike in 1890, the miners' strike at Broken Hill in 1892, and the series of shearers' strikes culminating in 1894. The strikes at Broken Hill both in 1892 and in 1909 were to have a particular significance not only for the mining industry, but also for the history of labour relations in the iron and steel industry. Australia's first major mining confrontation telescoped basic pressures felt throughout the metallurgical industries.

A characteristic of mining towns is their impermanence and few in 1890 would have expected Broken Hill to reach its centenary. Even by Australian standards Broken Hill was remote; its sunbaked landscape was arid and often burnt bare. The tin shacks inhabited by the miners and their families ensured that the pressures of a small closed community would be increased by a noisy and uncomfortable life-style. The basic amenities of nineteenth-century small-town life were largely absent, and they were not encouraged by the shifting presence of 'a large propertyless proletariat'.[13] Broken Hill is in the Barrier Range in western New South Wales but lack of overland communications meant that in the 1890s its easiest approach was the long route through Victoria and South Australia. Its isolation meant that social unrest had to be anticipated and, inevitably, the appearance of additional police before trouble actually erupted telegraphed intent and exacerbated already tense situations.

In 1892 the silver, lead and zinc deposits at Broken Hill were mined by a group of companies. These were dominated by the Broken Hill Proprietary Company, which operated the largest and most productive mine on the lode. By 1890 the easiest and richest part of the lode was nearly worked out and this coincided with two extraneous factors: depression and a sudden fall in the world price of silver. Between 1890 and 1894 the world price of silver fell by 50 per cent. The depression passed but the price of silver did not recover, reflecting international changes in coinage as most European countries came to depend upon gold rather than silver. (Britain, anachronistically, retained the name 'sterling' although it had adopted the gold standard.) By 1893, of the major consumers, only China retained silver as a standard store of value. In that year BHP shares fell from 91 to 41 shillings.

Moreover, by the 1890s major problems were emerging in the mines. These included the health hazard created by lead poisoning. There were also technical difficulties, such as the 'creep' caused by the inherent dangers of a traditional method of underground mining used when pit timber was scarce or, as at Broken Hill, not available. Theoretically the mine was developed so that it became a self-supporting honeycomb. But as the galleries became deeper, the dangers of a cave-in increased.[14] At the same time metallurgical problems were emerging, in particular the sulphide question. As the rich, oxidised top layer of the deposit was mined out, the problem of separating zinc from silver and lead in the unaltered sulphide ores found at depth became acute. Although the zinc was potentially valuable, its presence was detrimental to the operation of the furnace and this increased the cost of smelting both the lead and silver.

Apart from the serious hazard of lead poisoning inherent in this type of mining at that period, conditions at Broken Hill were, by comparison with other contemporary mining enterprises, favourable. Wages were good and all of the Broken Hill mines paid equal wage rates arranged by consultation with the unions. Most of the mines were sufficiently prosperous to allow for a degree of overmanning and consequently the pace of work was not excessive. The unemployed from other mining communities were only too anxious to find work at Broken Hill.[15]

To the uncertainties created by the threat of cave-ins and the metallurgical problem were added the natural fear of unemployment in a depression of hitherto unknown ferocity and the impossibility of the average miner earning elsewhere the high wages that then pertained at Broken Hill. Almost from the beginning labour at Broken Hill had been highly unionised, with the majority of miners belonging to the Amalgamated Miners Association. In 1892 they were led by Richard Sleath, a strong and vociferous Scottish migrant from Fifeshire. Many miners, frightened by the deepening depression, clung to the union for collective support. In July 1892 the union called a strike. This was marked by violent picketing.

However, by 1892 the mine managers, confronted with the falling price of silver on the international market and increasing technical difficulties in the mines, were well aware that their operating costs had to be reduced and that this could only be achieved by increased efficiency. The BHP mine, known as 'the Big Mine' was still making an actual, though greatly reduced, profit. Most of the other mines were making actual losses or at best only nominal profits. After an agreement, reached in 1890, the miners had been paid an hourly rate. A further agreement gave security against the use of contract labour. However, as the depression deepened, economic pressures tightened, despite the evidence that mine managers were genuinely anxious to avoid unemployment. In the existing state of the economy, they felt that this could only be achieved by increasing productivity. Given the previous fairly easygoing regime, they were convinced that this could only be achieved by some form of payment by results and they gave the unions a month's notice of their intention to introduce contract mining.

The unions led by Richard Sleath mounted a determined opposition to this idea. Contract mining, they declared, penalised the old and the slow, and it was dangerous.[16] Possibly the real fear was that the resulting pay differential would create an elite group and thereby break the collective power of the union. However, in the harsh economic climate of 1892, the union had miscalculated its bargaining power. By September 1892 strike support was dwindling. The mining companies lowered wages by 10 per cent, introduced a contract system and restored the 48-hour week. It has been estimated that one man now mined as much as two had done before the strike. This increased productivity enabled the Broken Hill mines to operate throughout the difficult 1890s.[17]

In October, after the strike had ended, nine of the leading unionists involved, including Sleath, were arrested on a charge of conspiracy. Because of local tensions they were tried at Deniliquin, in New South Wales, where seven were found guilty and given gaol sentences ranging from three months to two years. Richard Sleath, on his release, entered the New South Wales legislature as MLA for Wilcannia. He subsequently represented the miners' interests in successive Legislative Assemblies. The 1892 Broken Hill strike, along with the unsuccessful maritime and shearers' strikes of the same period, left a bitter and socially divisive legacy. The magnitude of these strikes clearly defined the attitudes of the managers and the unions. This marked the emergence of a pattern, which, as it developed over the ensuing decades, exerted a lasting influence on Australian government and institutions, as well as on Australian business, including the still undeveloped iron and steel industry.

As the depression progressed, industrial unrest became widespread and many people sought consolation and justification in a wide variety of socialist creeds. Small and varied groups of doctrinaire socialists had been active in Australia since the 1880s. They were usually more vocal than numerous. For example, in 1887 one of these small groups in the Sydney–Newcastle area formed the Australian Socialist League in New South Wales. Initally they had about thirty members and their numbers probably never exceeded a hundred. An early member described the party as 25 per cent philosophical anarchist, 25 per cent physical force anarchist, 25 per cent state socialist and 25 per cent laborite.[18]

The early socialists used the well-established didactic methods of the church to expound their views with what a contemporary described as 'the fervour and fanaticism of a new holy religion'. In 1908 the international communist Tom Mann actually established a Socialist Sunday School at Broken Hill. Children were taught to sing the 'Red Flag' and the 'Marseillaise'. The Socialist Sunday School Movement[19] reflected the conjunction of rationalism, evangelical enthusiasm and sentimentalism, all characteristics of the late Victorian society in which the labour movement originated, while the inclination of early industrial communities in Wales and the north of England to Methodism and various Nonconformist denominations is well known. At Broken Hill in 1897 Methodism appears to have been the leading denomination, although Congregationalists, Bible Christians, Baptists and the Salvation Army were well represented. These Nonconformists accounted for twenty out of the twenty-nine churches in the town.[20] The disastrous strikes of the 1890s further sharpened a consciousness of social divisions between capital and labour. This encouraged the development of social theories to explain and improve social conditions.

Australia attracted doctrinaire socialists from all over the world. They saw the vast and empty continent as a social laboratory where the iniquities of the old world could be remedied. Among the number of prominent social theorists who visited Australia at this time was Henry George, the author of *Progress and Poverty*. Although a free-trader, anti-unionist and anti-socialist, he was anxious to alleviate the harsher aspects of industrialisation. His theories, not always fully understood, lay behind the fiscal reforms envisaged by the Single Tax League. In 1888, the League's views were expressed when the Fifth Intercolonial Trade Union Congress met at Brisbane and resolved that 'a simple yet sovereign remedy which will raise wages, increase and give remunerative employment, abolish poverty, extirpate pauperism, lessen crime, elevate moral tastes and intelligence, purify government, and carry civilisation to yet nobler heights, is to abolish all taxation except that on land values'.[21]

When George visited New South Wales in 1890 he was presented with a free pass to the colony's railways by the Premier, Sir Henry Parkes. In Victoria his theories were taken up by the Melbourne journalist and intellectual Max Hirsh. Other visitors included the famous British socialists Sydney and Beatrice Webb, who visited Australia in their fact-finding tour of the British Empire. Among the more radical visitors who came to Australia in the decade before World War I was the educationalist and socialist suffragette Dora Montefiore, who visited Lithgow in 1911, a period of particularly tense industrial relations at the ironworks. These visitors must have done much to enliven and create debate in isolated communities, as political speeches and lectures, apart from any didactic value, performed a function similar to the media today.

During the 1890s left-wing socialists became increasingly disenchanted with the pragmatism of the New South Wales Labor Party. In 1898 they broke away to form the Socialist Labour Party with a formal policy of 'the establishment of a co-operative commonwealth founded on the collective ownership of land and the tools of production'. The Socialist Labour Party was indisputably Marxist: its motto was 'workers of the world unite' and members were enjoined to read *The Communist Manifesto, Socialism Utopian and Scientific, The Origin of the Family* and *Capital*.[22] In 1901 they sponsored six Senate candidates with a theoretical socialist programme in opposition to the official Australian Labor Party platform. One SLP candidate attracted 3109 votes. This was the peak of their formal political success.

More significantly, in 1890 the Labour Federation in Queensland had declared that the nationalisation of the means of production and exchange was the first plank in its political programme. In fact collectivism was at the root of nationalisation. Both were in antipodean eyes nothing more than benevolent government in action. The early successes of the miners' and shearers' unions in the 1880s had strengthened concepts of collectivism. These views were expressed in slogans such as 'collective strength inspired by collective thought for the collective good' and 'in union is strength'.

In 1901, when Federation finally came, the majority of Australians regarded the newly formed Commonwealth with cautious optimism. They hoped that the federal government would provide the economic and social solutions that had eluded the individual states. Government had played a larger part in the foundation of the Australian colonies than in any other British colonies. Thus a belief in the efficacy of government intervention, on the part of both management and workers, was stronger in Australia than elsewhere.[23] The Commonwealth government was willing to assume a paternalistic role, although the situation was complicated by the delicate relationship between the new federal and the older state governments. The 'new protectionism' aimed at fulfilling a dual role to provide support for the country's infant industries. A careful application of tariffs and bonuses was to be paralleled by ensuring that the working man participated in their anticipated benefits.[24] The arrangements whereby workers could share these benefits were to be supervised by the Commonwealth Court of Conciliation and Arbitration, established in 1904.

The Commonwealth Court of Conciliation and Arbitration grew out of earlier experiments in conciliation made by the various states. The philosophy behind the creation of both the Federal Court and the State Boards, or similar tribunals, was expressed by the South Australian and federal politician Charles Kingston, who, in giving evidence to the 1891 New South Wales Royal Commission on Strikes, declared that 'I think that the interests of the whole community may require that the rights of others should be settled by a competent tribunal rather than that the disputing parties should be left to fight the matter out simply by a strength test'.[25]

This idea was not unknown in nineteenth-century England, but there conciliation and arbitration tribunals were local rather than national. Until 1896 they depended upon consent rather than legislation. In Australia the same idea slowly evolved into a different system, tailored to the local conditions and the social attitudes of the individual colonies. In New South Wales, an Act in 1891 attempted to create the machinery for conciliation but the statute lacked the necessary compulsory powers for its effective operation, especially as the participants in industrial disputes still sought not a *conciliator* but an *umpire*, someone who would give decisive victory to one side or the other.

The New South Wales Labor Party's 1894 election programme attempted to remedy this defect by including compulsory arbitration in industrial disputes. This became law in New South Wales in 1901, when an Arbitration Court was established with the power to compel the parties to seek arbitration and to refrain from either strikes or lock-outs while the dispute was before the court. Thus the employer benefited from the fact that work was not stopped during a dispute. Furthermore, the court did not interfere with the actual management of the industry, although it could, and did, include in its award a clause enjoining 'union preference' in employment. Most importantly, by giving the unions an established role in the conciliation procedure, the court strengthened their authority.

Western Australia had established a similar tribunal in 1900, Queensland and South Australia followed in 1912. Victoria and Tasmania adopted a variant system and established wages boards. In 1908 New

South Wales combined both systems by adding a wages board to the existing court of conciliation and arbitration. One of the earliest boards to be established in New South Wales was the Iron Trades (Lithgow) Arbitration and Conciliation Board, set up in 1908 to settle long-standing labour problems at the ironworks.

Ultimately the concept of arbitration was to emerge as a powerful deterrent to the revolutionary solutions advocated by the Marxist doctrine of class warfare. After Federation the various states continued to operate their respective courts for the solution of internal disputes. But as industries became established on a national rather than a state basis, the influence of the Federal Court increased. From its inception the court offered a venue for settling disputes involving separate unions in more than one state.

The Commonwealth Court of Conciliation and Arbitration gained much of its reputation from its first president, Mr Justice Higgins, described as 'dour and almost always silent but at heart the kindest of men'.[26] The 1906 *Tariff Act* allowed a manufacturer to benefit from the payment of excise tariffs and the imposition of import taxes so long as his workers received 'fair and reasonable wages'. One of the first cases heard by the court involved the Sunshine Harvester Company, a manufacturer of agricultural machinery. In his judgment Justice Higgins defined 'fair and reasonable' in *social* rather than *economic* terms. The basic wage was to be tied to the normal needs of an average human being, whom Higgins envisaged as a man with a wife and two or three children living in a civilised country in a state of frugal comfort. Special skills were to be rewarded by additional payments known as margins.

Higgins's outlook was essentially humanitarian and infused with a desire to help the underdog; the débâcle of the union movement in the 1890s had convinced him that they were the weaker party in any confrontation with employers and he felt that the minimum wage would be a check on the abuses inherent in the contract system. He was convinced that an industry which could not pay a living wage had no place in a civilised community.[27] This outlook encouraged the co-operation of the union movement and ensured the popularity of the Federal Court. However, only interstate disputes were subject to federal jurisdiction. So the attitude of the Federal Court gave further encouragement to union consolidation through interstate federations. At the same time it encouraged national standards of labour in similar industries. Unfortunately it also led to a hardening of class attitudes. Many employers viewed the system with suspicion and, considering that the court frequently refused to recognise economic realities, they joined together to oppose it.

Government, employers and workers tended to adopt standard positions. Employers felt that their livelihood was being threatened by escalating labour costs. These would, in the short term, price their goods out of the market and, in the long term, prevent them from making the capital investment upon which their continuing profitability depended. The worker saw the higher standard of living of the entrepreneurial and managerial classes and felt that his contribution to that prosperity was undervalued. Both the federal and state governments, through legislative enactments and the industrial courts, were anxious to find a balance that would both satisfy their electors and encourage the geese to lay more golden eggs for the benefit of the community.

Meanwhile, the basic attitude of the states to federation remained 'the essential condition' formulated by the Queenslander Sir Samuel Griffith in 1891, namely 'that the separate states are to continue as autonomous bodies, surrendering only so much of their powers as is necessary to the establishment of a general government to do for them collectively what they cannot do individually for themselves and which they cannot do as a collective body for themselves'.[28]

One of the problems that the separate colonies had been unable to solve was the formulation of a national economic policy on questions of free trade and protection, especially as it affected the implementation of common tariffs and bonuses. Interstate free trade was guaranteed by the constitution in a clause that has subsequently been subject to much interpretative deliberation. However, at the time of Federation, there was majority agreement in principle over national protection for vulnerable industries. These included the native iron and steel industry. It was the form and conditions of that protection, and its social and economic implications, which ensured that it would be a matter of long debate. Consequently, although the concept of protection was accepted by the second decade of the twentieth century, the shape of the native iron and steel industry remained unresolved at the outbreak of World War I. The social arguments revolved around the doctrinaire question of whether the industry should be nationalised or left in the hands of private enterprise and, as it was now becoming increasingly obvious that the industry could not flourish without some form of state or federal assistance, the more practical question of whether any manufacturer should benefit as an individual from the taxpayer.

The argument for nationalisation was put by the Western Australian ALP Senator Hugh de Largie, a former miner who, on 13 April 1904, moved that the Senate affirm that 'the principle of an iron works being established and owned by the Federal Government for the purpose of manufacturing pig iron, and steel from native ore, believing this would be in the best interests of Australian industry, State rights, and Commonwealth prosperity'.[29] In the debate Senator Playford, a South Australian protectionist, pointed out that the Attorney-General had indicated that the principle was beyond the legal powers of the constitution.[30] However, the Senate supported de Largie's motion by fourteen votes to ten, refusing to await the opportunity to debate the question when the Manufacturers Encouragement Bill came before it. This Bill envisaged giving a bonus to the native industry.

The Commonwealth Political Labor Conference met in July 1905 and passed a resolution requesting Federal Labor MPs to urge the government to nationalise the industry. Although an increasing realisation of the size and complexity of such an undertaking was causing growing misgivings, nationalisation remained under consideration at state level until the 1920s. In Queensland the theoretical vision of a nationalised industry survived longest. New South Wales, having more practical experience of the industry and its requirements, had to confront the realities sooner but, even there, nationalisation remained an important issue in the period from Federation to the outbreak of World War I. During these years the unresolved issue undoubtedly hampered the development of a viable Australian iron and steel industry.

Apart from the adjustments required by Federation, the years between 1901 and 1914 were not easy for either management or labour. However, the disputes and confrontations of that period set the pattern for at least the next half century. Trade unions had previously been organised on a local basis, like the Eskbank Ironworkers, or a state basis like the Amalgamated Ironworkers' Assistants' Union of New South Wales or the Amalgamated Society of Ironworkers' Assistants of Victoria. After Federation, so long as a union remained within a state, it was subject to that state's arbitration machinery. However, some unions, such as the miners'—the Amalgamated Miners' Association (AMA) formed in 1874—had amalgamated before Federation. As an interstate union they immediately came under the Commonwealth court. The early organization of both mine employers and workers is indicative of the dominant position of mining compared with manufacturing in the Australian economy. In contrast the Victorian and the New South Wales ironwork-

Banner of the New South Wales branch of the Federated Ironworkers' Association of Australia, c. 1900. The banner celebrates the acceptance of an eight-hour working day in the previous century, and depicts the operation of a heavy forge in the propeller-shaft forging shop at Cockatoo Dock, Sydney.

ers' unions did not amalgamate until 1908 when they formed the Federated Ironworkers Association. They then became eligible for registration under the Commonwealth Court of Conciliation and Arbitration.

The Ironworkers Association was only one of the unions involved in iron manufacture. Coal-miners were part of the AMA and coal-mining also provided large-scale employment in the Lithgow valley. The principal industry dependent upon it was the iron and steel manufacture at Eskbank, although there were other related industries such as a gasworks, copper smelting and pottery. The service industries in Lithgow were largely dependent upon coal and iron for their prosperity. They in turn depended upon each other. The only alternative employment in the Lithgow area was provided by agriculture, and agricultural wages tended to lag behind those provided by mining. In addition much agricultural employment, for instance, shearing, was seasonal.

The mining industry has traditionally been dominated by coal, the basic fuel of the industrial revolution. The influence of coal upon iron manufacture is such that it cannot be ignored. There had been coal-mines owned by the Eskbank ironworks from the days of Rutherford, although the industry was also dependent upon other local collieries. The nineteenth-century coal trade in Australia had a typical early industrial history of erratic slumps and booms. These conditions were intensified by poor communications and the underdeveloped condition of the country, which had neither the industrial enterprises nor the population to provide an adequate home market.

In Australia coal was, and has remained, central to both industrialisation and to the export market. The scale and nature of the industry had clearly definable social and political consequences. Single-industry mining towns were usually geographically isolated from the rest of the community. Approximately one-third of the coal mined in New South Wales was exported between 1860 and 1914, but the export demand was unpredictable and linked to the availability of suitable land and sea transport. An attempt was made to regulate this economic uncertainty by fixing the amount produced at any given time among the various coal producers. This arrangement, known as the vend, was paralleled in the set daily production of the miner—the darg.[31] These arrangements had obvious social advantages and economic disadvantages.

Isolation and a common occupation combined to reinforce the strong trade union views that many of the miners had brought with them from Britain, while erratic economic conditions completed the foundation of traditionally difficult labour relations. From the 1880s an increasing feeling of class solidarity supported by communist and socialist views developed among the mining communities. In the years before World War I, the miners adopted a strongly socialist and pacifist outlook. They were influenced increasingly by the American syndicalist movement, the Industrial Workers of the World (IWW), which had been trying to spread its influence into Australia from about 1905. The IWW reinforced the miners' militant communist views as the movement accepted class hostility as axiomatic. The IWW considered that the only viable expression of the class struggle was for the working class to unite in one big union for the primary purpose of initiating a general strike. In the aftermath of the strike the victorious workers would be able to restructure society. Hierarchy divided the unity of the working class, so the IWW opposed the concept of the aristocracy of labour, labelling the craft unions as bourgeois. The IWW attracted socialists of more doctrinaire views, who found the pragmatic idealism of the Australian Labor Party, with its emphasis on evolution rather than revolution, difficult to accept.

## 5 TOWARDS A SOCIAL CONTRACT

In the decade and a half immediately preceding World War I the international aspects of the labour movement gained strength in Australia. Later they would be among the issues that would divide the nation at the height of the war. During these years, the ideals of this movement found their best-known expression in the 1909 strike at BHP's 'Big Mine' at Broken Hill. At Broken Hill both management and labour had remained highly organised in two combinations: the Mine Managers' Association and the Amalgamated Miners' Association. They negotiated agreements that applied uniformly throughout the Barrier Range area. Individual mines had varying and changing degrees of profitability, although BHP dominated the Barrier, employing three times as many men as any of the other mines. The Mine Managers' Association was chaired by BHP's general manager, Guillaume Delprat, who was commonly known as 'the king of Broken Hill', apparently as much for his personal qualities as for his position.

In the middle of the first decade of the twentieth century, lead prices were high and, in 1906, a very favourable agreement was reached between the Mine Managers and the AMA whereby the wages of the unskilled workers were raised by 15 per cent and the semi-skilled by 14 per cent. In 1907 prices remained high and, conscious that the 'Big Mine' was nearing the end of its spectacular career, Delprat took advantage of the high lead prices and mined 600 000 tons of ore in that year. Lead was £19 per ton and the BHP shareholders had a bonanza, particularly as their dividends were augmented by company savings. Delprat was shrewd and lucky, for, in the immediate future, no one would have benefited had the ore been left in the ground. Shortly thereafter lead prices fell sharply to £13 10s and, when the unions met to renegotiate wages, prices for zinc and silver had also fallen in world markets.

Conscious of the impending difficulties created by the altered world economic conditions, the Combined Unions Committee appointed the English labour agitator Tom Mann to organise their case. Tom Mann, who spent most of the first decade of the twentieth century in Australia, was a communist and a friend of Engels and of Marx's daughter, Eleanor Marx-Aveling. Although an international socialist, he had a strong belief in trade unions to whom he looked for assistance in the class struggle. He hoped to educate the Australian Labor Party to the socialist viewpoint and to this end he instituted a policy of co-operation. He was disappointed. Mann was particularly annoyed by the ALP's attitude to nationalisation. He felt that the ALP had betrayed the workers and that it had emerged as simply another party of the bourgeoisie. However, in 1905 he was instrumental in founding the Victorian Socialist Party.[32] Interestingly, the first edition of the party's journal, *The International Socialist Review*, carried an article on 'Revolutionary International Socialism' by a foundation member of the party—John Curtin. The future prime minister was then working as an estimate clerk with the Titan Manufacturing Company in Melbourne.

Meanwhile, at Broken Hill the combined unions pressed to have the 1906 wage levels retained despite the falling market and the Mine Managers, who had traditionally presented a united front, split. Nine mines agreed to continue to pay the higher wages, some with the proviso that they could not promise to remain open if commodity prices did not rise. The remaining four, headed by BHP, refused. On 20 November 1908 BHP left the Mine Managers' Association and Delprat resigned from its presidency the following day. BHP had started on its long road away from Broken Hill.

BHP lost its dominant position on the Barrier so quickly that the workers, pointing to the huge dividends of 1907, could not believe what had happened. Despite BHP's altered position, the Big Mine was still its major asset and the company was reluctant to close it, although this would have preserved its resources for an upturn in the market. Instead the company preferred to continue to operate, but on its terms. These were a reduction in wages to match the altered economic conditions. On 7 December a notice was posted at the BHP mine under Delprat's name, declaring that 'the bonus granted for two years, dating from January 1 1907, will cease on January 1 1909, and that the present rate of wages, less the bonus, will remain in force'. Possibly this wording was intended to provide a way between the mining companies that had agreed to maintain the 1906 wages and the dissenting companies. Delprat did suggest a sliding scale allowing for an improvement in wages should metal prices rise. The unions now fell back on Justice Higgins's concept of a living wage and, when the case came before the Court of Conciliation and Arbitration, Higgins supported them, handing down his decision on 12 March 1909. BHP then appealed to the High Court. The court declared against two of the six decisions in Higgins's judgment, which had extended to matters not under dispute.[33]

The dispute continued until 23 May 1909 and during its course attracted many of the more extreme labour agitators and militant socialists to Broken Hill. The disagreement, which left a legacy of unequalled bitterness and distrust, was essentially the result of a disastrous combination of economic events in a socially explosive situation. For many years after neither BHP nor the union movement was able to forget its legacy, while the other Broken Hill mining companies blamed BHP for an inheritance of soured labour relations. In 1910 Mann returned to England via South Africa convinced by his Australian experiences in Victoria and at Broken Hill that syndicalism, or working-class solidarity exemplified by one big union, was the only way forward. Before, during and after World War I syndicalism was a force in the Australian labour movement.

# 6

# PROMETHEUS BOUND

THE GENERAL DEBATE OVER nationalisation or free enterprise continued, and the specific question of protection for the iron and steel industry was among the earliest considerations of the federal parliament. However, the uncertainty engendered by the conflicting policies of successive governments undoubtedly had a detrimental effect upon the development not only of the iron and steel industry but of industrial enterprises in general. In 1903 the Barton government referred the bill relating to bonuses for the encouragement of manufactures to a Royal Commission (this continued the work of the House of Representatives' Select Committee). It reported to the Governor-General the following year. The twelve commissioners were evenly divided and the decision in favour of bonuses was made on the casting vote of the chairman, Charles Kingston, a South Australian protectionist. The report appended the opinion of the Attorney-General 'that the power of the Commonwealth to conduct manufactures is limited' adding that:

> No evidence has been produced which would lead your Commissioners to believe that any State Government contemplates undertaking the establishment of iron works or any abandonment of its position as indicated in the correspondence between the Federal Government and the States laid before the House of Representatives on the 29th July, 1902.[1]

They made two recommendations for inclusion in the Bill: to secure 'the equitable settlement by conciliation or arbitration of all industrial disputes in relation to any work for the earning of bonuses'; and 'securing to the Commonwealth or to the State in which the work for the earning of bonus is being chiefly carried on, a right of purchase of the undertaking after a fair interval at a valuation'. One of the six commissioners, E. Braddon, entered a caveat against the latter recommendation. Thus the vexed problem of nationalisation passed in effect to the government of New South Wales, which had emerged from the findings of the commission as the only state in which the industry was liable to succeed. At its conference in 1909 the New South Wales Political Labour League adopted nationalisation as official policy. Although the gap between agreement to this policy and its implementation proved unbridgeable, the unstable political atmosphere engendered by the policy inevitably had an unsettling effect upon the industry.

The commission's minority report agreed on the benefits that the industry would bestow on the nation as a whole. However, they had reservations over bonuses, pointing out that the Canadian experiment with bonuses, instituted in 1883, had not been an unqualified success. The system, instead of being a primer as anticipated, was still in operation. Furthermore, they had ideological difficulties with the Australian Bill:

> [It] provides for the payment of £324,000 of the people's money to private individuals engaged in an enterprise for their private gain. There can be no guarantee that the bonuses proposed would permanently establish the industry, though it is probable the inducements offered might be instrumental in forming speculative companies.[2]

The evidence before the commission did include one such speculative venture, that of the Blythe River Iron Mines Company. In 1891 the *Australian Mining Standard* reported on the successful smelting of iron ore from a deposit on the Blythe River near Burnie in Tasmania. This had attracted the attention a group of mining speculators, the Blythe River Iron Mines Company, with a nominal capital of £1 000 000 in £1 shares. The company aimed to attract British capital through its mining and industrial prospects and also through the anticipated protection of the industry by the federal government. The chairman of the Blythe River Company was William Jamieson, the first general manager of the Broken Hill Proprietary Company and a member of its Board from 1906 to 1926. His other interests included a directorship of the Mount Lyell Company. The commissioners regarded Jamieson's opinion with attention.[3]

Jamieson outlined a detailed plan prepared for the Blythe River Iron Mines Ltd by J. H. Darby, the managing director of the Brymbo Steel

Works in northern Wales. Darby had been carefully selected to give confidence to prospective British investors. His plan envisaged the expenditure of £1 109 000 on the construction of a complete iron- and steelworks, with two large blast furnaces each capable of producing 500 tons of metal a day. Certainly two such large furnaces would have had the benefits of economies of scale and continuity of supply in the event of one being unserviceable. But, when both furnaces were in blast, it was not clear how markets would have been found for such prodigious quantities of iron. Their production would have exceeded the total imports of iron and steel into Australia at that time. The works were to be situated on the Parramatta River, opposite Ryde in New South Wales, and materials were to be brought to the ironworks in the company's specially constructed fleet of ships.

William Sandford in his evidence to the same commission put forward an entirely different and much more cautious proposal, based on his own plans for a new blast furnace at Eskbank. On the advice of Enoch James, an English expert, who had visited Lithgow at Sandford's expense and been retained as a consultant, Sandford proposed a single, medium-sized blast furnace:

> The furnace we were going to erect would turn out 500 tons per week; but the same furnace would work up to 1,200 tons per week when required. We have machinery on the ground today to consume 12,000 to 13,000 tons of pig iron *per annum*. It takes some time to get new material into the market and we should go on as the demand increased.[4]

He estimated an expenditure of £100 000 to £125 000 on this single furnace, which would produce up to 170 tons of metal a day, with no provision for a steel-making plant. This was proportionately in keeping with Jamieson's more ambitious plans for the expenditure of £1 109 000 on two larger blast furnaces, together with steel-making and supporting facilities. The minority report emphasised Sandford's experience and inclined towards his lower costs and less ambitious plans. However, events within the decade were to show the logic of developing both a blast furnace and steel plant along the lines envisaged by Jamieson. Significantly, when Sandford actually built a modern blast furnace, although of a smaller size than that suggested by Jamieson, he went out of business because he lacked the capital to rebuild and modernise his steel-making activities.

Fortunately for Jamieson and his colleagues, the Blythe River Iron Mines Ltd did not develop as, although the deposits looked impressive, their appearance was misleading. Both the New South Wales government in 1912 and the federal government in 1918 considered purchasing them but pulled back on the advice of their experts. In the early 1920s Charles Hoskins, who was most anxious to find a reliable source of iron ore, offered £35 000 for the leases and his offer was rejected: 'How lucky we were!' declared his son in retrospect. 'It is debatable now whether it was worth £35 for a steel making venture.'[5] Jamieson, however, realised his vision of an Australian iron and steel company through his long connection with the Broken Hill Proprietary Company. From time to time Jamieson tried unsuccessfully to interest BHP in the Blythe River deposits, either as a flux for the Port Pirie silver smelters or as the basis of an iron company. It is a measure of Jamieson's confidence in the Blythe River deposits that he proposed to resolve his conflict of interests by resigning from BHP. As late as 1911 he wrote to the BHP Board that his position as a director of both companies was untenable but the Board considered that his offer to resign was premature.[6]

The Manufacturers' Encouragement Bill (Bonuses for Manufactures) took nearly a decade to come on to the statute book. After a long and uncertain career it finally become law in 1909. Sandford had been bankrupted in its expectation. Jamieson, whose evidence was taken on 25 September 1902, agreed that his scheme was entirely dependent upon a bonus or duty. Even then its delay had resulted in unsettling his prospective investors as 'we led them to believe that the bonus bill would become law much earlier than this'. William Sandford complained to the commission of a similar experience stating that:

> When I went home I saw a gentleman connected with one of the most successful ironworks in England, and he said—'If your figures are right, and the Bonus Bill passes, we shall be prepared to put money into it.' This was on bottom terms; I valued the works, and showed him my balance-sheets, and he said that he and others could make up £250,000, and names could be got making up £750,000 if necessary. We made an agreement to spend £250,000 and had books printed and everything ready to take up the work at any time; but members of the Commission knew what the result was following upon the uncertainty connected with the Bill.

One of the most interesting aspects of this episode was Jamieson's and Sandford's realistic estimate of costs for, at this time, neither the states nor the federal government could afford to create or purchase an industry involving an expenditure of this magnitude. The states already operated a variety of enterprises with very indifferent success.[7] Jamieson, when asked directly if he knew 'any reason why State iron works should not be successful within the Commonwealth', replied that he was personally of the opinion that 'no State industry can be carried on in as economical a manner as can a private enterprise', pointing out that the state would have to pay the manager an 'enormous' salary, not less than £6000 annually. Jamieson, on being pressed as to whether it was more difficult to run a large ironworks than a railway or the post and telegraph departments, replied that it was easy to run the last three whereas the first required highly expensive skills.[8]

Regardless of the social arguments being advanced for nationalisation or private enterprise, the economic arguments in favour of the industry presented an additional dilemma. The production of iron and steel was admitted in the *long term* to be the basis of industrialisation and of national defence. It had become increasingly clear that the very existence of the industry, particularly in its then undercapitalised condition, depended upon a high degree of protection. Furthermore, it was probable that only one state, and possibly only one firm, would be involved, at least at the beginning. Obviously, any action which would increase the price of pig-iron to the numerous manufacturers of iron products would be *immediately* considered detrimental to the economy and the nation as a whole.

The classical methods of protection are bonuses and tariffs. Bonuses, by directly subsidising an industry, enable it to compete in an open market, but they raise the problem of the taxpayer giving a specific person or company individual aid. Many considered that this was ideologically unacceptable; regardless of the fact that jobs may be created or sustained by this support, or that the nation would ultimately benefit by achieving a greater degree of market independence in a basic industrial commodity without, in the interim, increasing its cost to the consumer. The alternative method, the imposition of tariffs, offered immediate encouragement to struggling but established industries, while protecting existing employment and increasing the revenue. However, the imposition of tariffs immediately increased the price to the home market of basic or unfinished industrial goods, thereby creating a flow-on that increased the cost of living. Both methods were considered at length and eventually both were adopted by the federal government.

In view of the practical as well as the philosophical implications of the bonus question, it is not surprising that the Bill did not become law until 1909. Yet for most of the first decade of the federal parliament it was seldom off the parliamentary agenda. For instance, in 1904 it passed its first and second readings, only to lapse when the first Labor Party government, under J. C. Watson, took office. In the following year it was brought in again by Sir William Lyne and this time it passed all its stages in the House of Representatives before being thrown out by a hostile Senate. Lobbying for the Bill was a constant and time-consuming problem first for Sandford and then for Hoskins in their attempts to establish the industry on a solid economic foundation.

The Royal Commission on Customs and Excise Tariffs developed out of the 1902 Customs Tariff Bill and paralleled the enquiries of the Royal Commission on Bonuses. But while the bonus question had centered round the establishment of a native industry for the production of iron and steel, the tariff investigation surveyed Australian industry as a whole. As a domestic iron-smelting industry did not at this time exist, it was outside the commission's terms of reference. Evidence was sought from the Eskbank ironworks on bar iron, bolts and nuts, galvanised, corrugated and plain sheet iron. Inevitably the question arose of the necessity for home production of the pig-iron that was the raw material for these finished goods. The conclusions of the Commission in 1906 were that the market was insufficient for the continuous operation of the most efficient machinery to manufacture bolts, nuts and similar items, and that duties would, therefore, only increase the evil of excessive internal competition. Moreover, they would encourage the formation of a combine to force up prices and limit production.

Evidence over the manufacture of galvanised, corrugated, and plain sheet iron and tanks was conflicting and the commissioners, concerned about its flow-on to other industries, concluded that:

> the amount of labour concerned in the transforming of black sheets into galvanised sheets, and subsequently into galvanised corrugated sheets is insignificant especially so in the latter process.
>
> And as plain galvanised sheets are largely used in other manufactures in Australia which are being successfully carried on, and corrugated galvanised iron is in such universal request for roofing and other purposes, it is inadvisable to impose any charge thereon in order to stimulate the employment of labour the demand for which under any circumstances can only be very limited.[9]

The evidence elicited by the commissioners revealed the backward and perilous state of an industry composed of many small ironworks with neither the market nor the capital to make them efficient or competitive, while their position as industrial middlemen made the commissioners reluctant to increase the internal cost of their goods by the imposition of tariffs. However, certain other sections of the iron manufacturing trade, including some of the engineering industries, were given some tariff protection. As usual conditions were attached. Government remained anxious to exert social controls on any capitalist venture by ensuring that benefit would accrue to the worker as well as the manufacturer. To this end the newly erected Commonwealth Court of Conciliation and Arbitration was made the guardian of the *Tariff Act*.

When Charles and George Hoskins arrived in Lithgow, they were appalled at the state of the works: 'the present state of the works', declared George Hoskins, 'is almost paralyzing to any practical ironworker'. He made a preliminary statement to the effect that

> our firm's intention is to spend as little money on the old works as possible to enable us to cope with the government contract. After that we will thoroughly consider the question of establishing an up to date works. We quite recognise that in this case it is not so much the finishing off of a ten year contract, but the establishment of a permanent industry.[10]

Charles Henry Hoskins, *c.* 1900, an outstanding man of great determination who was the first to establish a viable steel industry in Australia. He was co-founder of G. & C. Hoskins Ltd, principal developer of iron- and steel-making at Lithgow between 1907 and 1925, and initiator of the transfer of these activities to Port Kembla.

From the information available it is possible to visualise the Eskbank works as they operated in the early years of Hoskins ownership, a period which proved vitally important for the subsequent development of the Australian iron and steel industry. The Lithgow plant[11] taken over by Hoskins in 1908 consisted of two quite distinct operations on separate sites.

- A 'modern' blast furnace with a nominal capacity of 1000 tons per week with three hot-blast stoves and a powerhouse containing boilers fired with blast furnace gas which raised the steam to operate the blowing engines, a hoist engine and water pumps. The furnace was, and remained, hand charged, a labour-intensive anachronism which was never altered.
- About a mile (2 km) from the new blast furnace, there was a rather run-down iron works, on the site of the original Rutherford works. This was arranged in classical style with a 'forge' consisting of four puddling furnaces erected in 1907 'feeding' a shingling hammer and a 16-inch 'muck' mill. The area also housed three small, open-hearth steel-making furnaces. The rolling mills were on the same site but separated from the forge. The two operations were conducted independently. The rough bars from the forge and ingots from the open-hearth furnace were allowed to cool before being transferred to the rolling mills where they were reheated in coal-fired furnaces before rolling. This made the works fuel- as well as labour-intensive. The preferred practice would have been to charge hot steel ingots into soaking pits, where their temperature was brought to the level required for rolling. Here they would be held until the ingots were needed in the mill. This practice was not adopted until the new bloom mill was commissioned by G. & C. Hoskins's successor, Australian Iron and Steel, in 1931.

The rolling mills had been modified and added to at various times during the Rutherford–Sandford years. Charles Hoskins described their layout as 'haphazard'. These steam-driven mills comprised:

- an 18-inch mill—producing intermediate sections (2–3-inch rounds and flats, sheet bars and billets) and fishplates. Apparently, in 1908, neither steel nor wrought iron rails were actually being rolled in Australia.
- a 14-inch merchant mill—producing finished rounds (1–1$^1$/$_3$-inch) and flats.

- a 9-inch guide mill—rolling billets from the 18-inch mill to $^3/_8$–$^7/_8$-inch rounds.
- two sheet mills—described as 'almost museum pieces'—rolling sheet bars to a range of sheet thicknesses (10 to 26 gauge), together with a galvanising plant described as 'very antiquated', and 'a very old fashioned corrugating machine'.

The origin of much of this equipment is obscure but an 18-inch mill was part of the original Rutherford plant in 1875. References to a 14-inch mill appear in 1898. A guide mill, sheet mills and a galvanising plant were in use in 1893 and a new sheet mill in 1898. The works were not electrified, there were no fixed lights and at night illumination was provided either by the furnaces or from slush lamps composed of 'great wads of cotton waste burning from the spout of a type of billy-can filled with either mutton or in some cases whale oil'. In 1909 Hoskins installed a 15-horsepower electricity generator that fed carbon arc lamps in various parts of the works.[12]

The Hoskins brothers had embarked upon their new enterprise at a particularly difficult time. Changing technology necessitated a very rapid

The 27-inch reversing mill at Eskbank iron and steelworks rolling 80-pound rails for the Commonwealth railway, c. 1915. Ingots are reduced to blooms and billets in the rolls at right, before being rolled to structural sections and rails in the rolls at left.

industrial expansion and this radically altered the traditional roles of both the entrepreneur-industrialist and the work-force. Despite improvements, the equipment still remained labour-intensive, as the available capital always fell short of large-scale mechanisation. Within a few weeks of his arrival Charles Hoskins was looking for suitable fitters to get the mills operating. An innovator of the old school, Hoskins's grasp of state-of-the-art ironworking and elementary concepts like division of labour was rudimentary. For instance, he could proudly say that 'the colonials were far ahead, as those who came out from the Old Country were accustomed to everything being done by machinery, whereas the men required at the ironworks were those who could make themselves handy with the hammer and chisel'.[13]

Three out of the four rolling mills had broken down and a 24-inch mill was not yet commissioned. It was for a short time operated by an engine formerly owned by the Botany Water Works which Sandford had managed to refurbish for use in the mill by adding a reversing gear. This enabled the mill to roll sizeable ingots, although a large diameter flywheel confined the engine to slow speeds. Among Hoskins's first actions was to order from England a second-hand reversing steam engine of 5000 horsepower, and a 'perfectly up to date' three-cylinder quick-reversing engine from Davy Brothers, Sheffield, which he had installed before the end of the year to drive the bloom and rail rolling stands of this mill.[14]

The industrial situation confronting George and Charles Hoskins on their arrival at Lithgow in the hot, dry summer of 1908 was already extremely tense and sensitive on both sides. In addition to their other difficulties a shortage of water was creating a serious problem for the ironworks as a whole. However, by 17 January the Hoskins brothers had restarted as much of the old works as was feasible. They could restart neither the sheet mill nor the galvanising mill because some workers, who had been employed in the sheet mill before the stoppage, had departed. This made it impossible to work either mill, for the one depended upon the other. The interdependence of the various sections of the works gave rise to a broader employment problem as a stoppage or go-slow in one area affected employment in others. When there was no work, the men were laid off.

The blast furnace had been restarted on 12 January but was kept damped down until 17 February. Sandford had been forced to augment the available coke by the undesirable practice of charging raw coal and this no doubt accounted for some of the subsequent operating problems.

The Hoskins brothers also had problems over the coke supplies for the blast furnace, but they resolved it taking over the entire output of the Oakey Park Coal and Coke Company.[15] A further complication, during the first half of 1908, was the falling price of pig-iron on the local markets. By June Charles Hoskins was in Melbourne, where the federal parliament met, expressing concern that unless 'some encouragement was given by way of a bonus, it was possible that the blast furnace would be a failure'. There were fears that the 'Bonus Bill', which had been read a second time in 1907, might lapse. A decision to hold the Bill over until later in the year had been taken when it had come before the House of Representatives in June 1908. One of the risks the Hoskins brothers ran when they took over Eskbank was that government sanction for the Iron and Steel Bill would be delayed.

Not only did the plant need modernising but so did the system of operating it. One of the earliest changes that Hoskins made was to bring the works under direct managerial control by substituting day labour for the traditional contract system. In the interests of efficiency the Hoskins brothers immediately started to introduce methods similar to those in their Sydney works, where moderately good labour relations prevailed. However, less than a fortnight after their arrival, the *Lithgow Mercury* reported a meeting of the Eskbank Ironworkers' Association of Mill and Forge Workers on the alterations in working conditions at the works, commenting that 'a feeling of soreness is being engendered among the men by the action of the heads of departments who, it is alleged, are trying to make a smaller number of men do the same amount of work as was done by a larger number of men during the time of W. Sandford Ltd.'

The union usually met on Saturday afternoon, and the following Saturday it was decided to widen their membership by accepting eighty blast furnacemen and opening membership of the Eskbank Ironworkers' Association to anyone employed at either the ironworks or blast furnace. This marked an increasing solidarity among the workers as previously only those earning at least six shillings per day had been eligible for membership of the union. At the same time it was reported that the executive committee had met

> one of the managers of departments on Saturday night and were informed that from the next day the complement of men usually employed by W. Sandford Ltd. in that particular department would be re-employed, in the opinion of both manager and men the number of hands employed in that department since the restarting could not get through the work.[16]

Labour unrest continued and in February 1908 the Eskbank Ironworkers' Association formally put before G. & C. Charles Hoskins Ltd a log of grievances. Charles Hoskins asked that the firm be given six months to get the works on a sound basis. He explained that the old works had been losing 'an enormous amount of money' and that at present the finished work did not cover the cost of wages, let alone materials and other charges. On 7 March the union wrote asking for the position to be reviewed 'in a couple of months'. A few days later the bar bank labourers, about thirty to forty men, struck for an increase to ten shillings a day on their present wage of eight shillings for an eight-hour day with overtime, stating that the work was too hard for the wages. Hoskins was not unsympathetic and assured them that, if they waited a month or two, labour-saving equipment would be introduced. The men refused and the strike continued. At the New South Wales Labor Conference held during the same month in Sydney, the Eskbank Ironworkers' Association proposed that 'union hours and wages shall be demanded on all government contracts without exception'.[17] The success of the Eskbank works depended upon the government contract which Hoskins had inherited from Sandford.

Despite their deficiencies, parts of the works were operating well and a record output from these areas was anticipated. By April 1908 the blast furnace was performing satisfactorily and plans were underway to improve the brickworks by substituting steam for horse power. By May all of the mills were operational and the works were employing about 650 men. Everything appeared to be going smoothly when Hoskins suddenly upset the delicate labour relations at the works by announcing that 'on and after Monday 13th April smoking will not be permitted in any part of the works during working hours'. This was immediately a matter for union discussion and a deputation was sent to Hoskins stating that smoking had been customary at the works for many years. In reply Hoskins pointed out that it was not allowed at ironworks in Sydney. However, he agreed that men who were working an eight-hour shift without a meal break could have a fifteen-minute smoking break at an officially arranged time, but those whose shift included a meal break must smoke at that time. The smoking ban continued to cause resentment both for its own sake and possibly because it offered a focus for underlying unrest.[18]

Unfortunately the market remained sluggish. Charles Hoskins warned: 'we are putting out considerably more pig iron than there is sale for, with the result that it has to be stacked. This emphasises the need for either a bonus or a duty'. About a week later twelve to sixteen men employed to stack the surplus pig-iron at the blast furnace struck for a wage increase of a shilling per day. Hoskins had cut down the number of men per shift. The union representative maintained that the stoppage was caused by the men having to carry whole pigs instead of half pigs—a pig weighed about a hundredweight and a shift was $8^3/_4$ hours per day (Monday to Friday) and $4^1/_4$ hours on Saturday.

Hoskins refused to discuss the strike in view of the surplus production from the blast furnace, then producing about 700 tons of pig-iron a week. This was proving unsaleable in face of foreign competition. Despite the falling price of pig-iron—the Melbourne price dropped by nine shillings per ton in the six months before June 1908—there were justifiable fears that the Bonus Bill would again be shelved, leaving Hoskins to reiterate his warning that 'unless some encouragement was given by way of a bonus, it was possible that the blast furnace would be a failure'. In these circumstances, the strike was mistimed. When the blast furnace manager advertised for replacements, some men came back and the strike collapsed. The rest of the men then tried to make terms with Hoskins but he refused to see them, declaring that they had waited too long.[19]

In an attempt to defuse the situation Hoskins and three of his staff made a statutory declaration before J. W. Spooner, JP, that there was an actual money loss of three shillings per ton on the 8000 tons of pig-iron on the order book. In addition there had been an Iron Trades Award following on the tariff concessions granted to certain iron manufactures. It was anticipated that the unions would demand a flow-on throughout the industry. When asked about the effects of this Hoskins replied that:

> I think Lithgow is being squeezed in a vice from which she cannot get out. First of all I take it that the award has been given because the manufacturer has received customs duty from which he has benefits. In the second that the iron trades have had a fairly prosperous time. Unfortunately for Lithgow neither of these things has happened. Last year there was a very heavy loss on the works, and, as everybody knows, up to the present moment we have not had the advantage of the customs duties . . . [but] it is quite likely that we shall be called upon to pay the increased wages.[20]

Despite these problems, Hoskins was spending a considerable amount on modernising the works which, it was admitted, 'wear a brighter aspect than at any other period during the past 20 years'.[21] This money was drawn from the engineering works and indicated the necessity of being able to balance losses in the iron and steel industry from another enterprise. The Hoskins brothers were fully aware that even relying on two relatively stable, and certainly preferential, outlets (the New South Wales government contract and their own pipe works), they still had to get the price of pig-iron down to the market level.

On the other hand their skilled employees at the ironworks, such as rollers, were alienated by the changes in their working conditions, which they undoubtedly construed as a loss of both independence and status.[22] Advances in technology were not only providing financial problems for management, but were isolating it from its natural supporters as the traditional hierarchy of labour was breaking down. An interesting sidelight on this aspect of industrial relations is shown in the evidence given in 1908 to the Iron Trades (Lithgow) Wages Board by Herbert Bladon:

> Rollers commanded high rates, because it was a trade peculiar to itself . . . He was a skilled man with knowledge gained by practical work. His duty was to see that the iron was not too cold and not too hot. He had been a roller for 35 years, and was not proficient yet; he could learn all his life. In the actual handling of the metal there was a knack that all men could not acquire . . . The head roller has always been recognised as the man in charge of the mill, and is responsible if anything goes wrong in the mill . . . To be a roller a man must start as a boy and rise bit by bit . . . He became a roller at 18 years old and was with his father from the time he was twelve years old . . . one of his sons was head roller [on the night shift], and the other assistant roller . . . He did not think that piece work would be disastrous to the industry.

Managerial conflict became evident when Hoskins declared that he had threatened Bladon repeatedly that if he did not keep his mill tidy he would be dismissed. Bladon agreed but stated that 'the mill is being gradually fixed up'. Furthermore, Hoskins was far from happy about overmanning in Bladon's mill and dubious about Bladon's son's abilities. Bladon, however, was a senior employee. He had been a head roller at the works for about fourteen years. He had given evidence to the 1903 Select Commission on Bonuses for Manufactures and had been 'elected at a large meeting' of the union to represent the workers at the Wages Board.[23] The strongly established hierarchy of labour was undoubtedly a major impediment in Hoskins's determination to modernise the works as quickly as possible. It was often supported by a family infrastructure and sustained by a rigid conservatism rooted in the genuine fear that change would erode hard-won status. Meanwhile the increasing number of unskilled workers saw evidence of prosperity in the installation of new machinery and, according to the norms of the day, wanted a flow-on to wages.

Unprofitability persisted as the federal government procrastinated over the Bonus Bill. Early in July 1908 an important meeting was held between Charles Hoskins and the Eskbank Ironworkers' Association to discuss Hoskins's expedient proposal of a temporary reduction in wages pending a firm indication that the Bonus Bill would be passed. The men, remembering the cuts imposed by the Industrial Court in 1903 as well as prior cuts in the 1890s, made a counter suggestion: they would continue for three months under the existing agreement and during this time they promised to agitate for the passing of the Bonus Bill. Robert Pillans, speaking for the workers, recalled that the 1903 cut had been made 'for a certain time' until the industry recovered; yet the workers still awaited a restoration. Irritated, Hoskins responded that the cut had been made by a court decision. As he had not made the promise to restore wages, he told them to forget it. He added that he would give them the title deeds of the works before he agreed to their claims. Pillans, a labour leader with a community appeal that later made him mayor of Lithgow, pointed out that the prosperity of the town depended upon a duty or a bonus, adding that Lysaght's had recently lost that 'duty or bonus' by not paying reasonable wages.[24]

Hoskins objected to Pillans's implications. He judged the purpose of the dialogue to be to arrange cuts until the Bonus Bill passed and not to discuss alternatives. He added that his firm had never been in court and that they had not had a strike for twenty-five years (a statement curiously at variance with another report that 'the Boilermakers' Society has been on strike against G. & C. Hoskins for a full 20 years').[25] Furthermore, it was the company's intention to pay a fair wage and, indeed, there were some men in the works to whom he would like to pay a higher wage. This was confirmed by the fact that on arrival he had raised some wages and reduced some hours. Hoskins added that he hoped for cooperation from the work-force at this difficult period, particularly in view of the fact that at Eskbank, unlike in some Sydney ironworks, 'they got constant work and constant wages'. Nevertheless, he was aware that anomalous conditions existed under which one man was paid £2 per week and another £2 per day. This desire to alter the customary wage structure was probably another cause of dissatisfaction among the traditional leaders of the ironworking community.[26]

The Hoskins brothers were self-made men[27] and from personal experience they were well aware of the difficulties faced by some of their employees. George Hoskins emphasised to the workers' leaders that he and his brother were not unaware of the hardship involved. They had exempted from the reduction all those with incomes under 7s 6d per day; above that figure he suggested a sliding scale of reductions from 7.5 to 12.5 per cent. He explained that they were a small firm with a turnover of about £300 000 a year, most of which was absorbed in wages. For instance, their labour costs to operate the blast furnace were three or four times those in England. Similarly the cost of puddling iron in Australia was 18s per ton against 8s 6d in England. The steel furnaces, or apologies for them, operated at such a loss that he hardly dared mention them. He could not go on running the works for another three months like the last. When the union secretary had come to see him, he had been considering closing the works. Instead he had agreed to this meeting. The men, on their part, reiterated that the status quo should continue until the fate of the Bonus Bill was known. In an attempted compromise Hoskins suggested that he keep the money saved by the proposed wages reduction in a trust fund, until the fate of the Bonus Bill was finally decided. The firm would only retain the money if the Bill did not pass. He further agreed that at that time, regardless of the outcome, he would hold a meeting with the men to discuss wages.[28] Nevertheless, after some discussion as to what constituted a day's work, it was decided that the workers should vote on the issue. Hoskins refused to state how he would react to a negative answer.

The union officials then balloted the men, waiting upon each individual with a pencil for 'convenience'. The result was an overwhelming 'No' to any reduction in wages. On 9 July Hoskins closed a section of the works, partly as a warning and partly from necessity. Interviewed by the press, George Hoskins said that the closure was necessary for essential repairs, including the rebuilding of the Siemen's furnace, the installation of new high-pressure steam boilers, and rebuilding the foundations under two of the mills, and he said that he was 'sorry that the men look upon this stoppage as a lock-out. Most of them must know that a stoppage must take place for the new installations'.[29] Nevertheless, the timing of the stoppage undoubtedly left it open to other interpretations. It is difficult not to conclude that mutual antagonism had reached a point where neither party was co-operating.

Four days later, on 13 July, the Eskbank Ironworkers' Association decided to register under the New South Wales *Industrial Disputes Act* and they voted for the establishment of a Wages Board. The union's solicitor, G. S. Beeby, telegraphed Hoskins asking him to withdraw the closure notice in the public interest. The *Lithgow Mercury* approached William Sandford for comment, but the press was denied the copy it obviously expected as it reported that 'Mr Sandford was not inclined to say anything about the position'. Instead, the paper concentrated on the importance of obtaining reliable supplies of iron ore, a problem which Hoskins already had under consideration. Hoskins stated that while work was suspended the firm would take the opportunity to remodel the shops and install the machinery imported from England. During this period they would offer as much employment as was required for these tasks. The railway spike-making department continued to operate, and between this and those redeployed on refurbishing the works nearly 200 men, slightly less than a third of the normal work-force, continued to be employed.[30] For many, the period of unemployment was short as workers were reinstated when the various sections of the works became operational again.

Judge Heydon, although nervous that he was over-extending the provisions of the recent *Industrial Disputes Act*, agreed to recommend the establishment of a Board. The Wade ministry confirmed his decision and the Iron Trades (Lithgow) Wages Board became one of the first boards to be established under the New South Wales Act. After some discussion about its composition it was agreed that the Board would consist of three representatives from each side. The union representatives declared that they had asked nothing from Hoskins that they had not previously asked from Sandford. Nevertheless, some idea of the workers' distrust can be deduced from the fact that the union executive told the *Sydney Morning Herald* that the employers had closed the works to take temporary losses against long-term gains, and they had concluded that the Hoskinses' Sydney workers enjoyed better treatment. The Sydney employees had in fact publicly expressed their support for the management.[31]

The newly established Wages Board met under the chairmanship of Judge Scholes, who agreed to the appointment of an accountant to investigate the financial position of the works thoroughly. Hoskins offered to pay the accountant's fee, but wanted the men to choose him.[32] Eventually Horace Allard of Lyell & Allard (Public Accountants) was suggested by Judge Scholes and appointed as an official of the court, which formally accepted Hoskins' 'generous offer' regarding Allard's remuneration. Allard's brief was 'to report to the Board as to whether the industry is financially capable of paying an increase of wages, &c.; and secondly, whether the financial capacity of the industry is such as to call for a decrease of wages'. He reported on 16 September 1908 that the industry was 'not capable of paying an increase of wages' and he was of the opinion that the financial position of the industry called for a decrease. At the same time the unions argued in the New South Wales Industrial Court that Hoskins, in contravention of the 1908 *Industrial Disputes Act*, had precipitated the dispute in order to lock the men out while he was reorganising the works. The union received the support of the Sydney Labour Council and Judge Heydon found for the plaintiffs, fining G. & C. Hoskins Ltd £50 with £10 costs, and Hoskins, who protested the verdict, was personally fined £10 and £10 costs.[33]

Both Charles Hoskins and his employees at Eskbank then turned to lobbying for the Bonus Bill. On 9 October 1908 the *Lithgow Mercury* published a statement on behalf of the Ironworkers Union and the town of Lithgow:

> The general conclusion that wages must be considerably reduced if the industry is to be continued on its present basis is very difficult to answer. With our full knowledge of the industry, we think that the present wages will be maintained by the Wages Board, and that the industry will expand considerably, and employ a much larger number of men if the proposed bonus on pig iron, steel ingots and puddled bars is granted . . . [the reduction of wages here foreshadowed affects nearly 1000 people] . . . there is no doubt that the present company is losing on each ton of pig iron sold.

The letter concluded by emphasising that the passing of the Bonus Bill would not increase the price of iron to Australians. Later in the month it was reported that there was a 'dullness' at the works and that 300 men had been thrown out of work because of a lack of orders. However, despite the depressed state of the market, the refurbishing of the works continued.

Finally, on 11 December the *Lithgow Mercury* was able to report triumphantly that Mr Hoskins had wired from Melbourne that the Bonus Bill had become law and that it would operate from 1 January 1909. Hoskins returned to an enthusiastic reception from the Lithgow Chamber of Commerce. The health of Hoskins' sons was proposed by Robert Pillans, who declared that 'nothing had taken place during his experience of Hoskins Ltd. that prevented him proposing the toast in the heartiest manner possible'. The Bill provided for the payment of a bonus on the production of pig-iron, steel, puddled bar and galvanised sheets. Over the next nine years it amounted in total to £205 823; almost certainly it saved the Eskbank ironworks.[34]

Meanwhile, the Wages Board had continued to sit, awaiting the outcome of the Bonus Bill. On 23 December 1908 the *Lithgow Mercury* announced that the Board would adjourn until 14 February 1909 when it would continue its meetings until it reached a conclusion, which it did the following month. At this time, the Board reviewed the structure of work at the ironworks and its decisions laid down the subsequent pattern for the industry. There was to be a 48-hour week of five and a half days on day shifts and six days for night shifts. Overtime was to be paid at time and a quarter for the first two hours and time and a half thereafter. Sundays, and the eight public holidays established by the award, were to be paid at time and a half for day workers. There were to be three 8-hour shifts. The minimum wage was fixed at seven shillings per day with margins for skills, shift work and other inconveniences. Despite strong opposition from the rollers, time rates replaced contracts, thus tightening the central control of management. This was balanced by a preference being given to employing union members being written into the award, thus strengthening unionism in the works. At the end of June 1910, a labourer at Lithgow was earning between seven and nine shillings per day.[35]

An uncertain economic climate and uneasy labour relations throughout Australia continued during 1909, the year of the great strike at Broken Hill. At Lithgow problems arose with the blast furnace, which resulted in it being shut down for some months for modifications. In addition there was a strike in the ironworks colliery that was only settled after an appeal to the Wages Board. However, unemployment was at a comparatively low level and it was anticipated that the new contract for steel rails, which had been awarded to the Hoskins company, would provide additional work. The isolation of industries in the Lithgow valley had created an introspective clannishness and suspicion of outsiders that did not encourage amalgamation. Nevertheless, unionism had a long tradition in the area, and although it had been economically weak in the iron and steel industry, it had often been reinforced by an almost suicidal stubbornness.

By 1910 changing technology and its effects, particularly on the blast furnace and its ancillary workers, encouraged a more conciliatory approach to the overtures of the New South Wales branch of the Federated Ironworkers' Association. In January 1911 the Eskbank Ironworkers' Association of Mill and Forge Workers amalgamated with the Federated Ironworkers' Association of Australia.[36] Economic uncertainty created, and conflicting social philosophies justified, defensive fears on the part of both management and labour. Lines of confrontation hardened. This encouraged, or forced, increasing government participation in the problems of the industry. At the same time the indecisiveness of government policy and its lack of continuity (aggravated by short-term parliaments) had a detrimental effect upon Australian industrial development at a crucial period.

# 7

# NATIONALISATION OR PRIVATE ENTERPRISE?

NATIONALISATION OF THE iron and steel industry was a long-standing ambition of many Labor politicians at both state and federal level. It was, however, the point at which social theory and economic reality confronted each other. The enthusiasm of the federal ALP politicians had declined as they slowly realised the practical difficulties involved in financing and operating a business of such magnitude. As each year passed the magnitude of these difficulties increased. At the same time procrastination hindered the free enterprise development of the industry.

The New South Wales Labor Party had adopted nationalisation of the industry as a policy in 1909. In October 1910 the Liberal–Reform government in New South Wales was replaced by the Labor administration of J. S. T. McGowan. The new Minister for Labour and Industry was G. S. Beeby, who had been a solicitor for the Eskbank Ironworkers' Association in 1908. The new New South Wales Labor government gave such a high priority to a nationalised iron and steel industry that, almost immediately he was elected, Premier McGowan left for Great Britain to find a suitably qualified expert to assess the feasibility of such a enterprise. He chose F. W. Paul, manager of the Steel Company of Scotland. In order that he might have the fullest authority, Paul was appointed a Royal Commissioner. The Royal Commission was officially established on 15 August 1911.

The Paul Commission took its evidence at a time when turmoil in the iron industry had become acute; indeed, Paul's appointment and new outbreak of labour unrest shared a common origin, the fall of the Liberal–Reform government. At Lithgow the election of a Labor government pledged to nationalisation intensified the unrest among the workers. For both Charles Hoskins and his employees, wider ideological considerations were now the underlying issue. The tension erupted on February 1911 when some of the iron ore miners at Carcoar, who claimed to be outside the jurisdiction of the Lithgow Wages Board, struck for a pay rise of approximately eight shillings per day.[1] Some men employed at the blast furnace at Lithgow had also been agitating for a wages increase. They now joined in the dispute. Hoskins dismissed both these claims.

Charles Hoskins advised both groups to return to work, assuring them that the men employed at the Carcoar mine as well as those at the blast furnace would be kept on and he would employ as many of the strikers as the works required. However, all who had been on strike, whether they were re-employed or not, would face prosecution under the *Industrial Disputes Act* and, Hoskins pointed out, the longer the strike lasted, the fewer men would be required. He believed that the strike was caused by some forty 'agitators' whose aim was to close down the blast furnace by withholding supplies of ore. Agitation was also a popular topic for workers. Their view was summed up by James Dooley MLA, the Lithgow tailor and ALP politician,[2] who declared that 'we require some men of the agitator type if we are to reach the standard of civilisation which we hope to attain in Australia'.

Dooley's wishes were shortly granted in the shape of the educationalist and socialist suffragette, Dora Montefiore, who visited Lithgow in 1911. She delivered an encouraging speech on 'Revolutionary Socialism and Industrial Unionism' to an interested audience from the balcony of the Grand Central Hotel in mid March. The *Lithgow Mercury* reported that

> The Speaker gave an exposition of what was meant by the Marxian interpretation of Socialism—that the workers never receive the reward of their labour, but receive only the market price for it. The remainder was kept by the capitalist and put aside, being termed 'capital'. Really it was the surplus value of the labour of the worker.

The dispute escalated when an engine driver, Syd Kelly, who was also president of the local branch of the Federated Engine Drivers and Firemen's Association, was dismissed. His colleagues came out in support. The secretary of the Railway Workers and General Labourers Association then accused Hoskins of a 'thinly veiled attempt to break up tradesunionism in connection with the industry'. He said that Hoskins had refused to see him and had told the men he would give them a rise if they would keep out of the union. Beeby, as Minister of Labour and Industry, came to Lithgow to assess the situation for himself but, at the time of his visit, Hoskins was in Sydney. Beeby informed the men that they could ask for a Board. At the same time he told Hoskins that he could guarantee that work would be resumed if the engine driver was reinstated.

A few days later the strike was settled 'somewhat unexpectedly' as a result of an informal meeting at the Lithgow Show between Hoskins, Dooley and two other politicians.[3] Their agreement was afterwards endorsed by the unions concerned, who had been afraid that, despite worker solidarity, the strike would be broken by economic necessity. Kelly was to be reinstated and, so far as possible, there was to be a return to the situation that had existed before the strike. It was a truce rather than a final settlement.

On 12 July 1911, in this atmosphere of mutual distrust, fear and suspicion, the delegate of the Ironworkers Tunnel Lodge, James Cairns, asked permission to absent himself from work at the Ironworks Tunnel Colliery on the following day to attend a union meeting in Sydney. Coalminers worked on a tonnage basis so the question of a day's pay was not relevant. Instead the main issue was absenteeism and its resulting lack of productivity. The colliery manager, Mr Spooner, did not specifically forbid or approve of Cairns's trip; instead he emphasised that the works was very short of coal. Some of the miners had been ill the previous week and the firm had been obliged to purchase sixty tons of coal from Oakey Park colliery. Spooner pointed out that when that was used up 'we shall have to stop the ironworks almost at once'.[4]

Subsequently Charles Hoskins stressed that a large part of the problem was that Cairns, regardless of the labour shortage at the mine and its possible consequence, had gone without providing a substitute to work his shift. This omission was exacerbated when the union did not complete its business in the day and Cairns was again absent on the following day. Realising this complication, both Cairns and Truscott, the secretary of the Western Miners' Association, wrote to Spooner to explain the circumstances. However, Spooner suspended Cairns. The other miners immediately came out on strike. This created further trouble. The preceding February, the miners had accepted two pence per ton above the hewing rate then current in the Lithgow valley. In return they had given a specific undertaking that they would not strike.[5]

Hoskins then wrote to Truscott stating his regret that the men had gone on strike, as, in view of the previous agreement, they would now have to accept a cut of two pence per ton in their wages. Hoskins and the local labour leaders met at the tunnel mouth at 8 a.m. on 17 July. Hoskins suggested that the men should go to work leaving Cairns suspended, pending a further discussion between himself, Spooner and Cairns. The men declined to do so, pointing out that the attendance of delegates at union meetings had been a convention, whereupon Hoskins answered that it was not a legal right: there was 'nothing in an industrial award' about it. Truscott replied that the custom had been established for twenty-five years and that when he had received Hoskins's letter about the two-pence cut he thought that the whole business was premeditated.

Hoskins argued that the men had tried to 'put a pistol' to Spooner's head by refusing to go to work. To this Bernard Scully, the president of the Western Miners' Association interjected that 'they were united to protect each other. Men had laid down their lives for unionism and he was prepared to do the same'.

Hoskins retorted, 'You'd like to have a halo, there will always be a class struggle while men like you are about'; he then pointed out that the whole business could have been settled in ten minutes.

Scully responded that 'it would have been a breakdown of principle. The principle of the Union is involved'.

Hoskins, furious and immune to the placatory appeals of other unionists, declared that he had paid the extra two pence as an insurance against strikes but 'you beggars, you strike when you like'. At the same time he said that he bore no personal animosity against Cairns. Drinks were brought out and passed around. Despite the now convivial surroundings further conversation failed to resolve what had become on both sides an impasse of principle.[6]

Hoskins telegraphed Beeby to come to Lithgow to settle the dispute. Beeby suggested that the previous state of affairs should be restored, pending arbitration over the extra two pence per ton. Hoskins misinterpreted this advice and replied that 'we accept your suggestion: extra 2d not to be paid pending arbitration award'. Beeby, not surprisingly, was furious and issued a public statement blaming Hoskins for the whole affair because his colliery manager had violated one of the established customs of coal-mining. He believed that 'the trouble is one that should never have arisen. What has grown into a serious matter could easily have been avoided'. The miners were naturally encouraged by Beeby's support. On 25 July a mass meeting of miners from the western coalfields was held in the Lithgow stadium. Here a decision was taken to give unanimous support to the miners of the Ironworks Tunnel Colliery. By now the effects of the stoppage had resulted in nearly 600 men being stood down. Charles Hoskins considered it outrageous that thirty coalminers could hold to ransom an industry employing approximately 1000 men. He prosecuted Cairns in the Lithgow Police Court. The magistrate dismissed the case. Hoskins then issued summonses against the men for refusing to work.[7]

The New South Wales government appointed a Wages Board under the chairmanship of Judge Scholes, by now well acquainted with labour problems at Lithgow. The Mayor of Lithgow, Alderman Pillans, who as a miner had a long association with the ironworks, tried to resolve the crisis. Neither he nor Judge Scholes were able to reconcile the parties. A further mass meeting of the Western Miners' Association resolved not to recognise the Board until the men were allowed to work under the old conditions. On 15 August, the day on which the New South Wales Royal Commission to inquire into the Iron and Steel Industry was established, strike funds were distributed among the members of both the miners' and the ironworkers' unions at Lithgow.[8]

Meanwhile, within the works, Charles Hoskins started to erect sheds with cooking and bathing facilities for the accommodation of non-union labour. Both sides settled in for a protracted struggle. On 19 August there was a mass meeting of all the unions in the Lithgow valley. Encouraged by reports that money for the defence fund was being subscribed 'very freely from all parts of the State', they passed a resolution urging the federal government to take immediate steps to 'repeal the Manufacturers' Encouragement Act until such times as the employees in the various industries receive union rates and conditions'.[9] A ballot of men working at the blast furnace decided by a narrow majority to remain working until such times as they were asked to handle coal obtained by non-union labour. There were about 180 men employed at the blast furnace and on 23 August a number of these, probably about half, joined the strikers. The union then disowned those who remained at work and began to negotiate with the other unions represented at the works for their support.

The strike escalated. The Federated Engine Drivers and Firemen's Association had long-standing disagreements with the Hoskins company, which they felt had on numerous occasions breached state awards. When they had served Charles Hoskins with summonses to this effect, he had reacted by immediately dismissing their members. On 24 August the fitters and moulders employed at the ironworks came out on strike. By this time very few men were employed at the ironworks, although the coal-mine and blast furnace were working with non-union labour.[10]

On 26 August the strike entered its seventh week. Hoskins, continuing to employ non-union labour, maintained that production was only down by a few tons a day and that before long he expected to be doing better than before. However, as the non-union labour was being intimidated by the strikers, police protection was introduced. The situation grew increasingly tense. On 30 August the *Sydney Morning Herald* described how a meeting of strikers and sympathisers resolved that

> in the opinion of this meeting the police of Lithgow are exceeding their duty in acting as messengers for Messrs Hoskins Ltd., by going to the houses of free labourers in order to bring them to their work at the blast furnace and, further, that the foregoing be sent to the Acting Chief Secretary, Mr Flowers.

Despite the clearly escalating crisis, on 29 August the *Sydney Morning Herald* had optimistically reported that 'though the feeling is naturally very strong, apart from the usual demonstration at the change of shifts there has been very little evidence of bad temper'. The next day the *Lithgow Mercury* carried banner headlines: 'Riot at Lithgow'.

About 6 p.m. on 29 August 1911 a crowd of strikers and their supporters, accompanied by a band playing the 'Dead March', had gathered as usual to picket the change of shift at the blast furnace. Non-unionists came out to see what was happening and some youths in the crowd started to stone them. The police, also the victims of crowd violence, were helpless to prevent the crowd from rushing towards the furnace. The non-unionists retreated into the engine-room and barricaded the doors. Charles Hoskins arrived at the blast furnace after the trouble began. He parked his car at the top of the road leading to the blast furnace and managed to enter the engine-room by the back door where he joined his three sons. He later revealed that 'we were fully armed, and had they broken down the doors there could be no doubt that it would have resulted in very serious bloodshed'. (It was not unusual for senior executives to carry arms in early industrial enterprises.) Fortunately, although all the windows were broken, the doors of the engine-room remained intact.

The next day the *Lithgow Mercury* reported events in detail. Senior Sergeant McKenzie of the Lithgow Police had arrived on the scene about 7 p.m. and called his men to stand in front of the engine-room with their revolvers drawn. Legalists among the rioters pointed out that the *Riot Act* had not been read and therefore the police could not shoot. The reference was to the British *Riot Act* of 1716, which was the principal method for controlling public disturbances before the development of the modern police force. Its terms required a magistrate to confront the rioters and to read to them, in a loud voice, the appropriate section of the Act. If, following this, the crowd did not disband within an hour, the army was called out and the rioters became guilty of the capital charge of felony. On this occasion McKenzie retorted that 'it matters not to me whether the Riot Act is read or not. The riot is here, and if you press further I shall certainly shoot, but for heaven's sake don't compel me to'. McKenzie tried unavailingly to have Hoskins confer with the demonstrators; they turned to other destructive activities. Hoskins's two automobiles were near by. One was damaged, and the other, his personal Renault 16/20, was rolled down an embankment and burnt. By midnight the rioters had gained control of the works. Meanwhile the crowd ransacked the quarters of the non-union labourers.

Police reinforcements were hurried in from neighbouring towns. A special train carrying police officers from the metropolitan division left Sydney Central Station at 12.30 a.m. However, by the time they arrived the local force, with assistance from Orange and Bathurst, was in control. Dawn on 30 August 1911 revealed a scene of incredible confusion as the strikers had done a considerable amount of superficial damage. Nevertheless, Charles Hoskins was once more in possession of the works and by 9.45 a.m. the furnace was once again in blast. He defiantly told the press that 'nothing but an earthquake will stop these works'.[11] Within six days he had replaced his Renault with an identical model.

These events can be interpreted in several ways and with varying degrees of emphasis. Much of the blame must lie on the equally intransigent attitudes of Hoskins and the union leaders. Hoskins was a self-made man at a period in which bankruptcy always dogged the entrepreneur. He must have felt that the political and philosophical tide of the times, impregnated with the doctrines of the Industrial Workers of the World, was running strongly against him. His fear of unionism was obvious. At the same time the ALP state government was committed to

Charles Hoskins on the morning of 30 August 1911, looking up at the blast furnace from the engine room, where he had been besieged overnight by rioting strikers.

nationalisation and he was under pressure from the Royal Commission. This was already sitting in Sydney and he had some cause to feel that its single commissioner, F. W. Paul, was unsympathetic, if not hostile, to him. In the short period that Hoskins had been operating the works he had certainly put more into them than he had taken out.

On the other hand the early industrial working conditions at Eskbank were harsh. Furthermore, conditions of work were changing throughout the entire labour hierarchy and, unless the benefits of change were obvious and immediate, labour attitudes to change were traditionally recalcitrant. The contract system, despite its potential for abuse, had provided an obvious hierarchical structure and a linkage with market conditions, connections which the wages boards were still struggling to establish.

## 7 NATIONALISATION OR PRIVATE ENTERPRISE?

The abolition of contract work had alienated the workers' natural leaders, such as the rollers, from the management at a time when unionists and politicians were extremely active and management needed all the support it could find. Some of the union leaders undoubtedly felt that they were crusaders. To the average worker the real economics of the situation were probably camouflaged by the amount of money being spent on improving the works, while none appeared to be available to increase wages. The financial connection between the Hoskinses' various enterprises probably did not occur to them. Moreover, there was the evidence of wealth shown by the Hoskins family, particularly their passion for spectacular cars. These were a constant source of comment in the local paper and it is possible that their destruction had a symbolic connotation for the rioters.

The Lithgow riot had much in common with the traditional unrest of labour in any early industrial society. Its major importance was that, like the strikes at Broken Hill in 1892 and 1909, it set the atmosphere for future labour relations in the iron and steel industry. However, both sides sought more immediate causes for the disturbance. The secretary of the Federated Ironworkers Association, John Dixon, claimed firstly that 'the non-unionists brought it upon themselves by Mr Hoskins bringing the men down and parading them before the eyes of the unionists' and secondly that 'if he [Hoskins] had only consented to confer the disturbance would have terminated very quickly'.

In *The Hoskins Saga*, written many years later, Sir Cecil Hoskins, who was present at the riot, wrote that his father did offer to receive a deputation. Charles Hoskins had told the union officials, through the closed door of the engine-room where he was besieged, to 'come and see me in my office at nine o'clock tomorrow morning' and that they did not appear. Conceivably, in the circumstances, they neither heard nor understood him. At the time Charles Hoskins attributed much of the trouble to the fact that many of the rioters had been drunk: 'in my mind, one of the causes of the men losing their self-control was that the strikers had received their fortnight's strike pay, and, in addition, I am informed that there was an abundant supply of free beer'.[12]

Both parties were now entrenched and desperate. In defiance of nearly eighty police the strikers resorted to guerrilla tactics. The 'man-hunting' of non-unionists continued as strikers attacked the undefended houses of 'loyalists'. A bomb was exploded on the doorstep of one house in Tank Street. The police were forced to charge one large crowd to enable the non-unionists to leave the ironworks in the evening. At the end of August

James Dooley addressed a mass meeting of unionists. He expressed the view that the harmony between employer and employee in the Lithgow community had been unnecessarily disrupted as 'since the arrival of this gentleman there had been dispute after dispute, almost every week, showing that though Mr Hoskins knew his business and could manufacture iron, he could not realise that his employees were human beings'. The meeting, fully aware of the political climate and of the Royal Commission, then sitting in Sydney, passed a unanimous resolution: 'we, the citizens of Lithgow, are of opinion that there will be no permanent prosperity in this district until the State controls the iron industry, or, failing the State, some reasonable person that will deal fairly with his employees'.[13]

Dooley had listed some of the grievances felt against Hoskins. The reduction of the men's wages soon after his arrival (although the Wages Board had agreed that this was an economic necessity). The 'accidental' weeding out of unionists after his take-over from Sandford. His failure to keep his promises to puddlers whom he had brought out from England. Finally, the introduction of non-union labour to replace unionists on strike. Hoskins's argument was that industrial promises are linked to industrial conditions over which he had little control. As a self-made industrialist, Hoskins had probably a very realistic understanding of the feelings of his work-force, but coupled with this was his knowledge of the slender economic line that separated success from the failure that would destroy them all. At the same time the aggression, which had ensured his business success, undoubtedly made him appear less than sympathetic to the immediate and basic demands of his employees. Convinced of the fragility of Australian industry in general, and of the iron and steel industry in particular, he undoubtedly sought to abridge the power of the unions.

After the riot an uneasy peace returned to Lithgow. On 1 September 1911 the *Sydney Morning Herald* commented that 'Lithgow resembles nothing so much as a brimming cauldron, bubbling and simmering, and threatening each minute to boil over, yet keeping somehow within bounds'. Over 100 police were now in Lithgow guarding the works, patrolling the streets, and delivering the 130 summonses issued in the aftermath of the riot. Charles Hoskins was angry and defiant, particularly over the victimisation of non-unionists and their families:

> If this is the method of combined unionism to attain its end, then all I can say is, God help the country. I am a believer in unionism so long as it is conducted in a reasonable way. But to my mind the unionists can never

succeed until they are determined that whatever happens they will not strike, but redress their grievances through the industrial courts established for that special purpose.[14]

On 5 September 1911 John Dixon (the secretary of the Federated Ironworkers Association), Bernard Scully (president of the Western Miners' Association), James Cairns (the delegate from the Ironworkers Tunnel Lodge) and five other leading unionists were secretly arrested on a warrant charging them with riot on 29 August. Dixon, Scully, Cairns and four out of the other five unionists were committed for trial at the Bathurst Circuit Court on 11 October. The trial finished on 14 October when Mr Justice Pring told the jury that:

> in civilised communities such as that in which they lived every man who had a wrong had a court of law to address, from the ordinary Police Court to the Supreme Court, and in more recent years the Court of Arbitration; but if people took upon themselves to redress their own wrongs they were getting back to a state of savagery.

Pring argued in support of 'the right of any man to carry on his own business, no matter whether that man was a large or small employer or a workman engaged at daily or weekly wage', stating that 'if anybody interfered with or hindered any such man he committed a very, very serious wrong indeed'. Finally the judge concluded that 'the riot was preconcerted and that it was organised with a view to forcing Mr Hoskins to grant the conference and of preventing free labourers working'. The jury found Bernard Scully, William Charles Hayes and Edward Williams guilty, they failed to agree in the cases of James Cairns and John Dixon, and they decided that Ross Kennedy and Ernest Alfred Cooper were both not guilty. The *Sydney Morning Herald* was critical both of the release of Dixon and of the attitude of the government.[15] The strike dragged on until April 1912, when a compromise agreement reinstated the miners' delegate and non-union labour was forced to join the union or leave the works—but wages were again cut.

Meanwhile, sitting in Sydney, the Paul Commission continued its investigations into the feasibility of nationalising the iron and steel industry in New South Wales. The commissioner was asked to comment specifically on five points:

> (a) The suitability of ores within our said State, or within other States, of our Commonwealth for the manufacture of Iron and Steel;

(b) The cost at which the various classes of Iron and Steel required by our Governments of our said Commonwealth and States could be produced from local ores;

(c) Whether the arrangement entered into by our government of our State of New South Wales with Messrs. G. and C. Hoskins, Limited, for the supply of Iron and Steel, is beneficial to our said government;

(d) What is a satisfactory price for the supply of steel rails for railway purposes produced at the works in New South Wales of Messrs. G. and C. Hoskins, Limited, aforesaid; and

(e) The approximate cost of a plant capable of producing the Iron and Steel likely to be required in the future by our Government of our Commonwealth of Australia and of our several Australian States.[16]

Charles Hoskins must have been well aware that such an inquiry would unearth some questionable activities in connection with the New South Wales contract upon which the viability of the works depended. Certainly, when he came before the commissioner on 22 and 26 September, he responded in the abrasive fashion that he normally showed under what he construed to be hostile conditions. Paul started off by assuring Hoskins that he would receive the most studied and unbiased consideration. Hoskins replied that he considered that it would be impossible for Paul to do so and satisfy his employers, the New South Wales government. It was on this note that Hoskins eventually walked out in a real or simulated rage. Paul was also exasperated and complained in his *Report* that

> I found the greatest difficulty in extracting evidence from many material witnesses, and this reticence was displayed not only by those whose interests were bound up with the Contractors, but by a number of Government officials. Finding that it was useless to expect evidence to be volunteered to guide me in coming to a fair and equitable decision, I was forced . . . to submit witnesses to a species of cross-examination.[17]

Doubtless the introduction of an overseas expert inevitably encouraged an instinctive cover-up on the part of Hoskins's employees. But it did likewise with the government officials. They felt that they might be accused of negligence, or find that their behaviour was remembered against them either on another occasion or by a succeeding government. Foreign experts come and go, local employers and governments are constant. One of the witnesses, expressing a cautious sympathy with the commissioner in his attempts to uncover the truth, added, with disarming candour:

> I do not know whether there is any connection between the fact of the Labor Party being at present in power and the action that might be taken by some new party at a future date . . . I am wondering whether my position will be jeopardised in any way. I am a married man with a family to maintain . . . so that I cannot say that I have a great deal to say, unless I have some guarantee that I would not suffer as a result of my evidence.[18]

Perhaps it was not surprising that the 1911 New South Wales *Report of the Royal Commission on the Iron and Steel Industry* revealed a lack of understanding of the history of the local industry. It contained a mixture of fact and interpretation, which in places verged on personal comment. Commissioner Paul concluded, mainly on the basis of geological reports and other documentation, that there were known, adequate and available supplies of iron ore if not in New South Wales then elsewhere in Australia. New South Wales certainly had adequate coal supplies in the northern and southern coalfields. Paul considered that 'there is little doubt that there would be found sufficient enterprise among the colliery companies' to install the necessary coal-washing plants and by-product coke ovens required, provided a good and regular market was assured. Regarding the economical production of the various classes of iron and steel required by the states and the Commonwealth, he pointed out that 'it may be accepted as an axiom that, provided raw materials can be produced at moderate prices, the question of economy of production depends in a great measure upon the magnitude of the output'. He felt that 'Australia's requirements demand an iron and steel works of such magnitude that economical production would be assured' apart from any consideration of a bounty.

From an interpretation of Hoskinses' blast furnace wages sheets and other records, Paul estimated that the cost of manufacturing pig-iron at Lithgow did not exceed 58s per ton. Charles Hoskins complained that this figure was unreal. It excluded costs associated with capital investment and strikes. Given modern equipment and a blast furnace with a capacity of 5000 tons per week, Paul further lowered his estimated cost to 54s per ton. He concluded that he 'could see no practical reason why Australia should longer delay in taking her legitimate place as one of the great producers of iron and steel'. Paul envisaged an industry 'approximating to a turnover . . . of from £3,000,000 to £4,000,000 *per annum*' and, he concluded, that it only remained for him to point out that for 'an iron and steel works on such a scale . . . an expenditure of approximately £1,500,000 would be entailed'. Doubtless aware of the shock he was inflicting on the aspirations of the New South Wales government, he suggested that such an expenditure could be incurred 'by a process of gradual development'. Thus he neatly side-stepped the fact that the bulk of that sum would still be required to make the enterprise operational.

Regarding the present contracts between the government and the Hoskins company, Paul condemned the existing situation absolutely: 'my investigations, however, have demonstrated that as matters have been conducted in the past, and exist at present, the quality of the material supplied is, in many instances, absolutely bad'. There was undoubtedly a quality control problem at Lithgow. This was not helped by Hoskins ignoring the rejection of material by the Government Testing Engineer at Lithgow and fulfilling the contract with already condemned iron and steel. It also transpired that the former Testing Engineer, a Mr Burrow, had been under a pecuniary obligation to Hoskins.[19] Finally, although the contracts were supposed to be supervised by a Conference Board this body had adopted 'a policy of *laissez faire*' and was admitted to be useless. 'Another serious matter', continued the commissioner, 'which tends to show the lack of *bona fides* on the part of the Contractors . . . is the fact that it transpired from the evidence that they were in the habit of using German steel in large quantities in the material supplied to the Government under the contract, which is based on the condition that steel made from native ores will be supplied'.

Furthermore, although some of the German steel was made by the open-hearth process, most of it was made by the basic Bessemer process. This was considered by Lloyds and the British Admiralty to be dangerous for certain construction purposes. 'I consider it', the commissioner declared, 'little less than indifference to the safety of human life on the part of the Contractors that such material should be allowed to go out of their works for constructional purposes'. This was because such steel contained a high percentage of phosphorus, which would have made it brittle. Finally, Paul pointed out that the connection between the Hoskinses' pipe-casting factory and their Lithgow operation allowed them to transfer imported iron and steel from one works to the other, confusing both the origin of the basic materials and the bookkeeping. He concluded that in a separate contract between the Government and Messrs. G. and C. Hoskins, Limited, for the manufacture of cast-iron pipes and special castings at their Ultimo works, a provision is included that the pipe contractors must purchase all pig-iron required in the carrying out of that contract from W. Sandford Limited Lithgow. The Lithgow works now belong to Messrs. G. and C. Hoskins, Limited, so it is competent for them to charge their Ultimo works with the pig-iron used for the carrying out of the pipe contract at any price they choose . . . an inspection of their books will show that the pig-iron used for the carrying out of the pipe contract is charged at 77s 6d. per ton, while for other works, outside the contract with the government, the charge is 66s. 6d. per ton.

Not surprisingly, Paul's verdict was that 'in answer the question whether the contract with Messrs. G. and C. Hoskins is beneficial to the State, my answer is in the negative'.

There can be little doubt that by the time he came to write his report, Paul had minimal sympathy either with Charles Hoskins as a person, or with the problems that confronted him at Lithgow. To these he made no reference whatsoever. Instead Paul, on his own admission, went out of his way to comment on the pipe contract and he further insinuated that 'whether Mr Hoskins wished to avoid scrutiny of the contract prices, or whether his sudden determination to close his evidence was to evade examination on the various other matters connected with his maladministration of the contract, I know not'.

Paul concluded that 'bringing him [Hoskins] to a sense of his liability under the law' was a matter for the Government to consider. The Commission had sat in secret, much against Hoskins's wishes and his usual preference for open enquiries. On 2 November 1911 the *Report* was presented to the Minister of Public Works, Mr A. Griffith. Much of it had been leaked beforehand and when it was first released it was not printed in full. Hoskins's reply was immediate and indignant. He did not so much deny Paul's findings as accuse him of stating 'skilfully hidden' half-truths. He also pointed out that Paul, who in his report had declared that steel-rail making at Lithgow was impractical, had during his tour of the works commented that the rail mill, was 'a very fine mill and can easily roll 300 tons of rails per week'.[20]

The Hoskins brothers, it must be remembered, were leading figures in the Sydney business community. In 1895 Charles Hoskins had been the first president of the re-established Chamber of Manufactures of

New South Wales. They were not without friends. An immediate storm broke out in the press as well as in the Legislature. A week later the New South Wales Attorney-General, W.A. Holman, made an official statement to the press denying that the appointment of the commissioner was in any way 'political' and the Premier confirmed that 'no suggestion as to Nationalisation was ever made to the Commissioner'. However, the Premier explained disingenuously that the government had reason to believe that 'the proposed contract with Messrs. Hoskins Ltd., for the supply of steel rails was against the interests of the State, and they had thought it best to have the matter thoroughly inquired into by an outside expert', who would, at the same time, also advise the government 'as to the development of the iron industry in this State'.[21]

On 21 November the Attorney-General indicated that the government contracts held by Hoskins would be cancelled. This brought a response from C. A. Lee (Secretary for Public Works in the preceding—Liberal—ministry and in that capacity responsible for the original Sandford contract taken over by Hoskins). His opinion from the opposition benches was that 'the methods adopted by the Commissioner were not those best calculated to obtain a just and fair verdict, and that his conclusions were not borne out by the evidence'. In its 1912 new-year issue, *Australasian Hardware and Machinery* announced that the *Report* 'is a stinging indictment of manufacturing methods at Lithgow, but is discounted in our opinion by the manner in which the inquiry was conducted'. In particular, Paul's report was condemned for giving no indication of the extent to which the Hoskinses were trying to put the plant in order and for making no reference to the industrial trouble in the works at the time. 'A perusal of this document leaves the impression that an adverse finding was a foregone conclusion.'[22]

Paul had also responded negatively to the federal government's question as to whether Hoskins was conforming to the conditions governing the bonus awarded by the *Manufacturers' Encouragement Act* (1908). The federal bonus was briefly suspended but the decision was revoked in view of the fact that there was some Australian content in the pig-iron used in the goods manufactured at Eskbank. However, although the state government removed the Hoskinses' contract, it did not prosecute Charles Hoskins. Hoskins, on the other hand, sued the New South Wales government for £150 000 damages for breach of contract! In 1913 the case was settled out of court: Hoskins was cleared of many of Paul's charges and found to be eligible for future government contracts. At the same time the state government was found to be justified in revoking the

## 7 NATIONALISATION OR PRIVATE ENTERPRISE?

contract. Mindful that legal processes 'cannot ruin a government, but . . . can ruin an individual', Hoskins decided to settle for a *de facto* return to the previous situation and within a few years he was once again in receipt of substantial government contracts.[23]

The Hoskins brothers had long been aware that their viability as ironmasters was going to depend upon economies of scale. To achieve some market stability they depended upon a combination of government contracts plus the demand from their own pipe works. This may in part explain why Charles Hoskins considered it essential to sue the New South Wales government and then to agree to an out-of-court settlement, thus ensuring that he would continue to receive government contracts. Nevertheless, despite the settlement, the dispute had a considerable aftermath as it was revived in 1914 during the Interstate Tariff Investigation Commission.[24]

The strike and the loss of the state government contracts very nearly ruined the Hoskinses, who were only saved by the award, in 1912, of a federal contract for steel rails to connect Canberra with the New South

The blast furnace plant at Lithgow, *c.* 1925. The original Sandford furnace at left was augmented in 1913 by Hoskins, who added a second, outwardly similar, furnace at right, and who also increased the number of stoves from three to four per furnace. This raised the combined weekly production to 3000 tons of pig-iron.

Wales rail system at Queanbeyan. In addition, Lithgow was chosen by Lord Kitchener as the site for a small arms factory. When this opened in 1912, it offered a further, though limited, outlet for Hoskins iron and steel.[25] Restored government support and an increasing demand from the Ultimo pipe factory now encouraged Charles Hoskins to add a second blast furnace to the Eskbank works.

The new furnace was commissioned in May 1913 and a festive Lithgow, proclaiming 'Success to Local Industry' closed ranks to greet the guests. Charles Hoskins's blast furnace was claimed to have a rated capacity of 2000 tons per week, twice that of the Sandford blast furnace, largely attributable to an increase in the hearth diameter from nine to eleven feet and an increased blowing capacity of about 25 per cent. In spite of these changes it was outwardly a twin of the Sandford furnace to which it was linked. It was, with the exception of the turbo blowers and the boilers, an all-Australian furnace, made entirely from local materials at Ultimo and Eskbank, but, like the Sandford blast furnace, it was charged by hand, a labour-intensive anachronism.[26]

The Hoskins brothers were skilful and inventive engineers and they put to good use the knowledge they had acquired during their short and troubled period at Eskbank. The No. 2 blast furnace was blown in with fewer problems than its predecessor and, as comparative industrial peace returned to the works, production recovered. To provide sufficient coke for the two blast furnaces a new battery of eighty coke ovens of Belgian design was added to the plant[27] and a new colliery was opened to provide coking coal. Fortunately ore supplies for the expanded operation were adequate as, in 1910, the company had already opened a new quarry of magnetite ore at Tallawang, 126 miles by rail from the works. This supplemented hematite ore from Carcoar, ninety-six miles away. Later, in 1918, a third quarry was opened at Cadia near Orange, as the Carcoar deposits were becoming depleted.

The critical step in the rationalisation of production facilities was the opening, in 1914, of a works railway between the blast furnaces and the steel-making plant. This allowed liquid blast furnace iron, 'hot metal', to be transported in 30-ton capacity ladles for direct charging to the open-hearth furnaces,[28] thereby shortening the time required to make a 'heat' of steel and reducing the fuel used in the steel-making process. This finally converted Lithgow to an 'integrated' steel operation.

G. & C. Hoskins had taken over a very dilapidated ironworks consisting of outmoded puddling furnaces and rolling mills, together with two uneconomically small Siemens acid open-hearth furnaces of $4^1/_2$-ton capacity and a somewhat larger, basic open-hearth furnace of 15-ton capacity. Charles Hoskins appreciated from the start that he needed to convert the ironworks into a steelworks. Steel was the product of the future and he had to replace the puddling furnaces with steel furnaces. Immediate necessity had forced him, shortly after he took over the works, to add four new puddling furnaces, and he was only able to finally phase out the manufacture of wrought iron during World War I. Thus, although at the time of the take-over he had a significant asset in the newly commissioned modern blast furnace, production and demand still had to be achieved, while a concurrent modernisation of the steel-making and rolling facilities was imperative if the enterprise was to survive.

The first of the new basic open-hearth furnaces, of 30-ton capacity, was installed in 1911. It was shortly followed by one with a 50-ton capacity. A two-stand 27-inch reversing mill to roll billets, sheet bar and heavy rails and sections was also completed in 1911. This mill, which was to roll the first steel rails in Australia, was converted from the 24-inch mill purchased, but never commissioned, by Sandford. Subsequently the 27-inch mill was upgraded to 28 inches. The introduction of the heavy mill was followed by the installation of duplicate 10-inch bar mills. These replaced Sandford's 9-inch guide and 14-inch merchant mills and rolled billets from the 27-inch mill to rods, bars and light sections. All the Lithgow mills were steam driven. Hoskins's changes would have significantly improved the profitability of the business; in particular they allowed the closure of the two small $4^1/_2$-ton open-hearth furnaces, the eventual closure of the puddling furnaces and, as the new heavy mill could accept much larger ingots, the maximum size of ingot could be increased fivefold: from six cwt (300 kg) to thirty cwt (1500 kg).[29] The commissioning of the second blast furnace in 1913 and increased demand for steel during World War I led to a decision to build a new open-hearth furnace of 75 tons capacity. This was first tapped in 1915.

The construction of the 75-ton open-hearth furnace completed the primary iron- and steel-making facilities at Lithgow. However, further investment in this area was required before all steel-making ceased in 1931: the capacity of all the open hearth furnaces was later increased, and a new blowing engine for the blast furnaces was purchased in 1923 from Thompson & Co. of Castlemaine in Victoria at a cost of £17 000.

To understand the magnitude of Charles Hoskins's task and his achievement, it must be realised that all of this modernisation was being undertaken by a man who had only become an ironmaster at nearly sixty years of age. He was working against the background of a government

Charging ingots into a coal-fired reheating furnace prior to rolling in the 28-inch reversing mill at Eskbank, *c.* 1925. The absence of soaking pits is a noticeable disadvantage.

planning the nationalisation of the industry and in face of a rebellious work-force, which had sacked the works, threatened his own life and the lives of his sons. Hoskins represented a fairly common figure in early British industrialisation—he was an 'industrial squire' a visible owner-manager living in a community that looked to him as a major employer.

## 7 NATIONALISATION OR PRIVATE ENTERPRISE?

Teeming steel from an 80-ton ladle into two-ton ingot moulds, Eskbank, c. 1925. The back of an open-hearth furnace is visible to the right.

The relationship between Charles Hoskins and his workers was complex.[30] Underlying the often bitter conflicts between him and his workforce there was a personal relationship which surfaced in various ways. For instance, the social event of the Lithgow year was the Ironworkers' Picnic. This survived the transfer of the works to Port Kembla. Hoskins and his wife not only generously supported these festivities but always attended them. In October 1912 Hoskins's daughter, Hilda, was killed in an accident. The citizens of Lithgow sincerely shared the family's distress and, differences forgotten, the union officials attended the funeral.[31] We have examined the early disputes between Hoskins and the Eskbank ironworkers in some detail for two reasons. They set the pattern for subsequent industrial relations, not only at Lithgow but also at Port Kembla, and the narrative of turmoil is a necessary illustration of the problems of the industrial development of Australia, which might be misrepresented by analytical discourse alone.

The pattern of industrial relations at Eskbank was not one of a mentally rigorous seeking of clear objectives based on optimum solutions but, for both parties, it was a case of random action based on traditional expectations. For example, on one occasion the Federated Ironworkers' Association complained that by operating the blast furnace on Sunday Hoskins was in breach of the *Sunday Observance Act*; further, the FIA submitted that a Sunday shift was 'unnecessary' and took Hoskins to court, although it was common knowledge that a furnace in blast had to be operated continuously. The court found in favour of the company. To the union, and arguably to Hoskins, the tactical thrust was the main point of the exercise.[32] Tactical flourishes, drains on time, confidence and emotional energy, signified no more than a habitual polarisation leading nowhere. For their part, except for vague gestures to innovation, the Hoskins brothers also clung in spirit to the first generation of the industrial revolution. Neither the Hoskinses' experience nor that of their workers' representatives had conditioned them to seek optimum pragmatic solutions as goals; instead, both sides believed in ideological finalities. This caused compromises to be indistinguishable from tactics, and it also explained why the cordiality between the adversaries had little practical use. Such tactics belonged to the bygone era of early British industrialisation. Theoretically, they might have been expected to have no place in a goals-oriented frontier society. But in practice, the dead hand of the colonial immigrants' cultural baggage gripped long and hard.

Sir Cecil Hoskins later claimed that under G. & C. Hoskins Ltd the labour force at Lithgow trebled, adding that during their years at Lithgow 'they had no more than their fair share of industrial stoppages'. Nevertheless, the Hoskins fully participated in the labour unrest that marked the industry during these years—an unrest for which their special circumstances made them particularly vulnerable. The causes were multiple. In

## 7 NATIONALISATION OR PRIVATE ENTERPRISE?

addition to the attitudes of both management and labour, the economic demands of the industry and the climate of the times all contributed to a background of uncertainty and social instability. As the labour requirements of the industry rose, its pivotal position in the economic development of the country was understood and it increasingly attracted both the support and the surveillance of state and federal governments. Both were ever conscious of the immediate demands of their electorates as well as, and sometimes to the detriment of, the long-term requirements of the state or the nation. This dual interest in itself created uncertainty. 'It was' writes Sir Cecil Hoskins in retrospect 'a difficult, often dangerous period in which the masters had as much to learn as the men'.[33]

In the United States and Germany, where life was more precarious and the stakes higher, the implications of the earlier British industrial experience had long been digested and rejected. Here emphasis was on technical education and the possibilities of 'scientific management'. To these new industrial giants, random thrusts, tactical flourishes and Fabian futures were seen as misuses of human resources by labour and capital alike. Even if they still had before them a long history in many Australian industrial ventures, the new overseas influences were shortly to make themselves felt in developments in the Australian iron and steel industry.

# 8

# INTERSTATE AND INTERNATIONAL

THE ADVOCATES OF NATIONALISATION, selectively reading the *Report* of the Royal Commission on the iron and steel industry, had drawn encouragement from Paul's conclusion that 'he could see no practical reason why Australia should longer delay in taking her legitimate place as one of the great producers of iron and steel'. In January 1912 the fifth conference of the Australian Labor Party resolved that a publicly owned ironworks was an 'urgent necessity'.[1] Despite its reservations over the practical implications of such an enterprise, the New South Wales government decided to take the initial step of introducing an enabling Bill for the establishment or purchase of a state iron- and steelworks. The still-striking ironworkers at Lithgow lobbied strongly, seeing in nationalisation the panacea that would solve the industry's difficulties and secure their own futures.

Armed with this political and ideological support, Arthur Griffith moved, on 22 February 1912, that the New South Wales Legislative Assembly form itself into a committee to consider the desirability of bringing in such a Bill. On 12 March the Legislature resolved that 'it is expedient to bring in a bill to authorise the establishment or purchase of a state iron and steel works'.[2] The Bill received its first reading very early the following morning. It was passed by thirty-three votes to twenty-one. It then lay on the table until 28 August when, under radically altered circumstances, it was resumed. What happened in the intervening five months was to change the course of the industry completely and, except in Queensland, to make nationalisation a dead issue.

## 8 INTERSTATE AND INTERNATIONAL

The *Report of the Royal Commission* contained a serious error, partly recognised and certainly suspected at the time: its defective assessment of the quantity and suitability of the iron ore deposits available for the projected iron- and steelworks, most notably those at Cadia in New South Wales and Blythe River in Tasmania. The Hoskins brothers subsequently found to their cost that both of these deposits were inadequate.[3] In 1912 Australia's richest known resources of iron ore had been for over a decade in the possession of the Broken Hill Proprietary Company.

BHP was from its inception and has primarily remained a resource development company, concentrating successively on silver, iron ore supported by coal and later by non-ferrous metals, oil and gas. A fortuitous combination of circumstances made its name synonymous with iron and steel in the mid twentieth century. It did not begin the century as a manufacturer of iron and steel but by the mid 1980s its shareholders were informed that 'the Broken Hill Proprietary Company Limited ... is Australia's largest integrated resource developer' with additional interests in 'international mining, manufacturing and trading houses with people, offices and investments in more than 15 countries'.[4] How this came about is complex and fascinating story, but only parts of it are relevant to the history of the Australian iron and steel industry.

On 20 June 1885 the Broken Hill Proprietary Company published its first prospectus. The new company held mineral leases for 297 acres on and around Broken Hill in the remote west of New South Wales. These mineral deposits proved to be fabulously rich, for the mines of Broken Hill produced not only silver but other metals including zinc and lead. A number of companies quickly joined BHP in taking up unpegged lots on the north and south of the coat-hanger-shaped lode. Of its original seven blocks in the center of the lode BHP itself retained only three. Within the first three years of BHP's existence,[5] the remaining four were profitably floated off as independent companies. On 13 August 1885 the Broken Hill Proprietary Company was registered and incorporated in the colony of Victoria. Its Board normally met in Melbourne. From its beginning the company was national. Broken Hill was located in New South Wales, but the company's communications with the outside world were through South Australia and it was registered in Victoria. These interstate connections gave the new company a considerable degree of independence from the government of any one state.

BHP was a distinctly different type of entrepreneurial operation from owner-managed businesses, such as those of William Sandford and Charles Hoskins at Lithgow. This fundamental difference has lain at the root of many subsequent misunderstandings. William Sandford and Charles Hoskins were local ironmasters living at Eskroy Park near their works at Lithgow, and as local industrialists they had a specific role in the community. BHP was a syndicate whose members were engaged in a variety of activities connected with commerce, agriculture or mineral exploration. Neither the directors nor the shareholders of BHP lived at Broken Hill. Nor was there any particular reason why they should live there, any more than on the site of one of their other enterprises, for example, Mount Lyell or Blythe River. Geoffrey Blainey has described their contribution to Australian industrial development:

> In the generation after the finding of Broken Hill there was a great revival of base-metal mining in Australia, and in the early years of virtually every important field promoters from Broken Hill played a crucial role . . . The history of many of the companies in which these men were involved has yet to be unravelled, but it seems that their main financial contribution was not large sums of capital but small sums which they invested in the first years when the risk of failure was high. They were entrepreneurs rather than capitalists . . . Their contribution was distinctive for they mostly ventured into mining fields which others shunned.[6]

BHP's directors and shareholders were still shrewd and cautious investors. Their interests in Broken Hill were safeguarded by appointing the best internationally proven mine managers, leaving them to manage the mine and rewarding them accordingly. The managers' reports and recommendations were as carefully considered as the mines' returns. From its inception BHP had a high regard for ability, reflected in the company's willingness to import the expertise considered essential for its purposes. William Jamieson, emphasising the expense of such expertise, told the Royal Commission on bonuses in 1902 that 'the company with which I am associated pays large salaries to its head men at Broken Hill, and I am sure that we would prefer to increase them by 50% rather than lose their services'.[7] In an enterprise of this nature, capital and management were separate, although complementary, components. BHP had from its inception a corporate philosophy that was in step with the global leaders of the second, or technocratic, industrial revolution.

BHP's connection with the iron and steel industry began in November 1899 when the South Australian government granted the company the leases for Iron Monarch in South Australia. Their application for these ironstone leases was not from a desire to become involved with the iron and steel industry. It was linked to BHP's decision to smelt ore concentrates from Broken Hill at Port Pirie. Ironstone flux was essential for this operation. Retrospectively, the question of why BHP chose to establish smelters at Port Pirie proved internationally important, particularly after 1914 when war broke out in Europe where most Broken Hill companies sent their ore concentrates to be smelted. However, in a purely Australian context, BHP's decision led to the company's acquisition of Iron Monarch and eventually to the establishment of an economically viable Australian iron and steel industry. The decision to establish the smelters at Port Pirie was obviously finely balanced and the favourable freight rates offered by the South Australian government may have been the final inducement.[8]

In the course of its meeting on 14 November 1895, the BHP Board minuted the purchase of a lease, with an option to purchase, of the Waratah site on which part of the Newcastle steelworks now stands.[9] On 28 and 29 September 1896 the Board considered 'a statement comparing costs at Broken Hill, Waratah and Port Pirie, from which it appeared that the most economical work was at Port Pirie'. A month later the Board was still debating the comparative costs of 'treating sulphide concentrates at the Mine, Port Pirie, Newcastle &c.' and 'in view of the costs therein shown, and the General Manager's recommendations it was decided that the smelting operations of the Company should be carried on at Port Pirie'. The smelters became operational in 1897 and, although only capable of smelting a small part of the entire output from Broken Hill, the works included 'perhaps the biggest single lead smelter and refinery in the world'.

Ironstone flux was now urgently needed.[10] J. H. Howe, a director of the Mount Minden Mining Company and a shareholder in BHP, suggested that the BHP officials prospecting for iron ore might look at Iron Monarch. Koehler, BHP's assistant general manager and a metallurgist, inspected the site and realised that it was 'an enormous formation, and can furnish infinitely more iron than the Mine would ever need'.[11] The Mount Minden Mining Company was an unlimited company[12] formed in 1890 by Ernest Siekmann, who had discovered and pegged the iron ore leases at Iron Monarch. Siekmann was aware that he had a valuable resource, but he appears to have been uncertain as to the best way of exploiting it. Iron Monarch was isolated and its only communications with the outside world were by horse or bullock cart. Considerable expense would have had to be incurred to start mining in what was a remote, waterless area. The company did not have capital on that scale and the enterprise was still-born in the economic conditions of the 1890s.

The site remained untouched. By 1896 the Mount Minden Mining Company's rent was three years in arrears and, in addition, the company had been unable to fulfil the labour conditions of the leases. Under South Australian regulations the leases were forfeited, because the company had failed to comply with the conditions under which they had been granted. On 13 May 1896 John Darling, acting on behalf of BHP, wrote to the Mines Office, stating that he understood that the leases were forfeited, and applied for them. On 26 December 1896 the leases were duly gazetted as forfeited.

On 1 April 1897 BHP's general manager, Alexander Stewart, telegraphed 'understand Adelaide Syndicate is being formed to secure all South Australian iron ore claims' and advised that the company lose no time in securing Iron Monarch.[13] The decision to peg out the leases was taken on 8 April and four days later nine claims of forty acres each had been pegged out for BHP. On 15 April these were registered as mineral claims, which gave BHP a legal right to the leases. Florenz Bleeser, another director of the Mount Minden Mining Company, now decided that he would apply for the gazetted leases on his own behalf. Bleeser was verbally informed, by the warden of the goldfields, Lionel Gee, that there was no opposition to his claim, whereas he should have been informed in writing that in view of the claim of BHP, established some six weeks earlier, his application could not be granted. BHP promptly protested. Bleeser offered to withdraw his opposition in return for a down payment of £2000 and a third share in the mine. John Darling described the proposal as little more than 'blackmail'.[14]

Siekmann now claimed that BHP had taken advantage of the Mount Minden Mining Company by using information about Iron Monarch given in confidence and with a view to establishing a contract for supplying flux. Certainly BHP may have lulled Mount Minden into a sense of false security as, although BHP knew that the leases were forfeited in December 1896, there was in the early months of 1897 a correspondence between BHP and Mount Minden about supplies of flux.[15] Until March 1897 Siekmann appears to have been unaware that his company no longer held the leases. Subsequently Siekmann acknowledged BHP's legal claim but felt that it had acted immorally in 'jumping' his claim. In the last resort, however, he had been careless in complying with the formal requirements of his lease and he had had ample time, over six years, to find a use for his discovery. BHP undoubtedly had the large financial resources required to develop the site, and to exploit its potential in such a way that its benefits would be maximised in Australia. Probably it was the only Australian company in this position at the time.

By 1898 the prices paid by BHP for ironstone flux had 'increased enormously'. The Board decided that 'steps should be taken to obtain the leases with as little delay as possible'. Darling was asked to 'do all that was necessary' to finally secure the leases for BHP. There was vociferous opposition to BHP from certain sections of the South Australian legislature; C. C. Kingston, for instance, declared 'that they kept their eyes on it . . . until they got their hands on it'.[16] In these circumstances BHP considered it prudent to wait until after the parliament was prorogued in December 1898 before making any overt moves. Although Darling was confident that the company would be successful by the following September, BHP only obtained the leases in November 1899. Once BHP knew it would obtain the leases, a private railway bill was prepared for submission to the South Australian parliament.

In May 1900 Darling, who was a member of the Legislative Council, was able to report that the Cabinet was 'favourable to the scheme and would assist the company as far as possible' being particularly desirous of furthering the already established link with Broken Hill. Shortly after the South Australian government formally announced that it would support the Bill. The BHP Tramway Bill was presented on 26 September 1900 by John Lewis, whose son, Essington, was later to play a prominent role in the company's affairs. Lewis was a shareholder in BHP but he sold his holdings on 24 October, two days before he was appointed chairman of the select committee to enquire into the Bill. The other members of the committee were J. G. Bice, K. W. Duncan and T. Pascoe.[17]

BHP had the numbers in the Legislature, but it was fearful that the debate over the leases might have harmed the company's reputation. Darling reported that some members of the committee seemed to be unreasonable and 'very suspicious' and also that there was 'a very large element of sentiment, with some of those who are opposed to the Bill'. This was hardly surprising given BHP's 'tall poppy' reputation and the ideology of the times.[18]

Much of the opposition failed to make a lasting impression, even as propaganda, because it did not address the basic issue: BHP, like most significant corporations, was a combination capable of handling projects that would have been difficult for an individual entrepreneur. The fact that the company was an umbrella for some of the tallest individual poppies and toughest Australian businessmen may have been a public relations liability but it was one the company, in the event, could afford. Eventually the committee's report, which incidentally endorsed the legality of the way in which BHP had acquired the leases,[19] was presented to the Council on 21 November. It passed the same day, although some of the members complained that the report of nearly one hundred pages had only been circulated at the eleventh hour.

Within the space of fifteen years the two richest metal deposits then known on the continent had come into the possession of the same enterprise. BHP was, from the beginning, very well aware that it had not acquired an ordinary flux deposit but 'an immense deposit of iron of particularly good grade . . . a body of almost unlimited extent'. After inspecting the company's new acquisition, the chairman, Harvey Patterson, was even more overwhelmed by its magnitude and its implications for BHP as 'a smelting company'.[20] The significance which the company attached to the deposit was reflected in the quality of the tramway and jetty that BHP hastened to erect.

Manual quarrying operations at the initial Iron Knob quarry, Middleback Ranges, South Australia, 1915. Ore from this quarry was analysed as containing 68 per cent iron and underpinned the financial success of the BHP Newcastle steelworks.

In 1902 the chairman informed the shareholders that, when the Minister of Public Works and other members of the South Australian parliament visited Iron Knob in November 1901, 'much surprise was expressed at the substantiality of the line ... the declaration was made that it was quite up to the standard of any of the Government lines of South Australia', while 'general regret was expressed that such splendid iron ore ... should find no further use than for flux for smelting purposes'.[21] Harvey Patterson, chairman of BHP until his resignation in 1907, saw Iron Knob as the centre of an Australian iron and steel industry and his successor, John Darling, was equally enthusiastic.

The perceived imperatives of mining economics at the silver mine played a crucial role in BHP's moves towards iron. As early as the 1890s the BHP Board, though more sanguine than its advisers,[22] was becoming worried about the long-term resources of the Big Mine. The life of a mine, however rich, is of limited duration. Successive general managers, John Howell and Alexander Stewart, had stressed that the Big Mine's days were numbered and would be short. Both were men of international standing in the mining world. They based their opinions on falling world markets and the impending exhaustion of oxidised ores. Large quantities of complex sulphide ores remained, but these could not be treated successfully by existing technology. The price of silver, which varied between 50 and 47.5 pence per ounce when the company was formed in 1885, had fallen to 30 to 23.75 pence in 1897 and, although it fluctuated, the overall trend was downward. Between 1897 and 1912 the price of silver never rose above 33.13 pence; in only four of those years did it rise above 30 pence.[23] As the mine became harder to work, the metallurgical difficulties appeared intractable. The BHP Board began to search for an expert who could solve their increasing problems.

By 1898 the BHP Board was worried. Careful enquiries preceded their offer of the position of assistant manager to Guillaume Delprat. It has been suggested that Delprat first came to the attention of the BHP directors through an article he published in 1892 in *Transactions of the American Institute of Engineers* on 'Extraction of ore from wide veins or masses'. It is very probable that this was borne in mind by Stewart when, in January 1898, he recommended Delprat to the Board. They offered him the position of assistant manager on a three-year term with an annual salary of £1500 and a house. Delprat declined. Stewart then indicated his intention of resigning to become general manager to the Chillagoe Company, although he remained a consulting engineer with

BHP. Stewart's period as general manager was short but he left the company three significant legacies: Iron Knob, the Port Pirie smelters and G. D. Delprat.

Accepting Stewart's recommendation, the Board now made private enquiries as to Delprat's suitability for the position of general manager. The London Board reported difficulty in obtaining information about Delprat without his knowledge but that he was 'believed to be dependable, able Manager—straightforward'. Stewart now suggested that they should contact Delprat directly and ask his terms. Delprat replied that he would accept a three-year engagement at an annual salary of £2000 and a free passage for himself and his wife and seven children.[24] At the same time the Board received a cable endorsing not only Delprat's capabilities but also his private character. In accepting Delprat's terms, BHP acquired the architect of its twentieth-century success.

Delprat was appointed general manager of the Broken Hill Proprietary Company on 12 May 1899, a position which he was to hold until his retirement in 1921.[25] The original vision and the managerial skill that laid the foundation of twentieth-century BHP must be attributed to Delprat and to the confidence placed in him by John Darling, the chairman of the Board during the important transitional years. Sadly, Darling did not live to see the Newcastle works completed. Others were to expand Darling's and Delprat's plans and build upon their achievements but the latter's shrewd and courageous realism laid the foundations for the development of a viable Australian iron and steel industry, and ended the prolonged and damaging nationalisation debate.

In the twentieth century the Board of BHP has combined to an extraordinary degree the pursuit of excellence in its chief executives with an ability to arouse in them an unswerving loyalty to the company, which they normally serve for life. Delprat was the first of BHP's outstanding chief executives to remain with the company for the rest of his working life. Although he became an Australian citizen in 1904, Delprat was the only twentieth-century chief executive who was not Australian-born. He was born in 1856 into a prominent Dutch family with a strong tradition of professional public service. The family is commemorated in the name of a street in The Hague, where his father, Major General Delprat, served as Minister of War. Delprat's education combined the practical and scientific training that was so marked a feature of late nineteenth-century Europe. He served his engineering apprenticeship in Scotland on the construction of the ill-fated first Tay Bridge. At the same time he took night classes in science and physics at St Andrews University. Here

Guillaume Daniel Delprat, 1857–1937, General Manager of BHP 1899–1921, c. 1915. A Dutch mining engineer who recognised the potential for BHP to enter the steel industry based on the rich iron ore from Iron Knob, he convinced the BHP Board to commit to steelmaking in 1912 and oversaw the construction and development of the Newcastle steelworks until his retirement in 1921.

he won, as Queen's Prize for Physics, a book with the prophetic title *The Management of Steel*. On his return to the Netherlands he was employed as assistant to the world-renowned Professor J. van der Waals, Professor of Physics at the University of Amsterdam.

Delprat's mining career began with the Tharsis Company in Spain, where he probably met Alexander Stewart, his predecessor as general manager of BHP. In Spain Delprat gained, among other things, a considerable reputation for locating and working forgotten Roman silver mines. By the mid 1890s he was well known as a mining authority in Norway, Mexico and North America. He was a man of extraordinary physical strength with the knack of doing most things well. An accomplished linguist, his broad interests included fencing, lawn tennis, billiards and ju-jitsu as well as sculpture, music and French literature. He shared his countrymen's interest in gardening, growing prize-winning dahlias. In 1929 a bust of Braille, which he sculpted in retirement, won him a silver medal from the French government. He obviously found challenges immensely stimulating and he was probably more interested in solving problems than making a fortune. At his death, his estate was probated at under £60 000. Some insight into his mentality can perhaps be deduced from the fact that he was acknowledged as a master chess player. At the same time his diary, with its numerous references to dinner parties, the theatre, performances of light and classical opera, reveals a naturally gregarious and cultured man. His daughter, Lady Mawson, in her biography of Delprat, *Vision of Steel*, reveals a happy and stimulating family life, while his diary indicates an affectionate though possibly autocratic father.[26]

Taken in its global context, Delprat's career, before joining BHP, was typical of a generation. Previously traders, military engineers and soldiers of fortune had been the main agents of diffusing expertise beyond the established centres of industry. This was changed by the second industrial revolution of the late nineteenth century. There was a new understanding of the optimal use of capital, and a revolution in world transport, communications and applied science. The age of capital metamorphosed into an age of expertise. This produced a generation of foot-loose elite technocrats, who followed paths determined by the location of industrial activity. A significant proportion of such people were resources experts and mining engineers. They were typified by men such as Delprat and Herbert Hoover, later President of the United States of America. Hoover, in his wanderings in the resources diaspora, briefly took part in the Australian mining industry; for a short time he was superintendent of the Sons of Gwalia mine. Often these men were businessmen with a scientific training that enabled them not only to anticipate market opportunities but to check them against likely directions in research and development. Such men were scattered thinly, and their loss, as in the case of AEG's Walter Rathenau, assassinated in Weimar Germany, could be significant. A new resources company in Australia that perceived the need for such men, and persevered with obtaining their services, automatically set itself apart from those which were still involved with early industrial ideals.

Delprat's arrival in Australia coincided with the final stages of the negotiations for the Iron Knob leases, although his attention was quickly directed to other matters. A few months after his arrival the Board directed that 'in order to have the fullest information before them before taking the final step . . . the Secretary should ask Mr Stewart that either he or Mr Delprat, or both, should inspect and report fully on the property'.[27] On his arrival at Broken Hill Delprat found great accumulations of zinciferous tailings and slimes. One of his most notable achievements was to discover a way of extracting metal from these waste products. Delprat, assisted by his more sceptical chief metallurgist, A. D. Carmichael, tackled the problem enthusiastically and found a method of separating metals by a flotation process. This was particularly novel in making use of the fact that sulphides floated on air bubbles to the top of an aqueous solution rather than dissolving in it or sinking to the bottom. The technique became known as the Potter–Delprat flotation process and BHP became a world leader in recovering metals by this method. Delprat's work was subsequently refined by others, the chief among them being BHP's Leslie Bradford. Bradford developed techniques of selective flotation that separated zinc and lead sulphides. These contributed significantly to the profitability of BHP during the crucial pre-war period. The flotation process and its refinements were a technological advance of world-wide importance; selective flotation is still in use today.

The timing of Delprat's discovery was important. It coincided with the growing use of electricity and the international rearmament movement. Both of these increased the demand for lead and zinc, which the company was now able to market in increased quantities. In 1905 BHP decided to add a spelter (zinc) plant to its works at Port Pirie at a cost of £17 000. The initial plant had one blast furnace and in 1908 nine more were added making the capital outlay on the spelter plant about £100 000. The production of the ten furnaces was estimated at 8000 tons a year, 'for all of which', the chairman, John Darling, informed the shareholders on 28 August 1908, 'a market is available in the Commonwealth and the East'. The previous month Delprat had told the Board that he estimated that there was 'sufficient material on hand and being produced to give 38 years work'.[28]

This increased profitability bought time for a cautious assessment of the company's next move. Moreover, it allowed BHP to wait until the social and economic ideals of the immediate post-Federation euphoria had settled, and until concepts of federal protection and a measure of state support for the development of native industries had become accepted. Although labour relations remained difficult, they were an acknowledged phenomenon of the industrial world, a problem within reluctantly defined economic, if not philosophical, boundaries.

Despite the solution of the sulphide problem (that is, the efficient separation of zinc and lead from sulphide ores), BHP's time at Broken Hill was running out. By 1908 the Big Mine had ceased to be the dominant mine on the lode and, finally, in 1912, Delprat warned the Board that 'if we decide not to go in for steelmaking, we will still have a few more years of prosperity, as long as prices keep up and our reserves at Broken Hill hold out, but the output will gradually diminish; profits will do the same; and, within a few years we will cease to exist altogether'. The BHP mine had been threatened with extinction within half a dozen years of its birth, but so many difficulties had been overcome that in 1912 the New South Wales government, investigating the mining prospects of Broken Hill, decided that it was 'impossible to express any definite opinion as to the possibilities of Broken Hill'.[29] In fact BHP was to continue operating at Broken Hill on an ever-diminishing scale until 1939, but, sometime between 1909 and 1912, the fates of BHP and Broken Hill parted. The focus of the company changed as the real question ceased to be the unpredictable future of the Big Mine, but the full exploitation of BHP's mineral resources, especially the development of Iron Knob.

Inevitably, from the time that BHP acquired the Iron Knob leases, the question had arisen as to whether the company would use these resources to expand its activities into the manufacture of iron and steel. In 1904 the chairman, Harvey Patterson, foreshadowed his hopes that 'our Federal Government elects to offer a bonus for the manufacture of pig iron in the States, to see this prodigious deposit availed of and put to an even more profitable use than at present'. By 1907 the shareholders were being told that 'we are conducting experiments with a furnace for the production of pig iron . . . there is no reason why its manufacture should not form an auxiliary to our extensive businesses'. Six months later, in August 1907, the new chairman, John Darling, revealed that 'your Directors . . . were particularly gratified with the developments which have taken place as the result of prospecting at the Iron Knob, and disclosed a very much larger quantity of hematite ironstone than was previously anticipated as existing. It is of high grade, and the quality in every way suitable for iron smelting'. Two years later Darling reviewed the company's assets as 'approximately 3,000,000 tons of tailings on the dumps containing zinc, lead and silver, which will keep our plants running many years, and with several million tons of ore in the Mine . . . and a property like the Iron Knob which is bound in the near future to become an enormous asset'.[30]

By 1911 Darling and Delprat judged that the moment to alter the company's interests from silver and zinc to iron and steel had finally arrived. On 2 June 1911 the Board met at Port Pirie to discuss the project. It was divided: Hugo Muecke, the son of a Lutheran pastor from the Barossa valley, a powerful and influential figure in the business life of

John Darling, 1852–1914, a director of BHP from 1892, and Chairman from 1907 until 1914, *c.* 1914. As Chairman he strongly supported the proposal for BHP to move into iron and steelmaking but died before the steelworks at Newcastle were commissioned.

Adelaide and on the Board of BHP, was strongly against the proposal. He did not consider that the project should even be investigated. William Knox was also against it, but not adverse to further investigation. Delprat was worried at Muecke's opposition 'but Darling helped me', he noted in his diary. '[I] had a chat with him before meeting—agreed at once and promised to help.' The Board divided five to two in favour. It was a triumph for Darling's persuasive powers just as his confidence in the scheme, and Delprat's ability to implement it, was to be a tribute to his business acumen and judgement of men.

Neither BHP nor Delprat had any experience in the internationally sophisticated manufacture and marketing of iron and steel. However, the company had considerable expertise in smelting other metals and it was well accustomed to surmounting commercial difficulties. BHP was rich and its name inspired the market confidence needed to encourage the investment essential to the success of the project. Given the company's established policies, ignorance was clearly not insurmountable. Experts could be employed and knowledge could be acquired. The Board agreed to give Delprat approximately six months' leave of absence to visit Europe and America. The shareholders were alerted to the need for the company 'to keep well ahead of the times' and that to this end the general manager would visit Europe and America to acquire the latest information 'and, if necessary, secure the services of experts for the development of industries kindred to our resources, as yet barely touched upon'.[31]

Delprat left for Europe on 21 July 1911. In the course of his tour he visited twenty-three iron and steel works: twelve in England, seven in the United States, three in Germany and one in Sweden. In 1920, looking back on these visits, Delprat commented that he had straightforwardly explained to his various hosts that he intended to set up a steelworks in Australia and 'without any exception I was given the very fullest information I could possibly have desired' until

> I made my way to the Continent and visited Germany. Here I had quite a different kind of experience. Hardly any information was given to me that was of any value, except the information that they were quite willing to supply all the necessary plant and machinery, and also the experts to work the plant. Further, they were prepared to take a large financial interest in the undertaking, which set me thinking . . . call it luck, or instinct, or foresight . . . we decided to place the orders in America and engaged American experts, and turned our backs to the financially more enticing offers from Germany. This was before the War.[32]

As a Dutchman Delprat knew and understood the European mentality. At the same time he spoke English so perfectly that some of the German executives he visited thought that he was Australian-born. He did not disabuse them of this opinion—until a friend recognised him and addressed him in fluent German! Leaving Germany, he went on to New York where, on 8 January 1912, he called upon James Gayley, the first vice-president of the United States Steel Corporation, with an introduction from Karl Eilers, a Dutch mining engineer and friend, then living in New York. Gayley recommended that Delprat should consult David Baker of Philadelphia as a 'first class expert on steel'.[33]

Delprat and Baker shared similar educational backgrounds in the theoretical and practical application of science. Baker, who was born in 1861, graduated from the Massachusetts Institute of Technology in 1885 with a degree in mining engineering, and his career had been in metallurgy and blast furnace technology. He had spent twelve years with the Pennsylvania Steel Company, where he had been blast furnace superintendent both at Steelton and Sparrows Point, and then he spent three and a half years with the Illinois Steel Company as superintendent

David Baker, 1861–1942, *c.* 1915. An American steelworks engineer, Baker was responsible for the successful construction, staffing, commissioning and operation of the BHP Newcastle steelworks from 1912 until his retirement in 1925.

of furnaces at its South Works, near Chicago. Next Baker moved to Canada for three years, first as general manager and then as general superintendent of the Dominion Iron and Steel Company in Nova Scotia. Finally he returned to the United States where he had now spent eight years as a consulting metallurgical engineer in Philadelphia. This role had enabled him to come into contact with most of the steelworks in America.

In the last quarter of the nineteenth century the American steel industry was dominated by the Scottish-born steel king, Andrew Carnegie. Carnegie's profound belief in education is attested to by the numerous libraries, trusts and foundations that bear his name. In his steelworks he operated a participatory incentive scheme, believing that 'every year should be marked by the promotion of one or more of our young men . . . we cannot have too many of the right sort interested in the profits'— although it was said that Carnegie never wanted to know the profits, only the costs. While many of Carnegie's men rose from the shop-floor, by 1901, the time he sold out to J. P. Morgan, the managerial ranks were increasingly being filled by college graduates whose youth was a continual source of surprise to foreign visitors. Brains, education and flexibility were the hallmarks of rapid promotion.

The industry was geared to the immediate and continuing reduction of costs. This meant reinvestment and innovation as well as economy. The theories of 'Scientific Management' were developed in this atmosphere. Their author, Frederick W. Taylor, had worked in the Midvale Steel Works as a labourer, foreman and chief engineer before becoming an engineering and management consultant in Philadelphia. Baker would certainly have studied his views and he probably knew Taylor. Taylor's theories were the subject of a highly publicised congressional inquiry in 1911 and would undoubtedly have been a subject of conversation at the time of Delprat's fact-finding visit. It was alleged that his emphasis on economy of labour encouraged assembly-line techniques and reduced workers to machines. Taylor's approach was open to abuse and even more to misrepresentation. Taylor himself believed that good management, based on a systematic study of the most economical way to perform a job, should lower labour costs and thus raise wages. He was a firm believer in incentives.[34]

American industry depended upon low production costs to sustain high wages. Consequently a high premium was placed on the proven results of good scientific training. Baker's career was very typical of this new managerial class.[35] At the Pennsylvania and Illinois steel companies Baker had been up against the Carnegie system of rigorous cost economy, managerial incentive and cut-throat competition. At the same time he had seen the managerial techniques of Judge Elbert H. Gary, the Methodist lawyer whom J. P. Morgan made chairman of Illinois Steel and then of United Steel. In the reorganisation that followed the establishment of the United States Steel Corporation, over thirty obsolete works were closed, streamlining the industry, making it more cost effective and ensuring its world domination during and after World War I.

Gary, supported by Morgan, pioneered a new style of management based on consultation and co-operation. He recognised the importance of the media both for communication and propaganda. To this end he held his famous dinners and encouraged the formation of the American Iron and Steel Institute.[36] He wished to substitute 'stability' and the 'law of reason' for cut-throat competition in establishing steel prices. Gary firmly believed the best business results were obtained through motivation. To this end he supported higher wages, safe, sanitary working conditions and the open shop. Gary in Indiana was built as a model industrial town. At the same time, Gary himself was an inflexible opponent of organised labour. His managerial skills made him the most effective opponent of the unionist Samuel Gompers, and secured the collapse of the 'Great Strike' in 1919–20.

Baker's practical expertise and scientific reputation were in the very important area of blast furnace technology, in which the United States then excelled. As early as 1890 Sir Lothian Bell, on a visit to the United States, had been amazed by the American practice of driving the blast furnaces at such a rate that they had to be relined every three years. The Americans were equally astonished to find that the linings of British furnaces in the Cleveland district lasted seventeen and a half years, but in that time they only produced as much iron as the American furnaces during their much shorter working life.[37] The American practice, with no penalty for the amount of lining consumed per ton of iron, clearly allowed much greater furnace productivity. Baker himself was to contribute to the effectiveness of American blast furnace operation by demonstrating that the decrease in lining life, caused by the adoption of mechanical filling, could be remedied by installing a rotary top to ensure a more even distribution of the fuel, flux and ore. Baker was the author of numerous technical papers. He was also a member of the British Iron and Steel Institute, the American Iron and Steel Institute, the American Society of Mining Engineers and the Geological Society of the United States of America.

Baker and Delprat met on 10 and 12 January 1912 and in the words of Delprat 'discussed everything fully'. Baker later recalled that Delprat had stated that his mission was:

> to secure an engineer who would visit Australia and report on the proposition 'Could good steel be made from the company's ore and at a cost that would make the undertaking profitable?' He stressed the importance of such development to the Australian Government, but emphasised the fact that the adventure must promise sufficient profits to justify the large expenditure.

Delprat told Baker that he had discussed his plans with a number of engineers without commitment. He added that he needed an engineer capable not only of making the report but, if the project proved feasible, 'of furnishing plans and estimates, supervising the construction, and, after completion, organising and starting operations, continuing the management and training Australians who would, eventually carry on the works'. Baker gave Delprat his curriculum vitae and was invited to come to New York the following day with his terms for the work.[38]

The BHP Board moved quickly. Baker sailed from Vancouver early in April, arriving in Australia on 12 May 1912. On 13 May there was a meeting between Delprat, F. M. Dickson (BHP's secretary) and J. H. Cann (MLA for Broken Hill and the New South Wales Treasurer) at which the New South Wales government learnt officially of BHP's intentions: given a favourable response to its enquiry as to whether 'we could count on the good will of the Government to assist us in a friendly way', the Broken Hill Proprietary Company had finally made its decision to enter the iron and steel industry.

The Premier, J. S. McGowen, mindful of the State Iron and Steel Bill already before the legislature and conscious of the economic problems, cautiously replied that 'any industry that may be established in the State of New South Wales will receive encouragement and consideration from my Government'. Caught between the imperatives of politics and economics, the Premier resolved his dilemma by reminding BHP that 'it is the policy of this government that the production of iron and steel from ores should be a national industry' and of the government's intention 'to carry this policy into legislative effect in due course'. BHP indicated that it welcomed competition: Delprat explaining that 'I should like to have other people to compete against [for] we have such faith in the development of Australia that we think a tremendous amount of steel will be required, in fact more than we or the Government or Mr Hoskins could supply'. In private Delprat expressed his concern that 'for the sake of competition, the book-keeping of a government industrial undertaking will be more elastic than ours'. Confirming the points raised at the meeting, Delprat, who was a past master at diplomatic bluff, wrote that 'it would pay us—all conditions being equal—to erect them (steelworks) in New South Wales, as there would be an advantage in carrying the iron ore to the coal rather than carrying the coal to the ore. This advantage is, however, not very great'. The company would forgo it if the New South Wales government viewed BHP's proposal 'with displeasure'. The works could be built in South Australia.[39]

Delprat now produced a list of enquiries: would the state government agree to the establishment of the works in New South Wales; would the government be willing to give BHP an extended lease on government land, supposing the company selected government land as the site for its works; could BHP count on the friendly disposition of the state government to assist it without financial assistance or concessions; and could the company be assured of a 'fair deal', even against the projected state iron works, if their products could be offered at a competitive price.[40] Delprat knew that BHP's combination of the control of Iron Knob, the richest source of iron ore then known in Australia, and the company's financial strength put it in a special league that would make either state competition, or the compensation required for subsequent nationalisation, extremely difficult. Under these circumstances, it did not greatly matter whether the Lithgow works became a state enterprise or remained with the Hoskins brothers.

Meanwhile, on 7 June 1912, a momentous day in the annals of the Broken Hill Proprietary Company, the full Board was called to the Melbourne offices of the company. John Darling was in the chair and the general manager, G. D. Delprat, was in attendance as was David Baker, whose reports were before the Board. The Board questioned Baker and asked him to prepare a supplementary report 'dealing more particularly with the ironstone in respect of utility for the manufacture of steel and the quantities available'. Probably their own past experience, the Hoskinses' difficulties and history of the Tasmanian deposits had increased the company's natural caution on the eve of so large an undertaking. After Baker had left the meeting, the Board had further discussions with Delprat before finally resolving that 'the Board favoured the policy of undertaking the project of the manufacture of Iron and Steel provided satisfactory financial arrangements could be arranged upon the position being legally approved'.[41]

The BHP Directors, finally convinced by the information that they had received from David Baker, accepted Delprat's advice. Later that day Delprat formally wrote to Darling, as Chairman of the Board, outlining Baker's career and recommending his appointment:

> From what I have seen of him I consider that he is the very man we want for the position of Superintendent of our project Steel Works, and I have no hesitation in recommending him very strongly to the Board for this position. In making this recommendation I thoroughly realise the great responsibility which attaches to this recommendation. If we select the wrong man we run the risk of making our venture a failure. I have considered the position carefully, and I am quite prepared to shoulder the responsibility of recommending Mr Baker for the position. I would suggest that the appointment be made for a term of five years . . . it will take 2 to 3 years to properly construct the plant, and two years more is not too much to enable Mr Baker to prove that the plant will fulfil his promise.[42]

Baker's principal report, dated 30 May 1912, was considered by the Board on 7 June. A further document, dated 10 June, revised and confirmed various costs and statements that he had made to the Board on 7 June. Finally, a six-page summary of his initial report was prepared on 29 June. All of Baker's reports were optimistic: on 30 May he emphasised that 'now is the psychological moment to start a modern steelworks in this country, and that an important advantage will result to you if this work is undertaken as recommended promptly and pushed to completion vigorously'. On 7 June, after meeting the Board, he pointed out that the 'estimates of cost and operation are safe ones, and I believe that you have a rare opportumty to establish a very profitable industry in the manufacture of steel in Australia'. Summarising his reports, Baker presented his conclusions to the Board in a letter dated 29 June 1912, in which he indicated that he 'considered the Company would be able to produce Iron at a lower cost than is possible by the United States Steel Corporation'.[43] Baker gave careful consideration to resources, markets, plant and site. His reports were framed as letters to the Board. Their simplicity and clarity gave them an apparent informality that belied their shrewdness. Delprat had chosen his expert well, for within a few decades BHP was to make the chcapest steel in the world.

Baker discovered, as Paul had found a few months earlier, that Australia required sufficient tonnage of steel to ensure the profitability of a moderately sized steelworks, provided the cost of raw materials was low enough. In 1913 less than 20 000 tons of ingot steel were produced at Lithgow and 750 000 tons of steel of all types were imported.[44] Baker was convinced that BHP possessed the raw materials in sufficient quantity and quality to produce the steel required in Australia. The immensity of the Iron Monarch deposit, its availability and quality were such that BHP had iron ore supplies for at least a generation. Even so, it subsequently transpired that only part of the deposit had been discovered. By 1922 exploration in the vicinity of Iron Knob had added two further deposits, Iron Prince and Iron Baron, to the company's resources. BHP's limestone quarry, conveniently situated at Wardang Island in the Spencer Gulf, had an abundant supply of flux. In 1916 further and better deposits, also convenient to the same sea route between Whyalla and Newcastle, were opened up near Devonport in Tasmania.[45]

Regarding the other major resource requirement, good coking coal, there were large deposits of low sulphur coal of adequate coking quality readily available in the neighbourhood of Newcastle and Port Kembla in

New South Wales. In fact it was the New South Wales coalfields and their geographical location that determined the most desirable location for the steelworks. Using steel rails as an example, Baker explained to the Board that 1.74 tons of ore were required against 2.44 tons of coal to produce a ton of steel rails. When the cost of freight was taken into consideration, it followed that 'the works should be nearest the coal, other considerations being equal, such as water supply, harbour facilities and nearness to market'.[46] South Australia, Delprat's suggested site, was immediately vetoed by David Baker, despite the richness of its iron ore deposits and its connections with the BHP Board.

South Australia was clearly not the most economic site for the industry. Of the two obvious choices, Newcastle or Port Kembla, Baker preferred the former. The reasons for his choice were that Newcastle had the largest supply of good coking coal of a quality then suitable for blast furnaces, the harbour facilities were better (Port Kembla's harbour was small and poorly protected), BHP already possessed land at Newcastle with good water frontage and ample adjoining space to provide for future growth, the site was located about a hundred miles from Sydney on a main railway line, and it offered excellent shipping facilities to other parts of Australia. Furthermore, the depression in the coal industry had created a surplus labour force in the area and Newcastle was an established town with a number of manufacturing companies already operating in the locality.

In the immediate future, Baker envisaged rails as the staple product for the new steelworks. Mills to finish other products could be added later. By first making steel rails BHP would both fill a government need and also pre-empt any potential competition in the manufacture of 'this most important steel product'. Rails were the product that the government required in the greatest tonnage. They were essential to the development of the country, and they were very satisfactory to produce 'for orders are always large, reducing the cost of manufacture'.[47] Federation had emphasised the need for improved communications between the states and in the years immediately before 1912 the country's requirement for rails had increased sharply (as can be seen in the table). On June 1912, in proposing the manufacture of iron and steel to the BHP Board, Delprat had emphasised that the 'contemplated Transcontinental Railway will require enormous quantities of rails and other material, and it is clear therefore that there will be no difficulty in disposing of our products'.[48]

**Government Railways—Mileage**

|      | Under Construction | Authorised |
|------|--------------------|------------|
| 1907 | 732.25             | —          |
| 1908 | 685.25             | 906.75     |
| 1909 | 996.25             | 584.00     |
| 1910 | 1046.50            | 1140.25    |
| 1911 | 2633.50            | 1644.75    |
| 1912 | 3161.00            | 1309.75    |

Source: *Commonwealth Year Book*, 1913

The apparent haste surrounding BHP's final move into the manufacture of iron and steel probably had its origin in three factors. First, there was the political dilemma of the New South Wales parliament. Members of both parties had begun to realise that the Bill to establish a state iron- and steelworks was, regardless of its ideological significance, a financial impossibility. The government was clearly under pressure to abandon a long-standing political commitment. Secondly, the goodwill of the New South Wales government was essential to the success of any company embarking on the venture. This would obviously be more difficult, if not impossible, to obtain once the State Iron and Steel Bill became law as the government, whether it built its own plant or purchased the Eskbank ironworks, would be operating in the same business. Thirdly, in 1907 the federal government's Transcontinental Railway Bill had provided £20 000 towards a preliminary survey for a railway line connecting Western Australia with the eastern states.

The survey had been completed in 1909. It estimated the cost of the railway from Port Augusta to Kalgoorlie, 1063 miles, at approximately £4 000 000. In December 1911 the Commonwealth parliament had passed a further Bill authorising the construction of the railway. This started on 14 September 1912. It provided an immediate financial incentive. Delprat, giving evidence before the New South Wales Select Committee on the Newcastle Iron and Steelworks Bill in October 1912, emphasised that BHP was extremely anxious to establish its works, because the company wanted 'an opportunity of quoting for the supply of rails for the Transcontinental Railway'. Delprat may also have felt, in view of the nicely blended political and economic attitude of the New South Wales government towards the State Iron and Steelworks Bill for the creation of a publicly owned works, that there were tactical advantages in pressing haste; certainly he requested the government for a speedy reply insisting that 'we have little time to lose'.[49]

In 1910 about 150 000 tons of rails were imported into Australia and Baker believed that BHP could make nearly that tonnage immediately. To this end he recommended the initial installation of one modern, mechanically filled blast furnace with a daily capacity of 350 tons; three 65-ton basic open-hearth stationary steel furnaces, producing 500 tons of steel ingots per day; one blooming mill, equipped to roll 500 tons of steel ingots per day to 8-inch square blooms for the rail mill; and a heavy rail mill, with cooling beds and finishing equipment for a product of 400 tons of finished rails per day. Although Baker considered the Bessemer method 'the quickest and cheapest' steel process, he feared that BHP's iron ore was too close to the Bessemer limit in phosphorus. This led him to recommend the basic open-hearth process. All of the plant was to be equipped with the latest labour-saving devices and to be capable of easy expansion in the future. Baker also recommended the installation of by-product coke ovens at Newcastle (BHP already had a battery of non-recovery coke ovens at Bellambi, on the south coast of New South Wales). Finally, Baker pointed out that BHP would have to import sufficient skilled workers from overseas to train the local work-force.[50]

Baker's reports were still before the Board when, on 26 June 1912, Delprat met Arthur Griffith, the New South Wales Minister for Public Works and his under-secretary. At this meeting BHP asked the state government for six concessions to make the projected enterprise viable. These were: to dredge the Hunter River in front of land owned by BHP and to build a 600-foot wharf; to cede the foreshore between the proposed wharf and the high-water mark; to hand over to the company the land known as the Botanical Gardens; to cede a triangular piece of land between BHP land and the railway yard; to close certain roads in Waratah and Wickham and to resume the railway embankment belonging to the Caledonian Coal Company then dividing BHP property in two, should that firm be unwilling to sell it to BHP at a reasonable price.[51]

The BHP Board met on 28 June 1912 and minuted, in the Board's condensed style, their decision that they were

> after due consideration of situation, convinced now psychological moment to start, important advantageous result if work undertaken promptly, vigorously . . . Directors feel strongly Iron and Steel Works will ultimately be started here and as this Company has own immense iron deposits,

tramway, jetty, also large organization already formed, it is particularly adapted to embark on operations and the present time most opportune to take advantage of position to forestall opposition.[52]

On 13 July 1912 the New South Wales Premier announced that 'the Government will place no obstacle in the way of the enterprise'. In connection with the public assets that BHP wished to acquire, the state government would be willing to assist the company by selling the Botanical Gardens site at market value; resuming the portion of the Caledonian Coal Company's railway and reselling it to BHP at a reasonable (probably nominal) price; undertaking the dredging of the river and erection of wharves in front of the whole area, charging the company the value of any reclaimed land and some reasonable payment for the added value of the area to cover part of the cost of dredging; either selling or granting on a long lease at a moderate rental the portion of crown land fronting on the river; granting a long-term lease for the wharf on a fair rental based on cost; grant leases for the extra land required by BHP for fifty years (any charge made to be 5 per cent of its present value); also, the Government would waive all charges for silt pumped on to BHP land during dredging and would maintain the deep-water channel.[53]

The position of the New South Wales Labor government now became extremely complex. Six weeks later, on 28 August 1912, Griffith, the Minister for Public Works, moved in the Legislative Assembly that the State Iron and Steelworks Bill be resumed at the point at which it had been interrupted in the previous session. This resolution was agreed. The next move came on 1 October when J. W. Cann, the state treasurer, moved on behalf of Mr Griffith that:

> this House will, on its next sitting day, resolve itself into a Committee of the Whole to consider the expediency of bringing in a Bill to ratify an agreement made between the Honourable the Premier and the Broken Hill Proprietary Company Limited, for the establishment by the said company of iron and steel works near Newcastle; for the purpose of carrying out such agreement to provide for leasing lands to and for vesting other lands in the said company; for resuming lands; for closing roads; to amend certain Acts; and for purposes consequent thereon or incidental thereto.[54]

This question was then put. It passed. On the following day the legislature consented to ratifying the agreement. The way was now clear for the New South Wales legislature to consider another iron- and steelworks Bill, the Newcastle Iron and Steel Works Bill. This was read for the first time on 3 October. It was moved that the Bill be read a second time on 10 October. The Bill was referred to a select committee consisting of Griffith, Grahame, Lee, McGarry, Cohen, Page, Lonsdale, Henley and Perry. Delprat, on behalf of BHP, gave evidence before the committee on 23 and 30 October 1912.

His evidence, playing on a well-worn theme of New South Wales politics, strongly supported the concept of free enterprise. In the course of his evidence Delprat was questioned by the Chairman, John Perry:

> CHAIRMAN: Is it the intention of the Broken Hill Proprietary Company to start smelting works which may be detrimental to the health of the people of Newcastle?
>
> DELPRAT: No. Steel Works make hardly any smoke.[55]

This extraordinary answer was accepted.

The select committee reported favourably on 31 October. On 6 November the Bill was read a second time and debated. It received its third reading on 13 November when it was passed in the Assembly, fifty-one votes to fourteen. The Bill was debated in Council on 27 November and returned to the Assembly without amendment. On 6 December 1912 it received the Royal Assent. The way was now clear for BHP to establish the Newcastle steelworks.

The New South Wales State Iron and Steelworks Bill had received its second reading on 15 October 1912 and its third reading on the following day. It was passed by thirty-four to twenty-five votes, but in the Legislative Council it was left to lie on the table. Then on 19 August 1913 and again the next day the Assembly debated and agreed, thirty-five to thirty-three votes, to send a message to the Legislative Council requesting that the Bill be proceeded with in council. Council, however, did not proceed and the Bill lapsed. BHP's timing had pincered the government between its desire to establish the industry in New South Wales and its adherence to the party policy of nationalisation which the state could ill afford being, in the graphic metaphor of J. C. L. Fitzpatrick, MLA for Orange, 'as destitute of financial resources as a frog is of feathers'.[56] Confronted with the stark decision of jobs versus ideology, the state government decided for the former, although for many committed Labor politicians it was a bitter decision. Arthur Griffith, the Minister for Public Works, tried to resolve the apparent contradictions by arguing that

> the fact that we propose to establish certain works for our own use ... is not regarded by the Government as a reason why we should refuse to

facilitate the proper and reasonable investment of private capital in industrial undertakings. The Government welcome the development of this great industry in one of our seaport towns.[57]

McGowen made the conciliatory gesture that 'while the works are in New South Wales we can nationalise them'. W. H. Wood, a member of the Opposition, stated that 'the Premier . . . knows very well that there is no intention to nationalise these works—that the Government have not the means to do so, and that no other Government in the near future will have the means'. Commenting on the State Iron and Steelworks Bill, Wood noted that 'this iron flag is to be kept flying like many other interesting flags which have to be flown in the political breeze when an election is coming on . . . the proposition of the state ironworks is as dead as Julius Caesar'.[58]

Ideologically committed Labor members like McGarry found themselves arguing from different and sometimes conflicting standpoints. Debating the projected resumption of the Caledonian Coal Company's land, McGarry indignantly commented that

> we are going to interfere with vested rights . . . it is the first time that any confiscation of this kind has been attempted . . . I was elected on a given platform . . . that great industries of this kind should not be left to private individuals . . . If I vote for this bill I break the pledge . . . They did not consult the Party before they introduced the measure.

T. H. Thrower, MLA for Macquarie, equally indignantly commented:

> I object to handing over the people's heritage [the site for the Botanical Gardens] to a private concern . . . We do not want to have it said that in times of stress we have to go to a company manipulated in foreign parts [sic] for permission to get the necessary equipment for the defence of the Commonwealth, and to keep it white for the people of Australia.

However, the citizens of the then depressed city of Newcastle were quite willing to sacrifice their undeveloped Botanical Gardens site for the employment that the steelworks would provide. Mr Earp MLC, a Newcastle merchant and sometime president of the Newcastle Chamber of Commerce, announced that 'in the history of Newcastle, I suppose there has never been a proposal of greater import to the port and district of Newcastle than that contained in this bill'.[59]

Antagonism to BHP was reflected in speeches such as that of R. D. Meagher, who questioned the government's granting of concessions to 'the Broken Hill Proprietary Company . . . [which] . . . for many years trampled upon unionism in Broken Hill . . . I see no reason why, if favours are to be bestowed, they should be given to a company whose conflicts with wage-earners should not exactly endear them to a Labor Government'.[60] On the same theme R. Hollis declared his desire 'to see the State iron industry controlled by the State and not by some jackanapes who will be out of touch with democracy'. The debates in the New South Wales legislature were undoubtedly rowdy, colourful and divisive. The government was frequently goaded by both its supporters and opponents over its conflicting ideological and pragmatic views. Delprat, a shrewd psychologist, who would have known some of these politicians from Broken Hill, had carefully injected a note of urgency mixed with promise into his evidence to the select committee. He made such statements as 'I am prepared to start right away, and I can carry out the work in two and a half years' and 'the moment Parliament gives me my Bill I am off'. The parliament did not have the benefit of Baker's report to the BHP Board, and the possibility that the works might be sited in South Australia must have appeared to them as a very real danger.

Under the Labor premiership of W. H. Holman the dream of a nationalised steel industry in New South Wales still had official substance, although this quickly vanished under the realities of war and the rise of BHP's works on the eastern seaboard. In January 1914 G. & C. Hoskins, foreseeing future difficulties, actually called the government's bluff. They offered to sell the government the entire Lithgow ironworks,[61] only to have the offer refused. Charles Hoskins's problems were quickly highlighted when, in May 1914, he lost the state government contract for steel locking bar pipes to German suppliers as, although he was allowed to tender twice, 'the Germans beat us hopelessly'. The *Sydney Morning Herald* alleged that the Germans were subsidising their steamers to Australia to the extent of £500 000 per year. Confronted with this situation, Hoskins immediately applied to the Interstate Tariff Investigation Commission for a protective duty on iron and steel. Its investigations had barely commenced when World War I began on 4 August 1914, and completely altered the economic scene.

Despite the outbreak of war, the Interstate Tariff Investigation Commission continued hearing evidence and, in November 1914, the manager of the Australian Wiredrawing Company, North Melbourne, told the commission that 'the English rods were not imported here, as they were too expensive. The German rods used to be imported here so much cheaper than the English could be'.[62] In fact the extent of German infiltration into the Australian market before World War I can be illustrated by the import market in plain wire. In 1880 98 per cent of the Victorian market was British; by 1908 this had fallen to 5.6 per cent while German imports had risen from 2 to 56.4 per cent. Imports to New South Wales and Queensland followed the same pattern, slightly less dramatically. The American share of the market was also increasing: between 1893 and 1900 the US share of the Victorian market rose from 1.1 to 47.1 per cent and in New South Wales from 0.2 to 41.4 per cent. In 1908 the total quantity of plain wire imported into New South Wales, Victoria and Queensland was just under 50 000 tons; in Victoria and Queensland, Germany had 56.4 and 57.2 per cent of the market respectively, but in New South Wales the German advantage over the Americans was slight—39.3 to 38.2 per cent.[63]

The consequences of Germany's interest in the base metal market before World War I have already been noted with regard to the Port Pirie smelters. But this was only one, although an important, aspect of an increasing German interest in the Australian market as a whole. Many Germans had settled in South Australia, particularly in the Barossa valley. At the outbreak of war in 1914 the chairman of BHP was Hugo Muecke, the German Consul in Adelaide, a South Australian merchant, who had been openly against the company's venture into steel.[64] For Germany, as well as for Britain, Australia offered the double advantage of a market for manufactured goods and a source of industrial raw materials. Furthermore, in view of Germany's underdeveloped colonial interests in the Pacific, a commercial attack on Britain's principal sphere of influence in that area was not without strategic significance. This probably explains Delprat's feelings when he visited Germany on his 1911 fact-finding mission.

In 1914 Germany's steel capacity (17 million tons) was considerably more than that of Britain (7 million tons) and France (5 million tons) combined. However, Germany was far outstripped by the United States, which in 1913 had a steel capacity of 31 million tons. This highlights the importance of America's friendship and eventual participation in World War I.[65] Even before World War I Great Britain had already lost much of its Australian market in certain key expanding areas. The uncertainties of the world economy in the inter-war period only slowed its perception of this fact.

A footnote to the nationalisation debate occurred in Queensland, where a Labor government was returned in 1915. In 1918 the Queensland Royal Commission on the State Iron and Steel Works unanimously recommended the establishment of a nationalised industry. This was essentially a statement of principle. Regarding the practicalities, the commission reported that 'even now we are without the necessary information to answer all the questions submitted to us' and that 'very little is known as to the quantity and suitability of ores in the state', while further research of a 'scientific and technical nature' would be necessary. The commission recorded its thanks to BHP in some detail, acknowledging that the company had helped them in every way.[66] Indeed, Delprat had even told them:

> to start straight away with the manufacture of iron and steel in Queensland, in order to take advantage of the high prices ruling at the present time. He generously offered to help the venture in every way and agreed to enter into a contract with the Queensland Government for the supply of iron ore from Iron Knob until such time as Queensland could rely on her own resources.

Delprat believed that in the developing Australian market there was room for all, particularly if the Queensland government was willing to rely upon BHP for its ore. Although BHP's interests were undoubtedly uppermost in any advice which Delprat gave to other concerns, at the time it was given, his advice was commercially sound. But, one of the major problems of the iron and steel industry is the volatility of the market and the time lapse between the formulation of a policy and its maturity. This ensures that plans made under one set of conditions come to fruition under other, and often radically different, circumstances. In 1918 the future of BHP depended not only on the success of its new venture into iron and steel, hitherto protected by the war, but also on the exploitation of its great mineral resources, not at Broken Hill but at Iron Knob in South Australia. The Newcastle works in New South Wales with their modern equipment and highly skilled management could easily cope with any competition likely to arise within Australia, while guaranteed sales of iron ore would give some security against the uncertain markets of a post-war world. Delprat knew the international market, and it is unlikely that a man of his acuteness did not have worries about how the still inexperienced and idealistic Australian governments would handle the long-established ruthlessness of overseas competition.

The Queensland government continued with its plans and as it tried to turn its ideals into commercial reality it ran into the usual problems of resources, costs and expertise. The scheme eventually foundered in the difficult economic conditions of the early 1920s, but before this occurred the government attempted to solve their resources problem by the acquisition of the iron ore leases for Cockatoo Island off Western Australia. Not only was Cockatoo a desolate, waterless island but local tides made shipping very difficult—conditions that had earlier dissuaded the Japanese, also looking for suitable resources of iron ore. The Queensland ironworks was to have been sited at Bowen in northern Queensland and it was planned to bring the ore there by building a transcontinental railroad across northern Australia.[67]

# 9
## THE NEWCASTLE STEELWORKS

THE IRON AND STEEL INDUSTRY'S combination of enormous capital investment with market volatility emphasised the need for an external cash flow to support it in times of low market demand. This was already evident from the Hoskinses' combination of the pipe works in Sydney with the ironworks at Lithgow and, in April 1912, Delprat urged the BHP Board to 'lose no time in getting to work so as to have the Steel Works earning their living before the time arrives when the old Mine is unable to further nurse it'.[1] BHP's timing attracted the good fortune essential for the success of any great enterprise. Two years later the outbreak of World War I brought a dual advantage: wartime demand and scarcity revived the profitability of the Broken Hill mine; at the same time isolation automatically protected the newly established iron and steel industry. Although mining was intermittent in the 1920s and 1930s, the Broken Hill mine did create vital income at strategic periods in the steelworks development, particularly in the mid 1920s and late 1930s. Until 1928, when the slimes and tailings were largely exhausted, the flotation processes introduced by Delprat and developed by Bradford provided essential additional income. (The mine was finally closed on 28 February 1939 and the leases were relinquished three years later.)

The contribution from the company's activities at Broken Hill was not merely financial. It was also source of trained technical and managerial staff. Among the many Broken Hill staff transferred to Newcastle were

Essington Lewis, Leslie Bradford and F. M. Mitchell. Without this reservoir of managerial talent it would have been virtually impossible to embark upon an enterprise of the size and complexity of the Newcastle iron- and steelworks in a country with a small population, engaged in fighting a major war overseas. The decline of the BHP mine at Broken Hill and the rise of the steelworks were inextricably intertwined.[2] It can be argued that the Big Mine at Broken Hill laid the foundation of viable heavy industry in Australia.

If, in the early twentieth century, no Australian government could have financed the construction and development of an economically viable steelworks, neither could any Australian company without raising considerable external finance. How BHP raised the additional capital for this venture is an extraordinary story in itself. On 19 June 1912, while Baker's final report was still pending and before the Board made its final decision on 28 June, the company secretary was instructed to meet brokers to discuss 'the question of the most expedient manner to be adopted in raising the necessary capital and submit a scheme to the Board'. BHP wished to raise £1 000 000. The London Board made enquiries and cabled 'first impression £1,000,000 with periodical payments as proposed, not business proposition for underwriters here'. To the London financiers 'BHP was a mining Company'. The Bank of Australasia was also approached. It indicated that, despite BHP's high financial standing, it might have difficulty in raising so large a sum for investment in an area in which its expertise was unproven.

The Board responded to this problem by resolving on 17 July 1912 that steps be taken 'for the purpose of increasing the capital of the Company by the creation of 540 000 new shares of 8s. each to be issued as fully paid-up and to rank equally in all respects with the existing shares'. These amounted to 960 000 fully paid shares of eight shillings each. The new issue would increase the capital of the company from £384 000 to £600 000. This proposal was unanimously approved at an Extraordinary General Meeting on 27 September and confirmed at a further meeting on 14 October 1912. BHP then decided to issue 240 000 of the new shares to the shareholders and the public at forty shillings per share, a premium of £1 12s per share. Within a fortnight they had raised £422 112 in new capital; the prospectus was published on 25 January 1913 and 211 056 shares had been allotted by 8 February. John Darling was among the underwriters.[3]

Like its Australian predecessors BHP soon discovered the iron and steel industry's voracious appetite for capital. By April 1914, over a year after the first increase in capital had been successfully achieved, more was urgently needed. The problem was solved by a mixture of good management and a fortuitous accident. Delprat was at the Newcastle Club where, in the course of social conversation with a group of bank managers, he learnt that the Commonwealth Bank apparently had 'plenty of money to invest'. He passed this piece of information on to BHP's company secretary, F. M. Dickenson, for his consideration. Dickenson made further enquiries. He had to act cautiously as a rejection would have impaired BHP's chances of attracting other financial support in the money market. Dickenson discovered that the Act incorporating the Commonwealth Bank gave wide powers to its governor, Denison Miller, to whom an anonymous and circuitous approach was now made. BHP was informed that a proposal could be considered if the security was adequate. Furthermore, the governor of the Commonwealth Bank was in Melbourne that day, 1 May 1914. A meeting was hastily arranged—there was not even time to locate a director—and at it Miller announced that he was prepared to entertain an application from BHP. The negotiations were finalised by mid June. On 6 July BHP published the prospectus of an issue of 6 per cent debentures with a face value of £600 000. These were priced at £97, had a currency of twenty years and were part of an intended issue of £1 000 000. The prestigious Commonwealth Bank had underwritten the largest part of the loan.[4]

The move was beneficial to both parties as the bank was trying to win increased recognition as a general banking institution. By underwriting the BHP loan the Commonwealth Bank entered a new area of development. However, the bank's participation caused an immediate furore. The storm centred round the perceived role of the bank. It had been established, in 1911, by the Fisher government as the fulfilment of a Labor ambition, formulated during the depression of the 1890s, for a 'people's bank'. When Senator Clemons, Minister without Portfolio, was questioned in the Senate as to whether BHP had received a loan from the Commonwealth Bank, he replied that 'in spite of every effort to obtain an answer' he was 'unable to supply one'. The governor of the Commonwealth Bank was under no obligation to answer such questions and neither the Senate nor the House of Representatives had the power to make him do so.[5]

World War I broke out a month after the loan was arranged. The financial market was dislocated, and raising capital on this scale would have been impossible. Further capital was realised in June 1915, when Broken Hill Associated Smelters Pty Ltd took over BHP's Port Pirie works for £350 000 and 150 000 shares. These shares could be liquidated if a future redistribution of the company's assets was required. Meanwhile, the remaining £400 000 of the debenture issue was floated in 1916 to meet the increasing capital expenditure on the plant, in particular the second blast furnace and the supporting battery of Semet–Solvay coke ovens. By 1918 more than £3 000 000 had been expended on developing the works. At this time the financial structure of the company was altered to provide greater flexibility. BHP was now an industrial as well as a mining enterprise. The share unit was changed from eight shillings to £1. There were 318 994 eight-shilling shares unissued and these were issued to the shareholders at £2 per share for every two and a half shares held. This was followed by a bonus issue of twelve-shilling shares. The two sets of shares were then consolidated into £1 shares. The result of this capital restructuring was that shareholders now held 140 £1 shares in place of every 100 eight-shilling shares.[6]

These financial developments were paralleled by the construction and operation of the steelworks. David Baker had returned to America and on 29 August 1912 BHP cabled to offer him a five-year contract first as engineer in charge of construction and then as manager of the steelworks. Baker accepted. His agreement with BHP was finalised on 4 October 1912. In the event he worked for BHP until his retirement, aged sixty-four, in 1925. Based on the plans that Baker drew up in Philadelphia, work began on reclaiming the Waratah site in January 1913. Piles had to be driven into the mud, which was submerged at high tide, to support the concrete foundations for the plant and heavy equipment. The whole area had to be raised above the high-water level in order to construct a blast furnace, two open-hearth furnaces, a blooming mill, a rolling mill, a battery of by-product coke ovens as well as a building for the administrative staff.

Baker returned to Australia on 18 March 1913. He submitted detailed plans to the Board. By the end of the month orders had been placed with US firms for the blast furnace castings, plate and structural work. Before Baker left Philadephia, the proposed orders had been inspected by his former partner James B. Ladd, a mechanical engineer, who later represented BHP in the United States for several years. In Philadelphia Ladd's office had adjoined Baker's, and the original plans for the Newcastle steelworks were drawn up there. These general plans were finalised on site on 22 April 1913.[7]

In 1912 Delprat had predicted that the steelworks could be built and commissioned within two and a half years. To the amazement of his contemporaries he not only justified his prediction but beat it by four months—and this in face of the added difficulties created by shipping plant and people to the Australia under wartime conditions. Looking back on this triumph of management and organisation Baker recorded that:

> It was the General Manager's idea that dates should be fixed for the completion of the foundations of each department, the start of erection and the completion of erection. These dates I was requested to figure out and commit myself to, and Mr Hacke prepared a blue print on which were blocked each job, time of starting, and of finishing. At each visit of the General Manager to the works he would colour with red pencil the progress made to date.[8]

Baker also reported that some of their fellow residents in the Great Northern Hotel watched Delprat and himself with considerable curiosity, declaring 'that scheme of BHP to build a steelworks in Newcastle will come to nothing. See, the General Manager and the Manager go to work in a penny tram'![9]

The weather was appallingly wet—54 inches (137 cm) of rain fell on the Newcastle area that year—but by April the plant positions had been staked out, even though the site was still under water.[10] The first shipment of machinery arrived on 1 January 1914 and by the outbreak of World War I on 4 August construction was well advanced, with the exception of the Semet–Solvay coke ovens plant which had been ordered from Belgium. This was later successfully delivered in spite of the wartime dislocation of shipping services. The blast furnace was blown in on 8 March 1915 and tapped two days afterwards. A month later, on 9 April, the first open-hearth steel was made. Trial rails of soft steel were rolled on 24 April and two days later the mills began to roll rails for the New South Wales government. Meanwhile, in South Australia, a new iron ore mine had been established at Iron Knob. The tramway to the coast was reconstructed to carry the heavier traffic and new crushers and loading facilities were installed at Hummock Hill, renamed Whyalla in 1920. On 8 January 1915 the first shipment of 2800 tons of ore was made on the SS *Emerald Wings*.

Delprat's managerial skills and David Baker's abilities were fully vindicated by the remarkable achievement of not only building but bringing into operation a complete steelworks in such a short time. Shortages of imported steel, following the outbreak of the war, made the achievement even more spectacular. Inevitably there were initial problems; Baker

Opening the taphole for the first cast of No. 1 blast furnace at the BHP Newcastle steelworks, 9 April 1915. The absence of protective clothing is typical of the era.

reported some of them in his diary when in the course of four days the following incidents occurred:

    28 April —Wednesday 4 a.m. . . . iron broke out deep down in hearth pocket under cinder notch. Two dull reports . . . shut down for thorough cooling off of hearth and repairs.

| | |
|---|---|
| 30 April | Started furnace about 6 p.m. Each course of main foundation of furnace . . . filled solid with concrete in place of sand. |
| 1 May | Hard tap hole at furnace . . . five heavy explosions—9 a.m. Cast at tap hole—6.30 all right again.[11] |

The technological advances embodied in the blast furnace changed the skyline of Australian steelworks. Previous furnaces, either open top or single bell, had required no structure above the stack. With the advent of mechanical charging, the top of the furnace became dominated by mechanical superstructure and ductwork. In later furnaces this rose half as high again as the top of the stack. These changes may be seen by comparing the Newcastle steelworks in 1915 (p. 191) with the Sandford–Hoskins furnaces (p. 145), built within the same decade at Lithgow in 1907 and 1913. The stack of the BHP blast furnace rose 98 feet above the ground. It had a maximum external diameter of $26\frac{1}{2}$ feet. Internally the furnace was 20 feet in diameter at the bosh and 13 feet at the hearth. The blast furnace, with a nominal daily capacity of 350 tons of iron, required charging with some 1000 tons of ore, coke and limestone each day. If this had been 'hand charged', it would have been very labour intensive, as was the case with all earlier Australian blast furnaces, where barrows of raw materials were lifted to the top of the furnace and then tipped by hand on to the bell or into the open top of the furnace.

In line with Baker's belief that costs should be kept low by minimising staff, the new furnace was mechanically charged using skips which were loaded with raw materials, raised up an inclined hoist and dumped into a hopper over the top of the furnace. All these operations were done automatically. They required the use of a double bell and cone-top sealing system to distribute the charge uniformly into the furnace and to avoid unnecessary loss of valuable 'top gas'. In these respects it was at the forefront of the best world technology. Both of these innovations had been introduced in the United States in 1883. By 1915 they were slowly becoming accepted world-wide; in 1914 sixteen of the forty-two blast furnaces in Ohio were still charged by hand, while in Britain a decade later the National Federation of Iron and Steel Manufacturers found that of the 350 blast furnaces in the firms they surveyed only eighty-six were mechanically charged.[12]

The BHP plant was the first in Australia to break away from dependence on British technology. From this time onwards orders for steel plant and equipment for the growing Australian industry were eagerly contested by suppliers from around the world. The construction of

Newcastle No. 1 blast furnace marks the half-way point between the beginning of iron making in Australia and the large capacity furnaces of the 1980s. When Baker's furnace was finally dismantled in 1985, the largest blast furnace in Australia, Port Kembla No. 5, had more than ten times the productive capacity of the furnace which Baker blew in seventy years before, in March 1915.

The opening of BHP's iron- and steelworks on 2 June 1915 by the Governor-General, Sir Ronald Munro-Ferguson, accompanied by the governors of New South Wales and Tasmania, was a national occasion. The guests represented the federal and state parliaments and 'almost every important manufacturing and commercial centre within the Commonwealth'. The seating plan for the luncheon is still extant and both the Hoskins brothers and William Sandford were among the guests.[13] Many of the guests arrived by special train from Sydney. On arrival in Newcastle they embarked in boats provided by the city. Approaching the works by water they were able to appreciate not only the extent of the enterprise but the significance of its coastal location, particularly for a country of vast distances with a small population. Afterwards Delprat

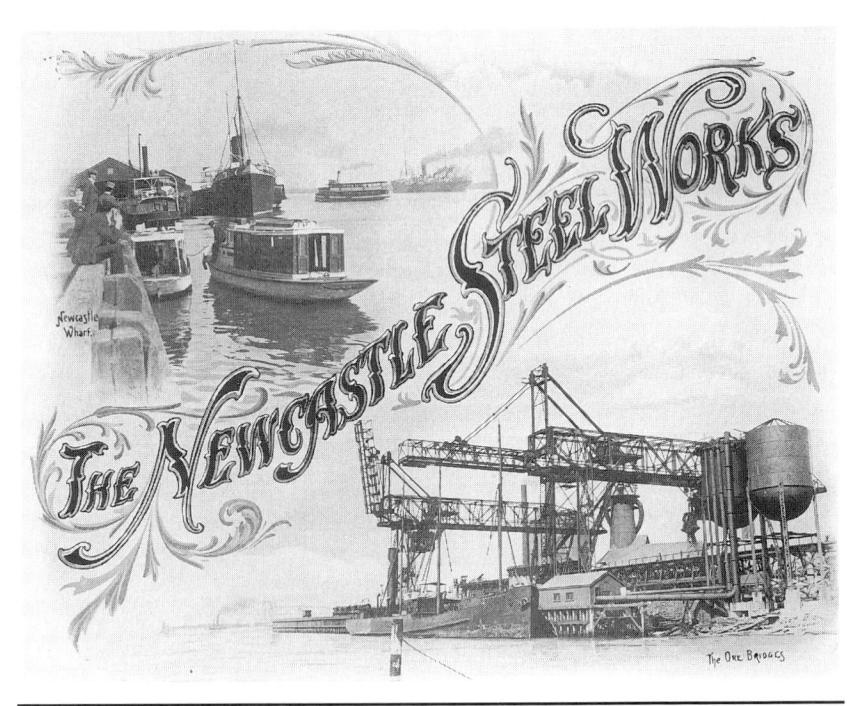

The frontispiece from *Souvenir of Opening the Newcastle Steel Works June 2nd 1915* emphasises the importance attached to having a waterside location for the new steelworks.

Tour of inspection after the official opening of the BHP Newcastle steelworks by the Governor-General, Sir Ronald Munro-Ferguson, 2 June 1915. Prominent are the blast furnace, hot-blast stoves and blower house.

wrote to his wife that 'everything went like clockwork'; Baker recorded in his diary that 'everything passed off smoothly assisted by beautiful weather'.[14]

The occasion was not entirely without incident for, as the Governor-General prepared to address the distinguished guests, 'all at once the safety valves on the mill boilers commenced to blow off . . . the Governor-General waited while an urgent order was sent to Mr Lindsay to stop that racket'. However, this was not allowed to mar the otherwise technical perfection of the day. The Governor-General confidently predicted that 'we may rest satisfied . . . that the steel products of the Newcastle Works will achieve a world-wide reputation'. The industry had come a long way from Governor Du Cane's reservations at the opening of the BTCIC furnace forty years before. As the applause from the Governor-General's speech subsided, 'there came flashing along the rollers, within the immense 950ft. building, a square mass of hot metal. It was a fascinating spectacle . . . to watch each movement that converted the red-hot mass into a perfectly formed steel rail'.[15]

In the speeches after the official luncheon, the chairman, Duncan McBryde, proposed the health of the Governor-General and used the occasion to point out that:

> as it has taken close on £1,500,000 to complete the works and develop the sources of the iron and limestone supplies required, it will be realised that the company can only be reasonably looked to enlarge the works when the orders coming in warrant such a step being taken. The Governments and the public, therefore, practically have it in their own hands to decide whether or not extensions shall be made . . . we have embarked on a very large undertaking, which we hope may prove profitable to ourselves as well as of great value to Australia, and should such prove to be the case all will have reason to be satisfied.

At the same time the chairman tempered his remarks with the company's traditional mixture of caution, optimism, commercial acumen and patriotism by pledging that:

> After the works have been in existence for a time, and the quality of the iron and steel produced has been satisfactorily demonstrated, we firmly believe that a number of industries not yet in Australia, unless to a very minor extent, which require manufactured steel as their raw material will spring up around the Steel Works and so confer yet another material benefit upon our country. Should such industries hesitate too long in coming, I fancy they will find that our Company will itself establish such works, and prove strong competitors to those who prefer to manufacture in other countries and export here.

He concluded his speech by stating that 'no one is better pleased than the Directors, knowing they have done something that will be of lasting benefit to what will ultimately become one of the great nations of the world'.

Allowing for the usual compliments, the speech-making was singularly apt. All the speakers underlined the theme later historians identified as central to the age: the symbiotic relationships between large corporations and the modern state. The forces generated by such relationships were inexorable, and they could neither afford to wait upon ideologies nor allow crises to deflect them from their path. The Governor-General stressed the patriotic theme emphasising that the reputation gained little more than a month before at Gallipoli by Australia's soldiers would be equalled by the industrial workers at Newcastle as all 'put their best into the common fold'. At the same time he carefully avoided the ideologies, then becoming an increasingly divisive element in the nation, by declaring that 'the best security for the industrial and social well-being of a community lay in giving equal freedom for public and private initiative'.

In retrospect, Delprat's own speech is particularly revealing in its pre-emptive approach to conflict. Delprat concentrated on the scale and scope of the works, pertinently identifying the ambition of the company 'to supply all the wants of the Commonwealth with the co-operation of his friend Mr. Hoskins'. This set the official tone of public amity between the two companies during the period of their independent operation. More importantly, it anticipated a goals-oriented managerial style, later to be nicknamed 'conflict resolution', which fitted well with BHP's record of pragmatism and good luck. Delprat had built on his European experience with his recent exposure to the latest ideas in the United States. He was influenced by Judge Gary, the chief executive of the United States Steel Corporation (US Steel). Gary was a firm believer in constructive emulation as opposed to the cut-throat competition that characterised the American industry at the end of the nineteenth century. The respect appears to have been mutual. In 1919 Delprat was a guest at one of Gary's famous dinners and Gary provided him with information on the organisation of US Steel.[16] Baker, as the American builder and manager of the new works, was perhaps only too aware of the emotional needs of his audience. He emphasised that 'the plant was erected with Australian labour, and 98% of the men employed in the works today were Australians'.[17]

With the opening of BHP's Newcastle works Australian industry entered a new phase of industrial maturity. The successful construction and financing of such an enterprise during a major world war and at so great a distance from the main centres of technology and finance was an incredible achievement. The timing of BHP's entry into the iron and steel business was undeniably auspicious. Almost immediately the company had a full order book, and the plant was operating to an ever-increasing capacity. Within the first four months the Newcastle steelworks produced 36 214 tons of pig-iron, 17 134 tons of steel blooms and billets and 11 574 tons of rails.

Apart from its initial problems, the blast furnace worked well, although it was not trouble-free, partly due to inexperience on the part of the workers and partly to the quality and availability of the coke. For instance, on 7 July, four days after the spectacular opening, the blast furnace was stopped by a mishap which caused iron to get into the tuyères. In contrast, during the early years of the plant, the open-hearth

Ingots being stripped from their moulds prior to either stocking or reheating in soaking pits, BHP Newcastle steelworks, 1915

furnaces gave considerably more trouble. This was to some extent due to the wartime shortage of refactories, fluxes and recarbonisers.

Refactory problems were eventually solved by the local manufacture of suitable silica bricks by Newbold & Co. of Lithgow. Local resources improved with the discovery of large deposits of magnesite (used as a refactory in the hearths of basic open-hearth furnaces) at Attunga and Fifield, about 200 and 422 miles by rail from Newcastle but within New South Wales. The importance of Baker's extensive contacts to BHP in its early days as a steel manufacturer should not be overlooked. As a consultant before his appointment with BHP, he knew the American specialists in the various sections of the industry. When Newbold visited the United States he carried letters of introduction to the leading silica brick-maker in Pittsburg, the Harbison-Walker Refactories Company, and 'was thus able to obtain full information on the manufacture of the bricks widely used in the steel furnaces in the United States, supplies of which were obtained to build the Company's [BHP's] furnaces'.[18] On his return Newbold rebuilt his Lithgow plant and greatly improved the quality of his product. Later he found a better source of raw materials and eventually built a plant near Newcastle.

Meanwhile, the problems of poor open-hearth performance were becoming increasingly serious. Delprat was a mining engineer and Baker was an expert on blast furnaces. Unless a speedy and satisfactory solution to the problems confronting the steel manufacturing side of the works could be found, there was going to be a mounting difficulty created by surplus pig-iron. Moreover, the country was at war and quality steel was needed for munitions. In these circumstances Delprat and the Board became increasingly worried by the seemingly intractable problems of this department and concerned lest BHP steel should acquire a bad reputation. These problems were surprising as the open-hearth superintendent, a Mr MacKenzie, and the three foreman melters had come from the Lackawanna Steel Company in Buffalo, New York. They were all experienced in open-hearth steel-making. Baker later described the problem in his 'Reminiscences':

> in addition to the lack of steel tonnage, the steel failed to meet the specifications due to the phosphorus being too high. The open hearth tests taken before the steel was tapped would show the phosphorus eliminated to a point well below requirements, but the next test taken after the steel was teemed showed the phosphorus content too high to pass inspection. The open hearth superintendent could suggest no remedy and therefore Mr Bradford, Chief Chemist, was asked to make a study of the problem, and to report. His conclusion . . . was that more lime was needed in the furnace charge. An increase in the lime content of the furnace slag meant risk of gobbing the furnace up with viscous slag.

In the meantime, confronted with this apparently insurmountable problem, the department's morale had collapsed. It was at this point that Leslie Bradford, who had already established the chemical and testing laboratories, was moved to the open-hearth department where he was given the somewhat anomalous position of assistant superintendent. At the same time Delprat asked Baker, possibly to both Baker's and Bradford's chagrin, to suggest an open-hearth expert who could be brought over from the United States to advise Bradford. Baker suggested Henry Hibbard, who arrived in late November 1915. Apart from recommending a few minor changes Hibbard confirmed what Bradford was already doing.[19] Unfortunately Hibbard also gave Delprat advice that conflicted with advice already given by Baker, who later recollected that:

> Mr Hibbard stated to Mr Delprat in my presence, that satisfactory wire rods could not be produced from open hearth steel, and that it was

necessary to have Bessemer steel for this purpose. I disputed this statement at once ... [but] Mr Hibbard had a very good reputation in the United States as an expert in open hearth steel manufacture and his opinion carried weight.[20]

The seemingly insoluble problem with the steel-making department was extremely worrying and its consequences potentially very serious. Not being a steel man, Delprat was dependent upon expert advice. But this incident undoubtedly marked a managerial rift.

In fact the problem had nothing to do with the making of steel in the open-hearth furnace itself. The problem was phosphorus reversion and while Bradford's suggested remedy was logical it was not effective. A search for fluorspar to improve the capacity of basic slag to hold phosphorus was immediately and successfully instigated, and the company acquired mineral leases at Carboona, near Tumbarumba, in New South Wales. Subsequent research has shown that phosphorus reversion is caused by silica from the ladle refactories dissolving in the ladle slag. This reduces the slag's ability to hold phosphorus which then reverts to the steel.

Leslie Bradford was born in Delhi on 9 March 1877. His father was an Indian civil servant who, in 1892, retired to Adelaide, where Bradford completed his education at the South Australian School of Mines. After a short career with the Block 14 Company, he joined the BHP laboratories at Port Pirie and shortly afterwards was transferred to Broken Hill where he worked at, and improved upon, the Delprat flotation process. Dissatisfied with Delprat's lack of recognition of his services he left the company in 1906. Shortly afterwards he returned as chief metallurgist at BHP's mine at Broken Hill. Here he invented a selective flotation process patented in 1910, and further important refinements were patented in 1912. Three years later he was transferred to Newcastle where he set up the laboratories at the new steelworks. Quiet and sensitive, Bradford had outstanding scientific abilities and very considerable managerial skills. Bradford managed to reorganise and extend the plant from three to seven steelmaking furnaces and by April 1918, when he was sent to America to investigate and study open-hearth furnaces and techniques, it was operating fairly smoothly. If John Darling, G. D. Delprat and David Baker were the architects of BHP's twentieth-century steel manufacture, then, along with H. G. Darling and Essington Lewis, Bradford, who died while chief executive in 1943, had claims to be one of its consolidators.[21]

## 9 THE NEWCASTLE STEELWORKS

Leslie Bradford, 1877–1943, c. 1943. His wide experience at BHP led to his succeeding David Baker as manager of the Newcastle steelworks in 1925. He steered the works throughout the difficult depression years until 1935, when he moved to Melbourne to become General Manager of BHP, a post he filled with distinction until his death.

Wartime demand led to immediate extensions to the original plant. The decision of the Board, announced on 28 July 1916, to build a second blast furnace, with the addition of three extra open-hearth steel furnaces to convert the additional iron into steel, more than doubled the capacity of the works.[22] The No. 4 open-hearth furnace was commissioned in March and the 18-inch mill began production seven months later in October 1916. They were followed in July 1917 by the 12- and 8-inch mills. By the end of 1917 the rod mill was in operation, thirty-three new coke ovens, a 1000-ton hot metal mixer and three new open-hearth furnaces, making a total of seven, were all in production. At the same time a 1000-kilowatt generator had been installed. By July 1918 the steel foundry was in operation. A few weeks after the armistice No. 2 blast furnace was commissioned on December 5 1918. After the war the plant continued to expand until 1922, although at a slower rate. A second rod mill came into production in September 1919, a further rod mill in 1922 and in the same year No. 3 blast furnace was commissioned. Finally, in 1922, sixty-three further coke ovens became operational as did a benzol and solvent naphtha plant to utilise the by-products of the ovens. The Semet–Solvay coke ovens used at that time had been Baker's third choice, after Koppers and the American design of the Semet–Solvay ovens, both of which were unobtainable. They were never satisfactory and the production of coke remained a problem until three batteries of Wilputte ovens were installed in the 1930s.[23]

During the war, the Federal Munitions Committee assigned the Newcastle works the task of manufacturing the rail and munitions steel urgently required by the Allies. The quality of the 16 000 tons of munitions steel and the 16 000 tons of steel rails provided by BHP brought favourable comment from the imperial munitions authority. A shell-making annexe was also built at the works but, as the specifications for light artillery shells were changed before the machinery was installed in the specially built munitions shop, the machinery was never used by the company. After the war some of the American-made machine tools were sold to the small arms factory at Lithgow. The shop became part of the Newcastle steelworks general store.[24]

The federal government also requested BHP to build a small blast furnace to supply its needs for foundry iron. A furnace, known as Maggie, was quickly designed and built beside the water to the west of No. 1 blast furnace. Built in an emergency out of local materials, much of its technology was outdated, with such features as the utilisation of pipe stoves, hand-charging and an uncased brick shaft. The furnace was lit on 17 July 1918, but proved capricious, never producing more than 100 tons in any one day. It operated spasmodically, producing both foundry iron and ferro-manganese for use in steel-making. It was finally blown out on 12 September 1925, and ultimately demolished to make room for works expansion in 1934.

Work also proceeded during World War I towards making the works more efficient. Ingot moulds had initially been obtained from outside foundries which remelted pig-iron but Baker, following United States practice, decided to cast ingot moulds using liquid iron obtained directly from the blast furnace. This 'direct metal' foundry, which was located close to the blast furnace, produced ingot moulds at lower cost and with longer lives than those bought externally. This practice was later adopted at all BHP steelworks. The foreman of this foundry shop was one of the men successfully relocated from Broken Hill. Baker recollected that the foreman 'was so competent that we soon added a crucible furnace to the equipment, and he made copper and brass castings, including coolers and tuyères required at the furnace'.[25]

Plate rolling was another enterprise undertaken in response to the national emergency. BHP had considered embarking on shipbuilding in view of the New South Wales government's desire to dispose of their yard at Walsh's Island. Delprat, however, had reservations about the company embarking on an enterprise of this complexity, writing in a 'confidential' letter to Baker that:

> My opinion is that Australia's best policy would be to send the steel home to England as Billets, and have it rolled into plates there, to be used in their ship building yards where every facility is available. This to my mind will be a much wiser course than our attempting to build ships here, where we are faced with the scarcity of skilled labour and a lack of properly equipped ship-building yards. I may or may not be able to convince the Government of this, but I believe that one of the things they will ask me will be, how long it would take to put up a Plate-rolling Mill . . .

However, Prime Minister Hughes was anxious to build Australian ships as a federal enterprise.[26] By November 1917 the works were rolling plates to replace ships sunk by enemy action, and also for the construction of the No. 2 blast furnace. The plate rolls were imported from the United States. When the blooming mill housings proved inadequate for the strain that this new operation placed upon them, new housings were successfully cast at the works, although each required some 50 tons of open-hearth steel. This made moving them for finishing and installation a major problem.[27]

Apart from the demands imposed by the wartime emergency, the symbiotic relationship between government and industry was expressing itself in other ways. It is an understatement to say that the structure of Australian society and the past history of the iron and steel industry ensured government a role in any industrial success. In 1913 the Interstate Commission of Australia had been requested by the government to 'report and investigate generally upon the effect and operation of the Tariff Acts at present in force and to indicate industries in need of tariff assistance, anomalies in the existing Tariff Acts' and 'the lessening . . . of the cost of the ordinary necessities of life, without injury to the workers engaged in any useful industry'.[28]

The commission, which was to sit for seven years, first met in 1914. The commissioners decided that in their deliberations they would ignore any effects resulting from wartime conditions, as their future impact upon the industry was unpredictable; instead, they would concentrate on the state of the manufacturing industry in 'normal' (pre-war) times. A quaint

Bloom being rolled from an ingot in the bloom mill, BHP Newcastle steelworks, 1915

statement to the modern reader, but the idea of 'normality', long part of Victorian semiotics, died hard. Nor were the commissioners alone in this error. Later the actions of the British Treasury during the crisis over the gold standard showed that the idea never occurred to them that 'normality' was gone. The long *pax Britannica* had, despite some vicissitudes, created concepts of 'stability' and 'normality' unknown today. These ideas carried over into the very unstable post-war era. The 1915 *Report* of the Interstate Tariff Investigation Commission presents an interesting survey of attitudes towards industry and industrial problems when Australia was on the eve of becoming an industrial nation.

When his New South Wales state contracts were undercut by the Germans in 1914 Charles Hoskins had applied to the Tariff Board for support. BHP supported Hoskins's application despite its firm declaration that it would require no public assistance, given to the New South Wales Select Committee on the Newcastle Iron and Steel Bill two years earlier. In part this about-face was due to policy developments and a deepening understanding of the optimum use of the works' capacity. As the works were being erected, Baker had advised Delprat to install plant giving the works maximum flexibility and allowing for a gradual and controlled development for 'this would make the Company a feeder for numerous industries in the hands of firms skilled in the business, and, in the future, the Company being the controller of the steel supply, could purchase any one of the finishing plants when a favourable opportunity offered.'[29]

Such an arrangement gave BHP financial flexibility while limiting the risks involved in over-extending existing enterprises and establishing new ones. BHP pursued this plan in the inter-war period, but the policy actually dates from the erection of the Newcastle works. The Morgan continuous rod mill, commissioned in 1918, was an important part of this general plan.

Delprat's evidence to the Interstate Commission was interesting. He candidly reiterated his original opinion, given, in 1912, to the New South Wales Select Committee that he did not require duties to produce rails and similar items. Rail production had been BHP's original intention but now he declared, 'I have altered my policy, and prefer to be a big steelmaster, rather than a small general trader'. In line with this development he was already contemplating a second blast furnace, although the first was not yet blown in. In fact, this new ambition meshed more closely with both the aims of the commission and the realities of the situation. Delprat was under no illusion that economies of scale were essential to produce the cheap steel that would make the industry both viable and profitable. Attracting dependent industries so as to increase steel demand was of fundamental importance, and he argued that 'if there are no increases of duty I do not think other factories would be put up, and we should be at the expense of putting up the factories ourselves'. He supported tariffs 'in order that I can enlarge the industry. It will enable us to establish the steel industry on a broader basis'.[30]

On 25 June 1914, in a summary report to the BHP Board on progress at Newcastle, Delprat had expressed the view that 'the production of more varied products will of course in the near future demand an additional blast furnace to produce more raw material for the larger quantity of finished products'.[31] To the tariff commissioners he quite simply explained BHP's interest in encouraging subsidiary industries: 'here are two reasons why we favour this policy. One is that if we did all the subsidiary works the supervision would be enormous, and the other is that if we keep our money to enlarge the blast furnaces, we shall have a larger output and a cheaper management.'[32]

Delprat gave evidence to the commission on 14 July and again on 28 July 1914. On both occasions he emphasised the need for economies of scale combined with the necessity of not over-stretching the quality of BHP's management. This could be best achieved by encouraging other firms to establish factories within easy marketable distance. A double advantage would accrue, that of providing outlets for the large capacity of the works and releasing the company's capital resources for further expansion. Delprat was a skilful and persuasive advocate and on 29 July he reported to the company secretary that 'the Commission seemed to be quite of my way of thinking and practically said so'.[33]

In 1914 both Charles Hoskins and Delprat, then only a potential steelmaster, gave evidence to the commission. Hoskins gave evidence twice in public and twice in private. Relations between BHP and G. & C. Hoskins were from the start friendly, if cautious, in view of both firms' belief in free enterprise. Both sides were well aware that their common interests were better served by a united front. At a personal level Hoskins and Delprat had complementary as well as disparate qualities and, before the commission, these probably combined to their mutual advantage. Hoskins's abrasiveness and his established position in the New South Wales business world made him a perfect foil for the urbane and internationally oriented Delprat, particularly as the latter must have been well aware of the xenophobia never far below the surface in Australia. Before the commission Delprat gave a deferential support to Hoskins's seniority and experience, although he reported to BHP that in his evidence Hoskins 'made so many contradictory statements, and also statements which on the face of them were exaggerations, that his evidence did not seem to carry much weight with the Commission'.[34]

Hoskins's meeting with the commission was turbulent. The controversial chief commissioner, A. B. Piddington, subjected him to a rigid cross-examination not only on the evidence of the 1911 New South Wales Royal Commission, but also on the part which he had played in lobbying for the *Manufactures Encouragement Act* in 1908. Particular focus was given to the influence which Hoskins might have exerted to secure the inclusion of a clause nullifying one in the New South Wales government's contract that he had inherited from Sandford. Piddington based this investigation on the importance of 'the question of past fulfilment of important government contracts for State purposes' claiming that he had to be satisfied that Hoskins was not seeking the imposition of duties because these were less subject to government supervision.

C. H. Hoskins and A. B. Piddington represented two very different facets of late nineteenth-century Australian society. Commissioner Piddington was a prominent figure in the literary and intellectual life of his day.[35] When he died in 1945, aged eighty-three, his obituary in the *Australian Law Journal* mourned the passing of 'one of the few remaining links with mid-Victorian academic, legal (and let us add with happy recollection, the bohemian) life of Sydney'. Piddington was well travelled; he was an accomplished linguist in Spanish, Italian, French and German. He was, according to the *Daily Telegraph* in 1898, 'the possessor of a clear incisive and persuasive eloquence, and of an analytical lucidity of argument'.[36] Piddington, who took the gold medal in classics in his year at Sydney University, was noted for his intellectual brilliance, keen wit and unfailingly liberal outlook. His social conscience was reflected in 'his zeal for fair economic treatment of the worker'; like H. B. Higgins, with whom he had much in common, he came from a Methodist and Low Church Anglican background. In 1931 he resigned from the presidency of the New South Wales Industrial Commission, considering that, in dismissing the Labor Premier, J. T. Lang, the Governor, Sir Philip Game, had committed an 'unconstitutional act'.

While hardly a fanatic, Piddington, as a true Victorian liberal, distrusted all structures of which the sole purpose appeared to be money-making. He, like his friend Higgins, always insisted that the primary role of all structures was to fulfil social responsibility, encapsulated in expressions like 'fairness', 'philanthropy' and 'humanitarianism'; wealth itself could be created through the free-trade mechanism. Such individuals refused to believe, until they were later persuaded by Keynes, that the long-evolving nexus between the firm and macroeconomic policy could handle identical goals more effectively. They would have been sad, as Hoskins would have been glad, to have foreseen fewer men educated in classics in the coming *dramatis personae* in politics and administration.

Tempting as it might be to pass over the Piddington–Hoskins episode as a psychological curiosity, it does raise a point of wider significance to the history of a technical industry. The episode polarised influences that were felt daily in industries' relationships with politicians, bureaucrats and other elites; it was one of those revealing occasions when unspoken assumptions became the basis of a public scrap. A precursor of what C. P. Snow's generation was to identify as the problem of the two cultures, the Hoskins–Piddington encounter bore testimony to the existence of an elite opposition to entrepreneurs, engineers, technologists and mechanics in general. Such an opposition, anthropologically familiar in most societies, was particularly insidious in societies like Australia, in possession of or emulating the intellectual traditions current within the nineteenth-century English intelligentsia.

Among the industrial leaders, England was alone in upholding the pre-eminence of a classical and literary education over a pure or applied scientific one. This partly lay in the continuing ecclesiastical associations of Oxford and Cambridge universities, which dominated the English educational system. Apart from the production of clerics, their principal concern was to educate the sons of the nobility and gentry, future politicians and imperial administrators. For all of these a classical education was considered the most suitable. England, therefore, had no equivalent of MIT and an applied scientific education was considered to be inferior, although there were places where it could be obtained, such as Firth College in Sheffield. Even pure science, apart from mathematics which was linked with logic, only enjoyed a limited appreciation. There was no sympathetic infrastructure of laymen comparable to those existing in the United States and Germany, and science as mental training was still thought inappropriate for a gentleman. Thus public administration in the new industrial age typically fell to an administrative elite of classics experts, who used their not inconsiderable abilities to seek a moral justification for exercising authority in fields in which they were untrained.

At least some Australians, including Piddington, had fallen under such influences. Their posturings were irrelevant to people like Delprat who, together with the Americans, Germans and even Scots, shared a broader-based academic lineage which made the 'two cultures' problem less acute. However, self-taught Englishmen like Hoskins tended to feel the attacks of men like Piddington as slurs upon their self-worth, while resenting their ability to destroy what they were trying to create. How Hoskins stood up to the test was a measure of the man.

Chief Commissioner Piddington succeeded in irritating Hoskins to the extent that he finally walked out, announcing that 'I have more profitable business to do . . . I do not want to hear this balderdash'. The other two commissioners, Swinburne and Lockyer, subsequently recorded strong objections to Piddington's attitude in their majority report, published two years later in 1916. Swinburne, after carefully rehearsing the history of the bonus, the Royal Commission and its aftermath, emphasised that all of this was now past history remarking:

> with regard to the evidence submitted during the whole of the inquiry it shows that both Mr Sandford and Messrs Hoskins have had one of the

stiffest up-hill fights that any men could have in endeavouring to establish this iron industry at Lithgow . . . and as far as I am concerned, the examination into these matters had nothing to do with this inquiry, and will not affect me in any decision.

Commissioner Lockyer agreed with Swinburne, adding 'nor have I any sympathy whatever, with the very adverse comments which the chairman has passed on Mr Hoskins'.[37]

Hoskins, aware of the potentially catastrophic consequence of antagonising the commissioners, returned to Lithgow and ordered the preparation of a publicity statement which, with the minimum of words and a lavish use of photographs, would show off the industry, its problems and, hopefully, counteract any unfavourable impression that he might have given to the commission. The result was an exceedingly interesting book with over sixty pages of photographs, carefully chosen to illustrate various aspects of the industry, interspersed with brief historical, explanatory or statistical information. It is a fascinating document, capturing the state of the Lithgow iron and steel industry at the moment BHP was opening its Newcastle works. In the introduction, dated 20 April 1915, Hoskins wrote: 'this Book has been compiled with the objects of—Firstly: Shewing the development of the Iron Industry at Lithgow, and Secondly: To impress upon the Federal Parliament the necessity of encouraging and maintaining the industry by the help of a Customs Duty'.[38]

It was a clever device. Although the commission's overall report was completed on 22 April 1915 and ordered to be printed within the week, the separate reports on the various industries were prepared later. In the event, the three commissioners could not agree on a common finding for the iron and steel industry and the *Iron and Steel Tariff Investigation* findings were contained in majority and minority reports. These were not handed down until 3 August 1916, while directions for their printing were delayed until 28 September. Hoskins's statement was widely available for about a year before the commision's report was prepared.

There can be little doubt that any commission brought out the worst side of Charles Hoskins. His approach to the commissioners was, not without cause, truculent, aggressive and defensive. Seldom a diplomat, and probably understanding optimal solutions as much as his workers understood Karl Marx, Hoskins nevertheless knew people and was in turn recognisable to them as an honourable example of a passing generation of industrialists. There is no doubt that Hoskins's powers of endurance commanded respect: between 1911 and 1914 he had faced the physical danger and the destruction of the Lithgow riots, the ominous implications of the Royal Commission into the New South Wales iron and steel industry, and the death of two of his daughters, aged nineteen and twenty respectively.

The commissioners were united in their conclusion that support of some kind was essential for the development of the industry. However, they disagreed so profoundly over the form this support should take that they presented the Hughes government with two separate reports. The majority report of commissioners Lockyer and Swinburne advocated tariffs; the minority report of the chief commissioner, Piddington, recommended bonuses. The commission had met and reported during wartime. This precluded any immediate action being taken and the problem was shelved until the pressing economic difficulties of the postwar era necessitated the passing of the *Customs Tariff Act* (previously the Industries Preservation Bill) in 1921. The 1915 Inter-State Tariffs Investigation Commission did, however, indicate an important development in the dialogue between industry and the paternalistic government. The debate had now definitely moved from the question free-trade or nationalisation to protection as a many-faceted tool within the framework of a mixed economy.

The commission considered that where tariff assistance was required it should, first, be sufficient to 'enable the Australian manufacturer, under an efficient system of production, and with modern business methods, to compete with outside competitors'. Secondly, tariffs should give particular weight to those industries that would 'materially strengthen national resources' but are, by 'a frank disclosure (confidentially made)', proved to be in need of tariff assistance. In addition, special consideration was to be given to such industries as would increase 'employment for labour under satisfactory conditions, and at fair and reasonable rates of remuneration' without being 'injurious to the health of employees'. The commissioners agreed that, despite the remarkable progress of manufacturing industries during the years 1908 to 1913, nevertheless:

> we cannot well anticipate that, in the open markets of the world, Australia may successfully compete with the manufactured products of those countries whose larger populations enable them to manufacture in quantities much larger, and consequently at a cost much less than is possible here under our present conditions.

The idea was accepted that tariffs could be imposed to compensate for high wages in undercapitalised and underdeveloped industries. At the same time they commented on cost increases for which they considered the 'extremely likely' cause 'a lessening of work done by the average employee' even when wages had been increased and hours reduced. They were aware that any comment of this nature would be countered by the argument that any falling off in output in recent years simply represented a check on the unfair demands made upon the workers in other countries. On this opinion the commissioners felt unable to comment. They did, however, remark on the low wages of women, less than half those of men. They found that wages were depressed in many industries, suggesting 'the necessity for a wiser discrimination, so that those industries employing labour at fair and reasonable rates of remuneration should receive preference when the tariff is under consideration'.

At the same time the commissioners declared that manufacturers were entitled to 'a fair and reasonable' profit in return for embarking on the risks of industry. They considered that 'of vital importance is the urgent necessity for a greater appreciation of the value of industrial efficiency'. They noted that, while a local prejudice against Australian goods still existed, it was diminishing. Careful discrimination was necessary 'when the finished article of one industry is the necessary raw material for another' so that 'suitable tariff assistance under such circumstances should be extended to that industry which promises the greater success, as being likely to employ the greater proportion of skilled and other desirable labour'. Similarly local production of raw materials could be encouraged by a bounty. This would not have the same flow-on costs as import duties. Tariff assistance was to be viewed in the light of 'the total of industrial development'.

In passing, the commission highlighted another important issue, the problem of high interstate freight charges. Astonishingly, it was cheaper to ship some goods from Europe than between Australian ports. On this important and intractable issue they made no recommendation, simply commenting that:

> many witnesses complained of what they deemed to be the excessive freights charged by the inter-state shipping companies, which, between certain ports in Australia, were frequently in excess of the freights to Australia from oversea countries. The high rates of wages and other labour conditions have naturally enhanced the working costs of the local shipping trade in common with other Australian enterprises.

The commissioners reported that, with the time at their disposal, they were unable to investigate and to decide on the merits of these claims but they considered that the charges should be 'fair and reasonable having due regard to the cost of management, upkeep and a reasonable profit to the shareholders'.[39] However, while the war continued it provided a natural protection which accelerated the development of Australian industry.

It was at this propitious time that the Newcastle steelworks came into production. Australian industry matured under the demands of World War I. Isolation made self-reliance essential and, in consequence, long-established patterns of trade were irrevocably altered. Restricted shipping facilities affected imports which became either extremely limited or non-existent. The total tonnage of overseas shipping entered and cleared from Australian ports was 10 500 000 in 1913. By the end of the war it had fallen to 5 000 000 tons. Delprat's conviction that there was room for both BHP and Hoskins was fully justified as, protected from European interference by the demands of war, the iron and steel works at both Lithgow and Newcastle flourished and rapidly expanded. Ancillary industries developed in an attempt to supply goods formerly imported, as well as to contribute to demands generated by the war.[40]

In fact, in the years immediately before the war, the federal government, increasingly conscious of the nation's vulnerability, had established a number of defence-related industries. One of these was the small arms factory established at Lithgow in 1912. In June 1914 it employed 1070 workers. By 1916 it employed between 2500 and 3000 and had a turnover of approximately £1 000 000.[41] Although the enterprise was modest and its products fairly simple: rifles, bayonets, scabbards, spare parts and similar items, its expansion was symptomatic of what was happening in various areas throughout industry.

# 10

# MANAGEMENT AND LABOUR

A T THE OPENING OF THE PLANT in 1915 Baker had prophesied that 'organisation and this combination of modern equipment and skilled management spelt success and prosperity for the industry'.[1] The size of the Newcastle works and the speed and conditions under which they developed inevitably created organisational stresses. In addition, there were the demands of the supporting operations associated with the company's diversification into iron and steel. These included the new mining operations in South Australia and Tasmania, the transport infrastructure and the continuing operation of the quite different, but crucial, mining activities at Broken Hill. This resulted in a managerial overload. Delprat was always very conscious of this possibility and he had on a number of occasions alerted the Board to potential managerial problems which, in fact, only became clearly manifest in the unsettled period after the end of the war. Delprat's fear was common to the industrial managers of the period.

In 1899, when Delprat became general manager of BHP, his role was typical of an industrialising society; Pollard, in *The Genesis of Modern Management* , sums it up as follows: 'the manager is a dominant individual who extends his personal control over all phases of the business. There is no chartered plan of organisation, no formalised procedures for selection and development of managerial personnel, no publicised system of wage and salary classifications'.[2] At the time of Delprat's appointment the company's interests were restricted to the Big Mine at Broken Hill and the Port Pirie smelters. When Delprat resigned twenty-two years later, BHP had interests not only at Broken Hill and Port Pirie, but also iron mines at Iron Knob, mechanised shipping facilities at Whyalla, limestone quarries in Tasmania, a number of other resources ancillary to the iron and steel works, such as magnesite, fluorspar and dolomite, and there was the nucleus of a company fleet. Company coal-mines were under consideration, although Delprat, perhaps influenced by what he saw in England, was in two minds about the company owning coal-mines.[3] In addition he had used his influence to persuade the company to provide some basic housing and amenities at Iron Knob and Whyalla, while some provision had been made for the American workers at Newcastle. Companies were becoming increasingly aware that they had a social responsibility for the welfare of their workers,[4] but anything approaching a company town lay in the future.

Always interested in scientific education, Delprat had plans for training apprentices at the Newcastle steelworks and utilising the library which was being created there.[5] He was one of the foundation members of the Executive Committee of the Institute of Science and Industry. The institute was the antecedent of the Commonwealth Scientific and Industrial Research Organisation. However, Prime Minister Hughes was somewhat suspicious of scientists and the Council for Scientific and Industrial Research (CSIR) was not established on a permanent basis until 1926. It did not evolve into CSIRO until 1949—after World War II. In January 1920 Delprat wrote a short article for the journal *Science and Industry*, expressing his disappointment that the institute had not yet been made permanent, warning that:

> Australian Industry wants all the assistance that science can give to it. Australia has got a splendid chance but cannot afford to ignore the example set by other countries. The war awakened Great Britain to the value of science. America realised it before the war, but in many directions, now that peace has been restored, that country is increasing her subsidy to science.[6]

Under Delprat, BHP had an unusual number of managerial staff with academic qualifications as well as practical experience. Among these were Delprat himself, Horwood (the manager at Broken Hill), Baker (the manager at the Newcastle steelworks) and Leslie Bradford. As the company diversified, Delprat became increasingly concerned about its managerial structure and repeatedly reminded the Board of the need to consider this problem. To use Drucker's famous analogy the company had outgrown its skin and required to be transmogrified into a different species, an animal with a skeleton.[7] The internal difficulties of such a transformation were magnified by the circumstances of the immediate post-war era. Furthermore, the very strength of the managerial team which Delprat had gathered around him, and in many cases the length of their service to the company, provided its own set of problems.

The development of large-scale organisations in the late nineteenth century, their labour problems and the role of government in relation to them, encouraged managers with contemplative as well as practical capacities to provide their work with a theoretical framework. In Britain, despite some interesting theories on labour relations, the practical emphasis on learning from experience continued to dominate.[8] Moreover, imperial administration absorbed and diverted a considerable amount of managerial talent. Thus it was from Europe and America, where Delprat and Baker had been trained, that important theories of management emerged.

In the late nineteenth and early twentieth century the employment of labour had been most intensive in mining and the iron and steel industries. Many of the contemporary theorists, therefore, came from the managers of these organisations. One of Delprat's many interests was reading French and one of the leading theorists was the French mine manager Henri Fayol, who in 1916 published in the *Bulletin de la Société de l'Industrie Minerale* an article entitled 'Administration Industrielle et Générale—Prévoyance, Organization, Commandement, Coordination et Contrôle'. In it he attempted to define, with Gallic precision, management and managerial activities. In America the theories of Frederick W. Taylor, who had worked in the Midvale and Bethlehem Steelworks, on Scientific Management had been the subject of a United States House of Representatives Special Committee in 1911. As has been noted, it was a *cause célèbre* about the time Delprat and Baker met. Taylor had stressed the mutual interdependence of management and workers. He queried why, in view of this interdependence, there was so much antagonism and inefficiency. Taylor stressed the need for a systematic study of work and management. He emphasised that all would benefit from high wages and low labour costs. In so doing, he laid himself open to the charge of 'mechanising labour'.

Almost certainly Delprat, Baker and possibly also Essington Lewis had read Andrew Carnegie's *Gospel of Wealth*. Carnegie held that economy and growth were achieved by reinvesting profits and the shrewd purchase of plants in difficulties, which had the potential to be made profitable. He believed in managing by strict accounting, and incentive.

To this end he encouraged rivalry, promotion from the ranks, and share and bonus schemes. The bonus scheme was later developed by Charles M. Schwab at Bethlehem Steel.

Both Delprat and Baker knew Schwab. On 11 April 1919 Delprat wrote to Dickenson, the company secretary, about his visit to the Bethlehem Steel Works and their bonus system:

> No officer in this company—from the very top—gets a salary of more than $12,000 (dollars) or about £2,500. The President [General Manager] gets this and all the others get less—BUT—every one of them gets a monthly bonus . . . calculated so that they can get several times the amount of their salary through the year . . . this system I had heard about before but it had never been so fully explained to me and I feel confident that if we wish to be successful we will have to adopt it also. I would like you to show this letter to the Board as I know it is against their well established policy. We cannot expect to get the best men from America—nor the best work out of the Australian—if we do not make them have a *personal financial interest* in their own results—and bring this home to them every month.

This was the background to the bonus incentive scheme developed at Newcastle. Shortly after the war a system of productivity bonuses was instituted and fixed rates were paid per ton for productivity above a certain level.[9]

Finally, we know from Delprat's diary and reports that he discussed managerial problems with Judge Elbert Gary. On 2 February 1920 Delprat sent another memorandum for the Board's consideration to the company secretary, F. M. Dickenson, with a covering letter saying that 'I cannot help feeling that it would be wise and advantageous to introduce some modifications in our own organisation and the perusal of the memorandum may suggest some of them'.[10]

Carnegie, Fayol, Taylor and Gary are only examples,[11] although leading ones, of the capitalist managerial counterblast to labour's Marxist class confrontation now being intrepreted by Lenin. Herbert Hoover and Thomas J. Masaryk represented other American and European facets of the same phenomenon. Australia produced Elton Mayo (1880–1949) the founder of the human relations movement and an important figure in the development of industrial psychology. After quarrelling with the university authorities at the University of Queensland, Mayo went to Harvard to make his career in America. Mayo, like his almost exact contemporary Essington Lewis (1881–1961), was an old boy of

St Peter's School in Adelaide and Lewis, Gibson, and probably Bradford, almost certainly knew him from their early days in Adelaide.

An important feature of this interest in managerial analysis was the role of the state in a modern industrial society. Among those concerned with this aspect of the debate was the German industrialist-statesman Walther Rathenau.[12] Rathenau was convinced that society as a whole would benefit from the participation in government of those with a wide experience in business and that economic forces should govern relations between management and the work-force. He had been manager of the Elektrochemische Werke, a subsidiary of AEG; as a manager and a director of the board, he had been principally involved in the electro-technical industries and the construction of power stations in Germany and abroad. His publications were widely read and influential in the early decades of the century. Rathenau was the industrial man in a nationalist context. After the war he became foreign minister in the Weimar Republic. In this capacity, he had been negotiating with the Allies over the complex question of German reparations when, on 22 June 1921, he was assassinated by a right-wing group of anti-Semites who mistakenly considered him to be a socialist. His death was a prelude to the post-war collapse of the German economy.

In post-war Australia, the rich if confusing overseas ferment of managerial practice put strains on an innovative company such as BHP. To the pressures of rapid expansion and diversification was added a real, if unhostile, lack of managerial homogeneity, for Delprat, Baker and the BHP Board represented European, American and British concepts in an Australian context. The plant was American both in design and equipment and, in accordance with Baker's wishes, it was managed along American lines. Delprat, open-minded but possibly concerned about local conservatism, agreed to see how this worked, although it was not what he was used to. Baker described his system as follows:

> Each department of the works was to be in charge of a specialist in that particular kind of work.
>
> An office was to be provided in each department so that the superintendent would always be near his work.
>
> The works were to be divided into the following main departments: Coke ovens, blast furnaces and ore docks, open hearth steel furnaces, big rolling mills, mechanical department, chemical laboratory, physical laboratory.
>
> Mechanical repairs would be in charge of skilled mechanics in each department, while the repair shops, water supply, and all repairs outside

of the departments would be in charge of a master mechanic who would have general oversight over the leading mechanics in the departments.

'The necessity for skilled managers and superintendents for the various furnaces, mills etc. was paramount', wrote Baker ' . . . so from overseas were brought men of skill and experience to guide the industry through its infancy'.[13] These men were selected by Baker and included, as superintendent of the blast furnaces, H. F. Noyes, a graduate of MIT; he was supported by three blowers, David Baker Jr, Royce A. Field and a Mr Aubel, each of whom took charge of one of the three eight-hour shifts, ensuring that expert assistance was always at hand. The open-hearth superintendent came from the Lackawanna Steel Co. of Buffalo, New York, and the head roller at the blooming mill was Warren A. Saul, from the Dominion Iron and Steel Company. The roll designer, William Jones, came from either the Illinois or the Carnegie Steel Company; Baker exercised particular care over this appointment for 'very little variation is permitted in the dimensions of rolled bars, especially rails, and failure to produce a rolled product true to dimensions means a heavy loss to the Company'. These men were enticed to Australia by large salaries and the company's willingness to pay their Commonwealth income tax.[14]

The heads of the various departments met each week to discuss and co-ordinate the overall activities of the works. In May 1918 Delprat suggested that these meetings should take place in the evenings and that those attending should be compensated. Baker was to receive an additional £5 and the others £1 per meeting. Baker, however, did not consider that evening meetings would be efficacious.[15] He guarded his authority jealously and, as the manager of the steelworks, his opinion on its method of operation was paramount.

Baker's extensive knowledge of and reputation in the industry enabled him, with almost unfailing accuracy, to find and persuade the right people to come to the new works and Delprat invariably supported his recommendations. Given the circumstances, it was inevitable that the management should be very largely American. In consequence, many of the managers had very little knowledge of Australian workers and attitudes to labour. Psychologically, the Americans and the Australians regarded labour from the opposite ends of the democratic spectrum. At Newcastle, this created a dichotomy which, particularly in labour relations, continued long after the original management and labour had retired from the works. Basically, the Americans regarded the advancement of society as the product of individual effort that ought to be not only handsomely rewarded but also emulated; the Australians, seeking collective security, banded together to denigrate the image of the 'tall poppy'.

In advising the company to transfer its energies from mining to manufacturing, Delprat was well aware of the magnitude and complexity of the potential labour problems. The iron and steel industry required a wide variety of skilled labour, while concentrating unskilled labour in unusually large numbers. The problems at Broken Hill were still prominent in the directors' minds. Similar conflicts would have to be continually guarded against at Newcastle. Nevertheless, in 1912, Delprat had pointed out to the Board that labour unrest was not a national but an international phenomenon. Viewing it in that light, he concluded in 1912:

> Labour conditions are certainly not ideal; and if other countries enjoyed a perfect calm and contentment, it might be unwise to embark on any industry in Australia. This, however is not the case. All steel producing countries have their labour troubles, and I would be much mistaken if these troubles do not assume a very acute form in England and Europe generally at no distant date.[16]

Workers returning to Newcastle from the steelworks, 1915

This was already true of the United States where the industry had been disturbed by the strikes at Homestead in 1892, US Steel in 1901 and 1909, and Bethlehem in 1910.

In the first quarter of the twentieth century, labour problems were universal. Although most disputes had local elements, underlying all of them were the issues created by mass industrialisation and the increasing political influence of the mass electorate expressed through the ballot box. Work in steelworks was heavy and demanding, and conditions were often unpleasant and dangerous. Moreover, it was an integrated industry and disputes in one section automatically flowed through to another. Even a small stoppage could have a disproportionate impact upon the works as a whole. The industry could also be disrupted by external disputes in related industries, such as shipping or coal-mining; for instance, the 1917 railway strike closed the Lithgow works for eleven weeks.

When war broke out in 1914 the Australian labour movement was bitterly divided. The Industrial Workers of the World sympathisers on the radical left viewed the war as a capitalist plot for which the workers would suffer. Initially, despite its vocal expression, this attitude did not attract much sympathy. In the early years of the war many unionists enlisted. (BHP paid the salary differential between the wartime and civilian remuneration of its employees in the armed forces.) But as casualties mounted and war-weariness set in, radical opinions became more attractive.

At this point another divisive element appeared in the shape of the the leading Roman Catholic ecclesiastic, the Irish-born Archbishop Mannix of Melbourne. Catholic influence was strong in the ALP and many of the Catholic clergy had been trained in Ireland. Archbishop Mannix had previously been in charge of the famous Irish seminary at Maynooth, whose influence was felt not only among Australian clergy but throughout the world. In 1916 two events heightened the tension within the Australian Labor movement: the Easter rebellion in Ireland, and the conscription crisis in October. This split the ALP.

Early in 1916 the Federated Ironworkers' Association (FIA) Council had only voted for an anti-conscription resolution by eleven votes to ten. The even refused to discuss the case of Tom Barker, a gaoled IWW journalist. However, as the war continued, their opinions hardened. Marxist unionists tended to think in terms of two great opposing forces, capital and labour. They translated the war into men versus money. This simplistic view led to statements like that of the FIA Adelaide secretary,

Martin Collaton, who declared, in 1916, that 'if they want to conscript flesh and blood, let them conscript wealth first'. The Lithgow branch removed its president for supporting conscription and emphatic protests were launched against Prime Minister Hughes.[17] The success of the Russian Revolution in 1917 further emphasised the concept of an international class struggle. The idea of class struggle remained a dominant element in labour relations for most of the twentieth century. It was understandably strong during the inter-war depression, and aspects of it were seen even during World War II. It only lost its virulence in the prosperity which followed World War II and in the diaspora which brought many to Australia with personal experience of communism and its practical implications for the worker.

Government and employers were convinced that the Industrial Workers of the World influenced the 1917 general strike.[18] Certainly its leadership was clearly visible in the syndicalist movement for 'One Big Union'. In November 1918, immediately after the war, Delprat was warned by the company's industrial relations department that:

> the labour position as to the workers at the Steel Works and other industries in Newcastle in particular will become very unsettled in the near future. That being so employers especially those in the new industries, should be prepared to meet any emergency as to the efforts of those who are trying to foster the One Big Union Movement on employers and their employees.[19]

In view of this projection the company decided to surreptitiously encourage its workers to become members of the single industry union that it was trying to foster. Foremen were verbally instructed to, as far as possible, employ workers who were not subject to the rules and decisions of unions whose members were employed in operations outside of the iron and steel industry. Foremen who did not comply with these instructions were to be dismissed. Finally the company was advised to immediately contact satellite industries, such as the Austral Nail Co. Ltd, Lysaght's Ltd and the Commonwealth Steel Products Co. Ltd 'with the object of placing before them the advisability of encouraging a Union of Workers whose policy is to keep apart from the One Big Union Movement and to discountenance strikes'.

A sharp watch was to be kept for known agitators, such as John Storey, who as president of the Federated Engine Drivers and Firemen's Association, had taken a prominent part in the September 1916 strike, and Hector Sutherland, who had declared that he would revenge himself against BHP for not employing him or his brother. Enclosing this information, Delprat wrote to warn Baker that employer solidarity was not to be relied on, commenting that:

> In connection with this matter however, I think we will require to be exceedingly careful in any dealings we may have with any other Companies, as from my past experience at Broken Hill I often found that other Companies sometimes overlooked matters of a confidential nature such as this, and introduced them to the very people for whom they were not meant, in order to curry favour.[20]

Although the Industrial Workers of the World was banned in 1918, the 1919 conference of the New South Wales Labor Party was dominated by the struggle between the One Big Union, with its international overtones, and the Australian Workers' Union, the indigenous equivalent. Both adhered to the idea of collective ownership of the means of production, distribution and exchange, while seeking to promote the idea of one big union for Australian workers. The Australian Workers' Union, with a membership of approximately 100 000, was strongly entrenched throughout Australia: twenty-five unions were amalgamated to it. On the other hand, many craft unions, tending to see both unions as threats to their autonomy, stood aloof. At the conference a proposal for support of the OBU was defeated by fifteen votes, 127 to 112.[21]

After the defeat of the One Big Union, the Marxist left split into a number of small antipathetical groups. Some of these later coalesced, in 1920, to found the Communist Party of Australia, which, through the Militant Minority Movement formed in 1924, sought to infiltrate the union movement in the inter-war years. Between 1916 and 1920 the leadership of the FIA in Queensland, New South Wales and South Australia changed. Some of the new leaders, inclining to the Industrial Workers of the World, held syndicalist views. In 1921 two founder members of the Communist Party of Australia, Handcock and Denford—from Sydney branches of the FIA—were prominent members of the Third Communist International. Denford, however, resigned from the Communist Party when, in 1924, the ALP decided to expel all communists.[22]

Most of the unskilled and semi-skilled ironworkers belonged to the Federated Ironworkers' Association. By 1912 unionists among the unskilled and semi-skilled workers at the Eskbank works had been officially absorbed into it. Nevertheless, their very strong local identity remained; in the 1920s the Lithgow branch threatened secession. The fierce independence of many local branches, for example the Balmain branch in

Sydney, frequently made difficulties for the union's central administration, for the FIA covered a large number of metalworkers apart from those involved in the primary production of iron and steel. This automatically created a major problem as the physical conditions and economic circumstances under which its members worked varied considerably from employer to employer. In addition, people doing similar jobs could belong to different unions. This resulted in inter-union competition for membership. Eventually the FIA and the Australian Workers' Union both competed for membership in the iron- and steelworks.

The 1911–12 strike had highlighted the Industrial Workers of the World views held by certain labour leaders at Lithgow. In joining the FIA these men found that the spitting black cat and wooden shoes, the insignia of the IWW, were not unfamiliar to many of their new brethren.[23] Naturally these associations did not commend the FIA to the American management of the new steelworks or to the BHP Board, especially in the aftermath of the long-remembered 1909 strike at Broken Hill. The divisiveness of that long-and bitter strike lived on in the memory of not one but both protagonists. It left an inheritance of bitterness and suspicion that flowed through to future negotiations.

The FIA was a relatively new union and correspondingly unsophisticated. It was not a craft union and it certainly felt weak and vulnerable in face of the power and reputation of BHP. This probably encouraged the more extreme rhetoric of its leaders. The FIA was anxious to gain strength from amalgamation. It had not been very successful in making its claims effective. But it was only after its overtures to the Australian Workers' Union were rebuffed,[24] that the FIA turned to the One Big Union movement. The OBU's involvement in the 1917 strike was considered by many to be unpatriotic. It convinced employers of the need to control the unions or to expect future industrial strife. At the same time the unions were convinced that the employers were using the war to cripple, if not destroy, them.

Craft unions were considered to be divisive of the labour movement and, as such, they were deemed heretical by Marxist sympathisers. Nevertheless, for skilled workers and tradesmen there was the traditional multiplicity of craft unions. Thus the management of a large enterprise was automatically involved with the individual and competing demands of a wide variety of separate unions. In 1914 the problem of how and to what extent individual unions could or should be subsumed into a corporate labour movement was a major problem in the union movement. It remained unresolved. Furthermore, advancing technology had produced new conditions of employment. David Baker commented that 'the establishment of the iron and steel industry in Newcastle introduced a large number of skilled positions not covered by previous awards in that district. In many respects the work was different from that which obtained at the Hoskins Iron and Steel Works at Lithgow'.[25]

BHP management was very conscious of the power of the unions to strangle the new industry at birth. There was a mutual wariness between the company and the individual unions, each of which had a different style. The deep rifts in the Australian labour movement added a further complication. More positively, all the unions regarded the new works as a panacea for the unemployment problem in the Hunter region, where there was, despite the war, a surplus of labour. This reinforced labour caution as many workers were unwilling to endanger their jobs. BHP itself increasingly favoured either no unionism or an American-style company union. The latter would probably have been more responsive to the company's view of the state of the industry and it would certainly have simplified negotiation.

Through all of this long-running ferment, the core of the labour movement remained socialist, but not communist, and continued to be more concerned with employment, pay and conditions than ideology. Only a few of the union leaders were either communists or syndicalists. Fear encouraged both employers and unions to retain their entrenched positions throughout the economically difficult inter-war years. Some indication of FIA support for the One Big Union and the areas from which it came can be gauged from the table.

**FIA Referendum For and Against Joining the OBU—1919[26]**

|  | Actual Votes |  | Majority |  |  |
| --- | --- | --- | --- | --- | --- |
|  | For | Against | For | Against | Informal |
| Newcastle | 226 | 174 | 52 |  |  |
| Sydney | 907 | 379 | 528 |  | 49 |
| Balmain | 305 | 429 |  | 124 |  |
| South Australia | 184 | 95 | 89 |  | 37 |
| Queensland | 61 | 25 | 36 |  | 2 |
| Victoria | 242 | 237 | 5 |  | 5 |
| Castlemaine | 6 | 87 |  | 81 |  |
| **TOTALS** | **1931** | **1426** | **710** | **205** | **93** |

Source: FIA Council Report, 1920, in Merritt, A History of the Federated Ironworkers' Association of Australia.

The Newcastle works were established during the years when confrontation between capital and labour was at its most acute in Australia. In war-torn Europe patriotism masked this underlying conflict but in the United States President Wilson's administration had given new hope to the American Federation of Labour, to the great concern of the American steelmasters.

Baker shared the views of his American colleagues. At Newcastle, American engineers and technicians had been brought in to install and operate the new plant. They worked alongside local men and those transferred from Broken Hill. Although Australian workers were gradually trained to replace the overseas experts, this took a number of years and the plant was always to bear the imprimatur of its American origins. While well-versed in, and sympathetic to, the American view, Delprat knew that unions were a fact of industrial life in Australia. He warned Baker, who was inclined to think that BHP should also emulate American policies in this area, that

> the rates of wages and conditions of employment were fixed in Australia by the courts through awards which should be adhered to exactly; otherwise the Company would be under heavy penalty. He also stated that the [BHP] Board reserved to itself the right to depart from the awards; that is to pay more than the awards required.

Realising Baker's unfamiliarity with the system, Delprat worked to establish conflict resolution on local principles. He created a labour department in the hope that it would avert disputes, particularly strikes of the Broken Hill pattern. H. A. Mitchell, a former secretary of the Federated Engine Drivers and Firemen's Association at Broken Hill, was appointed labour officer. The department was soon so busy that he was allocated Arthur Burgess, who eventually succeeded him, as an assistant.

The first Newcastle Steelworks Award was handed down by the New South Wales government-appointed Steelworks Board in October 1915. This award attempted to establish margins for the new skills created by the works. As the plant was modern, the Board considered that the work was less arduous than at Lithgow and consequently the rates were lower. Not surprisingly, this caused universal dissatisfaction. In addition Mr Justice Edmunds had reluctantly reduced the basic wage by three shillings because of the economic evidence put forward by BHP.[27] Discontent was usually, but not always, checked by the availability of alternative labour. Baker considered that underlying discontent contributed to the coke workers' walk-out on 23 June 1916 when 'in spite of efforts by the

Arbitration Court, all coke workers 'walked off the job . . . not waiting to finish the shift'. Delprat reported that the day before 'a deputation of coke workers had informed him 'that they considered 22 ovens enough for a day's work', thereby attempting to establish a darg, or work quota, as was customary in the coal industry where many of them had previously been employed. Delprat replied that the furnace was operating badly for want of coke. 'This, they said, did not concern them.'

In these circumstances the general manager's decision to reline the blast furnace was, perhaps understandably, suspected by the men of being a lock-out. Nevertheless, the blast furnace was operating poorly and the Semet–Solvay coke ovens were never very satisfactory, despite numerous efforts to improve them. The shut-down of the blast furnace was used to try to overcome deficiencies by changing the system of handling coke. Inevitably this altered job specifications and Baker declared that 'we could not promise the men that they could have the same positions on resumption of work—hence the walkout'.[28] Then on 16 September at 4 p.m. the engine drivers and firemen's union went on strike 'claiming back pay before the award was issued'. This was a serious dispute as good internal rail communications were vital for the efficient operation of the steel works where hot, heavy and bulky loads were continually on the move from shop to shop.

The Arbitration Court, to whom both sides appealed, censured the union for striking, whereupon the latter decided that attack was the best defence. A striking worker always put his job at risk and, with this in mind, the engine drivers attempted to prevent 'victimisation'. In a secret ballot they voted 102 to 47 'not to submit to any men being excluded from the works'; Delprat had told them 'point blank' that 'undesirables would not be taken back'.[29] The men then declared that 'they were fighting for a principle'. Prime Minister Hughes was gravely concerned at the worsening labour relations at Newcastle, especially in view of the conscription crisis. He decided to intervene, although the matter was then before the industrial courts in New South Wales. Hughes contacted the chairman of BHP, H. G. Darling, offering to telegraph the union secretary. He asked Darling to telegraph the general manager of BHP, to see if a conference could be arranged in a spirit of 'give and take'.

Alarmed at the Prime Minister's action, and the ramifications of federal intervention, Delprat telegraphed the Board:

> no useful purpose will be served by taking this matter out of the hands of the Arbitration Court of NSW and putting it into the hands of Mr Justice

Higgins ... *This is a fight whether the men will control the works or the Company and not a question of grievances at all* [italics added]. The only point in dispute is whether we will or will not take back the ring leaders who tried to ruin our Open Hearth Furnaces by not allowing their men to tap molten steel ... I am very sorry that PM has taken action in the matter—this will tend to prolong strike.

Delprat was also fighting for a principle, and arguably a higher one than the workers, at least from a pragmatic viewpoint. Win or lose, the workers would be left with the dogma of class conflict unimpugned and there had never been any conclusive evidence that the Australian worker was committed to much more. On the other hand, a loss for Delprat was tantamount to an abrogation of management, a finality in itself and incompatible with his technocratic training. Just as the reforming Judge Gary would be prepared to draw the line at the workers' demand for a closed shop at US Steel in 1919–20, so Delprat judged it proper to go to the brink to exclude those agitators whom he perceived not as advocates but as wreckers. It was a topical question, on which a short time later the *Sozialdemokratische Partei Deutschlands*, the world's greatest Marxist party, would carve itself apart in the bloody street-battles of post-Armistice Berlin. In the cases of Gary and Delprat, the managers maintained ranks by shifting modes from conflict resolution to crisis management, a jargon neither knew personally even if each contributed substantially to its subsequent renown.

Supported by his Board, Delprat arranged to meet the union secretary who, after a few days' delay, came to the conference. Delprat reported to the Board that the union leader informed him that 'I have nothing to propose and nothing to give'. Delprat suggested to the Board that the number of those excluded be reduced from six to three, pointing out that one of the three excluded men was an Industrial Workers of the World supporter. This proposal was conveyed to the Prime Minister by Darling and McKay. However, the union secretary responded that the 'men will not resume unless all are reinstated' adding that 'not one [was] IWW'. The impasse was resolved by leaving the issue of reinstatement in the hands of Justice Edmunds.[30]

Eventually, on 11 October, the men decided to return and 'were taken on as required'. The blast furnace was blown in on 15 October and the new coke handling system came into operation. Then on 31 October 1916 the coal-miners in the area went on strike in support of an eight-hour bank-to-bank agreement, leaving the works with only 6000 tons in hand. Finally on 26 November the engineers, fitters and turners struck at midnight. An obviously exasperated Baker recollected that although

> the Roll Turners from the United States under contract violated their agreement . . . followed suit remaining out until January 10 1917.
>
> We showed these skilled workers that the plant could be operated without them . . . A good stock of turned rolls and the substantial character of the new machinery enabled the foremen and the staff workers to carry on without the fitters and turners.[31]

Inevitably the works were affected by the unrest of 1916 and 1917. Baker recorded that at this time 'there were many strikes',[32] an understatement in view of the fact that it has been calculated that nearly fifteen weeks' work was lost in the thirteen months from July 1916 to August 1917. Then, on 11 August 1917, Baker wrote in his diary that there was a 'strike at the works commencing afternoon and night shifts due to works being declared black'. In September 1917 the New South Wales Arbitration Court, at the request of BHP, deregistered the FIA and it was not re-registered until August 1918.[33]

Concerned about the consequence of sudden stoppages, BHP had a skeleton system of staff workers who could operate the plant in such an emergency. After the engine drivers' strike, Baker noted that 'in spite of this walkout of an important Union, the works operated nearly as usual by means of the staff workers'.[34] Naturally this arrangement was anathema to the unions, which felt that the company should trust their good sense not to do anything which would damage the livelihood of their members.

Significantly, there is evidence of a deliberate policy of minimising the seriousness of these early labour disputes. Delprat, possibly enjoying the rhetorical device of saying the unexpected, told the Millions Club at a luncheon held in his honour in 1920 that:

> You will be astonished to hear that our men really give us no trouble at all. They number among them a great many who take a pleasure in their work. We treat them as fairly as we can, and in spite of the fact that these are times of many strikes, we have really never had a strike at the works since commencing. Once or twice there were sympathetic strikes, but our men never had a dispute that could not be settled in the works. They have treated us exceedingly well, and I wish to give them this public testimony of my gratitude.[35]

On the other hand he may have viewed the Newcastle labour disputes in a global context.

## 10 MANAGEMENT AND LABOUR

Mill operators controlling the bloom mill at BHP Newcastle steelworks, 1920

In 1920 when the Prince of Wales visited the steelworks, Baker noted that 'among the invited guests were the leading Union secretaries of the district, who were especially invited by the General Manager. During the trip round the plant Mr Delprat arranged to present to H.R.H. each one of these secretaries in turn, which delighted them very much'.[36]

Ideally, men like Baker wished to view labour relations solely as a company problem, as indeed they would have liked to see capital, technology and management exclusively in terms of the firm. In part this was because many modern managers carried the genetic code of utopian socialism. This predisposed them to an Owenite ideal-community mentality that had become a fixation with an older generation, including Sandford and the Hoskins brothers. In fact, it was clear that, as with any business, the substantive tasks of establishing an iron and steel industry in Australia had been complicated by macro-economic twists and the impact of belief systems outside the firm. Although the subtleties of the relationships between micro-economics and macro-economics were not properly considered before Keynes, the ferment between the modern state and the modern firm was already plain. External shocks and pressures deprived the firm of its ideal exclusivity. Outside the factory gate there was the ballot box, and this dominated the politician's world.

In the case of BHP many of these complications were intensified because the reorganization of the firm occurred at the actual, rather than the chronological, watershed of nineteenth-century political economy. World War I brought to a head the changes prompted by the revolution in the scale and size of industrial enterprises in the previous generation. Despite expressions of public interest in government control of industry, the political system under which BHP entered the iron and steel business was not socialist, but neither was it free enterprise. In its obtuseness the system reflected most of the perceived virtues of a mature free-trade latitudinarianism. Many still believed in the civilising message of free trade even if immediate interests suggested otherwise. Such well-intentioned attitudes, aimed at the appeasement of perceived challenges to social equipoise, had the disadvantage of delaying the rehabilitation of government regulation and protection as morally acceptable links between business and government. This required such a radical rethinking of economic and political concepts that long public debates were guaranteed. These were seldom constructive to the tasks and goals of industry in Australia. In the meantime, the natural tensions between entrepreneurial industry, government and society were open to distortion rather than resolution and, except for minimal trade-offs, the process of achieving an optimally co-ordinated effort between macro- and micro-economic activities was delayed.

# 11

# A NEW WORLD

IN 1917 DELPRAT AND BAKER disagreed, apparently over the expansion of the works. The foundations of the second blast furnace and the ancillary battery of coke stoves were under construction as were the foundations for the 1000-ton mixer and four additional open-hearth furnaces. Baker considered that his control at the works should be paramount. He was very sensitive to anything that he considered an infringement of his authority and BHP was almost wholly dependent upon his expertise. In March 1917 J. McMeekan, who had been in charge of construction work, went on extended leave. Essington Lewis replaced him and, as construction supervisor, Lewis installed the Morgan rod mill. Baker wanted Lewis to remain at Newcastle in charge of the building programme. Delprat, who had other plans for Lewis, refused. But Lewis remained on friendly terms with Baker, who noted in his diary on 13 November 1917 that 'Messrs Darling and Lewis had an informal dinner with us—both most agreeable company'.[1] This is interesting because Darling and Lewis were subsequently known for their dislike of social occasions.

Essington Lewis belonged to a prominent South Australian pioneering family. He was educated at St Peter's College and the South Australian School of Mining which, at that time, probably provided the best practical training in mining and metallurgy in Australia. In 1905 he graduated with a Diploma in Mining, having done his practical work as an underground miner at Broken Hill. After completing his diploma,

Essington Lewis, 1881–1961, c. 1930, devoted his whole career, 1904–1961, to BHP, rising from a miner at Broken Hill to Managing Director in 1926 and Chairman in 1950. A man of great energy, he was a driving force in developing the steel industry at Newcastle and subsequently at Port Kembla and Whyalla.

Lewis returned to Broken Hill where he worked as a shift boss at the sulphuric acid plant and then in the zinc flotation plant where, if he did not already know him from Adelaide, he would have met and worked with Leslie Bradford.

The Lewis and Darling families were both prominent members of the South Australian establishment. Lewis knew H. G. Darling as a student and through his sporting activities. In fact he probably knew him from childhood as, although Darling went to the rival Adelaide school, Prince Alfred's, both of their fathers sat in the South Australian parliament. John Darling and John Lewis knew each other well. They had both been involved in the legislation for the Iron Knob tramway at the time when BHP acquired the Iron Knob leases.

Delprat recognised Lewis's abilities early and by 1912 he was acting manager at Port Pirie. When BHP decided to manufacture iron and steel, Delprat sent Lewis to supervise the South Australian side of the operation. Lewis prepared the quarries at Iron Knob and supervised the relaying of the rail track from Iron Knob to Hummock Hill (now known as Whyalla) to carry the heavier traffic from the ironstone quarries. At the same time he directed the expansion of the harbour for the ore ships. The jetty was lengthened to 2290 feet and equipped with the latest technology for the mechanised loading of iron ore. In addition Lewis was responsible for opening up the limestone quarries at Port Turton and Wardang Island. Lewis remained in charge of the Port Pirie works until Broken Hill Associated Smelters took over the plant in 1915, when he was moved briefly to Melbourne. Next he opened the limestone quarries in Tasmania and then went to Newcastle to assist McMeekan with the development of the plant. The munitions section of the plant was established as a separate company, BHP Munitions Co. Pty Ltd, and Lewis was responsible for its establishment and operation. In 1916 he attempted to enlist but was frustrated by Delprat's claiming that BHP required him in the national interest. By 1917 Essington Lewis's knowledge of the company was second only to that of Delprat himself. In 1918 he became technical secretary to Delprat and deputised for the general manager when he went overseas immediately after the war.[2]

In 1917, when he withdrew Lewis from the Newcastle steelworks, Delprat transferred his former secretary, F. M. Mitchell, from Broken Hill to Newcastle as chief accountant. Mitchell was later company secretary and possibly Lewis's most trusted subordinate. The son of a Ceylon tea-planter, Mitchell was intensely Australian, even to the point that it was said he would only have Australian-made goods in his house. Like Dickenson, Mitchell had been trained in William Knox's office in Melbourne. Knox was the first secretary to the company and the chief strategist behind the company's early development.[3] He was responsible for its initial organisation. Not the least of his services was the training both of his own successor, the Melbourne stockbroker Frank Dickenson, who played such an important part in the Commonwealth Bank loan in 1914, and Dickenson's successor, Frank Mitchell. On resigning from BHP, Knox entered Victorian politics and was subsequently the first federal MP for Kooyong. Like Jamieson, BHP's first manager, Knox afterwards sat on the BHP Board. Mitchell was probably transferred to Newcastle not only to strengthen the accounting side of the operation, which appears to have been weak, but also to increase the senior management at Newcastle and perhaps equally importantly to increase its Australian component. In fact there is some evidence that not only national, but even state, balance within the company was a potential source of friction. For instance, in December 1920 H. G. Darling was complaining that 'there is far too much Sydney management about the whole show with the result that Melbourne knows nothing'.[4]

Accounting was becoming more and more vital as unaccustomed inflation was already evident. Even if Australia was spared the horrors of the post-war inflation in some European countries, inflation among the developed nations was on a scale that was unknown to those born in the Victorian era. It was to make it extraordinarily difficult to estimate costs of even Australian raw materials. For instance, the price of coke was 6s 6d per ton in 1915 and 17s 9d by 1920. Overseas purchases, such as new plant, were even more difficult to estimate.

In November 1918 Delprat obtained the Board's approval for the appointment of a construction engineer to oversee the development of the Newcastle site. But such was the delicacy of his relationship with Baker that on 22 November, with the approval of the Board, Delprat wrote to Baker to assure him that:

> The Board does not for one moment doubt that our present staff, under your guidance, could carry out the construction work now contemplated, but this would not exactly suit their views. The Board feels that we are on the eve of a very severe struggle, now that the war is practically finished, and that the question of cost of production is the vital point which will determine our success or failure. For this reason the Board wants to have the full weight of your experience and knowledge concentrated on the operation of the present Plant, so as to reduce the cost of production to the lowest possible minimum. They fully realise that this is no easy matter, but feel confident that if your attention were not diverted in other directions, but given solely to this, this desirable end would be obtained. For this reason they wish to engage a highly skilled and experienced constructing engineer for two or three years—as may be necessary—to whom you could leave this construction work without your own time being encroached on. This man would of course, be under your supervision, but should be a sufficiently big man to do this work—with only such general directions as you might give him from time to time . . .
>
> The Board fully appreciates your wish to promote an 'esprit de corps' amongst the Staff, and realise that you have been very successful in bringing this about; also the desirability of proving to officers that promotion follows on good work done. This has been the Board's policy for many years; but, of course, this does not mean that officers should be promoted to positions for which they may not have the necessary qualifications . . . You might think the position over, and on my next visit we can discuss

it more fully. Perhaps by that time you may have thought of some Constructing Engineer in U.S.A., whom we might be able to engage for a period.

Shortly afterwards Alexander Gibson, Professor of Mechanical Engineering at the University of Queensland before the war, was appointed. Baker recorded in his 'Reminiscences' that Gibson was given 'full charge of construction, engaging his own assistants, and receiving his orders directly from the general manager, Mr Delprat'.[5]

Delprat revealed very little of his thoughts or his intentions. But there is strong circumstantial evidence in the way that Lewis was switched from one position to another that Delprat was training him for the succession, although he always seems to have felt that Lewis required a firm hand. For example before Delprat went overseas in 1919 he noted in his diary 'long talk with Lewis about his grievances—he asked for an increase in salary' and the following day he told the Board that 'he had been approached by an officer of the Company for an increase in salary and reported his views as to being unable to recommend the same, which course the Board approved'.[6] This may have been the famous occasion when Lewis went to confront Delprat with his grievances, only to be offered a chair and a cigar, and be told 'What is that idiom you have in English, Lewis? That fleas are good for a dog; they keep him from brooding over being a dog. Now put that in your pipe and smoke it'.[7] Lewis's day lay in the future and Delprat had good reasons for not emphasising it at that moment.

Apart from Lewis, Delprat was well aware of a group of men, who, now that the works were established and the war was over, felt that their contributions to the company should be recognised in various ways. Under Delprat there were two managers, Edward James Horwood at Broken Hill and David Baker at the Newcastle steelworks. Although the Big Mine no longer dominated Broken Hill, BHP's operations were still sizeable and its manager a formidable presence. Horwood had a first-class Master's degree in engineering and it has been said that 'no mine manager in Australia could surpass Horwood's blend of academic and practical qualifications'.[8] Born in 1864 he was eight years younger than Delprat, while Lewis was Horwood's junior by seventeen years. These sensitivities may explain why Lewis was not given the title of assistant general manager while Delprat was overseas in 1919.

As early as August 1916 Delprat had been anxious to establish an infrastructure of experienced deputies at the steelworks and he brought this subject periodically before the Board. In July 1918 he again 'gave the Board an outline of his ideas in this matter',[9] although he realised that nothing satisfactory could be done during the war. Both Delprat and Baker had been anxious to underpin the management and operation of the steelworks securely. Part of this arrangement had been the system of staff workers who could operate the works during an emergency. The other part was establishing the system of managerial 'understudies'. One of the problems of this type of scheme was that it required a degree of stability to operate, enabling people to be switched around. Too long a tenure as an understudy in one postion created undesirable side-effects, especially by inflating expectations to the succession. Although in 1915 BHP was by Australian standards large and complex, it was not large enough nor was its steelworks sufficiently long established to provide this degree of flexibility.

Immediately after the war, from March to November 1919, Delprat went on a fact-finding tour of Europe and America. This timing was unfortunate as the true nature of the post-war economy had not emerged. On 23 May he attended one of the famous American Iron and Steel Institute dinners presided over by Judge Gary. During this visit he talked over managerial problems with Gary who supplied him with the information on the organisation of US Steel, which he subsequently relayed in a memorandum to the BHP Board.[10]

In 1919 most of the managerial tension centred around Baker and who his understudy should be. Baker intended to retire within the next few years and whoever was appointed to that position would obviously be marked to succeed him. Delprat appears to have favoured Bradford, but Baker wanted H. F. Noyes, who was like himself a graduate of the Massachusetts Institute of Technology. In 1918 Noyes had been appointed 'understudy to the Manager in respect to the management of the works', but the question of ultimate succession had been postponed because the arrangement was concurrent with Bradford going to the United States to investigate the rival merits of the open-hearth and duplex steel-making processes, for adoption in the future expansion of the Newcastle works. In fact both appointments were confirmed at the same Board meeting. The duplex system was being investigated as a possible remedy to the ever-present problem created by the shortage of the scrap essential for open-hearth steel-making, but the system was relatively new and it was untried using Australian minerals.[11]

However, Delprat considered that the Noyes arrangement had not been satisfactory, giving as a reason that production at the blast furnace had declined. As a result Noyes was reinstated as head of the blast furnace department and on his return from the United States Bradford had resumed his position at head of the open-hearth department. This was the situation when Delprat left on his world tour. This delicate balance was soon upset. Delprat left in March 1919. In April two of the directors, Jamieson and Darling, visited the works. Baker prevailed upon them to approve the appointment of Noyes as assistant manager of the steelworks; Lewis, as *de facto* acting general manager, concurred.[12]

Delprat returned to Melbourne on 4 November 1919. Within three weeks the arrangement had been reversed. Delprat explained to the Board that

> it was of the utmost importance that the Blast Furnace should receive individual attention as the production of pig iron was the base of all operations . . . He had since his return, discussed the position with Mr Baker and he had agreed that Mr Noyes should return to the Blast Furnace. Apart from this some feeling had been created amongst other officers of the Company at Mr Noyes being put into a position over them . . . The necessity for Mr Baker having someone else under him as an understudy was referred to and Mr Delprat advised he had brought Mr Slee from Broken Hill to the Works because he would be most useful as an understudy in some direction, he had considerable personal ability. Kendall was also a good man in the Open Hearth Department, Henderson at Broken Hill was also good, of the Bradford type . . . In case of Mr Noyes leaving consequent upon his being returned to the Blast Furnace work he anticipated no difficulty in replacing him. Mr Brassert, the American Blast Furnace expert was quite equal to securing someone suitable.[13]

On 24 November Bradford's salary as steel superintendent was increased to £1600 and the increase was backdated to 1 November. The next day Bradford's salary was again discussed but the Board decided to defer the matter for future consideration.

On 17 November, less than a fortnight after his return, Delprat recommended to the Board 'that Mr Lewis be appointed Assistant General Manager and that he be given 12 months' leave in order to visit America and Europe in the interests of the Company. During Mr Lewis' absence he would propose bringing Mr F. M. Mitchell from Newcastle to Melbourne.' The Board considered this recommendation on 23 November. In view of the good work which he had done in Delprat's absence they agreed, and increased Lewis's annual salary to £2500, also giving him a bonus of £500. Mitchell, with his legal and accounting skills, was needed in Melbourne to look after the company's interests in the projected tariff legislation. Two days later, on 25 November, Delprat tendered his resignation to the Board, writing in his diary that:

> I considered I was getting too old for the position. The Board agreed but no time was fixed to allow them to make arrangements. Was asked if I considered Lewis would do for the position—said *Yes*—that he was rather young but would soon get over that. No further mention made of the matter—all apparently friendly—but felt for some reason or other they had lost the old confidence in me.

The issue was then shelved for the immediate future and six months later the Board raised Delprat's salary to £8600. Delprat did not emphasise words frequently or indiscriminately; he appears to have done so only when he felt strongly about an issue.[14]

Almost immediately after Lewis was appointed assistant general manager, Horwood resigned as manager at Broken Hill and moved to Melbourne. Delprat advised the Board to offer Horwood's position to Slee, and, if he refused, to Lindsay, the chief engineer, who had worked at both Broken Hill and Newcastle. Slee's acceptance was noted by the Board on 9 January 1920. Bradford and Noyes were still at Newcastle when Baker indicated that he wished to go on holiday. The Board decided to appoint F. M. Mitchell as assistant manager of the works during Baker's absence. This was probably intended as a neutral decision particularly as in addition to his secretarial-accounting background, Mitchell was rather older than the others.[15]

About this time Noyes's mother fell ill and he went to the United States on a mixture of recreation leave and business. Whether Noyes's intentions were known before or after Mitchell was appointed is uncertain. However, Noyes later joined Darling and Lewis in America where he declared his opposition to the adoption of the duplex process in steelmaking. This method had been supported by Bradford, and continued to be supported by Baker and Delprat. The duplex disagreement had an important role in precipitating changes in the company's management.

On 19 January 1920, almost immediately after Mitchell's appointment, Bradford wrote to Delprat expressing his dissatisfaction.

> On the occasion of your first visit to Newcastle subsequent to your absence from this country, I told you how I felt in connection with the appointment of Mr Noyes as Works Superintendent, and you gave me to understand that you were not in favour of this appointment, and that it

## 11 A NEW WORLD

was made without your knowledge or consent. You assured me that this would be altered, and that the Works did not require an Assistant Manager. At the same interview I let you know how I felt about matters here, and that I would not be content unless I had your assurance that my case would be considered when the time came for anyone to be appointed second in command on these works. Acting on the assumption that this last move has been made with your approval, I can only conclude that you have weighed the matter, and do not think that I am the right man in the organisation to fill such a position.

Bradford went on to outline his claims 'to the position of No. 2 on these Works'. A copy of this letter was sent to Lewis endorsed 'Dear Essie, for your information'.[16] Delprat laid Bradford's letter before the Board where it was inconclusively discussed on 6 and 7 February. On 16 February Delprat noted in his diary: 'had a talk with Bradford who went away quite satisfied—would have no grievance unless some one else was placed above him as Assistant Manager'. Delprat reported this to the Board on 20 February 1920.[17] But, despite Delprat's attempts at conciliation, Bradford remained offended.

Noyes had no sooner left Australia than Bradford resigned, asking to be relieved of his duties as soon as possible for he wished to sail for the United States at the end of April. As a flotation expert of international reputation, Bradford had been asked to appear as a witness in an action by the Mineral Separation Co. of America and he possibly felt, in view of his recent visit, that there was a market for his talents there. Baker was asked to suggest to him that he might take extended leave to pursue his business in America, but Bradford was adamant and the Board reluctantly accepted his resignation.[18] Once in the United States Bradford discovered the recent change in the economic climate: the firm that had bought the rights to some of his processes went out of business. Bradford then returned to Australia and established an electric foundry with E. J. Kendall. Part of the reason for the delay in Delprat's resignation was to allow Lewis, who had never left Australia, to go overseas to inspect the international steel world. In May 1920 Lewis, whose departure was delayed by the great strike at Broken Hill, left on a world tour, accompanied by H. G. Darling. By this time the senior management of the company was certainly overstrained. It was at this point that the duplexing controversy occurred.

Delprat's resignation has been attributed to the abortive attempt to introduce the duplexing system of steel-making into the Newcastle works and his clash with H. G. Darling and the latter's protégé, Essington Lewis. But the evidence indicates that this theory is probably incorrect or at best an oversimplification. In any case, the controversy was not so much about the process itself, and its defects, as about its profitability and suitability for the Newcastle steelworks. Nor was duplexing the only controversial issue surrounding Delprat's retirement. There was also the appointment of the American tin-plate expert Clement Poppleton and the projected tin-plate works. The role of the tin-plate plant and its ramifications was indeed more significant in the long-term development of the company. However, the real explanation was probably more in keeping with the character of the man: a combination of intensely private and universal considerations. Delprat's age, which he noted in the privacy of his diary, was central to the whole question of how the managerial problems consequent upon BHP's venture into iron and steel could be tackled. He was too much in touch with world affairs to believe that the war had settled anything. With the benefit of his European connections, he probably recognised some of the problems that Maynard Keynes was at that very time expounding in *The Economic Consequences of the Peace* (1919). Distance often sharpens the logic of a situation while proximity increases its emotional context. Undoubtedly the conviction that he had lost the confidence of the Board was a major consideration in his decision to resign, but this should be viewed against the wider background.

In 1919 the BHP Board was composed of seven directors. Four had been on the Board either virtually, or actually, since the foundation of the company: Bowes Kelly, Duncan McBryde, D. W. Harvey Patterson and William Jamieson. The other three were H. V. McKay of the Sunshine Harvester Company, R. O. Blackwood, son of the first chairman, and H. G. Darling, son of John Darling. At thirty-four, compared with the other directors, Darling belonged to another generation; he, like Lewis, deferred to the authority of the leading technocrat, but in a steel business this meant Baker, not Delprat. From the days of his prime at Broken Hill, Delprat recalled only too well the crucial distinction between a technocrat's authority and that of a secular manager. The latter's vulnerability increased more rapidly with age than the former's, as Baker's role showed clearly.

John Darling's vision and persuasive powers had carried the Board by a majority of one into the iron and steel business. Throughout the early stages of the transition from silver and base-metal mining and processing to iron and steel, Darling had given Delprat solid support.

## 11 A NEW WORLD

Harold Gordon Darling, 1885–1950, c. 1934, was appointed a director of BHP after the death of his father, John Darling, in 1914. His period as Chairman, from 1922 until his death, saw BHP consolidate its position as a steelmaking company of world standing.

Darling's untimely death had not only robbed him of seeing the works established but had removed from the Board Delprat's most astute and supportive critic. After Darling's death the Board depended increasingly and relatively uncritically upon Delprat's advice. In November 1917 they passed a motion of appreciation of their general manager's services over nineteen years, especially regarding the establishment of the iron and steel works. Delprat not only received a letter to this effect but a month later he was presented with an illuminated address.[19]

However, the able, cynical and dominant Delprat had made powerful enemies. During the first two decades of the twentieth century he was indisputably the most influential managerial figure in Australia. By birth and education he could claim equality with anyone in an Australian society that was isolated and ostensibly egalitarian. However, it was also acutely xenophobic. The 'tall poppy' image fitted Delprat like a second skin and inevitably created enmity, particularly in the Melbourne and Adelaide establishments. The Australian establishment was intellectually Low Church and liberal rather than Calvinist. It had inherited and developed that dichotomy of emotion and intellect that almost destroyed liberal England in the years between the wars. Thus, to men like Justice Higgins, Delprat was the embodiment of managerial capitalism, while W. S. Robinson and the Baillieu group considered that he had outsmarted them over the transfer of the Port Pirie smelters.[20]

Furthermore, Delprat had enemies within the company who quickly seized the opportunity when they perceived the first sign of apparent weakness. 'Somebody', wrote H. G. Darling to Lewis, 'knows that my feelings towards him are anything but pleasant. We met alright, but we understand each other perfectly as soon as our eyes met . . . he wishes to be on the Bridge the whole time and run every blessed thing'.[21] There can be little doubt that Harold Darling disliked Delprat, possibly on personal as much as business grounds. Delprat had been his father's friend and they belonged to different generations. As the war drew to a close Darling began to undermine the Board's confidence in its general manager.

Delprat's position had a fatal weakness. He was the general manager but not a managing director and, although he was frequently in attendance, he was never a member of the Board. This was a hangover from an earlier company structure and quickly rectified by Delprat's successor. After he returned from the United States in 1920 Darling wrote to Lewis, who was still abroad, that 'I had a real good go with the Directors . . . it is most difficult, as none of them know anything about the technical side and [find it] hard to follow an argument'.[22] The instability of the world economy in the post-war era was to give the shrewd, cautious and astute Darling his opportunity. In the circumstances his instinct proved correct and probably saved the company from being over-committed to the point of collapse.

In common with steelmen throughout the world[23] Delprat believed that the post-war era would bring boom conditions. From the beginning Delprat, and Baker, had been convinced of the need for economies of scale in the production of iron and steel and for satellite industries to absorb this excess capacity. Both were convinced that iron and steel manufacture could only achieve maximum efficiency through sufficient production growth to allow effective cost-cutting. Delprat's overseas tour in 1919 had coincided with the immediate post-war euphoria and his opinions had been confirmed as he saw a world preparing for boom conditions. Darling and Lewis, whose overseas tours were later when the chill winds of depression had begun to blow, gained a more realistic impression. Meanwhile, Delprat was determined that Australia would participate in the projected boom and that BHP would consolidate its dominant position in the industry, both in the home market and in the South Pacific region.

To take advantage of the anticipated boom Delprat began to press ahead with plans for expansion. Many of these were fulfilments of plans foreshadowed even before the works were commissioned, and most of them had been formulated before the end of the war. They required capital. Although the 1918 recapitalisation had raised approximately £638 000, on 22 September 1920, while Darling and Lewis were still overseas, the Board authorised an issue of 420 000 of the unissued £1 shares at £2 5s, to be first offered to shareholders on a one-for-five basis. A further £1 500 000 was to be raised by an issue of 15 000 second-mortgage debentures of £100 each at 7 per cent per annum.[24] By December 1920, when the debentures stood in the market at £94 10s, Darling could write, with the admitted benefit of hindsight, that

> everyone has been far too precipate & it would have been a great deal better if only one of the issues had been made. Either the shares or the debentures but certainly not both. Being wise after the event is always very easy but I really think the case is one where very little judgment has been shown.[25]

Darling was by now convinced that hard times were coming and he suggested that the company should buy in its own debentures to save paying the interest and as

> all gilt edge securities will advance & perhaps the time will not be far distant when our 7% will be over par. Money is getting very tight here due to the large expenditure of Federal & State Govt. & also importing houses carrying very large stocks . . . There is not shadow of doubt that Australia has been reckless due to Govt. extravagance.

Darling was concerned at the expectations aroused by the Federal Basic Wage Commission's decision of £5 10 0 per week as the basic wage when 'other countries are cutting back'. However, he thought that recession might 'mean the settlement of our labor troubles', pointing to the severe problems confronting the mining industry. For instance, 'there is not a copper mine in Australia paying at present' and although the long strike at Broken Hill was over, the Broken Hill Mines were working 'only 27.5 hours per week at the face, the future looks like shut-down for economic reasons'.[26]

Now that the war was over, Australia was no longer industrially isolated and protected from imports. A significant factor influencing the course of the post-World War I Australian iron and steel industry lay in the policy of the British towards their own so-called old industries and ancilliaries. Given the multifariousness of the British connection, Delprat had early recognised this as a wild card and devoted himself to it during the last days of his incumbency, although the question was beyond any one man to handle. Many British firms, realising that protection would be the normal order of trade even in their former imperial markets, decided to partially cut their losses by establishing branches in those overseas markets they had previously supplied from Britain. While he was overseas in 1919 Delprat had reported to the BHP Board that:

> Generally speaking—the conditions in England are at present so bad, that many large firms are looking round for new fields for their operations—and now is the time to induce them to come to Australia. We could now stipulate more favourable conditions than in the past, but as we only desire a contract that is fair to both sides over a long period, this does not really affect us.

Delprat went on to emphasise the necessity of encouraging British manufacturers to establish skilled industries which would absorb BHP's over-capacity in steel, and he continued:

> with this in view, I saw Mr Hughes the Prime Minister and explained these views, and asked him if he would favourably look on any effort on our part to induce one of the leading shipbuilding firms to came and build *English* ships in Australia. By English ships, I mean ships built of our steel but with the English excellence of workmanship . . . Ship building requires a lot of steel if carried on vigorously.

Among Delprat's plans were negotiations with Rylands, for the manufacture of wire netting in Australia. This fitted perfectly with the idea of BHP supplying iron and steel for other companies to finish.[27]

While overseas Delprat had started, or continued, negotiations with a number of British firms anxious to establish Australian subsidiaries. Some of these plans came to fruition during the inter-war years, others withered away in that hostile commercial climate. For instance, from 1918 to 1920 BHP was negotiating with Stewart & Lloyds regarding the manufacture of steel pipes. The contract which Delprat had arranged in England provided that the proceeds should be divided in accordance with the ratio of the manufacturing costs of each party. But the draft contract submitted to the Board in the harsher economic climate of September 1920 arranged for a ratio of six parts to Stewart & Lloyds and four parts to BHP. Delprat, advising the rejection of this contract, told the

Board that he had been contacted by Babcock & Wilcox who proposed manufacturing solid drawn steel tubes.[28]

In 1918 John Lysaght (Australia) Pty Ltd was formed to supply the Australian sheet steel market. This had previously been supplied by the parent company's works at Bristol in England. The original agreement was that two-thirds of the profits would go to Lysaght and one-third to BHP. This was adjusted in 1920, when Messrs Lysaght came to discuss the arrangement with the Board before the works came into operation in 1921.[29] Other finishing industries also became established at Newcastle despite the difficulties of the post-war years. For instance, in 1919, the local consortium Commonwealth Steel Products Ltd began operations. By 1921 in addition to John Lysaght, there was Rylands (Aust) Pty Ltd, the result of a merger of the Austral Nail Co. Ltd with the Australian interests and the expertise of John Rylands, Warrington, England. Another firm established to surmount the tariff wall and absorb excess capacity was the wire rope manufacturer, Australian Wire Rope Works Pty Ltd. This was formed by Bullivants (England) and BHP and, although not established until 1925, negotiations for its formation were begun in the immediate post-war era. All of the enterprises established immediately after the war suffered from the progressive decline in demand. Consequently they failed to absorb the excess capacity produced by the expanded steelworks plant.

This surplus created severe problems for the BHP management as, unlike Hoskins Iron and Steel Works Ltd, BHP did not have an assured outlet for all its product. Other negotiations for finishing industries collapsed in the deteriorating economic conditions of the early 1920s. The most important of these potential industries was the tin-plate industry. Consideration of this development continually recurred and lapsed throughout the inter-war period. The war had shown the importance of establishing a tin-plate manufacturing industry in Australia, to provide for example, containers for the export of fruit, jam and similar primary produce.[30] Tin-plate production was a sunrise industry in the post-war era and Delprat was most anxious that BHP should participate in it. From the 1890s refrigeration had vastly expanded the export of meat, indicating the potential export market for other types of agricultural produce—if they could be safely preserved. This proved to be a difficult problem, especially as failures eroded public confidence. Effective methods of canning milk, fruit and vegetables were not discovered until the twentieth century. The double-sealing of cans had to wait until 1923; this eliminated the use of sealing compounds, with their dangerous potential for disintegration.[31]

In 1918 BHP was looking for a second-hand tin-plate mill and 'Delprat's desire to have someone associated with the BHP Co. in the Tinplate industry of Australia' was so well known that the largest tin-plate manufacturers in Britain, Richard Thomas & Co. Ltd, who before the war supplied 80 per cent of the Australian market, became alarmed. They were not very anxious to establish an Australian works. Labour was a large component of the cost of tin plate and, at their site in Wales, not only were adult male wages very much cheaper than in Australia, but a considerable amount of the work was done by women and boys, reducing the cost even further. However, the carrot of government support was held out while the goad of tariff exclusion was threatened. At Delprat's request Prime Minister Hughes, then in London, was cabled to enlist the imperial government's assistance in obtaining an expert as 'the industry would be of national importance'. Meanwhile, on 31 May 1918, Delprat cabled BHP's American agent, J. B. Ladd in Philadelphia: 'can you secure services first-class Tinplate Mill Manager. Capable erecting and working mill here. Urgent'. A week later Elder Smith & Co. telegraphed its London office to tell them to urge Baldwins Ltd to send an expert stating that BHP would give 'all assistance possible'.[32]

The initial capacity from the tin-plate mill was to be 2000 boxes or about 100 tons per week. Ladd suggested 'going in on a larger scale . . . your location promises exceptional returns on Tin plant'. Delprat replied that 'we intend to start with this small quantity to get experience. The demand for tinplates in Australia is immense . . . good future'. On 23 September Delprat cabled Ladd to 'place advertisement in *Iron Age*: "competent man erect and take charge tinplate mills—*must be able to leave immediately*"'. Delprat, anxious to establish his plant before the pre-war market pattern become re-established, cabled London to 'suspend negotiations re expert—cannot afford to wait'. On 11 October Ladd cabled that Clement F. Poppleton was available; he had thirty years of experience and wanted an annual salary of £1500. Delprat replied immediately, agreeing to the terms.[33]

Two months later Ladd told Delprat that some of his Pittsburg friends had warned him that Poppleton was 'little more than a draftsman although he poses as an authority'. However, Poppleton had by then been engaged and was on his way to Australia, where he arrived early in January 1919. On 23 January he reported that 'there is no reason that Tin Plate should not be made in Australia as cheaply as anywhere on the face of the Globe . . . the manufacture of Tin Plate . . . will become a very profitable business besides filling a great need in all the states of Australia'.[34]

The appointment was a disaster from the start. Ladd's belated second opinion proved all too true. Poppleton was incapable of carrying out the work to the satisfaction of the Board and within a few weeks of his arrival the Board had decided that Delprat, who was preparing for his overseas visit, should look for a first-class manager to replace Poppleton when he was in the United States. Various expedients, including health, were considered as reasons for terminating the contract. Finally, in August, Poppleton was offered three months' salary and fares back to the United States for himself and his family. Delprat was by then abroad, and the arrangements were made by Baker, who neither offered nor was asked for an explanation for the cancellation of Poppleton's contract, remarking afterwards 'in fact, I did not think he was sober'. Darling was still reminding Delprat of this episode eighteen months later. Not only did it undermine the Board's confidence in the omniscience of their General Manager, but it impressed upon them the dangers of making appointments sight unseen. On 3 December 1920 the Board 'expressed a preference for engagements being made by personal interview rather than by cable'.[35]

After this episode, the Board returned to considering a British firm and embarked upon long drawn-out, and eventually abortive, negotiations for the manufacture of tin-plate with the famous Welsh firm Richard Thomas & Co. Ltd. Richard Thomas wanted to roll its own bars and to establish its own open-hearth plant, indicating that 'the steel they required had to be of the highest quality . . . a duplex plant would not give them the quality they required'. In reply BHP promised adequate quantities of good steel, but pointed out that 'the purpose of the projected contract is to find an outlet for our steel, consequently if you were to put up your steel furnaces, the main reason for making any contract would disappear'. Meanwhile, the market grew more uncertain. Two months later, in February 1921, Richard Thomas & Co. cabled 'in view of deplorable conditions of trade and high cost of erection feel compelled to postpone decision about erection of tinplate plant'. By the end of the month they were declaring that 'industry all over the world seems to have come to a standstill'.[36]

The idea lapsed until September 1924, when the new general manager of BHP, Essington Lewis, enquired whether Richard Thomas was still interested in establishing a tin-plate plant, as BHP had been approached by another party. In reply Richard Thomas lamented the 'very difficult times', complaining that tin-plate bars could be imported from Europe into Wales at £5 17s 6d—cheaper than they could be manufactured. Moreover, recent Australian legislation had prohibited Richard Thomas from importing tin plate into Australia under a preferential tariff.[37] The question lapsed again, this time until 1930, when BHP's construction of a plant was only halted by information that important technical changes in the industry were pending. In any case, finance was difficult as the world was sliding deeper into economic depression. Nevertheless the tonnage of steel represented in Australia's consumption of tin plate ensured that the manufacture of tin plate would continue to attract the attention of the BHP Board. On January 1932 Lewis called on the Minister for Trade and Customs to request that the Australian government would not yield to British pressure for the reduction of tariffs on tin plate at the forthcoming imperial economic summit, the Ottawa conference.

The question of the sovereignty of the former British dominions, acknowledged but not defined in 1918, was resolved over a series of imperial conferences during the 1920s and given legislative expression in the 1931 Statute of Westminster. Not surprisingly the 'nation of shopkeepers' and its former dependencies had found it easier to arrive at a political than an economic agreement. The question of imperial preference continued to agitate the newly established British Commonwealth of Nations. The Ottawa conference was called in 1932 in the vain hope of achieving consensus on the issue.

The British steel manufacturers were so concerned to retain their place in the Commonwealth market that Sir William Larke, Director of the National Federation of Iron and Steel Manufacturers, suggested the Empire's iron and steel producers might meet before the Ottawa conference to explore such common issues as mutual co-operation, market developments, reciprocal preferences and the establishment of an international cartel. AIS and BHP replied that they did not consider such a meeting would materially assist the Ottawa conference. The Federation then made a direct approach to the Australian government but, at Ottawa, when the British government pressed for the removal of the Australian tin-plate duties in the interests of their manufacturers, the Australian government, well briefed by Darling and Lewis, stood firm.

The question lapsed once more. Then in 1933, an agreement between BHP and Richard Thomas & Co. Ltd was negotiated by the chairman of Richard Thomas, Sir William Firth, a leading British steelmaster. Firth was on a visit to Australia to try to break down protection. The reasons that Firth gave for coming to Australia were:

> I visited Australia because of information received to the effect that it was their intention to produce tin-plates. Before going, it was my thought that I could organise the [Australian] consumers of Welsh tin-plates to protest against protection being given to local industry, which would have the effect of raising prices to the Australian Packing companies, but, during the voyage, I decided, before making any such attempt, to inspect the BHP property and endeavour to estimate its competitive strength. I was forced to the conclusion that it was futile to attempt to successfully counter them by protest and therefore decided to endeavour to persuade them to delay as long as practicable their tin-plate project . . .
>
> There are two important companies in Australia, the A.I.& S. Co. and the BHP Co. Of the two, the Broken Hill is the MOST powerful financially, the most efficient and the best balanced . . . the [BHP] Board is influenced by a far-sighted, progressive and wealthy Chairman, and a progressive and exceedingly efficient Managing Director.[38]

Under the agreement Richard Thomas was to help BHP to establish a tin-plate industry in Australia; BHP was to pay Richard Thomas £250 000 for its assistance and to refrain from manufacturing tin plate until the end of 1935. The agreement was to lapse if BHP had not started to construct its plant by 1937. Sir William Firth's visit was an extremely significant one because of the part that he played in the BHP–AIS take-over, the most important event in the inter-war history of the Australian iron and steel industry. However, in 1920, this was still far in the future.

Delprat, shielded by distance from the increasing chill in the current economic wind, was still anxious to effect economies of scale for anticipated post-World War I markets. On 27 April 1920, he obtained the Board's consent to the building of a third blast furnace of a rather greater capacity than either of the two already in operation. The cost of the furnace was estimated at £300 000, and a similar sum was required for the coke ovens to support it. Although they concurred in the policy of expansion, Delprat and Baker continued to differ. For instance, Delprat estimated that the furnace would take about eighteen months to construct, while Baker declared that it could be done in a year.[39]

The size of the Australian home market automatically restricted the amount of iron and steel it could absorb; consequently other markets had to be found for excess capacity. The search for post-war markets began almost immediately the works were opened. Early in 1916 copies of the *Souvenir of Opening the Newcastle Works*[40] were sent to the British Ambassador and Commercial Attache in Yokahama and in 1918 Delprat told the Board that he had sold 1500 tons of pig-iron at £9 18 0 per ton and a similar amount of plates at £50 to Mitsui Bussan Kaisha, Japan. Purely fact-finding enquiries on behalf of the Chinese government, asking for specific information about the iron industry, were refused but, in August 1918 Elder Smith, who represented the company in Queensland, reported an enquiry for steel from Jardine Matheson & Co., Shanghai. This enquiry was followed up in the ensuing November, when J. McGregor Forbes of Jardine Matheson & Co., Hong Kong, had lunch with the BHP directors at the Australian Club in Melbourne.

In May 1917 the BHP Board had advertised 'for a high class and fully competent man with a knowledge of the Australian market for Iron and Steel products to take charge of the Distributing Department' and R. H. M. Rowe was appointed. Agencies were established in the various states: Elder Smith & Co. held the agency for Queensland and Western Australia, Mr Kirk was the agent in Sydney and Mr L. A. Williams in Adelaide. There was also an agency in New Zealand. BHP was represented in Java by Overall & McCray Ltd and advertisements were placed in the *Dutch East Indian Archipelago*. The company's United States agent, J. B. Ladd of Philadelphia, was asked for information about the American market and enquiries were also made about the European market.

The company was already trading with South Africa and Malaysia as well as opening up other Pacific markets when, at the end of 1918, Prime Minister Hughes enquired if BHP was interested in exporting steel to Siberia. The Board replied circumspectly that 'they could not see their way to doing anything in this direction for the present'. Yet if the idea of trading with the Soviet Union in 1918 seems extraordinary today, it should be remembered that BHP would have been in extremely good company, as contacts with the Soviets were soon being made by both Germans and Americans, and in both cases by leading technocrat-oriented businesses. On 6 February 1917 the BHP Board had requested its Secretary to attend a meeting at Sydney Town Hall to consider ways and means of promoting trade and commerce between the Russian Empire and the Australian Commonwealth.[41] Although the Russian Revolution broke out in the following October, its long-term consequences remained obscure for some time.

It was against this background of expansion and international uncertainty that the duplex system of steel-making was considered as part of

BHP's plans for internal expansion. Some mention has already been made of the effects of this controversy on internal company relationships. It now remains to document the evolution of the problem, the cause of which is familiar to all steelmen. A serious concern was the limited supply of scrap. G. & C. Hoskins had established its claim to much of what scrap was available in New South Wales. BHP was largely dependent upon the scrap generated in its own works. This was less than that economically desirable for the manufacture of steel in its open-hearth steel furnaces. It was primarily to surmount this difficulty that Baker, probably early in 1917, suggested the duplex system of steel-making. By this process blast furnace hot metal is partially refined in a Bessemer converter before being transferred to an open-hearth furnace. Here the refining is completed and the temperature and the composition of the steel adjusted to the specification of the particular steel required. Much less scrap is required in this process than in the steel-making process then in operation at Newcastle.

Baker had originally decided against making Bessemer steel because of the phosphorus content of the South Australian iron ores. However, given the difficulties with the open-hearth process and Hibbard's adherence to the then-conventional view that Bessemer steel was essential for wire rods, Baker may have felt that installing a duplexing plant could solve a number of ancillary problems in addition to the paramount difficulty created by lack of scrap. Most importantly, to supply the anticipated finishing industries, a Morgan rod mill had been purchased in August 1915. For two years it had remained in store at the Morgan works in Massachusetts. It was not shipped to Newcastle until September 1917. This has been partly attributed to Hibbard's advice.[42]

At first Delprat was dubious about the idea of introducing duplex steel-making. He replied to Baker's suggestion by pointing out that:

> Open hearth plant. I have been reading in several of the latest books on steel articles regarding the duplex system, and I notice among others that Campbell, p.232, condemns the system as expensive in operation. Another French authority, namely, H. Noble in a very full book on the production of steel, mentions that this system is used at Witkowitz, where the pig iron carries a high silicon and phosphorus. This man affirms the cost of operation is very high. I merely mention these two points for what they are worth, as perhaps you have information which negatives them.[43]

Not being a steelman Delprat was dependent upon the recommendation of experts and his resident experts considered it would solve their principal problem, the lack of scrap. On Delprat's recommendation, and after some discussion, the Board decided, in March 1918, to send Bradford to America as soon as possible:

> to look into the use of the Duplex process which is now being extensively used in large works in America. By adopting the process he thought that there might be no necessity to increase the Open Hearth furnaces, as by the adoption of this preliminary process the daily capacity of the existing furnaces would be increased and be able to deal with the additional output available from the second Blast Furnace.[44]

Bradford's progress reports were tabled at Board meetings in July, August and October 1918 and on 25 October Delprat reported that 'after full consideration with Mr Baker and Mr Bradford he had decided to recommend the adoption of the Duplex process. The cost of the installment would be £200,000 and would include two Bessemer furnaces and a tilting furnace'. On 25 November 1918 the Board reaffirmed its earlier decision to adopt the duplex process. At the same time 'it was decided to obtain a report from the G[eneral] M[anager] setting out the recommendations and items of expenditure involved'.[45] New plant had to be imported and in the immediate post-war era inflation and variable exchange rates made costing exceedingly difficult. It made the rule-of-thumb estimates, which had given approximate costings in more stable times, totally meaningless.

In its size and international complexity the inflation factor was a new and, to businessmen trained in an earlier age, a very frightening phenomenon. Their other commercial ventures had made the directors of BHP acutely aware of this situation. In 1918 Bowes Kelly, then chairman of BHP, became a director of the National Bank of Australia, which had recently amalgamated with the Colonial Bank. The vice-chairman, Duncan McBryde, had, from 1910, been a director of the Commercial Bank of Australia. At this time gold could not be exported to balance debts incurred in the post-war imports boom and H. G. Darling thought that worry about currency exchange between Australia and London, contributed to McBryde's death. McBryde, who had been elected to the BHP Board at the company's first general meeting in 1886, was not one of the more flamboyant of the early directors of BHP, but he attracted real affection and his sudden death on 24 November 1920 was genuinely lamented.[46]

Meanwhile, on 20 December 1918 the Board on Delprat's advice decided 'that our needs for the present would be better served by the addition of three further Open Hearth furnaces'. The matter then went into abeyance probably to allow Delprat to investigate the process for himself while he was overseas. On 14 May 1919 Delprat, then in the United States, noted in his diary that he had discussed introducing duplexing at Newcastle with Mr A. Brassert, a blast furnace expert. Brassert advised against it as it would remove the manganese first and this was a mistake as the sulphur could not be lowered; Brassert considered that 2.5 per cent manganese in pig-iron was desirable. Confronted with conflicting expert opinion, Delprat returned home uncertain.[47]

A year later on 24 June 1920 Delprat opened up the question again, advising the Board 'that he wished to send someone to America to study the details of the Duplex Plant and gain experience in its working'. The Board agreed and Delprat recommended Yates, the understudy to J. A. Kendall who had succeeded Bradford as superintendent of the open-hearth department. Kendall, who had considerable experience of open-hearth steel-making in Canada, was proving very useful. He successfully reorganised the open-hearth shop, increasing production by an improved method of heating (a greater heat input was applied first and then reduced instead of vice versa). This reduced the time to make each heat of steel. In September the Board voted him a bonus of £200.[48]

In late June and early July 1920, while the arrangements to investigate the duplexing process further were being finalised, the Board was suddenly bombarded with a series of cables from Lewis and Darling. These first queried the the equipment ordered for the No. 3 blast furnace and then the suitability of the duplexing process itself. Noyes had told Darling and Lewis that a Mesta horizontal engine had been ordered for the new blast furnace. Lewis advised cancelling this in favour of an Ingersoll Rand turbo blower, as this was being universally used in new plants with excellent results. A bewildered Board cabled Delprat that 'Board attach great importance to opinion of Darling, Lewis and Noyes but would not like to go counter to you and Baker'.[49] The Mesta engine was eventually purchased. Then on 30 June Essington Lewis cabled from Ohio querying the whole duplex project. On 13 July Darling cabled: 'trust the Board of Directors will reconsider the whole question Duplex from information received consider first cost prohibitory—adoption likely to prove fatal to Broken Hill Pty. Co.—advise strongly against incurring any expense'. Lewis cabled on the same day: 'Duplex, after inspection of Donora Gary Chicago consider unwise at present to proceed with Duplex or Bessemer Converter—will telegraph further after inspection of Birmingham, Bethlehem'.[50]

Lewis had met Noyes in America and he had concurred with Lewis's opinion. The Board, now in a quandary, dispatched the following cable to Lewis:

> Board have discussed with Delprat the whole position and had advantage discussing with Herbert Wilson Director Cammell Laird who stated process ideal for Newcastle where question of scrap steel supplies most necessary—to run furnaces properly 33% minimum whilst at present furnaces only receiving 17% inclusive of our own scrap—outside supplies practically negligible quantity—Wilson further states quality steel equals any other and suitable rail plates—Baker strongly supports Duplex necessity view scrap position and this is supported by Bradford in his reports after late American visit—did you see or consult Bradford on matter and had you considered scrap position—matter such importance Board agreed proceed Duplex plant—meantime would like your reply fully as to any special reason outside of above which prompted condemnation process.[51]

Delprat, advising the Board, had referred to the Morgan rod mill and read to the Board extracts from the *Iron Age* 'shewing that at Bethlehem a Duplex mixer almost identical with our own arrangement was being installed'. The Board then authorised the expenditure of £238 500 out of the originally authorised £650 000 for the whole plant. At the same time the Board requested written reports on the whole question from Delprat, Baker and Kendall.[52] Baker produced an elaborate report with supporting evidence from a number of authorities and he concluded by stating: 'I am fully convinced that the Board, in deciding to adopt the Duplex process with 200 ton Tilting Furnaces for these works, has chosen the wisest course for the future success of the Broken Hill Proprietary Company'. Almost immediately after he had completed his report, Baker appears to have had a nervous breakdown and, until he left to convalesce in the United States some six months later, he was far from well. Kendall, who had actually operated a duplex plant at the Dominion Iron & Steel Co. in Nova Scotia, agreed with Baker, writing: 'I feel sure the Duplex process would be a success in this plant' and gave as his reasons the scarcity of scrap and the low phosphorus and sulphur content of the iron. In his report, Delprat stated that:

> the principal reason why I advocate the Duplex Process is that it uses exclusively molten metal and does not use any scrap . . . In Newcastle we have only sufficient scrap (mostly of our own making) to mix 17% scrap.

We have exhausted the scrap accumulated before our works started, and the quantity we can now buy (and at a high price) is negligible . . . if we establish the Duplex Process, we make an extra quantity of Steel, which produces the usual quantity of scrap in the Rolling Mills. The Open Hearth Plant would then receive the 17% it receives now, and in addition the quantity of scrap resulting from the additional quantity of Steel produced, and we could then count on at least 34% of scrap, and probably more, as more Steel would be made in the Duplex Plant, and a smaller number of Stationary O.H. furnaces would have to be operated. Hence, if we install the Duplex Process we will have two Plants which work under most favourable conditions. But if we add another Stationary O.H. Plant, we will have two 'scrap starved' Plants working under uneconomical conditions . . . My strong recommendation to install the Duplex Process must not be taken as a general statement that the Duplex Process is under all conditions preferable to the Stationary O.H. Process. This is not the case. I only claim its advantage at Newcastle situated as we are in connection with scrap supply, and the character of our iron and coke. In other localities where the conditions are different, there might be serious objections to the Duplex Plant.

Further cables arrived from Darling and Lewis. They had discussed the question with Bradford and Noyes and several American experts. They concluded that the tonnage of pig-iron available would be too small and that the plant was too expensive, for they estimated that 'Duplex will cost BHP erected between four and five million dollars' to make it a commercial proposition. In answer to this Delprat reminded the Board that the No. 3 blast furnace would come on line on 1 July 1921 and that, even if the duplex plant were ordered immediately, it could not be in operation before January 1923. By this time 324 000 tons of pig-iron would be available at an accumulated value of £1 500 000. Furthermore, the foundations for No. 4 blast furnace were already laid and by that time it would be ready to come into production. Even if delays and breakdowns eroded these figures, there would still be a great quantity of iron available.[53] The Board cabled Darling and Lewis to obtain further information.

In Darling's absence the Board was composed of a number of elderly gentlemen, whose business experience had been gained in a very different world. They were totally dependent upon their expert advisers in an industry that was completely new to them and one of these advisers, Kendall, having operated a duplex plant in Canada, spoke from practical as well as theoretical experience. In October Delprat, in reply to a question from the Board, 'advised that both he and Mr Baker were still of the same opinion as to the advisability of installing the Duplex plant', although he was now proposing a 130-ton tilting furnace instead of one of 200 tons and a 15-ton converter instead of a 25-ton one. He would arrange that Mr Baker would investigate the appropriate size of plant when he was in the United States.[54]

H. G. Darling was officially welcomed back on 12 November and on 19 November the Board decided that nothing further should be done until after Baker's visit to the United States. This was the end of the proposal for the introduction of duplex steel-making at Newcastle. BHP was spared a crippling expenditure on a process which was subsequently proved to be neither necessary nor desirable. Lewis was welcomed back on 27 January 1921 and Baker left for the United States on 4 February. On 11 February the Board minutes recorded that 'Mr Delprat laid before the Board the possible necessity for the reorganisation of the General Management of the Company and in that connection placed the matter of his agreement in the hands of the Board'.[55] Delprat was now in his sixty-fifth year and, in view of his often-expressed opinion on the need for reorganisation, this was the logical moment to activate his foreshadowed resignation. The Board discussed the situation on 15 February and again on 18 February, when the chairman reported that Delprat had accepted the position of consulting engineer and agreed 'to carry out such work as the Board might from time to time call upon him to do'. The new contract, which was to run until 30 September 1922, stipulated a salary of about £8000 (as per the agreement of 10 January 1918) and allowed Delprat to engage in private consulting. As foreshadowed fifteen months previously, Essington Lewis replaced him. The changeover took place on 25 February 1921 and, prior to Delprat's official resignation, both men went to Newcastle.

Undoubtedly there were personality clashes and circumstantial factors in the departure of one dominant personality and the rise of another. Such is usually the case and curiosity generally increases speculation, especially as both were intensely private men. Furthermore, on this occasion, the succession to and retirement from the management of Australia's largest industry took place against a background of unprecedented international economic instability. Nevertheless, mythology and speculation should not be allowed to obscure the basic logic of a situation dominated by two interlocking events: namely, that the managerial reorganisation of BHP was urgently necessary and that the economic and social aftermath of World War I took the vast majority of industrialists in the iron and steel industry by surprise.

The circumstances of the change-over highlighted a problem inherent in the industry, the constantly fluctuating relationship between supply and demand. Success or failure depends upon the accurate forecasting of demand and ensuring that the supply is available to meet it. Hampered by distance from the industrial centres of the world and being relatively new to this complex industry, Delprat made an incorrect commercial prediction. Despite the fact that the vast majority of the leading steelmen of the day held Delprat's opinion, it was still incorrect and the result could have been disastrous for the company that he had served so ably. On the other hand Delprat had trained Lewis well, even ensuring that he went abroad at that crucial period. For this reason Delprat's work survived and with it his reputation as the greatest managerial figure in Australia in the first two decades of the twentieth century.

Paradoxically, speculation was further highlighted by the degree of stability which Delprat's long dominance had given to the development of the company. When Delprat became general manager of the Broken Hill Proprietary Company, it was a mining company with a limited future, his predecessors having already foreshadowed the end of the Big Mine; when he left, BHP was already well on the way to becoming a national institution. The question can be asked why BHP was the only mining company to develop in this particular way at this particular time. Moreover, the fact that Australia produced such an enterprise when socialist theory was near its zenith in politics is in itself remarkable. The blueprint for this achievement and the company's development between the wars was indisputably the work of Guillaume Delprat and John Darling, but the equally challenging task of carrying it out belonged to their successors H. G. Darling and the new general manager, Essington Lewis.

# 12

# CRISIS AND SURVIVAL

THE DIFFICULTIES CONFRONTING Essington Lewis, the new general manager of the Broken Hill Proprietary Company, were massive. Domestically BHP faced the still unresolved restructuring problems resulting from its changing direction and rapid growth during the previous decade. Externally there were already visible national and international problems which converged with unprecedented severity during the following decade. At home, the tariff problem was recognised but only partly solved. Abroad, world over-capacity in the steel industry encouraged vicious price undercutting in the universal search for limited export markets. All of these difficulties were concurrent and they were aggravated by the financial instability and economic depression that marked the international economy in the interwar period. These problems underpinned world-wide labour unrest. H. G. Darling, who emerged as chairman and the driving force on the BHP Board, and Essington Lewis, the chief executive, were well aware that the company would either ride the storm with spectacular success or founder miserably. The margin between the one and the other would be very slender.

Lewis and Darling's visit overseas in 1920 had developed a personal friendship. This was now cemented into a working relationship, creating a unity of command during the dangerous years which followed Lewis's appointment as general manager and Darling's election as chairman of the BHP Board. These appointments were made when both men were at

## 12 CRISIS AND SURVIVAL

Ingots being teemed at BHP Newcastle steelworks, while an open-hearth furnace is being tapped in the background

the height of their powers and confidence. Both men were relatively uninfluenced by the views of those who had held similar positions before the war. Their lack of pre-war preconceptions was important, for the managerial and industrial world had been altered almost beyond recognition by the acceleration of change created by World War I.

Within the company the retirement of Delprat and the appointment of Lewis were the forerunners of widespread managerial changes. Circumstances beyond the company's control were forcing the pace of its transition from a mining and infant industrial enterprise into a mature multi-faceted organisation. The managerial change-over was timely. The order and the extent of the changes were also advantageous, for Delprat's resignation had allowed Lewis to become firmly established before the other replacements took place.

When Lewis became general manager in February 1921 there were two senior vacancies in the foreseeable future: the positions of company secretary and of manager of the steelworks. There was no immediate urgency in either case. Baker was overseas and F. M. Mitchell, whose all-round managerial skills were proving invaluable, was acting manager of the steelworks. Furthermore, there was a relatively clear field at the steelworks. As had been anticipated, many of the Americans who had been brought over to establish the works now wished to return home. Noyes, who was responsible for the blast furnace department, had announced his intention of resigning to educate his children in the United States and Kendall, who had succeeded Bradford at the open-hearth department, had also indicated his intention of resigning when Baker returned. However, no great changes were immediately envisaged in the American-style management of the steelworks, as on 24 March 1921 the Board requested Baker, then in the United States, to look for three senior men: an assistant manager for the steelworks, a rolling mill superintendent, and a constructional engineer under whom Gibson had agreed to work.[1] Meanwhile, Leslie Bradford's business venture in the United States had not prospered. He had returned to Sydney and become a partner in Bradford, Kendall & Co. Ltd., a steel castings firm. At the request of Lewis, who was obviously anxious to retain contact, the BHP Board appointed Bradford's firm consultants to the company.

The blueprint for the new organisation was envisaged as early as January 1922. On 6 January Darling wrote to Lewis:

> At the Board meeting yesterday it was agreed that the whole organization should be placed under one head viz. General Manager. This principle has now been adopted and the General Manager and his officers together with myself as Chairman be asked to draw up a plan of a rearrangement for submission to the Board for adoption. The Board desires this to be gone on with at the earliest and have asked me to be privy to the scheme so that when it comes before the Board no time need be lost.

The Company Secretary, F. M. Dickenson, was in poor health and Darling, anticipating a vacancy in this department, wrote:

> as soon as the plan of the new arrangement is ready a public announcement will have to be made (of course after Dickenson has been informed) stating that F.M.D. has retired and that Frank Mitchell has been appointed in his place. Now we are all supposing that Frank Mitchell will accept the Secretaryship and as far as I am aware no direct overtures have been made but no doubt you will be au fait with his feelings on this subject.

Lewis immediately replied:

> I am very pleased that the Board should agree that the whole organization of the Company, in the future, be placed under one head and that on my head the mantle is to fall. It is most comforting and encouraging to feel the confidence that the Board is placing in me;—I think it is a wise move that you should be in touch with the reorganization Committee as Chairman . . . Your supposition that Mitchell will take the position in the new organization as Secretary is well founded. I have his word today that he will accept the position when offered.

Nothing more was said for a year. Then, on 19 January 1923, the Board minutes laconically record that it had 'decided that for the future the whole organization of the company including the Melbourne and Branch offices shall be under the direction of the General Manager'. A week later, on 26 January, the Board advised that the subcommittee had met and a chart of the proposed rearrangement was submitted, which the Board then approved.[2]

Although the organisation remained untouched for the year after Lewis's appointment as chief executive, a number of significant staff changes occurred during that year. Warren A. Saul, the superintendent of the rolling mills, resigned. Saul had established this department bringing with him men and equipment. His two sons had worked as rollers in the blooming mill. Saul now wished to return to the United States. He was replaced by an Australian, W. J. Todhunter. Todhunter was to make a very considerable contribution to BHP. He was respected for his knowledge of steel-making, and he was held in affection for his skilful and kindly managerial style. In March H. F. Noyes suddenly reconsidered his resignation as superintendent of the blast furnaces. He was offered but declined the position of production superintendent at the same salary and he left Australia at the end of April 1922.[3]

Baker's return was expected at the end of October 1921. On 14 October the Board, at the suggestion of Lewis, indicated that it felt that Baker's role should be advisory rather than administrative. Mitchell was, for the time being, to remain at Newcastle as assistant manager and, as Kendall's resignation from the open-hearth department would take effect on Baker's return, J. McCrum was appointed to replace him. At the same time L. J. Griffith was appointed to succeed H. F. Noyes as blast furnace superintendent.[4] On his return Baker sought Lewis's approval to approach Bradford. This was given with the comment that Lewis did not think that he would succeed. Since his return from the United States, Bradford had been connected with the company as a consultant but, contrary to Lewis's expectations, he now agreed to become production superintendent. The Board was notified on 21 April and Bradford, who remained a director of Bradford, Kendall & Co. Ltd., took up his position at Newcastle on 1 December 1922.

There had been a vacancy on the Board since the death of McBryde in November 1920. On 23 June 1922 it was filled when the South Australian W. G. Duncan was elected. Then, on 27 October, there arose 'the matter of appointing a Chairman in the place of Mr. Kelly who expressed his desire to relinquish the position in accordance with the usual custom of the Board after the Chair had been occupied for a certain length of time'. After Kelly had been 'eulogised' for his services to the company and assured of the high esteem in which they all held him, 'at the unanimous request of the Board Mr. Darling agreed to accept the position vacated by Mr. Kelly'. Darling remained chairman until his death in January 1950. On 12 January 1923 James Campbell, the assistant company secretary who had deputised for F. M. Dickenson during his recurrent illnesses, also became ill. He was given twelve months' leave of absence with pay. Three days later Dickenson's resignation was accepted with regret and he was given a year's salary. Superannuation, even for senior executives, was still in the future. After these events, F. M. Mitchell was appointed company secretary on 19 January 1923.[5]

Mitchell had been assistant manager of the steelworks and on his appointment as company secretary he was asked to prepare a report on the steelworks. This report was considered by the Board on 16 February 1923. Mitchell recommended the introduction of a works budget and that costing should be on a monthly instead of a weekly basis. He also recommended the formation of a subsidiary by-products company, as BHP's relationship with De Merics for the disposal of coke oven by-products had amassed considerable debts and had not proved satisfactory. Finally, he pointed out that certain aspects of BHP's arrangement with John Lysaght had become 'impractical' in the prevailing circumstances; these needed to be sorted out and appropriately adjusted.

The Board agreed with all of Mitchell's suggestions. They also accepted the recommendation that Baker and Mitchell should prepare a bonus scheme for the steelworks and present it for the Board's consideration.[6] During his overseas visit Mitchell had investigated and been impressed with bonus schemes which he had seen operating in the United States. The bonus system allowed the company to adjust financial rewards to economic performance and market conditions on a non-permanent basis. It was particularly suitable for an industry that was subject to sudden changes in economic circumstances and sharply fluctuating supply and demand. Workers naturally preferred a predictable remuneration and for this, and other similar reasons, the system became a source of contention between the company and the unions. The recommendations accepted from Mitchell's report signalled budget projections, accurate costing and reports as an integral part of the new managerial policy.

On 1 June 1923 the chairman reported to the Board about 'an interview with Mr. Baker whose health precluded him continuing in his position any longer and asked to be released on 30th November next'. The Board decided that on the retirement of Baker, Bradford would be appointed as manager of the Newcastle steelworks. At the same meeting the Board was informed that its chairman, H. G. Darling, the new director, W. G. Duncan, and the general manager, Essington Lewis, had visited Broken Hill and Newcastle. They 'expressed their entire satisfaction with the way operations were proceeding'.[7]

Bradford was appointed assistant manager of the steelworks on 20 July 1923. L. J. Griffiths, who had been among those sent overseas in 1922, replaced Bradford as production superintendent. In September Bradford accompanied Lewis on his visit to Broken Hill. From then on Bradford was clearly marked as Lewis's 'understudy'. Bradford's position was further confirmed when he was appointed assistant general manager during Lewis's overseas tour in 1925. However, Bradford's brief was restricted. He was to remain at Newcastle and to attend Board meetings once in every five weeks. In August 1925, when the Premier of New South Wales was to discuss the 44-hour week with him, Bradford was instructed to defer the meeting, on the grounds that he had been urgently called to Melbourne, and to leave Darling to negotiate with the Premier.[8]

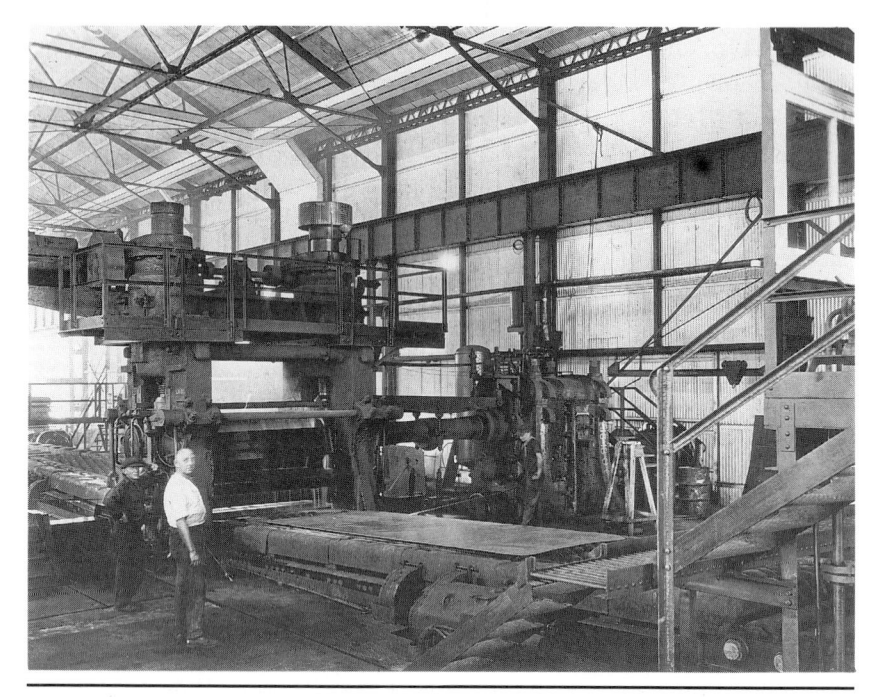

The 3-high plate mill at the BHP Newcastle steelworks, capable of producing plates up to 80 inches wide and down to three-sixteenths of an inch thick

Nevertheless, the hierarchy was clear and the new regime was to remain in place until the death of Bradford in 1943. Senior executives appointed at this time remained in office for life or until retirement. BHP's management now had an Australian homogeneity. Although the company's headquarters was in Melbourne and its principal sphere of activity was New South Wales, the origins of its management lay firmly in South Australia where Darling, Lewis, Mitchell, Bradford and Duncan had all grown up. They all remained intensely loyal to South Australia. It is not improbable that this loyalty was subsequently reflected in certain aspects of company policy.

On 31 August 1923 the Board met in Melbourne to confirm these arrangements. That evening the company gave a dinner for Baker and his wife, who sailed the following week for America. Baker's return to the United States was to be temporary as, now that the works were again in operation, the Board was anxious to retain his skills and connections, at least for a time, and at Baker's suggestion it accepted the following scheme for his retirement. Baker was to go to America at the beginning of September 1923 and to return to Australia in January 1924. He would finally leave Australia in June 1924. On his return to America he would act in an advisory capacity for the company for which he would receive a salary of £1000 a year; should he devote more than two months in any year to the company's affairs, he would receive additional remuneration, for the time involved, at the rate of his present salary.[9] This plan was agreed and for the rest of his long life—he died in 1942 aged eighty-one—Baker remained on friendly terms with the Board.

Changes in managerial style paralleled these changes in personnel. Three months after the resignation of Delprat, in April 1921, the Board, worried by the still-deteriorating economic conditions, appointed a committee to go to Newcastle to examine the estimates in connection with the proposed extensions. Darling, in particular, had been concerned about these for some time. The committee had before them a 'Statement of Capital Expenditure based on the General Manager's letter from Newcastle—3rd May 1920'. Delprat and Baker had, like many of their contemporaries in the stabler pre-war age, tended to work in approximate rather than actual figures. This had been further complicated by the fluctuating exchange rates of the post-war period. For instance, the Board had authorised £375 000 for the No. 3 blast furnace; of this £125 000 had been expended by January 1921 and there were orders outstanding for £194 000. But, before he left for America in February 1921, Baker had revised the original figure. He now stated that 'in his estimation the blast furnace would cost between £500,000 and £600,000 completed'.[10] There were also the partly completed orders in connection with the duplexing plant, the continuous mill, the sulphuric acid plant, and a bridge for stacking structural steel. All of these were in various stages of construction and there were varying states of uncertainty as to what exactly the estimates did or did not include.

The committee was composed of Jamieson, McKay, Darling (directors), Dickenson (company secretary), Lewis (general manager) and F. M. Mitchell (acting manager, steelworks). They all met at the Newcastle steelworks and conducted a thorough tour and investigation of the plant as well as of the company's associated interests. They decided to try to cancel any orders that were not immediately essential and any others that had not proceeded to the point where cancellation would be more expensive than completion. These included orders for a 40-inch bloom mill and the 18-inch and 24-inch continuous mills. An attempt to cancel the duplex plant or to sell it in the United States met with limited success as the Alliance Co., from whom it had been ordered, declared that it had been designed to BHP's specific requirements. They countered with the suggestion that the purchase be completed and that they would keep it in good condition and store it without charging rental. At the same time they pointed out that they too were in a difficult position as they owed the local bank sums at high interest; furthermore, a ship-stripping crane, store balance cranes and a charging machine were already boxed for shipment.

The committee also investigated the labour situation, in particular the effect Judge Beeby's decision to uphold the 44-hour week would have on the shift work essential for the continuous operation of the works. This resulted in a decision to write to the Premier outlining their special problems regarding labour and hours.[11] The tour of inspection was completed by a visit to John Lysaght & Co. Ltd and the Austral Nail Works Co. Ltd. As a consequence of this investigation there was a cut in proposed expenditure of about £2 000 000.[12] A rigorous system of accounting and inspection was instituted. Without reference to the Board, the managers at Iron Knob, Broken Hill and Newcastle could authorise the expenditure of £200 only and the general manager £2000. Accounting and inspection were to be the everyday characteristics of Lewis's general managership. They were used positively: to ensure that things were done efficiently and economically. To this end Lewis inspected the company's enterprises regularly. He gave due notice of his visits and expected everything to be in order on his arrival. Nothing missed his eye. At the same time he was an encouraging manager, praising warmly when he was pleased.

Meanwhile, demand was slackening, although more in some products than others. In September 1921, there was record productivity in the steel department, but the 12-inch and 8-inch mills had to be closed for lack of orders. The same happened again in December, when Lewis informed the Board that the 'pig iron outlook was disquieting'.[13] In fact there was a world surplus and Australian production costs were still high by world standards. Earlier that month Baker had reported to Lewis that the Governor of New South Wales, Sir Walter Davidson, whom he had met at a social function, had expressed concern over the cost of steelmaking. Baker had taken the opportunity to inform him of the necessity of reducing the cost of labour and coal to enable the industry to compete. The Governor replied that if the company would supply him with the figures he would try to influence the state government to secure some relief for the industry.[14]

By the second half of 1921 the Newcastle works were under severe financial pressure. In October 1921, the Board suspended all dividend payment 'until they can more closely ascertain the position as to prospects in the immediate future of the iron and steel industry having regard to the keen outside competition at present existing'.[15] The *Massey Greene Act* of 1920 had only partly shielded the industry from the dumping of cheap European steel finished, in whole or in part, in Britain. From Britain it was subsequently imported into Australia under the favourable imperial preference tariffs. The 1921 *Customs Tariff (Industries Preservation) Act*, was deliberately aimed 'to protect . . . the industries of the Commonwealth against unfair competition from overseas, especially from countries with depreciated currencies'.[16] Industries claiming such protection had to apply to a newly established Tariff Board. But it was only after full investigation that even partially effective tariffs were imposed in 1924, when the Tariff Board reported that:

> in order to protect the iron and steel industry, action had been necessary under the Customs Tariff (Industries Preservation) Act; and while the present conditions remain in Great Britain and the continent our iron and steel industry and the subsidiary industries will need the additional protection afforded by the Act.[17]

For the duration of the war, both G. & C. Hoskins and BHP had patriotically linked the price of steel to cost rather than demand. The Tariff Board was conscious of this important fact, noting in its *Annual Report* for 1926–27 that 'during the war . . . the prices of these products from overseas became abnormally high. It would have been possible for the local producers to have increased their price in keeping with those of the imported commodity but such action was not taken . . . Australia was saved £4 or £5 million'.[18] In consequence neither BHP nor Hoskins had been able to build adequate reserves to cushion the difficulties of the post-war era. In addition, there was a sharp rise in New South Wales rail freight charges and the supply of essential raw materials was further complicated by labour unrest.

Locally, the problems of 1921 were exacerbated by the inflationary spiral, which had started during the war and continued in the uncertain post-war economic conditions. This had flowed through to wage demands and created labour unrest. The long miners' strike at Broken Hill from May 1919 to November 1920 had not only involved the company directly but had also removed the income from the mine that could have ameliorated the difficulties confronting the steelworks. Then, the seamen's strike in 1919 had reduced the flow of ore from South Australia. The 1920 increase in New South Wales railway freight charges affected

Scrap being delivered by a works locomotive for charging to open-hearth furnaces at the BHP Newcastle steelworks. In the background a furnace is being charged with molten pig-iron.

the carriage of magnesite and other minerals mined within the state for use in the steelworks. Although this was a more serious concern for the Hoskins Iron and Steel Company than for BHP, it was worrying for both companies at a time when every effort had to be made to cut costs in face of British and foreign competition.

Dumping of cheap British and foreign goods remained a problem until the government, after the investigation by the Tariff Board, imposed an effective duty in 1924. In the early 1920s, exposed to foreign dumping and largely without the support of the Big Mine at Broken Hill, the new steelworks were close to bankruptcy. A falling market, combined with a rise in the basic wage and a 44-hour week, led to the temporary closure of parts of the works: as already noted, the 12-inch and 8-inch mills had to be closed for lack of orders for a week in September 1921 and again in December. Given the integrated nature of a steelworks, a stoppage in one department, for whatever reason, brought stoppages and lay-offs in others. On 15 December No.1 blast furnace was blown out and No. 2 blast furnace banked. The works were closed from Christmas to the end of January 1922, when BHP demanded a cut of a third in wages and the cost of coal to enable it to reopen.[19] The works were partially reopened while the company applied for a reduction in the basic wage. But, at the beginning of April, Justice Beeby rejected the company's request for an extension of time before implementing the 44-hour week. At this point, the Board decided that the only course available to it was to close the works.

On 18 April Lewis wrote a 'confidential' letter to Baker to inform him that 'we are closing down the whole plant and we none of us can tell how long we will be closed down. Therefore, it is wise at the outset to conserve all our resources and to bring our weekly out of pocket expenses down to an absolute minimum'. Baker was also requested to use only staff men once the works were closed. To this directive Baker replied that 'I am sure you are seized with the importance of retaining a nucleus of our skilled men, so that the starting up expense may not be too great. We have a number of skilled men outside of staff employees that I think it necessary to retain'. He then gave a list of jobs which he thought might be done.[20]

Lewis replied that the company would be delighted to do these 'right away' but for the present financial stringency and that they would be done at a later date. He re-emphasised the anxiety of the Board to have the work done by staff men—the company's emergency skeleton of skilled non-union men. Baker still protested, worried at the thought of losing the skilled work-force he had so painfully trained. Lewis wrote to him again on 5 May:

> From the line that you have taken in your letter I feel that I have failed to make myself explicit in my previous communications. The crux of the whole matter is one of finance; our cash position is that from now on practically no money will come in . . . our resources will be strained to the very utmost . . . the financial position controls the whole situation.

Lewis then went through the figures which Baker had submitted. He pointed out that they amounted to approximately one-third of the work-force when the plant was fully operative and he concluded: 'I am sure you will excuse my going into this matter so fully but I do wish you to be entirely informed of our actual position'. On 9 June Darling and Lewis reported to the Board that 'it had been arranged with Mr. Baker to limit the expenditure to £5,000 per week maximum'. F. R. Hockey, the superintendent at Iron Knob, was also told to reduce expenditure to an absolute minimum.[21]

To the Governor of New South Wales, Sir George Fuller, Lewis wrote a 'confidential' letter explaining that the company had been forced to close the works because

> we are unable to secure orders at the prices which we have to quote, since these prices are so much higher than the figures for which material can be imported from abroad after paying a substantial tariff. In Great Britain and in America they have been enabled to meet competition owing to the fact that they made adjustments in the price of coal and in wages to meet the altered economic conditions. During 1921 the wage reductions and the reductions in the price of coal in England were tremendous, whereas in Australia no apparent reduction in either of these two matters has been made.[22]

The real problem lay in the difference between the social standards acceptable to Australian society as defined in the Court of Conciliation and Arbitration, and those pertaining in the international commercial world in which the Australian iron and steel industry operated. To balance the gap between the two, either the price of goods had to fall or tariffs had to be further increased, thereby raising the price to local consumers. The price of goods could only be reduced by either obtaining cheaper coal, or the socially unacceptable lowering of wages, or a combination of both. The other alternative, correct tariff adjustment, particularly for a key industry, was a difficult and delicate task requiring more time than was available with a major industrial concern at a standstill. Similarly, although the works were modern and well run, the effectiveness of efforts to further increase efficiency could only be monitored after production recommenced.

Another remedy was vertical integration. Lewis had listed coal and freight as areas targeted for economies. Negotiations had begun to acquire a coal geologist from Britain. J. M. Morris was appointed and brought out to inspect the various options on coal land that BHP already held.[23] The escalation in the price of coal and the unreliability of its supply was a major and a continuing problem; for example, on 6 July 1923 the general manager informed the Board that the 'coal shortage [was] still causing great anxiety and becoming increasingly difficult. [He was] endeavouring [to] secure South Coast coke [to] keep two blast furnaces running—grave possibility [of] having to bank one Blast Furnace next week if position does not improve'. This recurrent problem was only solved when, after extensive exploration, BHP established its own coalmines. These were operated by a subsidiary company formed in 1923,

BHP Collieries Pty Ltd. In 1925 a Mr Fallins was appointed to manage BHP's first mine, the John Darling Mine. The mine began to supply the steelworks in 1927 and others followed thereafter.[24]

The shipping department, and the nucleus of the fleet, indicated the company's intentions regarding the sea-freight problem. In the early years of the steelworks BHP leased ships from Scott & Fell Ltd. In the post-war period the seamen's strike in 1919, and the shortages which this and other unpredictable factors created, encouraged BHP to develop its own shipping department. This began with the purchase of *Emerald Wings* and *Bright Wings* which were renamed *Iron Prince* and *Iron Baron; Iron* has subsequently been part of the name of most BHP ships and of all of those actually owned by the company. The shipping department, under the management of Mr Barter, was established in 1921 at the Melbourne head office.[25] The fleet did not get off to a particularly good start as in April 1923 *Iron Prince* was grounded off Cape Howe and subsequently declared a total loss. However, by August 1923 the Board had before it a sketch of a ship to be built to its own specifications. The Port Waratah Stevedoring Co. Pty. Ltd was also formed

The BHP ship *Iron Warrior* being loaded with finished products at the Newcastle steelworks wharf, 1938

in 1923 to operate harbour facilities. At the end of 1923 BHP had three ships, a new *Iron Prince* (formerly the *Dilga*), *Iron Warrior* and *Iron Knob*. By 1939 BHP had the largest coastal shipping line in Australia.

Similar attention was paid to the development of outlets for products, most of which had been foreshadowed when Lewis took office. By the end of 1924 the Board was inspecting a sample of the first wire rope made by the new Australian Wire Rope Pty Ltd established the year before. In the same year the by-product company De Meric & Co. Ltd was wound up and a new company, BHP By-Products Ltd, was established. The American input continued as J. B. Ladd (who continued to be the technical representative in the United States until his death in November 1931) was requested to find a by-product expert, particularly for tar, 'in connection with the management of the new company'. Mr Sibley was recruited and in August 1923 he sailed for Australia from San Francisco. In 1925 Ryland Bros (Aust.) Ltd was taken over by a share exchange, based on the closing price of BHP shares on 24 February 1925.[26]

During these years the pattern emerged for the establishment of other companies to finish or absorb BHP's basic product. Many of these companies, such as Lysaght Brothers & Co. Pty Ltd, started as subsidiaries of British firms and were eventually taken over by BHP. Britain had a reservoir of the skills required for finishing industries that was advantageous to both parties, particularly as the British firms knew the requirements of the Australian market. Furthermore, by the time they were taken over by BHP, the important financial hurdles associated with establishing a new enterprise had been surmounted, while BHP had consolidated its own industrial position. The forward and backward links developed during these years created a stable and independent organisation. Other companies, such as the Commonwealth Steel Products Coy. Ltd—for the production of railway wheels and axles—were started by Australian interests and subsequently attracted BHP investment.

There remained the labour questions of wages and hours, and throughout the early months of 1921 repeated and unsuccessful efforts were made to resolve this problem. Always suspicious of the Court of Conciliation's grasp of economic realities and ever conscious of the political dichotomy between government and industry, the BHP Board announced on 21 May that

> the compulsory arbitration of Australia is strangling the industries and crippling the economic progress of the country. It has already paralysed, as we have seen, the greatest of our national key industries and if it be not

promptly and effectively amended to permit of a mutual re-arrangement of wages, hours of work and coal prices . . . many other industries will soon inevitably fall into the same quagmire of stagnation in which the iron and steel industry is so unfortunately bogged.[27]

Five thousand men out of work in a key industry with a flow-on to other dependent industries created a serious, even an appalling, social problem, for there was little relief for those who were out of work. It was to this local and immediate problem that the judges of the Court of Conciliation and Arbitration addressed themselves, trying vainly to find an acceptable compromise. The militant labour movement, fresh from the long strike at Broken Hill, felt that BHP should carry the work-force through what they regarded as only a temporary downturn. The company, uncertain as to the nature or the duration of the economic recession, was convinced that without radical adjustments to local expectations the collapse of the industry in Australia was inevitable. Given the state of the industry in inter-war Britain, these fears were not unrealistic.

In August 1922 BHP applied for a wage cut of 10 per cent. But Judge Rolins questioned the Board's sincerity as, although they had stopped dividends, BHP had not reduced staff salaries or directors' fees. BHP replied that it would do so—and by 15 per cent—immediately the 10 per cent wage reduction was granted. The unions said that they would agree to these cuts on a temporary basis so long as BHP would agree to restore the present level of wages when the economy began to recover. BHP refused: the company did not believe that the industry could sustain labour costs at that level even under hypothetically normal conditions. Apart from a few reductions in high margins and overtime, Judge Rolin rejected the company's application.[28] BHP then appealed. The case was heard by judges Edmunds, Curlewis and Beeby, who rejected both the appeal and Judge Rolins's concessions, whereupon BHP declared that it had no intention of going bankrupt. Stalemate ensued. Shortly thereafter, H. G. Darling, now chairman of the BHP Board, declared that 'Industry is rapidly learning that no third party in the shape of arbitration courts can regulate business successfully. All settlements for the carrying on of business must come from within . . . The more courts there are, the more disputes become manufactured, and the greater the interference with industry'.[29] The retiring chairman, Bowes Kelly, had said a few months earlier that 'no government commands a magic wand by which the wheels of industry can, by a touch be set in motion, or an industrial Arcadia assured'.[30]

Eventually, in February 1923, the long dispute was brought to an end by a Conciliation Committee under the chairmanship of Judge Edmunds. It met in the board room at the Newcastle steelworks. BHP was represented by Baker and Bradford, with the company's industrial officers H. A. Mitchell and A. Burgess as alternates. The union representatives were Farquharson and Thomas. By this time BHP had ended its attempt to establish an American-style company union and accepted the Australian Workers' Union, much to the annoyance of the more militant Federated Ironworkers' Association. The reduction in wages now agreed was less than the 10 per cent originally demanded by BHP but the AWU agreed to a sliding scale which would relate increases and decreases in margins to the current state of the industry. During February 1923 the coke ovens and blast furnaces were relit and No. 3 blast furnace was blown in on 3 March. The various departments gradually came into production and by 4 May 1923 the general manager could report to the Board that the works were running smoothly and that the rod mill had started satisfactorily.[31]

Charging molten blast furnace iron into an open-hearth furnace from a 38-ton ladle, BHP Newcastle steelworks, *c.* 1930

The same drive for cost-cutting and long-term efficiency was applied to the quarries at Iron Knob. Mechanisation was increased and electrical power was provided from BHP's generators at Whyalla via a 33 000-volt transmission line to a substation at Iron Monarch. When Quarry E was opened in 1928, it was completely mechanised and a crushing plant was installed enabling the ore, which had previously been crushed at Whyalla, to be prepared at the quarries for shipment. This reduced the cost of the freight from Iron Knob to Whyalla, while handling the ore more economically. Quarry E supplied both Newcastle and Port Kembla from 1928 to 1935. Quarry A was then mechanised and reopened. At this juncture Quarry E was closed and its equipment was moved to Quarry F, which was then opened as a new, mechanised quarry. Quarries A and F met BHP's requirements for both export and domestic consumption until Quarry G was opened in 1954.[32]

BHP's leading quarry expert was F. R. Hockey. He was largely responsible for implementing these developments and, even more importantly, for establishing a group of BHP geologists trained to prospect in Australian conditions, about which very little was scientifically known at that time. Hockey joined the company in 1910. Since joining BHP he had largely worked under Lewis, first at Port Pirie, then he had been in charge of opening the Wardang Island limestone quarry before going to Iron Knob as a quarry officer in 1913. There he had been in charge of opening the quarries at Iron Knob and he had also been involved in supervising the construction work required to develop the harbour at Whyalla. In 1915–16 he was similarly responsible for opening up the limestone deposits and supervising the loading constructions at Devonport in Tasmania. In 1916 he returned to Iron Knob as superintendent.

Hockey had been among the first of the company's senior executives to go abroad after the war. His overseas report, written in 1921, is No. 4 in the company's archives (nos 1–3 are those of Delprat in 1919 and Lewis in 1920). From 1922 to 1924 Hockey and J. M. Morris, the consultant British geologist, were involved in BHP's coal feasibility exploration in New South Wales. At its successful conclusion Morris returned to England with a tangible expression of the company's gratitude in the form of a bonus, while Hockey went to head office in Melbourne as superintendent of mines and quarries. In 1932 he became general superintendent of mines and quarries and subsequently played a leading role in BHP's mineral diversification. Shortages of essential minerals, such as magnesite during World War I, had emphasised the need for finding reliable sources in Australia. Coal was also crucial to the industry. The rising cost of coal, combined with the restrictive practices associated with that industry, had emphasised the BHP's need to acquire a measure of independence in that area. The sale, at par, of BHP's 200 000 shares in Associated Smelters raised money to develop the John Darling Colliery.

Throughout the 1920s BHP employed specialists to advise and train its own geologists. They searched continuously for minerals connected with the company's activities. By the end of the decade BHP's geologists were the most highly trained team in Australia. When the depression emphasised the value of gold, Prime Minister Scullin suggested to Lewis that BHP might investigate the old Western Australian goldfields. In September–October 1931 Darling and Lewis went to Western Australia, via Whyalla, on a 23-day inspection of the various gold mining properties then under offer to BHP. In the course of this tour they covered 1750 miles. Hannan's North Mine was purchased and reopened. Apart from a few years during World War II, it was worked until 1951. Meanwhile, the search for gold continued. In December 1931 Darling and Lewis were investigating gold-bearing country on the Belubula River, near Mandurama in New South Wales. Small mining operations were opened, one near Cooma in 1936 and another near Wellington in 1938. These ventures (all in New South Wales), which were shut for some years during the war, brought barely adequate returns and they were finally closed in 1953 and 1958.

BHP's response to the Labor Prime Minister's suggestion was indicative of the co-operative special relationship that was gradually established between the Australian government and the country's largest industrial company. A strong Australian nationalism now began to permeate the company. It owed much to the personalities of H. G. Darling and Essington Lewis, both of whom were not only Australian-born but also products of the new Australian nationalism. The inter-war years marked the high tide of romantic or visionary nationalism. This was common to both the British Commonwealth countries and the new European nations acknowledged in the Treaty of Versailles. In 1942 Lewis refused a knighthood and shortly afterwards he wrote to Prime Minister Curtin to say: 'I feel I owe Australia everything and that Australia owes me very little'.[33] Thus, at the height of the depression, BHP diversified into gold, apparently for a mixture of patriotic and business reasons: the company had the expertise, the country needed gold, the ventures would provide employment and, hopefully, profit.

The BHP Board has always been singularly well informed of the current state of the industry throughout the world. From the end of World War I, BHP senior executives toured the world, continually informing the Board of economic conditions and the latest developments in technology. In the 1935 Jubilee Number of the *BHP Review* it was reported that, while it had been BHP policy 'almost from the very earliest days' to send officers abroad, since the inception of the steelworks this had increased and that:

> During the past fifteen years some seventy visits abroad have been made by numerous officers of the Company, and the information gained has in all cases been applied, resulting in increasing efficiency. In addition the Company's overseas technical consultants have visited Australia from time to time, for the purpose of studying local conditions and to confer with the Company's officers regarding plant and technical practice.[34]

In peacetime there was not a single year and probably very few months in which the Company was not receiving detailed reports from its executives overseas. This information gathering, while part of any efficient company, was, in the case of BHP, given an added impetus by isolation assisted by an independence, which had earlier shown itself in the establishment of the Port Pirie smelting operation at a time when most of the other mining companies were sending their zinc concentrates to Europe.

Under the long hegemony of Darling and Lewis, BHP consciously began to produce a company work-ethic. To ensure this, the company trained its own and, except under very special circumstances, promoted its own. This policy emerged early under the new regime. In 1925 Lewis wrote from London regarding a departmental appointment: 'I was hoping that it would not be necessary to import outside officers into this organisation, as I thought our policy was to bring along junior officers so that there would always be under-studies for the senior men'.[35]

When the works were shut down in 1922–23, BHP, although convinced that the works would ultimately reopen, had prepared for a long period of closure,[36] though not so long as eventuated. However, Lewis was determined that the time should be well spent and that its results would be apparent in increased efficiency when the works reopened. Throughout this period, company reorganisation was progressing. From this point of view the closure of the works proved valuable. Lewis, supported by the Board, was anxious that the heads of the various departments should be in touch with the latest overseas technology and the most recent developments in the industry. No less than nine senior executives went overseas during this period, many of them for the first time. Travel was still by sea and trips extending over a number of months were not always easy to arrange if the works were busy, or if there was a major problem which involved the expertise of a particular individual.

By 1924 trade was improving and all the major problems which had confronted the company appeared to have solutions. The directors could now contemplate further improvements and expansion. Baker was asked to investigate the De Lavaud process for making spun pipes and the Wilputte type of coke oven to replace the Semet–Solvay ones. The Semet–Solvay coke ovens, although the best available at the time they were installed, had never been satisfactory. On both subjects Baker sent back glowing reports, remarking that the De Lavaud process would displace sand-cast pipes for 90 per cent of pipe consumption.[37] Nevertheless, he considered that the patents were unduly expensive and that a new sand-spun process that was being developed might be an improvement.

On his return Baker began to write his final report. The installation of the new AC power plant in September completed the major refurbishment of the works begun during the closure. It was anticipated that the remainder of the work in hand would be completed by February 1925. Baker's original agreement was until the end of 1924, but, on 20 October 1924, shortly after he had completed his report, he was asked to stay until the end of March 1925.[38] The principal reason for this request was probably a scheme that Lewis brought before the Board in December 1924. By then it was clear that any further economies would have to come from increased capacity. With this in view, Lewis resurrected and brought before the Board the idea of duplicating the works. The sales department, under R. H. M. Rowe, considered that if steel was available they could sell over 7000 tons per week and the chief engineer gave a 'snap estimate' of £5 500 000 for the work. The question was how to finance it. The Board suggested that further and more precise details should be quietly obtained and that preliminary soundings should be made to see if the British firms Guest, Keen & Nettlefold & Co. Ltd and John Lysaght & Co. Ltd might consider having a financial interest in these expansions. On 23 January 1925 the Board considered estimates of £3 500 000 to £4 000 000, and suggested that Guest, Keen & Nettlefold might like to put in £1 250 000. To this end Sir John Beale, the chairman of Guest, Keen & Nettlefold, and the Board of John Lysaght were to be given all the technical and financial information they required to enable them to come to a decision on the matter.[39]

The time had finally come for David Baker to leave. He and his wife departed from Australia in a flurry of dinners (the one at Newcastle was attended by both the Hoskinses and the 83-year-old William Sandford), and a cascade of gifts. Finally, on 16 March 1925, the Board bade them farewell with a dinner at the Australian Club in Melbourne. The directors presented Baker with a tea and coffee service of Broken Hill silver, engraved with a view of the Newcastle steelworks, and Mrs Baker with a diamond watch.[40] An era had ended. The next day the Board was on its way to Newcastle to make one of its detailed tours of inspection,[41] and to discuss the future management of the steelworks with the new manager, Leslie Bradford.

Next month, Lewis, with his scheme for expanding the works in mind, left on a world tour of investigation and inspection. However, he was not long in Great Britain before he realised that any hope of finance from the British steel firms was likely to prove a mirage. By 1925 the financial dilemma confronting the British iron and steel industry had become acute. Not only was the industry in need of rationalisation, but many of the works were technologically outdated and had been sited to meet the needs of a former age. Although this had been the case for decades, in the inter-war years the problems facing the industry came to a head. Capital had to be written down and at the same time new capital had to be raised for modernisation. Works that had been expanded during the war in expectation of a post-war boom were faced with over-capacity.[42] In 1928 the *Iron and Coal Trades' Review* noted the fact

> that much capital, not only in ordinary shares but in preference shares and even debentures, will have to be written off is unhappily only too true, but this operation cannot affect production costs . . . if British industry is to keep pace with developments abroad, conditions must exist whereby profits can be earned to finance improvements. New capital must be provided for any scheme of rationalization immediately, as in most cases the last seven years have been a period of continued loss and it is impossible that new capital can be attracted under the present system of free imports.[43]

In Australia the fiscal and free trade policies of the federal government compounded the serious problem of foreign dumping. Until the imposition of effective protection, imperial preference had allowed foreign goods, with only a small British component, to flow through to Australia free of tax.

It was hardly surprising that, when he arrived in England, Lewis decided that the outlook did not justify investment discussions being continued at present. Shortly afterwards he recommended that they should be called off altogether. Pressed for the reasons that a financial association between BHP, Guest, Keen & Nettlefolds Ltd and John Lysaght Ltd had been abandoned, Lewis reported to the BHP Board that his reply had been that:

> the reasons generally were industrial and financial ones. Obviously his directors in Australia considered that at the present time the schemes as suggested were not propitious—would BHP approach same concerns later?—in General Manager's own personal opinion . . . such further approach was merely a matter of time.[44]

A consortium with British firms was unlikely to provide a sound financial basis. Other methods of expansion would have to be found.

Lewis, like Carnegie, was always particularly interested in production costs and his enquiries revealed that in Britain the production costs for pig-iron were high: 'practically nobody' Lewis reported 'is making pig iron for 60s. and that a very good cost for this material today is 65s'. However, this was balanced by the cost of converting pig-iron to steel which was 32 to 35 shillings a ton and for steel rail it was not expected to exceed 40 shillings per ton. At BHP's Newcastle steelworks the reverse was true for, whereas pig-iron could be made for approximately 60 shillings, converting it to steel was nearer 50 to 55 shillings and, Lewis wrote, 'now we have succeeded in getting our pig iron on a reasonable basis, we will have an opportunity of addressing ourselves more closely to the Open Hearth costs'.

> I mention these figures, and make these remarks for the sole purpose of making everybody realize that our efforts on the lowering of costs must not be relaxed. I think the officers at Newcastle have done marvelously well to get the costs they are now showing, and their efforts are entitled to the highest praise, and I am not overlooking this fact when I compare the English costs of operation with our present figures.[45]

Basic costs were not the only object of Lewis's investigations overseas. Knowing the international surplus capacity of the post-war industry, Lewis was well aware that import replacement offered the greatest scope for absorbing BHP's basic iron and steel. More than half of Australia's finished iron and steel goods were still imported. In Australia, there was a shortage of finishing industries and workers with the skills appertaining to them. Large contracts were usually dependent upon federal, state or local government projects of social or economic utility. It was with this in mind that Baker had originally recommended the production of rails. However, as the development of the communications system slowed down, the demand for rails, although always present to some degree, was a declining percentage of the total manufacture of ferrous goods. An important aspect of Lewis's overseas tour was to discover possible finishing industries, to persuade them to come to Australia and to establish markets for BHP's iron and steel on conditions favourable to both companies. Another possibility was for BHP to manufacture certain basic finished goods itself. Pipes were a particularly attractive commodity as, in the 1920s, they fitted in with the schemes of various governments to improve the standard of living. The reconstituted G. & C. Hoskins Ltd, the Hoskins Iron and Steel Company Ltd, had survived the vicissitudes of the early 1920s much more successfully than BHP, because they had greater vertical integration with their twin products of rails and pipes.

Lewis continued Baker's investigations into the De Lavaud spun pipe process. The English patent was held by the Stanton Iron Company Ltd, which had pioneered the process in 1919 and used it in its manufacture of both iron and concrete pipes. Lewis arrived in London on 5 July 1925 and was immediately pressured by Walter Wood, the representative of the 'so called independent Companies of the United States' who were also engaged in manufacturing centrifugally cast-iron pipes in a sand mould. They were very anxious that BHP should not finalise anything with Stanton Iron until BHP had seen a demonstration of its process, although Wood admitted that it was being challenged by the De Lavaud company as an infringement of their patents. The De Lavaud patents in the United States were held by the United States Cast Iron Pipe Co.: 'the principle of this process being the centrifugal casting of cast iron pipes in steel moulds'. Lewis then reminded the Board that, Baker 'has an intimate connection' with the US Cast Iron Pipe Co.[46]

Others besides BHP were interested in the De Lavaud process and shortly after his discussion with Wood, Lewis received a visit from Charles Hoskins, now on his last visit to the country which he had first left in 1852. Hoskins was also negotiating for the rights to the De Lavaud process. Confronted with two Australian suitors, the British firm tried to persuade BHP and Hoskins to jointly take out the Australian rights on the process. Hoskins suggested a territorial arrangement, namely, that if BHP took out the process then there should be an agreement between the two companies whereby Hoskins supplied New South Wales and Queensland, the Hoskinses' established pipe markets, and BHP supplied the other states. There should be a pipe plant in each state. Lewis did not rule out the idea of an arrangement, but he disagreed with the territorial plan and with the idea of establishing a separate plant in each state. The BHP Board came up with a different objection and cabled Lewis its resolution 'that the Board is opposed to linking up with Messrs Hoskins and unanimously and strongly against any form of monopoly'.[47]

Hoskins gave Lewis to understand that he was reluctant to see the expensive plant, which he had already installed in Australia, made redundant by this development. If BHP did not finalise its arrangements with Stanton Iron, neither would Hoskins, and the matter would be shelved until they were both back in Australia.[48] Shortly after his return, Charles Hoskins became seriously ill and died on 14 February 1926. His death was recorded in the Board minutes at BHP and a letter of sympathy was

Aerial view of the BHP Newcastle steelworks, *c.* 1927. The layout of the works allowed a logical flow of material from the wharves on the Hunter River inland through the blast furnaces, open-hearth furnaces and rolling mills. Service shops are towards the rear; coke ovens are on the right.

sent on behalf of the company. At the same meeting it was noted that Hoskins Iron and Steel intended to build two modern blast furnaces at Port Kembla. A year later, in 1927, Hoskins Iron and Steel acquired the sole rights for the De Lavaud process in Australia.

A few months later, on 8 May 1926, William Jamieson, the first general manager of BHP, died, and a seat on the BHP Board became vacant. The Board decided to offer it to its chief executive, Essington Lewis, who, in a very complex process, then resigned from being general manager to become, at the same salary, managing director. From that time onwards the company's chief executive has sat on the Board. The last piece of the gradual restructuring of the BHP administration, which had started with the resignation of Guillaume Delprat five years before, was now in place. BHP, despite many changes, was to retain the same administrative shape until after the resignation of Lewis twenty-six years later.

# 13

# THE AUSTRALIAN IRON AND STEEL COMPANY

AFTER THE WAR THE Hoskins enterprises had to face long-term challenges which, although not as pressing as those at BHP, were fundamental, even fateful. This was largely due to the fact that G. & C. Hoskins Ltd, and its successor, Hoskins Iron and Steel Company Ltd, belonged to an earlier managerial era when the owner and manager were indistinguishable. This arrangement had usually meant that the new manager, if not actually the son of the old manager, came from within the family group. Frequently this provided distinct and more intractable problems of succession than those that occurred in large public companies. By 1919 George and Charles Hoskins realised that the family business had to be reconstructed for the next generation. Their children could hardly be expected to share the close relationship that the brothers had forged during their early struggles.

Eventually the brothers decided that Charles should buy George out and, on 30 July 1920, G. & C. Hoskins Ltd became the Hoskins Iron & Steel Company Ltd (HISC).[1] The two businesses could not be split between the two families, for the iron and steel manufacture and the pipe works were interdependent. Indeed this vertical integration had kept the Lithgow works viable in the difficult years after the collapse of the postwar boom. The pipe market was so important that in 1921 Hoskins established another plant for making steel-locking bar pipes in Brisbane. This plant only operated for a few years before its activities were transferred to the company's principal pipe works in Sydney. But they were important years, as the company's presence in Queensland enabled it to

## 13 THE AUSTRALIAN IRON AND STEEL COMPANY

Arthur Sidney Hoskins, 1892–1959, a life-long supporter of the iron and steel industry. He was joint Managing Director of Hoskins Iron and Steel Co. Ltd from 1924 to 1928 and of the Australian Iron and Steel Co. Ltd from 1928 to 1935 in conjunction with his brother Cecil. After the latter company merged with BHP he became the manager of the Port Kembla steelworks until 1949.

tender successfully for contracts in Brisbane, Rockhampton, Warwick and Cairns, thus opening a market in Queensland for its iron and steel manufacture during a very difficult trading period.

Four years later Charles Hoskins officially retired and his two sons, Cecil and Sidney, became joint managing directors of the company, repeating the managerial pattern of the preceding generation. In the case of Cecil and Sid Hoskins the bond was further strengthened when they married sisters. At the steelworks they worked from adjoining offices and shared a common secretary, the able and formidable Bessie Foskett.[2] Sibling community of interest and absolute trust operated as a powerful supportive force within the partnership. It was a strength as long as it was confined to the family company, but there is some evidence that it did not translate as effectively into the management of a public organisation. Temperamentally the brothers were complementary; Cecil, the older, was the driving force with some of his father's abrasiveness, while Sid, who inherited some of his Quaker mother's attributes, was a listener and adviser.

Cecil Harold Hoskins, 1889–1971, c. 1950, a major force in the development of the Australian iron and steel industry. He was the Chairman and joint Managing Director of both Hoskins Iron and Steel Co. Ltd (1924–28) and of the Australian Iron and Steel Co. Ltd (1928–35). Subsequent to the merger with BHP he was General Manager of the Port Kembla steelworks until 1950. He was knighted in 1960.

What were the Lithgow works like and what problems confronted them at the formation of HISC after World War I? The illustrated book prepared to influence the Tariff Board gives a pictorial record of the works and their related activities in 1915. Further details emerge from a report on the works filed by Essington Lewis, who visited Lithgow on 24 January 1917.[3] Lewis noted that, while Hoskins had coal for raising steam-power located at the works and coke was being made from coal mined in the vicinity of Lithgow, the remainder of their raw materials had to be rail freighted, often from considerable distances, and, although Lewis did not spell it out, heavy freight costs also applied to the marketing of HISC products. Of the three open-hearth basic steel furnaces, one was still being built. The two in operation were small, with capacities of thirty and forty tons; however, the new one had an estimated capacity of eighty tons. At the same time, Lewis noted an important advantage, remarking that 'they use large quantities of scrap iron, a contract having been entered into with the NSW government'.

Unlike BHP's Newcastle works, the mills had no soaking pits; instead they depended upon small, coal-fired reheating furnaces. On being told that it was intended to install soaking pits, Lewis simply noted: 'these mills are very antiquated but the whole of this department is being remodelled and an up to date plant installed. A lot of iron puddling furnaces have been used but these are now closed down'. In the foundry he found that 'all the steel and iron rolls required are made by themselves'. At that time the iron and steel works employed about 700 men. A further 1000 were employed in the company's associated activities, including the Sydney pipe works. In general, he concluded, 'the whole works at present look rather dilapidated but they are now being brought up to a much better state of efficiency'.[4]

After the war Hoskins found himself in a position that was similar to that of many contemporary iron and steelworks of a similar size in Britain. The problems confronting him should be seen in this context. In Britain, at the end of World War I, both government and industry were well aware of the massive difficulties confronting them. Their failure to solve the problems of maturity and obsolescence had long-term national and international consequences. As early as 1916 the Asquith government had appointed a 'Committee on Commercial and Industrial Policy after the War'. Seven departmental committees of the Board of Trade reported to it. One of these dealt with the iron and steel trade. The evidence which came before the members of the iron and steel trades committee on the state of the industry was far from reassuring. For instance, they were told by A. K. Reese, the general manager of the Cardiff works of Guest, Keen & Nettlefold, that many 'modern' plants were in fact simply antiquated technology constructed on a larger scale. C. G. Atha, the general manager of the Frodingham Iron and Steel Company, pointed out that the industry was faced with a huge task, 'as the final aim must be nothing short of a complete replacement of the great majority of existing plants . . . and learning to manage and operate such [replacement] plants in accordance with modern practice and methods'.[5]

However, the problem lay not so much with capital-intensive technological replacement, enormous though this was, but with its social implications combined, in certain cases, with the inevitablility of mergers and relocation. Democratic opinion as expressed through the ballot box inevitably exerts a myopic influence on all governments. During the inter-war period successive British governments stopped short of the social and economic consequences of abandoning old metallurgical districts, despite their obvious logistical problems. They felt, probably correctly, that in the economic conditions of the inter-war years such massive changes would inevitably have placed intolerable strains on social order.

Shrewd, imaginative and courageous, Charles Hoskins was well aware of difficulties confronting him. His works had followed the pattern of the British ironmasters. He too had expanded old technology and, like his British counterparts, he not only needed new equipment but also suffered from the logistical problems of an out-of-date location. Here the similarity ended as he did have the opportunity to abandon an old metallurgical district and start afresh. Australian industrial society was still sufficiently new to adjust to so radical and painful a dislocation of labour. Sir Cecil Hoskins said that three major factors contributed to his father's final decision to move to Port Kembla: the 1920 increase in rail freight charges; the lack of good coking coal in the western coalfields; and the disappointing quality and quantity of New South Wales deposits of iron ore, which meant that this basic raw material would have to be brought from another state.[6] Together these imperatives meant that the works would have to be relocated on a coastal site.

It is uncertain exactly when Charles Hoskins realised that relocation was essential. Certainly, when he attended the opening of the Newcastle steelworks in 1915, he was too shrewd not to have realised the advantages of BHP's modern plant and, as he was ferried to the works, not to have envied their coastal site. Similarly, he would have been aware of the contemporary British debate on the future of their once famous industry and the dilemmas confronting it. When the New South Wales government announced its increased freight rates in January 1920, they provided both a catalyst and an excuse. Hoskins's reaction was immediate. Closing the works, he declared that 'the new freight rates dealt a death-blow at the establishment of manufacturing industries in country districts'. A few days later he announced that the new rates 'make it impossible to carry on the business at Lithgow, and we consider that, under the circumstances, the quicker we get out of Lithgow the better'.[7] Four months later HISC Board minutes recorded that negotiations were under way for the purchase of 380 acres of land from the Wentworth estate at Port Kembla.[8] The purchase was finalised in 1924, and the land became the core of the Port Kembla steelworks site. As at Newcastle, the area was subsequently enlarged by the purchase of various adjoining parcels of land, added as the works expanded and related industries joined the complex. In fact, the Port Kembla works had greater potential for immediate expansion than BHP's Newcastle works as, although the site had its own problems, it was not a tidal swamp.

Port Kembla was the obvious choice for a coastal site; in 1912 Baker had considered it before deciding on Newcastle. At fifty-five miles from Sydney, Port Kembla was the nearest deep-water harbour to the capital and business centre of New South Wales. Hoskins's business was very much New South Wales-oriented and, with his pipe works at Rhodes and Alexandria, he was still part of the Sydney business community. In addition, about seven miles from Port Kembla, Hoskins had coal deposits and coke ovens at Wongawilli, near Dapto. HISC also had limestone leases at Marulan. Marulan, although only about sixty miles from the projected steelworks, presented a logistics problem. It was on the tablelands near Mittagong and separated from Port Kembla, on the coastal plain, by a high escarpment. The existing railways ran from Sydney along the coast or direct to Victoria and Melbourne through the towns on the tableland. Hoskins required the co-operation of the New South Wales government to provide a direct rail link between Marulan and Port Kembla for there was no link between the tableland and the coast except a triangular one through Sydney. The escarpment ensured that such a link would be difficult and expensive to construct. After he had made his initial declaration, Hoskins moved slowly, implying that the Port Kembla works would be in addition to the Lithgow works. The impression was given that the latter would supply the west of the state, while the new works would develop the industrial potential of the south coast. It was difficult for the New South Wales government to refuse to support such a proposition and it was naturally attractive to local interests in Wollongong and the Illawarra. In 1923 Charles Hoskins successfully concluded negotiations for the New South Wales government to construct a branch railway line from Moss Vale on the tableland to Port Kembla. The agreement was ratified by his sons in 1927 against a promise by the Hoskins Iron and Steel Company to build an iron- and steelworks at Port Kembla in the near future. In addition, HISC undertook, giving a bond of £100 000 (to be returned as the work progressed), to spend at least £650 000 on the plant within three years.[9]

By 1925 the development of the Lithgow plant was virtually over. Apart from the No. 1 blast furnace, most of the equipment which Hoskins had acquired from William Sandford in 1907 had been replaced. In a publication of 1925, HISC stated that its assets at Lithgow included:

The steam locomotive 'Eskbank' c. 1936. The first locomotive used at Eskbank ironworks, it operated there from 1905 until transferred to AIS steelworks, Port Kembla, in 1927. It was finally retired in 1937.

2 blast furnaces—combined capacity of 3,500 tons a week.
A Power House.
Coke ovens.
Open-hearth steelmaking furnaces—2 × 80 tons, 1 × 70 tons.
28" rail & billet mill.
A modern 10" bar mill for rolling small bars.
Corrugated rolls.
Coal mines.
Maintenance & engineering shops.
Iron & Steel Foundry.
Locomotives & rolling stock.[10]

In 1968 J. Rue, who joined HISC as an electrical apprentice in 1928, when the Lithgow works were in their last stages, recollected:

> By modern standards the plant presented a somewhat tumbled-down appearance. Some parts of it may have been painted at one time but little evidence of this survived, but I suppose there was really no necessity for either protection or decoration. It was far from the sea and rust was no problem—besides paint cost money . . . There was no crane in the [work]-shop itself, heavy articles being either rolled or dragged . . . High on the

## 13 THE AUSTRALIAN IRON AND STEEL COMPANY

... wall was a long board and painted on it in letters a foot high the motto 'It can be done—It must be done'. And done it was—mostly by manpower and sweat.[11]

Mechanisation was minimal. There was a power supply of 480 volts created by four generators each of about 200-kilowatt capacity, directly coupled to vertical Bellis & Morcom steam engines. Electric lights were either 60 or 300 watt. Rails were rolled on a two-stand mill direct from steel ingots. To the end the Lithgow works were undercapitalised and poorly equipped for the tasks they were undertaking and 'It can be done—It must be done' led to *ad hoc* solutions that were often dangerous.[12] Although Essington Lewis had been told, in 1917, that changes in the works were imminent, post-war trade, after the short-lived boom, was not conducive to what shortly became interim remedial expenditure.

Once the decision to erect a steelworks at Port Kembla had been taken, the Hoskins brothers divided their responsibilities. Cecil Hoskins looked after finance and the company's Sydney interests, including the pipe manufacture, while his brother was responsible for the new steelworks. The Port Kembla plant was carefully planned to avoid the chaotic growth which had caused so many inefficiencies at Lithgow. Work

The BHP steamship *Iron Warrior*, with a cargo of 5000 tons of South Australian iron ore, unloading the first ore to be delivered at the AIS steelworks jetty, Port Kembla, 1928

AIS steelworks, Port Kembla, No. 1 blast furnace plant under construction, 1927. Steelwork for the American-designed blast furnace and hot-blast stoves is well advanced, as are the power-house and boiler house to the left. The locomotive 'Eskbank' (ex-Lithgow) is noticeable near the white building at left.

on the site began on 1 January 1927 with the laying of railway track and the construction of a deep-water wharf in Port Kembla harbour, the No. 1 blast furnace, a boiler-house and a power-house. The master plan for what was to become the No. 1 steelworks included four blast furnaces, three of which were eventually built (No. 2 in 1938 and No. 3 in 1952; in February 1987, although decommissioned, they were all still standing, complete with their blowing engines).[13] Two more blast furnaces were built in 1959 and 1972 respectively on the site of No. 2 steelworks. At Wongawilli, the battery of coke ovens was increased from eighty to 120 ovens to meet the requirements of the new blast furnace.

The blast furnace was of an American design supplied by Freyn Engineering, Chicago. It was selected by Sid Hoskins and his chief engineer, F. T. Merrett. Although small by present standards, in 1928, when it was blown in, it was declared to be the 'largest in the British Empire'.[14] With a rated production capacity of 800 tons per day, it was approximately twice the capacity of both of the Lithgow furnaces combined. It had a height to the stockline of 87 feet 6 inches and an 18-foot diameter hearth. On a flat and featureless site, the blast furnace, standing at an overall height of 160 feet, flanked by three hot blast stoves 105 feet high and 20 feet in diameter and neighbouring plant buildings, was an island of industrial activity in an otherwise deserted area. The furnace was blown in on 29 August 1928. It was lit by Charles Hoskins's widow, Emily Hoskins, and, following the American custom, named after her. It performed well until it was blown out for the last time fifty years later.[15]

A furnace of this size required considerable blowing capacity and this was provided by a Brown–Boveri turbo-blower of 60 000 cubic feet per minute capacity operating at thirty pounds pressure. In addition there was a reserve blower previously installed at Lithgow in 1923. This was a reciprocating blower made by Thompson & Co. of Castlemaine in Victoria and with a capacity of 45 000 cubic feet per minute at twenty-five pounds pressure. It was said to be 'the largest engine designed and made in Australia from Australian materials'. The blowers were located in the power-house adjacent to the blast furnace, which also housed two electric generators interconnected with the Public Works Department electricity supply. The generators were all supplied by steam raised in boilers fired either by blast furnace gas or fine coke and coals.[16]

Cast-iron pipes being made in the spun pipe plant at AIS steelworks, Port Kembla, using the De Lavaud process, c. 1929. Molten iron from a cupola is being poured into a rapidly rotating mould from a ladle at the rear.

After the blast furnace, the next major section of the plant was a cast-iron pipe-making facility commissioned ten months later on 26 June 1929. In 1927 HISC acquired sole manufacturing and selling rights in Australia and joint (with the Stanton Iron Works) manufacturing and selling rights in New Zealand of the De Lavaud process.[17] In this process the liquid iron was poured into a water-cooled steel mould that rapidly spun on its long axis, causing the iron to spread uniformly over the inner surface of the mould where it solidified to form a pipe. Four of these casting machines were installed producing pipes from four to twenty inches in internal diameter. They were fed by pig-iron remelted in two cupola furnaces, each with a melting capacity of twenty tons per hour. The process eliminated almost all of the flaws in casting and also greatly increased production as 'one machine would produce 47 pipes in an hour, whereas at the company's old works it took five men three days to turn out the same number'.[18] The technique produced a lighter and more uniform pipe than the conventional sand-casting methods and its superior qualities brought it a ready market.

The De Lavaud process was invented by a French engineer during World War I. In 1917 the National Iron Corporation's works in Toronto, Canada, proved that it was a commercial proposition. Within the next few years it was developed at the Stanton Iron Works in England and the United States Cast Iron Pipe & Foundry Co. The De Lavaud pipe-making facility complemented HISC's existing pipe works. Pipe manufacture was always an important part of HISC's business, and, during these years of increasing urban amenities, it was particularly valuable. The De Lavaud shop's advanced technology made it an important part of the Port Kembla works.

The discrepancy between Australian aspirations and capital was largely met by overseas borrowing. These loans were serviced by foreign exchange provided by the export of minerals and primary produce. However, in the industrial sector, where it was expressed in high wages incommensurate with productivity, the basic discrepancy between production and consumption remained acute. In 1929 Cecil Hoskins explained that wages represented 92 per cent of the cost of making steel. He illustrated this by stating that in England, where wages were lower, it cost £8 per ton to make steel rails, whereas at Port Kembla the cost for the same product was £12.[19] In order to reduce the high cost of labour, labour-saving equipment was introduced wherever possible in the new steelworks. Unlike the older-style hand-charged blast furnaces at Lithgow, the new furnace at Port Kembla was equipped with the latest

## 13 THE AUSTRALIAN IRON AND STEEL COMPANY

labour-saving devices. This was typified by the electrically operated charging system, which allowed one man to control the collection of burden (the ore, flux, coke and so on) from the bins, its transfer to the skip and elevation by the skip hoist to the furnace top, where it was fed into the stack through a McKee distributor and double bell and cone system. There was also a pig-casting machine, so that

> the molten iron is tapped into large enclosed mixer-type ladles. There are two of these, having a capacity of 125 tons of molten iron each. Carried on massive steel bogies, the ladle of metal is hauled by loco from the furnace cast house to the pig-casting machine where the liquid iron is tipped by the ladle's own electric motor into the launder feeding the moulds. The pig-casting machine is of the double-strand continuous-chain mould type ... Pigs weigh approximately 80 lbs. each. The pigs are water cooled in the moving moulds, and discharging direct into trucks for delivery or for the pig-iron stocking yard nearby.[20]

This saved the labour associated with casting into a pig-bed. At the beginning, before the open hearths or the spun pipe plant were completed,

Pig mill at AIS steelworks, Port Kembla, c. 1930. Molten iron from the blast furnace is being poured from a torpedo ladle and cast into chill moulds which form two continuous belts. This process superseded casting into sand beds, as practised at Lithgow.

these pigs were freighted to HISC's Sydney or Lithgow works or to the open market.

In his 1923 submission to the New South Wales government, Charles Hoskins estimated the cost of the new steelworks at £2 000 000. To raise funds for the new plant, a float of 300 000 £1, 7.5 per cent cumulative preference shares was launched in 1926 and oversubscribed. However, an enterprise of the size envisaged required capital on a scale which it would have been difficult, if not impossible, for what was still essentially a family company to raise in Australia at that time. The financial requirements of the Port Kembla steelworks led to the formation of a new company, Australian Iron and Steel Limited, in 1928. AIS was an amalgamation of Hoskins Iron and Steel Co. Ltd (share capital £1 000 000), Dorman Long & Co. Ltd (£600 000), Howard Smith Ltd (£400 000) and Baldwins Ltd (£100 000).[21]

This particular type of amalgamation was a common method of financing expansion at a time when the British imperial market was adjusting to the political and economic aspirations of the independent dominions. It was against this background that BHP had considered approaching John Lysaght Ltd and Guest, Keen & Nettlefold Ltd, before Lewis's overseas tour in 1925 indicated to BHP the full extent of the financial problems confronting the British iron and steel industry. The history of the Australian industry between 1928 and 1935 can only be fully understood if the ramifications of this imperial background are taken into account.

It has been estimated that 60 per cent of Australian demand for iron and steel in the 1920s was met by imports. Many British firms, realising that the imperial market was changing, attempted to safeguard their outlets by establishing wholly owned subsidiary firms in the dominions, where their traditional skills would be at a premium. It was anticipated that these enterprises would prosper in the expected post-war boom and provide an outlet for surplus capacity in Britain. Naturally it was hoped that they would provide the parent company with a value-added bonus in the profits from goods produced by their Australian subsidiary for the local market. This policy was quite explicit and, in August 1927, Sir Hugh Bell, whose own family firm had amalgamated with Dorman Long in 1902, wrote to Cecil Hoskins explaining that:

> our policy has been looking for an outlet for the produce of our English works in various countries of the world even when in order to accomplish this object, it was necessary to establish manufactories to use the steel we

## 13 THE AUSTRALIAN IRON AND STEEL COMPANY

imported ... in so far as your new enterprise was successful, it would go to defeat the object we had in view in establishing constructional works first at Melbourne and more recently in Sydney.

The letter emphasised this point before concluding that their desire to establish 'intimate relations between your company and ourselves might be accomplished if you are willing to come to some arrangement by which our investments of a permanent character in Australia were made to form part of your new enterprise'.[22] The final agreement between the co-operating firms included a clause stating that AIS would not purchase steel from Britain except from Dorman Long, which would quote AIS its most favourable price.

Baldwins Ltd, the other British firm involved in the consortium, was interested in disposing of surplus machinery that it had installed in expectation of the post-war boom, and also in establishing a tin-plate manufacture in Australia using the new Watkins process. They had initially suggested that the licence for this process should be acquired by themselves and Hoskins. The new company, Baldwins & Hoskins Steel Co., would undertake to purchase from Baldwins 'a full supply of sheared and open blackplate on a sliding scale on the market price of tinplate f.o.b. South Wales'. At the same time, Sir Charles Wright, the chairman of Baldwins, told Hoskins that he understood that Stewarts & Lloyd had been negotiating with BHP for steel supplies estimated at 40 000 tons annually. Wright indicated that he understood that Stewarts & Lloyd were not happy over the deal and suggested that Hoskins might try to attract them into his consortium. However, Hoskins replied that, much though he would like to have Stewarts & Lloyd, he did not wish to quarrel over their involvement with BHP 'as we are very friendly with the latter and wish to remain so'.[23]

BHP and Hoskins had been on friendly terms from the start of the Newcastle works. Both companies were aware that cut-throat competition would be mutually disadvantageous and that both companies faced common problems, such as overseas competition, tariffs and labour relations. They could and did assist each other; for example, when either company was relining its blast furnace, they supplied each other with pig-iron at an agreed price. They formed a cartel regarding sales to merchants and agreed the division of state and federal government contracts between them.[24] In 1935, on receiving the souvenir edition of *BHP Review*, Sid Hoskins congratulated Lewis, writing that 'although the book tells a wonderful story, it cannot tell the splendid part which you have played in it . . . I feel that on behalf of steel makers both here and abroad, I must take my hat off to you as an expression of sincere admiration from your brother craftsmen'.[25]

The state of the British iron and steel industry even before World War I had encouraged the formation of consortiums such as AIS. The overwhelming majority of British firms had originated as family businesses and the vicissitudes of time ensured that there would be a long tradition of mergers and take-overs; for example, Dorman Long & Co. Ltd had absorbed Bell Brothers (1902), North Eastern Steel Co. (1903), Sir Bernhard Samuelson & Co. (1917) and the Carleton Iron Company (1920).[26] These amalgamations had included not simply the iron and steel plants but a variety of assorted interconnected enterprises, such as ore- and coal-mines as well as finishing plants. But their subsequent development, often for historical reasons, had fallen short of the radical rationalisation that was needed. After 1921, when the immediate post-war boom ended, at least eleven British firms, including both Baldwins and Dorman Long, paid no dividend on their ordinary shares for a decade; Bolckow, Vaughan & Co. Ltd and the United Steel Companies Ltd were in the same predicament.[27]

By the end of World War I, the magnitude of the problem was finally realised, but for the social reasons already considered, the extent of such rationalisation was limited. Nevertheless, in an attempt at rationalisation similar to that which had taken place in the United States at the turn of the century, many historic steel firms were merged in whole or in part during the inter-war years. For instance between 1927 and 1929 the steel-making enterprises of Vickers, Armstrong-Whitworth and Cammell Laird were united to form the English Steel Corporation, while their engineering, armaments and shipbuilding components remained with the original companies. Another rationalisation was that of the steel-making enterprises in the Sheffield and Scunthorpe areas of Thomas Firth and John Brown to form Firth Brown; John Brown's coal and shipbuilding interests remaining separate. The formation of AIS reflected this type of merger. Indeed a merger with closer links to AIS was that in 1930 of Guest, Keen & Nettlefold's Dowlais and Cardiff works with those of Baldwins at Port Talbot, Margam and Briton Ferry in South Wales to create the firm of Guest, Keen & Baldwins.[28]

In 1927, while discussions on the formation of AIS were under way, the industry went through one of its periodic downturns and Dorman Long emphasised that one of its conditions would be that the necessary capital should be raised in Australia. The Hoskins brothers, who had hoped for British capital, considered 'that the present was not a favourable time for the issue of capital in Australia'. The delicacy of the economic balance was reflected a month later when Cecil Hoskins wrote to Dorman Long's Sir Hugh Bell that 'we have been blessed with satisfactory rain and a change of Government in this state, which will help to restore our normal prosperity'.[29] Although in 1928 the times were hardly propitious for raising capital in either Australia or England, they were infinitely better than they became a year later. AIS was able to raise a further £1 000 000 through a public share issue of 1 000 000 7.5 per cent cumulative preference shares. When applications closed in June 1928 the issue was oversubscribed. At 30 November 1928 the new company had an authorised capital of £5 000 000. This was divided into 3 400 000 ordinary £1 shares and 1 500 000 cumulative preference £1 shares. The issued capital was £3 100 000. The remaining 1 400 000 ordinary and 500 000 preference shares were reserved.[30] This enabled the steel-making facilities to be built and the installation of the heavy mills obtained from Baldwins in South Wales.

All the heavy mill equipment—the buildings, mills, drives and engines—was transferred from Baldwins' plant at Margam in South Wales, as were

The AIS 40-inch bloom mill. This electrically driven reversing mill was purchased from Baldwins Ltd of the UK and is shown installed in the Baldwins steelworks at Margam, South Wales, prior to dispatch to Australia.

The 36-inch structural mill at AIS steelworks, Port Kembla. A bloom is being rolled in the roughing stands on the left, driven by a 16 000-horsepower Galloway steam engine brought with the mill from Margam, South Wales. The finishing rolls at right are simultaneously rolling a structural section, which was possible because these rolls were independently driven by a 5000-horsepower Davy engine obtained from Lithgow.

the cranes, roller tables, hot saws, soaking pits and all auxiliaries. This extraordinary operation involved hiring special Norwegian ships with heavy lifting cranes to transfer the plant, in its entirety, from South Wales to Port Kembla.[31] The plant consisted of a bloom mill and structural mill. The single-stand 40-inch bloom mill had been built, in 1917, by Davy Bros Ltd, Sheffield.[32] It was driven by an 18 000-horsepower electric motor weighing 250 tons, which, in 1930, was described as 'one of the largest electric motors in the world'. The 36-inch structural mill, consisting of three stands of rolls, also came from Baldwins where it had been the largest and heaviest structural mill in Britain. Its two roughing stands were driven by a 16 000-horsepower reversing engine and the finishing stand by a 5000-horsepower reversing engine, both of which were steam powered. The 36-inch structural mill produced a wide range of rails, structural sections and billets. In addition the first finishing stand could be set up to roll plate. This equipment represented Baldwins' total contribution to the new company. It had purchased these large mills in the hope of the post-war boom. When this did not materialise, they were surplus to requirements.

As at Newcastle and Lithgow, the basic open-hearth steelmaking process was adopted. The arrangement with Dorman Long included its structural steel fabricating shops, except those required for the Harbour

Bridge contract. AIS had made the most of its assets and, in particular, the business reputation of the Hoskins family. Furthermore, AIS had been fortunate in its timing and opportunity. However, the available capital and the cash-flow position of the new consortium was, individually and collectively, vulnerable, particularly in view of the severe economic depression which confronted the new company before it was able to become securely established.

After World War I the financial centre of the world had moved from London to New York where, on 29 October 1929, the Wall Street securities market crashed. The ensuing depression highlighted Australia's position as a debtor nation and its dependence upon the climate of international finance for capital. In the scare that followed the Wall Street crash, credit came under severe international scrutiny. Australian overseas borrowing virtually stopped. At the same time the price of Australian primary products fell on overseas markets. As unemployment rose and revenues fell, the crisis was compounded. Rising expectations had encouraged wage increases in previous years that had not been balanced by increased productivity. An acute balance of payments crisis had been created by the dependence of the economy upon overseas borrowing and the need to service the loans. About 70 per cent of the Australian states' revenues was absorbed in servicing debt.[33] Much of this borrowing had been to develop social infrastructure (for example communications, housing, water and sewerage).

Public capital formation, in the aftermath of World War I, with its demand for pipes, rails and structural components, had increased the dependence of HISC, and its successor AIS, upon state and federal government contracts. Traditionally and, particularly while they were at Lithgow, logistically, they were closely tied to the economic fortunes of New South Wales. During the 1920s HISC's New South Wales connections and its public contract market orientation had worked to the company's advantage providing it with a reliable market. During the depression this changed, for, as the most industrialised state, New South Wales felt the depression most immediately and acutely; its government revenues were severely curtailed. In April 1934 Cecil Hoskins, commenting on the effect of these cut-backs on AIS, stated: 'When the company was formed . . . its basis for work was mainly governmental, but it had been affected seriously by the changed policies of the Governments, and, in consequence, business in such things as the railways was now almost non-existent'.[34] In contrast, BHP's market was broader based and more oriented towards the private sector, which recovered more quickly.

When the federal and state governments recovered from the immediate shock of the magnitude of the financial crisis, they were bombarded with conflicting advice. The conservative view was deflationary. It was shared by the international financiers, such as Sir Otto Niemeyer, whom the Bank of England sent to Australia to investigate the situation and advise them on the large outstanding federal and state loans. Australian governments hoped, unsuccessfully, that Niemeyer's appearance would increase international confidence in the Australian economy but, after a month's inspection, Niemeyer told the premiers:

> there seems to me to be little escape from the conclusion that in recent years Australian standards have been pushed too high relatively to Australian productivity and to general world conditions and tendencies. If Australia does not face that issue, she will not be able to keep even those standards which she might hope to carry by taking timely action, and she will see an inevitable increase in unemployment.[35]

Confronted with this analysis, the premiers agreed to cut costs and balance their budgets. The problem was the magnitude of the deflation required and the unacceptably high level of unemployment it would create. The ALP felt that the erosion of the working-class standard of living was to be avoided at all costs. Labor, therefore, advocated an inflationary solution: for governments to spend their way out at home and to adjust overseas finances through exchange control and currency devaluation.

Resentment was particularly strong in New South Wales. Here the union leader J. S. Garden protested that not only would the workers refuse to accept a 20 per cent cut in wages to meet the demands of the Niemeyer plan but, striking the racist drum, that 'they will not agree to pay any of the Shylocks of London if they will not agree to fund the debt free of interest for five years'. This became the central theme of the New South Wales election that took place in October 1930. There was a Labor landslide and the ALP took office under J. T. Lang. Lang, to the dismay of his fellow premiers, the ALP federal government, and the business and financial interests of the country (including the horrified Hoskins, Darling and Lewis, who thought that he had gone mad), embarked on a unilateral policy of interest repudiation.[36]

Under Lang's premiership New South Wales defaulted in 1931. To maintain external solvency, the Commonwealth government paid the debts and then proceeded against the state for their recovery. Eventually, in July 1931, Lang was forced to go to the Loan Council to meet the

Inside the cast house of No. 1 blast furnace, AIS steelworks, Port Kembla, c. 1930

state's wages and salaries bill. In return for assistance he agreed to resume payment of external interest. Lang's activities not only created financial uncertainty and instability in New South Wales—for instance, there was a run on the Government Savings Bank which closed on 23 April 1931—but at the federal level his maverick policies brought down the Scullin Labor government in November 1931. In January 1932 the New South Wales government again defaulted. This time the federal government called an emergency session and passed laws to collect money from defaulting states. To indicate the seriousness of the situation, Australian bond holders were left unpaid. Finally, when Lang directed the New South Wales treasury officials to act contrary to federal law, the New South Wales Governor, Sir Philip Game, dismissed him for acting unconstitutionally.[37]

The remainder of the plant at Port Kembla was completed during this time of political and financial instability. Seven weeks after the Wall Street crash, on 18 December 1929, the *Sydney Morning Herald* reported:

> In the presence of a large gathering of officials, the last brick of the first steel furnace stack for the Australian Iron and Steel Works was laid today by Miss M. Mortlock sister of Mr. W. H. Mortlock, general manager of the works. The stack is connected to the furnace, and is the largest of its type

in the British Empire. It is 200 feet high, and 750,000 bricks were used in the construction of the furnace.

Steel was tapped from the first 150-ton open-hearth furnace at Port Kembla on 5 November 1931. The furnace was known as No. 22 (the No. 2 furnace in AIS's second open-hearth shop). It was followed by No. 23 in October 1933, and No. 24 in April 1935. Two more open-hearth furnaces were added after AIS had become part of BHP: No. 25 in January 1937 and the pre-war installation was completed when No. 21 was added adjoining the original furnace (No. 22) in 1939. The furnaces were of American design, 45 feet long and 16 feet wide internally, and fired with producer gas. The two initial gas producers were the largest type made by the English firm Wellman, Smith & Owen and each was capable of gasifying 8000 pounds of coal per hour. Coke-oven gas was not available at the steelworks until 10 January 1938, when a new battery of Wilputte-type coke ovens and a by-product plant came into production at the works.[38] Before this coke for the blast furnace had to be freighted from the non-recovery coke-oven plant at Wongawilli.

From the blast furnace the iron was carried by rail to the open-hearth shop in 125-ton closed ladle cars built by Morts Dock & Engineering Co. Ltd of Sydney. Scrap was charged into the furnaces in five-ton charging boxes. The furnaces were, at that time, the largest in Australia and their technology, with electrically operated charging doors and extensive water cooling, was state-of-the-art. Finished steel was tapped into 150-ton ladles and teemed (poured) from them into five-ton ingots. Finally the stripping crane removed the mould from the ingot, which was then either stored or placed in a soaking pit until ready for rolling in the blooming mill. Four pairs of soaking pits were commissioned initially, followed by an additional four pairs in 1934. These pits were fired by producer gas and each pit held up to eight ingots. In 1938 three further pairs of soaking pits were added.[39]

On 21 November 1931 the *Sydney Morning Herald* reported that

> during the week Australian Iron and Steel Ltd., has been making trials with the blooming and billet sections of the large rolling mills which have been erected at Port Kembla. The trials have been very satisfactory ... The mill will now go into production and the large mill at Lithgow will be dismantled.[40]

The end of rolling activities at Lithgow appears to have come with the closure of the 10-inch merchant mill in December 1931. This mill

## 13 THE AUSTRALIAN IRON AND STEEL COMPANY

The 10/13-inch merchant mill, AIS steelworks, Port Kembla, c. 1935. Commissioned in 1934, this mill rolled all the merchant sections produced at Port Kembla. The finishing end of the 10-inch stands is shown; the 13-inch stands are in the background.

was in good condition and was transferred to Port Kembla complete with buildings, cranes and mill stands, and operated there for a short time. On advice from the Youngstown Sheet and Tube Company in Pennsylvania, this mill was subsequently updated with the addition of six new 13-inch roughing stands arranged in tandem so as to roll the incoming billets in a continuous fashion. The product from the roughing section was then rolled in four of the original 10-inch stands arranged 'cross country', that is, with the stands placed side by side. All these roll stands were electrically driven and the mill was recommissioned as the '10/13-inch mill' in January 1934, producing rods and small sections.[41]

The details of the gradual closure of the Lithgow operations are not entirely clear but the scaling-down appears to have taken place as follows: one blast furnace, making pig-iron for the local open hearths, was still in operation early in November 1928, but it closed on or before the end of the month and, on December 28, No. 2 blast furnace was demolished—like its Rutherford predecessor it was blown up.[42] Blast furnace No. 1 (Sandford's) was still standing; later, as AIS had definitely decided not to continue manufacturing iron at Lithgow, it too was demolished. Subsequently, the open-hearth furnaces were closed as orders declined: 'A' in March 1930, 'C', which had been scheduled for closure the following December, was temporarily reprieved when orders for 2000 tons of steel rails were received. This appears to have been the last burst of activity. After nearly sixty years of iron- and steel-making grass began to grow on the site of the old Eskbank ironworks. The men and the activity had moved to Port Kembla where most of the old works had been transported to use as scrap.

The dislocation of labour was a major social as well as an economic concern. The decision to finally close the Lithgow works was either taken slowly, or gradually became public, over a decade. When the final closure came at the height of the depression in 1931, Cecil and Sid Hoskins went to Lithgow and addressed a public meeting in Lithgow Town Hall, explaining the problems that confronted the new company, particularly in relation to overseas price-cutting and Australian labour costs. They argued that 'our high nominal wage in New South Wales has meant that neither capital nor labour has received an adequate return. Tonight we are here because we know so many of you and because we like you. If we can help it distress will be limited as far as is in our power. Unfortunately that is not very far'.[43] In fact, the final closure came at a period of unprecedented economic depression and widespread unemployment. By this time the company had undergone extensive changes. Charles Hoskins was dead and, despite the appearance of the Hoskins brothers, the old family company, Hoskins Iron and Steel Company, had vanished to be replaced with a new international consortium. It was in its name that the final closure occurred.

On 9 March 1928 the *Lithgow Mercury* announced the formation of AIS:

## 13 THE AUSTRALIAN IRON AND STEEL COMPANY

The intention of the new company is to continue to operate the collieries, steelworks and rolling mills at Lithgow, during the constructional period at Port Kembla. After Port Kembla Works are on production, various units of the Lithgow works will, from time to time be transferred to Port Kembla as the constructional programme warrants.

The Lithgow work-force was given employment preference at Port Kembla, but there was neither re-housing nor transfer assistance. In 1928 the Lithgow Wages Board was extended to cover the new AIS works, bringing with it the advantages that had been granted to the workers at Eskbank, benefits that were a carry-over from the more strenuous physical work required at the older works. These included an industry loading for working holidays and unpaid lost time as well as higher margins than those awarded for similar tasks at Newcastle.[44]

# 14

# A NATIONAL INDUSTRY

HISC, AND LATER AIS, had a serious underlying weakness. Both companies were dependent upon BHP for supplies of iron ore. In 1927 HISC had made a contract with BHP for supplies of iron ore. Anxiety over the transference of this contract to AIS resulted in legal advice being sought immediately after the formation of the new company. AIS's solicitors, the Sydney firm of Allen, Allen & Hemsley, replied that 'the contract with BHP for the supply of iron ore . . . contains no provisions that is assignable, but on the whole we are of the opinion that the contract may be validly assigned . . . we suggest that you should formally write to the BHP Co'.[1] This contract was important in both the immediate and long term, as none of the New South Wales or the Tasmanian sources available to HISC, or its successor AIS, proved viable.

In the immediate post-war period Charles Hoskins had searched for a reliable source of iron ore and in August 1926 HISC had purchased for £33 000 the mining leases for Cockatoo Island in Yampi Sound, Western Australia, from the Queensland government. HISC also held leases in Tasmania, which subsequently proved unsatisfactory.[2] Yampi Sound in the north-west of Western Australia was not only distant and isolated but Cockatoo Island had a tidal variation of thirty feet. Its development would be both difficult and expensive while HISC's requirements were immediate as well as long term. Thus, early in 1927, the Hoskins brothers had entered into a ten-year contract with BHP to purchase

Electric shovel loading blasted iron ore on the 100-foot-high Bench E of Iron Monarch in the Middleback Ranges, South Australia, c. 1935

200 000 tons of iron ore annually at sixteen shillings per ton delivered to Port Kembla.[3]

BHP was opening a new quarry, Quarry E, at Iron Knob, and when this was available it was agreed that the cost of ore per ton delivered would be reduced by six pence. So long as BHP controlled the only viable source of iron ore, Lewis could encourage AIS, as Delprat had encouraged the Queensland government. The Yampi Sound deposits represented a threat to this monopoly and they were carefully watched. For instance, in January 1935, there was a rumour in Perth that the Japanese were negotiating with AIS for the leases. This was fuelled by the appearance of Mr Burns, the secretary of AIS 'who arrived in Perth this week and conferred with the Japs for the best part of yesterday (Wednesday) afternoon'. Burns, refusing to give the press any information, announced that he was returning to the eastern states on Saturday. AIS only controlled the leases to Cockatoo Island as Cecil Hoskins had rejected an offer of £15 000 for the leases on the adjoining Koolan Island. The potential of Yampi Sound almost certainly contributed to BHP's interest in a take-over of AIS later that year.[4]

The BHP–HISC contract was originally negotiated in January 1927 and the following July Sid Hoskins indicated on behalf of HISC that it might require an additional 100 000 tons of ore per annum.[5] Lewis, agreeing to this, was concerned that it might temporarily strain BHP's existing quarries. Aware of this problem he wrote to Hockey that: 'It would be very bad business to let Hoskins open their own quarry by not supplying this additional 100,000 tons'. One of BHP's greatest strengths had always been that it was and remained a diversified mining company. Thus, in addition to having a cheap source for company manufactures, BHP was able to return a profit by the sale of raw materials on either the home or foreign market. The significance of this became increasingly apparent during the inter-war years. For instance, at AIS in the early 1930s ore purchased from BHP accounted for one-third of the cost of pig-iron.[6] Caught by the depression, Cecil Hoskins on behalf of AIS tried to renegotiate the contract in 1932 only to be informed by Lewis that 'I have placed your request for a decrease in the price of ironstone before our Directors. They think that, considering all the circumstances, the agreement is a very fair one and therefore they regret their inability to agree to your suggestion for a further reduction in the price of ironstone'.[7] The contract was a fair one at the time it was made. It had given satisfaction to both parties; this was the reason for the Hoskinses' desire to ensure that it would be carried over to meet the requirements of AIS. BHP had expanded its quarries to meet its increased commitments but shortly after the industry became confronted with an economic downturn of unprecedented severity, which then placed an unexpected strain on the newly established AIS.

The formation of AIS had been justified by the expectation of substantial profits and the strength adduced from the new company's alliance with two famous British firms. It was considered that the 'minimum net profits of the new Company are estimated at £213,758'.[8] It is probable that neither of the Hoskins brothers realised the degree to which the two British companies were financially straitened. In fact Howard-Smith Ltd, the fourth participant in the new company, wrote to Cecil Hoskins in May 1928 complaining of the delay in finalising arrangements:

> it seems extraordinary to us that two big British Companies could overlook in their negotiations with you such essential factors as in the case of Baldwins Ltd., their agreement with their Australian agents preventing their investment, and in the case of Dorman Long & Co. its Australian assets being encumbered.[9]

Dorman Long's Australian assets were encumbered along with its British assets with £4 000 000 of debentures. AIS had in fact paid cash for part of the Australian assets of Dorman Long. The agreement was 500 000 £1 shares fully paid calculated as ten years' purchase at the present annual profit of £50 000 for the goodwill of its business in Sydney and Melbourne; the stocks and work in progress were valued at approximately £413 000 and for these it would receive a further £100 000 in fully paid ordinary shares and the balance of about £313 000 in cash. However, the underwriters insisted on an independent valuation. This delayed negotiations for, after the valuation was made Laurence Ennis, who had been representing Dorman Long in Sydney, wrote:

> I had previously stated I thought it would be in the neighbourhood of £175,000 and Hoskins had stated that in their opinion it would be about £160,000. You can imagine' our dismay when the valuer returned £94,500. To be quite candid I thought that Howard Smith would not continue the negotiation on the old basis when the valuation was received, as he considered that it would be difficult to justify over £400,000 as goodwill.[10]

This last-minute discovery—Dorman Long's Board minute is dated 19 June 1928—led to certain additional assets, originally intended for the Sydney Harbour Bridge contract, to the value of £9165 17s 9d being included. Nevertheless, it is probable that Dorman Long's assets were over-priced. Ennis, who was later chairman of Dorman Long, was pleased with the deal, pointing out that, in addition to the tariff, there were several other difficulties in the Australian market that were likely to have a detrimental effect on British manufacturers. He noted that about a fortnight previously BHP had unexpectedly and 'very considerably' reduced its prices for angles and channels, while 'the consistent and ever increasing propaganda for preference to Australian manufactures is having its effect. Several tenders that have been let lately have specified materials manufactured in Australia and as much as 15% financial preference is being given'.[11]

Dorman Long was extremely anxious to obtain cash. On 12 June 1928 the secretary of Dorman Long's wrote to Ennis:

> I am glad the Australian business is settled at last . . . As regards payment for the stocks we have today received your cable saying that the money, namely £150,000 will be cabled here on the due date which is July 1. This will help us considerably. Our bank balance is in a deplorable condition. Trade was never so bad, we are hardly doing anything and money is difficult to get . . . Seeing how badly we need cash I hope you will keep an eye on the payments for us and see that we receive the money at the due dates as far as possible.[12]

Dorman Long's major Australian enterprise was its contract for the Sydney Harbour Bridge, which had been specifically excluded from the Australian enterprises made over to AIS. Even this was causing the company secretary concern: 'As regards the costs I am afraid that the position does not look quite as well as the engineering side appears to do . . . the debit balance may be rather a serious one unless costs can be cut down in the meantime'. He was also worried in case it was not completed within the contract time as 'every day of extension means heavy additional costs'. The Hoskins brothers had sunk their entire business assets in the new company but neither Dorman Long nor Baldwins, which had suffered severe financial problems in the post-war period, were in a position to provide AIS with financial assistance.[13]

Lewis's assessment of the capacity of British firms to provide capital for the expansion of the Australian industry had been quite correct. However, the Hoskinses had no choice. They could not remain at Lithgow. To prosper they had to build a modern works on a viable site and, to achieve this, they had to accept what assistance they could find. Few alternatives were available to them and in the circumstances their arrangements appeared to have much to recommend them. Their mis-

Reheating furnaces and roll stands in the sheet mill at AIS steelworks, Port Kembla, installed to diversify the company's output by producing galvanised sheets in competition with Lysaght's plant in Newcastle

fortune was to be confronted with the worst global depression that the industrial world had experienced.

The Hoskins period of plant development at Port Kembla was concluded by the introduction of sheet rolling in April 1935. The new sheet rolling and galvanising plant was a major development of US design, consisting of two reheating furnaces, a roughing mill, two finishing mills, annealing furnaces, and galvanising and corrugating facitilities.[14]

This sheet mill, being more modern and more highly mechanised than its Lysaght's counterpart at Newcastle, could have been expected to compete profitably against the established manufacturer. However, there were problems with the mill from the outset when the piling for its foundations proved unexpectedly difficult and expensive. In operation the 3-high Lewis roughing mill proved particularly troublesome with a succession of broken spindle boxes, gearboxes and rolls, while at other times 'a piece of steel being rolled stuck to the heated roll as though welded'. Such incidents involved the company in an expense it could ill afford, and to these problems repairs and maintenance added 10 per cent to the production costs. The American technicians who installed the mill were unable to solve these problems, although in many cases the difficulties appear to have been associated with poor operation of the

The 3-high Lewis mill at the sheet mill, AIS steelworks, Port Kembla, c. 1934. Repeated mechanical problems with this roughing mill contributed to the need for a merger of the Australian Iron and Steel Co. Ltd with BHP in 1935.

reheating furnaces and poor management of the roll separation at the 3-high mill. Finally the drive shaft from the reduction gearbox snapped and a new steel gearbox, which had been installed to solve the problems of the mill, broke. It seems probable that it was this final disaster which led the Hoskins brothers to approach Essington Lewis with a view to the absorption of AIS into BHP.

Ironically there does not seem to have been anything fundamentally wrong with the mill, as in the rationalisation that followed the merger with BHP, the sheet mill was successfully operated by Lysaght's in its original location at AIS. It was later made redundant when Lysaght's new plant was built at Springhill in the Port Kembla area. The mill was subsequently moved to Lysaght's works at Newcastle where it gave excellent service during World War II.

As a major event in Australian industrial history the ensuing merger of AIS into BHP generated its own, often very colourful, stories. On investigation, many of these are of dubious historical veracity, although, as reflecting folk memory and attitudes, they are of considerable interest. Quite simply, there appears to have been a cumulative series of disasters in which the workers' inexperience and the company's urgent necessity to obtain results probably played a considerable part. Although AIS's senior staff had followed BHP's example and inspected the latest technology abroad,[15] the episode highlighted the need to balance technology with skill and experience in the work-force as had been done at Newcastle some twenty years before. Many in the AIS work-force had been trained at Lithgow and had little experience of the now very complex technology confronting them at Port Kembla. In March 1935, shortly before the commissioning of the sheet mill, the AIS Board noted a works report to the general manager from L. A. Davison, the bloom and rail superintendent, that 'one of our weaknesses is the lack of competent rollers . . . I would suggest that steps be taken to obtain the services of at least one really good roller'.[16]

The failure of the sheet mill was indisputably a severe blow to the aspirations of the management, who had hoped that it would not only contribute to the capital necessary to complete the works but also provide the cash-flow for ongoing costs. AIS had been encouraged to challenge Lysaght's monopoly by the strong demand for galvanised iron, particularly by the reviving rural and construction industries. It was also an attempt to broaden the company's markets and redress AIS's dependence upon contracts associated with public works. Apart from operational difficulties, the danger of excessive reliance upon government contracts had been revealed at the height of the depression.

It might be tempting to dwell on the inevitable logic of the absorption of AIS into BHP. Delprat's significant emphasis on peaceful collaboration has already been mentioned but hard evidence of long-term intentions or even trends is scanty at best. Even so, there is no question of the absorption being sudden: the relatively smooth way it occurred is itself evidence of prepared ground. Furthermore, when it is remembered that the joining of AIS to BHP was consistent with developments overseas, the force of secular imperatives becomes obvious. As early as April 1933 Sir William Firth had written to Essington Lewis of a conversation he had had with the Hoskins brothers reporting that

> I ventured—rather impudently—I fear—to suggest to them there was only the *sane* solution to the Australian Steel Situation—i.e. an amalgamation of B[H]P and A[I]S via a sale of control or a Co. owned or controlled by the BH . . . The Hoskins appeared genuinely interested and I should judge them to be ready to talk *reasonably*.

Lewis had replied:

> I read with particular interest your remarks about the AIS and ourselves. Personally I feel that some such action is bound to take place; I also feel that perhaps the time is not yet quite ripe but it does seem foolish having two such large sized plants competing with one another for the limited amount of local trade.

The next day, 4 May, Sir William wrote again. He had visited AIS and remarked on their 'fine Blast Furnace Plant' but

> [they] are obviously short of outlet. On a toe to toe fight there could, I think, be only one result. But fighting causes bitterness & is always wastefully expensive—& the victor does not always vanquish . . . the chief interest the Hoskins took in me was to *separately* question me while going round their wks. as to *your* views on amalgamation of interests . . . *That they would like to have a deal with you I am quite positive* . . . Do hope you will recognise the sincerity of my intentions & forgive appearance of meddling.[17]

The AIS shareholders were becoming restive. A year later, on 18 April 1934, the *Age* reported the annual meeting of AIS at which some of the shareholders had protested at the company's failure to declare a dividend on the cumulative preference shares. The following October the *Herald* declared the 'Ordinary shareholders have not received anything since the establishment of the Company'. However, dividends were resumed in 1935 and on 4 April the *Herald* commented that 'the Company would appear to have definitely turned the corner'. The situation was far from settled as, after improving in 1934, profits fell back in the first part of 1935. Finally, on 27 July, the Hoskins brothers arranged to meet Lewis, who was *en route* from Newcastle to Melbourne, in Sydney's Central Railway Station. At this meeting negotiations for the amalgamation of the two companies were started. On 12 August the *Herald* carried the headline 'Steel Merger Rumours—BHP Officials Silent'. On the same day Cecil Hoskins wrote to Essington Lewis that

> all ordinary shareholding interests in Australian Iron and Steel Limited have agreed to accept the proposal for the acquisition by your Company of their Australian Iron and Steel Limited Ordinary Shares on the basis set out by the note handed to me by you in Melbourne dated 2nd August 1935.

The letter goes on to list the points agreed. These were:

1. An effective safeguard against block voting by the BHP shares allotted to AIS.
2. BHP will exchange for 2,700,007 ordinary AIS shares BHP shares to the value of £2,100,000.
3. BHP officials would be allowed to satisfy themselves regarding the value of AIS assets and to sight contracts.
4. All taxes, stamp duties and other costs to be borne by AIS.
5. No action to be taken until after August.
6. Shares allotted to us will rank for dividend in your Company from the date of issue.
7. Date of settlement of base price and transfer to be mutually agreed.
8. No AIS dividend in the interim.[18]

The stipulation about block voting proved to be one of the most difficult points in the negotiations. The British firms, Dorman Long in particular, were anxious to realise their capital. BHP was concerned about the possibility of a managerial take-over should the shares become concentrated and about the destabilising effect that the sudden disposal of such a large number of shares might have on the stock market. To avoid this, Dorman Long's agents explained to their principals, a trust composed of representatives of both AIS and BHP was to be appointed to hold the shares and

> no shares shall be sold without the consent of the Broken Hill Pty. for a period of 2 years from the 1st January next. After the two years period, the Trust is empowered to sell the shares up to the extent of 10% of the total holding in any one year. The shares at first to be offered to the Chairman of the Broken Hill Pty., at a price to be mutually agreed upon under an option of 21 days.[19]

If the two parties could not agree on a price then the chairman of the Melbourne Stock Exchange's arbitration would be binding on both parties. This agreement was to run for seven years, although the AIS negotiators tried to have it reduced to five and the period for the chairman's option reduced to fourteen instead of twenty-one days. The Dorman Long Board declared that it was 'very much surprised . . . and . . . disinclined to accept such onerous conditions'. In reply Frank Way of Allard, Way & Hardie explained the circumstances and how the negotiations were conducted:

> you will understand that up to the present, all negotiations have been carried through by Mr. Cecil Hoskins and Mr. Essington-Lewis [sic]: After each interview Mr. Hoskins had with Mr. Essington-Lewis, a meeting of the representatives of the ordinary Shareholders has been held to discuss the proposals or Agreements submitted, but no direct contact has been made with Mr. Lewis by any representative other than Mr. Cecil Hoskins.[20]

He continued that, although he and his partners agreed that 'the conditions imposed regarding selling the shares over so long a period are very onerous', BHP was adamant. However, this had to be balanced against the fact that 'the price offered for the shares is very satisfactory under the circumstances'. On 21 September F. M. Mitchell had written to C. H. Hoskins explaining BHP's stand on the seven-year delay before the shares could be freely traded as 'a matter of prudence' and adding a further clause to the agreement stating that 'any liabilities not disclosed by the Balance Sheet as at 30th November, 1934, shall be . . . a first charge on the shares held by the Trustees'.[21]

On 1 October Way wrote again to Dorman Long emphasising that AIS would not be able to carry on in opposition to BHP, pointing out the effect of the existing price-cutting and the undercapitalised nature of AIS, particularly in view of its need to expand. Both Hoskins and Howard Smith had already stated their intention of accepting and 'strongly advised' Dorman Long to join them as did Way, Dorman Long's agent. BHP shares had for purposes of the take-over been valued at £2 16s each, amounting to 750 000 shares in all. On this basis Dorman Long would be entitled to 166 666 BHP shares and, if the deal was completed almost immediately, BHP had agreed that it would also receive six weeks' dividend at 12.5 per cent per annum. BHP, explaining its viewpoint, gave a verbal intimation to Dorman Long's chairman, Lawrence Ennis, 'that moderate selling of shares during those [initial] two years will not be objected to provided the market can absorb such sales without undue disturbance'. Dorman Long agreed and received about £2400 in lieu of interest. Subsequent half-yearly dividends could be estimated at approximately £10 413 presuming that the dividend remained at its present level. Way concluded:

> I realise from communications received that there was a certain reluctance on the part of your Board to accept the Agreement, containing as it did many restrictive conditions. With the acquired knowledge I have of the affairs of Australian Iron and Steel Ltd., had the shares been my own I would willingly have sold on the terms stipulated.
>
> ... this transaction must be a matter of satisfaction to you; justifying ... selling the Dorman Long construction undertaking to Australian Iron & Steel Ltd. which has now resulted in a capital value of over *£450,000* with an annual return, under present conditions, of over *$20,000*.[22]

Most of the negotiations in Australia were conducted verbally and much of the business with AIS's overseas associates, Baldwins Ltd and Dorman Long & Co., was conducted by cable. However, Dorman Long's Sydney agents, H. B. Allard, Way & Hardie, Chartered Accountants, followed their cables with written airmailed reports. From these letters it appears that the terms were virtually dictated by Lewis. Way indicated:

> it would be necessary for all the present Directors to resign and that the new Board would probably consist of Mr. Darling as the Chairman and Mr. Essington Lewis as Deputy Chairman. Mr. Lewis and Mr. Sid Hoskins would be managing directors or in the alternative, some other office might be found for Mr. Sid Hoskins. Mr. Cecil Hoskins stated that in the negotiations no special provisions were made for either him or for Mr. Sid Hoskins as this was entirely left to the Broken Hill Pty. to decide ...
>
> The whole of the negotiations have been carried out by Messrs. Cecil and Sid Hoskins as it would have been impractical for all the Directors to be present while negotiations were conducted.[23]

No announcement was to be made until after the BHP shareholders' meeting on 30 August. It was BHP's jubilee year. The company had made a profit of £670 000, after deducting £541 000 for depreciation. A bonus issue of shares was expected. This would have had the immediate effect of 'watering' the shares and, until the market stabilised, it was difficult to calculate how many shares would come to AIS should the take-over occur. In fact there was no bonus issue. Instead provision was made to increase the capital of the company by £1 500 000 in £1 shares. These were offered to the shareholders at a premium of ten shillings per share; at the time BHP was standing at around £3 per share. The shareholders were also informed that 'conversations' were taking place with

AIS. At this stage BHP was allowed to inspect the assets of AIS but Way wrote on 6 August that 'it is not proposed to allow the Broken Hill Pty. access to the books of the company as, in the event of negotiations falling through, they would be possessed of information which it is not desirable for them to have as competitors'.[24]

Media speculation started almost immediately. The next day the *Argus*, under the headline 'Rumour of Iron and Steel Merger', suggested that 'the two English Companies, Dorman Long and Baldwins, may not wish to meet the uncalled liability on the shares that they hold, and that the introduction of new capital therefore would be welcome'.[25] On 12 August Lawrence Ennis received a long letter, dated 30 July, from Frank Way outlining the situation. Recommending acceptance Way wrote:

> Mr. Hoskins gave as his reasons for wishing to dispose of the Hoskins interests, mainly his fear that the Broken Hill Pty. Ltd. competition would eventually prove too strong for the profitable working of Australian Iron and Steel Ltd. He instanced the recent lowering of prices by the Broken Hill Pty. on those lines which had hitherto proved most profitable to Australian Iron and Steel Ltd. He also referred to the difficulties the Company has lately experienced principally in connection with the re-lining of the Blast Furnace, the failure of the Sheet Mill Plant and the probable serious position with regard to Spun Iron Pipes. He also referred to the insufficiency of the capital of the Company to provide for necessary extensions to the undertakings of Australian Iron and Steel Ltd.

Way noted that Mr Yarwood, who represented Baldwins, had indicated that his company with its comparatively small holding would 'no doubt ... be prepared to fall in with the view of the majority'. Way then gave Dorman Long his reasons for advising a similar decision. They were:

> 1. I think the Company is trying to do too much on its available capital and I do not think that we have men with sufficient experience to undertake some of the developments lately entered into, particularly the manufacture of Black and Galvanised Sheets.
>
> There has been a growing feeling ... that the Hoskins take too much upon themselves and do not take other Directors into their confidence. As a consequence we do not hear of any of the failures of the Company until they are accomplished facts, when of course, it is too late to suggest a remedy. I do not say this with any idea of harsh criticism and I have the most friendly feelings for both Cecil and Sid Hoskins, I do think, however, that

they are rather prone to rush into new undertakings without a full knowledge of all the difficulties to be encountered.

Recently we had trouble with the Blast Furnace—the relining of which cost nearly £22,000 and for a considerable time we had to purchase Pig Iron [from BHP] to the extent of about 9,000 tons. Then in order to keep faith with our customers, the work was rushed ahead and scrap and pig iron were used very often from the cold state.

A further difficulty was with Coke which had to be bought in as we were not supplying sufficient for our purposes.

Now we have to face the difficulty of re-organising the Plant for the production of black and galvanised sheets. We were assured in the first instance that the local rolls would be satisfactory. Later the estimates had to be revised as it was found that no progress could be made with our own rolls; consequently they had to be imported. We did not know until the last meeting of the Board that the new rolls had been continually broken and in that way a loss of capital of about £6,000 has to be made good.

The men brought out from America to superintend the manufacture of the sheets were found to be incompetent and an effort was made to carry on with our own men at Kembla—I am afraid with disastrous results . . .

2. Competition from the Broken Hill Pty. is now intense although there is apparently the most friendly feelings between the respective managements. The reductions in prices which took place recently will have a serious effect on the profits of Australian Iron and Steel Ltd. during the current year. The effect will not be fully realised until the latter half of the current financial year.

I understand that Mr. Lewis has already intimated to Mr. Hoskins that further reductions in prices will be suggested next year. The estimate of the Secretary is, that the present reduction will mean the falling off in estimated profits of the current year, of not less than £94,000 . . .

3. In view of the arrears of Preference Dividends and the unlikelihood of only [sic] moderate profits being made under present conditions, the possibility of a dividend on the ordinary shares is very remote; this of course means that the ordinary shares have approximately no market value . . . at present there is very little benefit as far as I can see to Dorman Long & Co. in being associated with Australian Iron and Steel Ltd. In fact I remember on one occasion that you informed me that you would be glad to get rid of the shares at a reasonable price. If, therefore, the negotiations can be carried to a successful issue . . . your Company would to my mind,

be in a much stronger position as it would have a negotiable security instead of a frozen asset.[26]

Finally, 750 000 BHP shares were exchanged for 2 467 507 AIS shares of which 950 000 were partly paid. At the time of the agreement BHP shares were approximately £2 16s and there were arrears in the AIS preference shares dividend amounting to almost £240 000. The document arranging the exchange was signed by H. G. Darling, R. C. Meares and F. M. Mitchell on behalf of BHP and by Cecil Hoskins and J. C. McGann on behalf of AIS.[27] The arrangement was beneficial to all concerned and it was conducted with the minimum of disruption. Shortage of capital, which had haunted the Lithgow works, had finally necessitated the amalgamation of AIS and BHP. The management of AIS had realised its limitations and BHP had patiently waited until AIS made the first move.

It is uncertain when Lewis first realised that the take-over, if not inevitable, was at least highly probable, given AIS's circumstances and the market conditions pertaining in the 1930s. After 1925 BHP had shelved the idea of expansion and instead continued on a period of consolidation, securing resources and markets and bringing the established plant to its maximum efficiency. This programme was justified by a recession in 1927 and in 1928 the directors commented that 'the policy of keeping the entire plant in excellent condition and making improvements had been steadily upheld, with the result that the plant has never been in better shape and we are ready to seize any advantage that may present itself when business improves'.[28] BHP had also broadened the base of its products: for example, in 1929 bar iron was being rolled in 18-inch, 12-inch and 8-inch mills. Integration, efficiency, economy and modernisation, including the electrification of the works, placed the Newcastle steelworks in an increasingly strong position to compete in the import replacement market, especially as tariffs were imposed to counter dumping in 1924, 1926 and 1929. In the mid 1930s bar iron accounted for approximately 30 per cent of the sales of both AIS and BHP, but BHP's volume was very much greater and its market more varied with greater linkages to the private sector. By the end of 1935 as a result of further modernisation, bar was being rolled at Newcastle in 18-inch, 12-inch and 10-inch continuous mills.[29]

BHPs strong financial position was an important element in its take-over of AIS. Throughout the 1920s BHP under Darling and Lewis had adhered to cautious, while at the same time far-sighted and efficient,

## 14 A NATIONAL INDUSTRY

The first coke being pushed from the by-product recovery coke ovens at AIS steelworks, Port Kembla, 1938. This coke was produced to augment the production from the outdated non-recovery coke ovens at Wongawilli.

Expansion at the AIS steelworks, Port Kembla, 1937; construction work on the No. 2 blast furnace in the left foreground, alongside the original blast furnace

financial practices. Between 1920 and 1935 no attempt was made to raise capital on the open market, although shares were issued to participate in subsidiary or associated enterprises, such as Ryland Bros (Aust.) Ltd (1925) and Lysaght's (Aust.) Pty Ltd (1929). The company did, however, obtain short-term credit from its bankers from time to time.[30] Slowly but steadily the debentures, to which Darling had objected so strongly in 1920, were redeemed and fixed interest upon borrowed capital reduced. BHP had two series of debentures, 'A' at 6 per cent and 'B' at 7 per cent, and throughout the 1920s the company had a sinking fund to redeem these debentures. In 1929 interest payments amounted to £81 094 but by 1934 the 'A' series was paid off and interest on the 'B' series reduced to £26 241.[31]

Both AIS and BHP had capital outstanding at fixed interest rates. The annual claim on AIS's preference shares was £75 000, reduced by 22.5 per cent after the adoption of the Premiers' Plan and the New South Wales *Interest Reduction Act*. Nevertheless, AIS could not meet even the reduced sum and cumulative payments were deferred between 1931 and 1934. By 1935 arrears amounted to approximately £240 000 and these were not paid off until 1940. During the depression, AIS paid no ordinary dividends and BHP stopped paying ordinary dividends between 1930 and 1932. BHP's depreciation policy was similarly strict and, despite completing and modernising the company's plant at Newcastle and Iron Knob, and developing various other assets, depreciation rates were, with the exception of 1932, steadily improved. Over the six years 1929–34, AIS's depreciation rate was 2.15 per cent and BHP's 5.40 per cent. At the nadir of the depression BHP had a reserve fund of £1 500 000, while in 1929 AIS's reserves only amounted to £15 711.[32] To develop its plant to a level of profitability under depression conditions AIS had to trade present solvency for long-term growth.

Furthermore, AIS's works, with their mixture of modern American and British equipment along with outdated and refurbished machinery from Lithgow, were unbalanced, making problems of organisation and production inevitable. These might have been avoided had adequate capital been available. For instance, although electrically driven mills were the current technology, steam-driven rolling mills had of necessity been brought from Lithgow. When the merchant mill brought from Lithgow was electrified and improved in 1934, the cost of production was almost halved.[33] By 1935 the remaining Lithgow mills had been scrapped. Problems on the production side were created not only by this mixture of equipment but also by the various purposes it was required to meet. For instance, the rolling of plates in the bloom mill was inefficient: the mill could not absorb the flow of steel from the open-hearth furnaces. Throughout this period the mainstay of the company was government contracts for the manufacture of cast-iron pipes by the De Lavaud process at Port Kembla and steel pipes at Alexandria in Sydney.

External assets might have provided valuable income to supplement vicissitudes in the company's cash-flow as was the case at BHP. AIS, like BHP, had considerable holdings in companies producing related products but, unlike BHP, not in enterprises sufficiently diverse to be removed from the same economic fluctuations. AIS held 138 229 8 per cent cumulative participating £1 preference shares paid to fourteen shillings in the Southern Portland Cement Co. Ltd, which supplied AIS with limestone, and 45 000 fully paid £1 shares in Southern Blue Metal Quarries Ltd. Unfortunately these companies also had to suspend dividends during the depression and could offer no more assistance than the British companies that were part of the AIS consortium. BHP was more diversified and had additional sources of income unrelated to the iron and steel industry. Between 1929 and 1933 these provided the company with an average external annual income of £135 237. At the depth of the depression in 1931 and 1932 they kept the company from having to use its reserves.[34]

During and in the aftermath of the depression it was impossible for AIS to find the capital necessary to complete the Port Kembla steelworks. AIS's performance did not make the company's shares an attractive proposition in the open market and AIS was therefore dependent upon bank credit or on intercompany loans. In February 1934 AIS secured a loan of £40 000 from Broken Hill Associated Smelters Ltd.[35] However, BHP, with its large internal resources, could command market support, as it demonstrated in 1935 when it increased the company's nominal capital by nearly half. Moreover, BHP had been considering expansion for at least a decade. AIS had the potential but BHP the capital for development.

The arrangements for the take-over were concluded at a conference held in Lewis's office in Melbourne on 22 and 23 October 1935 between Darling, Lewis, Bradford, Mitchell (secretary, BHP), C. Hoskins, S. Hoskins and R. J. Burns (secretary, AIS). The memorandum of the meeting records:

> There were many matters of mutual concern which would need to be discussed ... Mr Darling said the BHP Board had recently considered the

matter of personnel of the future Board of the AIS and it was thought that it should consist of the present members of the BHP Board, with the addition of Messrs. L. Bradford, C. and S. Hoskins. As to the Secretaryship, the BHP desired that Mr Mitchell should assume this office and that Mr Burns be the Assistant Secretary of the Company. Messrs. C. & S. Hoskins expressed the opinion that not only themselves but the whole of the AIS organisation would give whole-hearted support to the new management and would assist in every possible way.[36]

The conference then discussed the future management, the assets and the liabilities of AIS in detail. The managerial transition occurred swiftly and with the minimum of friction at the works. Furthermore, given BHP's perceived Victorian and South Australian orientation, the Hoskinses' established position in the New South Wales business community was a bonus. Cecil Hoskins was, as his father had been, a prominent member of the Chamber of Manufactures of New South Wales and New South Wales had the largest market opportunities in Australia.

AIS continued as a public company until 1949. The Hoskins brothers continued to administer it until Sid Hoskins retired as director and manager in November 1949 and Cecil Hoskins retired as general manager a year later. Cecil Hoskins remained a director of AIS until November 1959 and was chairman and managing director of the AIS subsidiary Southern Portland Cement Ltd until 1957. Cecil Hoskins, who took a keen interest in politics, had been a member of the executive of the conservative All for Australia League, a movement that had merged with the United Australia Party in 1932. Among his many business interests was the Australian Mutual Provident Society, whose Board he had joined in 1929. After World War II, in 1947, he became its chairman and in 1960, the year he relinquished the chairmanship of AMP, he received a knighthood. He continued on the AMP Board until 1963 when he retired. Both brothers, but especially Sid Hoskins, were interested in a wide spectrum of social and philanthrophic activities and both probably enjoyed a quality of life denied to many business executives at their level.[37]

The international background against which the amalgamation occurred significantly contributed to the event itself and the shape it took. The year before the amalgamation Lewis had gone on a world tour. In common with many industrialists, he had been alarmed at what he had seen in Japan, which he visited for the first time. He wrote to Darling saying that he saw Japan 'as a big gunpowder magazine and the people as fanatics and any day the two might connect'. He then went on to visit

Nazi Germany before returning to Australia fully aware of the country's isolation and vulnerability. More than most he must have known from the condition of Britain how little assistance could be given should a war break out in both Europe and the Pacific. Convinced that the country must prepare for war, he urged the government and the business community to stockpile essential resources and to embark on the large-scale manufacture of ships and aircraft.

BHP took over AIS against this background. The agreement was barely completed before BHP began to pour capital into developing its new acquisition: some £5 000 000 was spent almost immediately.[38] Wilputte-type coke ovens, allowing the recovery of valuable by-products, soaking pits for the open-hearth steel shops, and a second blast furnace were among the major items in a construction programme that continued until after the outbreak of war in September 1939. These helped to balance the works. In consequence it was possible to rationalise Australian iron and steel production. The Hoskins brothers fully shared Lewis's patriotism and concern.

By 1939 Australia was making arguably the cheapest iron and steel in the world. Metallurgical passion and business skill had combined in

The AIS steelworks, Port Kembla: aerial view of 1960 showing the original Hoskins No. 1 steelworks occupying a roughly triangular site in the foreground. Beyond the blast furnaces lie the service shops and rolling mills. The open-hearth shop is arranged diagonally on the right and the spun pipe plant is towards the lower right corner.

the creation of highly efficient, modern plants at Newcastle and Port Kembla. A bench-mark of national achievement had been set, even if the underlying reasons for success were not always clearly understood or appreciated. When war came to the Pacific, Australia had emerged as a nation with considerable industrial self-sufficiency, capable of making an effective contribution to its own defence.

During the decade after the war, the integrated steel industry was evolving rapidly on the foundations laid by BHP and AIS in the formative pre-war years. Industrial growth was fed by a willing immigrant work-force desparate to claw back the aspirations which the European war had snatched from them. For more than a decade after the end of hostilities the steel industry continued as the bell-wether for Australian industry, until the leadership of BHP dramatically broke from the confines of its traditional business, and steel-making became but a part of a complex mineral development enterprise although, in its turn, it was a valuable source of cash-flow for these future developments. The diversification and internationalism of BHP's operations will be judged by the appropriate yardsticks of future historians. However, by the standards of progress in the century or so before the outbreak of World War II the earlier generations of ironmen had fulfilled their task well.

# NOTES

## ABBREVIATIONS

| | |
|---|---|
| *ADB* | *Australian Dictionary of Biography* |
| *AHM* | *Australasian Hardware and Machinery* |
| *AI* | *Australasian Ironmonger* |
| BHPA | BHP Archives |
| C of A | Commonwealth of Australia |
| *PP* | *Parliamentary Papers* |
| RC | Royal Commission |
| *SAGCR* | *South Australian Gazette and Colonial Register* |
| *SMH* | *Sydney Morning Herald* |
| *V & P* | *Votes and Proceedings* |

## 1 BLUE SKY

[1] Dutton, *South Australia and its Mines*, p. 265. As a wood derivative, charcoal contained only traces of minerals that might react disadvantageously with iron ore. It had been used for smelting since the beginning of the iron age. Later it fired the Catalan hearths and bloomeries and, from the fourteenth century, the early blast furnaces.

[2] Quoted in G. B. Wilkinson, *South Australia: its Advantages and Resources*. See also *SAGCR*, 22 June 1847.

[3] *SAGCR*, 25 September 1847.

[4] See *SAGCR*, 18, 20, 21 April, 12 May 1849; *South Australian Geological and Mining Journal*, 19 April 1849.

[5] *SAGCR*, 12 May 1849.

[6] See G. N. Blainey, *The Tyranny of Distance*, pp. 232–4; D. Pike, *Paradise of Dissent*, p. 338; SA PPV & P, 1851, 3 September, item 9.

[7] SA *PPV & P*, 1851, no. 32, 17 October, no. 33, 21 October, item 12; *SAGCR*, 19 November, 18 December 1851.

[8] See R. E. Mitchell, 'Mittagong and District', for the most comprehensive study of the Mittagong iron industry.

## NOTES (CHAPTER 1)

9. *SMH*, 18 November 1889; *AI*, vol. 4, 1889, p. 419, vol. 11, 1896, no. 10, pp. 167, 195, vol. 12, 1897, p. 213.
10. Mitchell, 'Mittagong and District', pp. 420–1; *NSW Gazette*, 8 August 1848; *SMH*, 2 February 1849.
11. *SMH*, 8 April 1856, 8 December 1859, 17 August 1864.
12. Ibid., 10 August 1858.
13. Ibid., 22 March 1850.
14. Mitchell, 'Mittagong and District', pp. 421–2.
15. *NSW PPV & P*, vol. 1, 1854, pp. 1396–7—the evidence of F. J. Rothery in 'Report of the Select Committee on the Fitz Roy Iron and Coal Mining Co. Bill'.
16. *SMH*, 13 May 1859; see also *Australian Home Companion and Band of Hope Journal*, vol. 4, 1859, pp. 476–7.
17. *NSW PPV & P*, vol. 1, 1854—Rothery evidence, p. 1396.
18. *SMH*, 27 March 1852, 10 August 1858.
19. *Empire*, 2 September 1856.
20. *SMH*, 8 April 1856.
21. *Empire*, 19 August 1856.
22. Ibid., 16, 30 September 1856; *SMH*, 21 October 1856.
23. *SMH*, 21 October 1856; Mitchell, 'Mittagong and District', pp. 428–9.
24. *Empire*, 31 March 1857; *SMH*, 10 August 1858, 8 December 1859.
25. Mitchell, 'Mittagong and District', pp. 429–31; *SMH*, 13 May 1859.
26. *SMH*, 8 December 1859.
27. Mitchell, 'Mittagong and District', pp. 432–3.
28. *SMH*, 24 April 1872.
29. *Argus*, 25 July 1860.
30. Ibid.; Mitchell, 'Mittagong and District', p. 433; *SMH*, 24 April 1872; *AI*, vol. 8, 1893, no. 12, p. 393.
31. *SMH*, 21 July 1863.
32. Ibid., 21 July 1863, 21 April 1864.
33. *AI*, vol. 11, 1896, no. 9, pp. 276–7; *SMH*, 24 April 1872.
34. *SMH*, 2 August 1864; *Empire*, 19 August 1864.
35. *Empire*, 17 August 1864.
36. Ibid., 24 April 1872. By the 1870s these were old technology also.
37. Mitchell, 'Mittagong and District', pp. 435–6; *SMH*, 26 February, 6 June 1865.
38. *SMH*, 6 May 1865, 30 June 1868, 8 January 1870.
39. *NSW PP*, 1865, p. 729, 26 May 1865, 'Report of the Select Committee on the Fitzroy Ironworks Co. Bill'.
40. Mitchell, 'Mittagong and District', p. 437.
41. Pittman, *The Mineral Resources of New South Wales*, p. 194.
42. Mitchell, 'Mittagong and District', p. 438; *SMH*, 6 June 1867.
43. *SMH*, 31 May 1867.
44. Ibid.
45. Ibid., 31 May, 6 June 1867.
46. Ibid., 15, 23 June 1867.
47. Ibid., 30 July, 12 August 1868; *AI*, vol. 9, 1869, no. 9, p. 277.
48. *SMH*, 30 July, 12 August 1868, 14 May 1907, 11 January 1870; Mitchell, 'Mittagong and District', p. 442.
49. See *Iron*, 8 February 1873, for the prospectus.
50. Mitchell, 'Mittagong and District', pp. 445–6; *SMH*, 22 September 1876, 14 May 1907; *MJRCG*, vol. 46, no. 2125, 13 May 1876, p. 537; *Mining Journal*, vol. 1, no. 2319, 31 January 1880, p. 116.
51. *AI*, vol. 4, 1889, no. 10, p. 419; *SMH*, 18 November 1889.
52. Mitchell, 'Mittagong and District', pp. 448–9; Sandford, *Australian Pig Iron*, p. 1.

# NOTES (CHAPTER 2)

## 2 THE INTERNATIONAL IRON RUSH AND AUSTRALIAN REALITIES

1. 'Commercial History and Review of 1871', *Economist*, 16 March 1872, p. 4, 15 March 1873, pp. 8, 10; see also P. Deane and W. A. Cole, *British Economic Growth, 1688–1959*, pp. 226–8, and A. Birch, *The Economic History of the British Iron and Steel Industry, 1784–1879*, p. 226.
2. *Peaceful Conquest*, p. 219.
3. Quoted in D. Burn, *The Economic History of Steelmaking, 1867–1939*, p. 5.
4. Quoted in J. C. Carr and W. Taplin, *History of the British Steel Industry*, p. 48.
5. W. T. Hogan, *Economic History of the Iron and Steel Industry in the United States*, vol. 1, p. 11.
6. Ibid., p. 15.
7. *Iron*, 25 January 1873; *Vic. PP*, 1883, vol. 4, p. 731, *RC on Tariffs—Evidence*, 10 May 1882, Mr James Thompson, Manager of Langlands Foundry.
8. *Industrial Progress of New South Wales*, p. 452; *SMH*, 21 August 1868, 2 July 1932; *AI*, vol. 3, 1888, no. 9, p. 247.
9. *Illustrated Sydney News*, 26 October 1870.
10. *SMH*, 27 July, 12, 26 August 1868.
11. Ibid., 7 August 1868.
12. See J. Niland, 'In search of shorter hours', especially pp. 4–7, 11, 14.
13. *SMH*, 17 August 1868.
14. H. A. Clegg, A. Fox and A. F. Thompson, *A History of the British Trade Unions from 1889*, vol. 1, pp. 22–3; Carr and Taplin, *History of the British Steel Industry*, pp. 62–77, especially pp. 69–70. There are photographs of Dale and Kane following p. 65.
15. Clegg, Fox and Thompson, *History of the British Trade Unions*, vol. 1, p. 13.
16. *Argus*, 3 June, 5 August 1872; see also the *Argus* average of fortnightly quotations for the years quoted.
17. *Historical Records of Australia*, vol. 5, p. 547, Patterson to King, 18 January 1805.
18. 8 December 1873. An unpublished paper on the Tasmanian venture was read at ANZAAS 1982, jointly authored and researched by D. Cash, E. M. Johnston-Liik, G. Liik and R. G. Ward, A Dream Unfulfilled: The Rise and Fall of Iron Smelting in Tasmania, 1872–78.
19. *Cornwall Chronicle* (Launceston), 3 May 1872.
20. Ibid., 1, 25 November, 2, 8 December 1872, 7, 21, 23 April, 2 May 1873; PRO Victoria, C.O. 280/381, no. 64, Defunct Trading Co. Records, VPRS 932/255, resolutions passed at extraordinary general meetings, 23 May, 13 June 1873, statement of dissolution, 22 May 1874.
21. *Cornwall Chronicle*, 17 March 1875. For a description of the works, see *Launceston Examiner*, 10 June 1876; *Mercury*, 29 November 1875; *Australasian*, 24 June 1876; *Illustrated Sydney News*, 29 December 1875.
22. *Mercury*, 20 June 1876.
23. *Launceston Examiner*, 10 June 1876; *Cornwall Chronicle*, 31 May, 19 June 1876; *Mercury*, 20 June 1876; C.O. 280/383, Weld to Secretary of State, 6 July 1876.
24. *Cornwall Chronicle*, 27 November 1876; T. C. Just, 'Iron deposits of the River Tamar District', p. 460; T. C. Just, *The Official Handbook of Tasmania*, p. 29.
25. E. Riley, 'On Chromium Pig Iron produced by the Tasmanian Iron Company', p. 107; *Launceston Examiner*, 11 December 1877.
26. *Cornwall Chronicle*, 30 July 1877.
27. *Victorian Government Gazette*, 13 January 1873, p. 200; PRO Victoria, Defunct Co. Records, VPRS 932/266; *Launceston Examiner*, 2 Decmeber 1873; *Mercury*, 1 December 1873, 23 February, 18 April 1874; *Cornwall Chronicle*, 23 March, 15 May 1874.
28. *Cornwall Chronicle*, 25 December 1873, 10 July 1874; *Mercury*, 9 July 1874.
29. *Mercury*, 9 November 1874; *Cornwall Chronicle*, 28 June 1875, Letter from Diogenes, 26 December 1873; *AHM*, May 1902, p. 177, September 1905, p. 176.
30. *Cornwall Chronicle*, 27 May, 1, 22 June, 26 October, 9 December 1874, 31 November 1877; *Mercury*, 10 July 1877; W. H. Twelvetrees and A. McI. Reid, *The Iron ore Deposits of Tasmania*, p. 28.

## NOTES (CHAPTERS 2-3)

31. *Cornwall Chronicle*, 9 December 1874.
32. Ibid., 13 November (editorial). The paper was owned by T. C. Just, the local director of BTCIC. Eight of the fifteen councillors had large pastoral properties stocked with *c.* 40 000 sheep, see *Tasmanian Legislative Council Journals*, 1877, sess. 4, no. 6, 'Inspector of Sheep Report for 1876–7'.
33. *AHM*, September 1911, p. 300; *Annual Report of the Victorian Secretary for Mines 1910*; P. S. Staughton and R. W. P. Ashley, *The Lal Lal Blast Furnace 1876*, pp. 118–34 *passim*, p. 176; R. W. P. Ashley et al., 'The Lal Lal Iron Tramway', pp. 5–7.
34. Ashley, 'The Lal Lal Iron Tramway', p. 7; Staughton and Ashley, *The Lal Lal Blast Furnace*, p. 176–7; *BHP Review*, Autumn 1968, pp. 9–12.
35. *Vic. PP*, 1874, vol. 2, pp. 51–2, 'Mineral Statistics for Victoria, 1873'.
36. Ibid.; *Vic. PP*, 1875, p. 52, 'Mineral Statistics of Victoria'.
37. *NSW Gazette*, 10 December 1873, p. 3787; J. B. Jacquet, *NSW Geological Survey*, 7 April 1874; *ABP*, 8 April 1874.
38. R. I. Jack and A. Cremin, *Australia's Age of Iron*.
39. *Journals of the Iron and Steel Industry*, vol. 1, 1874, p. 412; J. F. Conigrave, *South Australian Manufactures and Industries*, pp. 13–14; H. V. L. Brown, *A Record of the Mines of South Australia*, pp. 52–3; *SAGCR*, 21 May 1874; R. L. Jack, *The Iron Ore Resources of South Australia*, p. 17; *SAGCR*, 1, 16 December 1874; H. Bauerman, *Treatise on the Metallurgy of Iron*.
40. *SAGCR*, 16 December 1874.

## 3 AN AMERICAN ENTREPRENEUR AT LITHGOW

1. *The Industries of New South Wales*, pp. 91–2.
2. *BHP Review*, February 1939.
3. *Bathurst National Advocate*, 14 October–11 December 1911, Rutherford's dictated autobiography. Unless otherwise stated, quotations attributed to Rutherford are from this autobiography. Rutherford died on 25 November 1911.
4. *ADB*, vol. 6, pp. 223–4; *AI*, vol. 4, 1889, p. 302.
5. *BHP Review*, August 1936, pp. 12–13. See also *SMH*, 4, 21 August 1868; *Illustrated Sydney News*, 28 October 1870; *AI*, vol. 8, 1893, no. 12, p. 393.
6. *SMH*, 24 April 1872; see also *Cornwall Chronicle*, 3 May 1872.
7. *Bathurst National Advocate*, Rutherford autobiography, 25 November 1911; *SMH*, 2 January, 20 December 1875, 9 February 1876.
8. *AI*, vol. 4, 1889, p. 212.
9. Ibid.
10. *New Zealand Herald*, 7 July 1890.
11. *AI*, vol. 6, 1891.
12. Ibid., vol. 4, 1889, p. 302; his obituary states that he was was 'known in political circles as "Honest" John Sutherland'.
13. C of A, RC *on Bonuses (1903)—Evidence*, p. 82 (1615, 1621); *SMH*, 6, 8 January 1920; *AI*, vol. 9, 1896, no. 9, p. 273; *AHM*, January 1901, p. 4.
14. *Australian Social History Association Newsletter*, vol. 10, 1980, no. 1; Mitchell Library, Sandford MSS; *The Hoskins Saga*, p. 34; *SMH*, 2 January 1875, 14 May 1907; 'Report of the Examiner of Coal Fields of NSW for 1877' in *NSW Mines Dept. Annual Report, 1877*, pp. 178–9.
15. *AHM*, November 1904, p. 339, December 1904, p. 374.
16. Ibid.; *Hoskins Saga*, p. 35; C of A, *RC on Customs & Excise Tariffs*, 1906, p. 257. William Thornley became general manager about 1901, *Lithgow Mercury*, 3 May 1907.
17. J. C. Carr and W. Taplin, *History of the British Iron and Steel Industry*, p. 14.
18. *Bathurst National Advocate*, Rutherford autobiography, 2 December 1911.
19. *BHP Review*, February 1939.
20. C of A, RC *on Bonuses (1903)—Evidence*, pp. 69–71; *SMH*, 16 January 1894.

## NOTES (CHAPTERS 3–4)

[21] A. Birch, T*he Economic History of the British Iron and Steel Industry*, p. 273.
[22] *New Zealand Herald*, 7 July 1890, gives a description of the Onehunga ironworks.
[23] *SMH*, 16 January 1894; *Lithgow Mercury*, 3 May 1907; *SMH*, 14 May 1907, 30 May 1932; *BHP Recreation Review*, vol. 9, no. 3, p. 3; R. W. Sandford, *Australian Pig Iron*, p. 1; *AHM*, June 1932, p. 178.
[24] *Bathurst National Advocate*, Rutherford autobiography, 2 December 1911.
[25] *AI*, vol. 6, 1891, p. 126.
[26] *Bathurst National Advocate*, Rutherford autobiography, 2 December 1911.

## 4 A PYRRHIC VICTORY

[1] A. H. Smith, The Australian Wire Industry 1870–1959, pp. 20, 104, 110; *SMH*, 14 May 1907, 30 May 1932; *BHP Recreation Review*, vol. 9, no. 3, p. 3; R. W. Sandford, *Australian Pig Iron*, p. 1; *AHM*, June 1932, p. 178.
[2] C of A, R*C on Bonuses (1903)—Evidence*, p. 69; see also R. Murray and K. White, *The Ironworkers*, p. 36.
[3] *BHP Review*, February 1939.
[4] C of A, R*C on Bonuses (1903)—Evidence*, pp. 70, 66.
[5] Ibid., pp. 64, 68. Bladon may have succeeded Miller as principal iron roller.
[6] *BHP Review*, February 1939.
[7] *SMH*, 16 January 1894, gives details of the ceremony and a description of the works. See also *AI*, vol. 8, 1893, p. 260.
[8] *AI*, vol. 13, 1898, pp. 385–6. For the works in 1903, see C of A, *RC on Bonuses (1903)*, p. 53.
[9] C of A, *RC on Bonuses (1903)—Evidence*, p. 53.
[10] Ibid.
[11] *SMH*, 25, 27 April 1900, 18, 21 March 1929; *AI*, vol. 15, 1900, no. 6, p. 199; *AHM*, 1923, p. 402. See also I. Jack, 'The Iron and Steel Industry'; B. Turner, 'The Lithgow Furnace'. R. I. Jack and A. Cremin, *Australia's Age of Iron: History and Archaeology*, 1994, appeared after the completion of this manuscript.
[12] *AHM*, December 1923, p. 402; *SMH*, 21 March 1929.
[13] *Australasian Trade Review*, 9 February 1887; *AI*, vol. 2, 1887, pp. 56–7; *SMH*, 26 April 1900.
[14] *AI*, vol. 2, 1887, no. 3, p. 57, vol. 3, 1888, no. 4, p. 110; *Australasian Trade Review*, 9 Feburary 1887; see also *Journal of the Royal Historical Society of Victoria*, September 1983, pp. 47–9; C. G. T. Weickhart, 'The First Foundry', pp. 47–9; *Argus*, 12 August 1887; *Australian Builder and Contractor's News*, 20 August 1887; *AI*, vol. 2, 1887, p. 288.
[15] PRO Victoria, VPRS 932/685, Defunct Company Papers, items 9–25, 39.
[16] Ibid., VPRS 931/1061, item 1; *AI*, vol. 2, 1887, p. 254, vol. 3, 1888, pp. 105, 288.
[17] *AI*, vol. 5, 1890, p. 41, vol. 6, 1891, p. 202.
[18] Ibid., vol. 3, 1888, p. 110, vol. 5, 1890, p. 41, vol. 6, 1891, p. 202, vol. 4, 1889, pp. 349, 424, vol. 15, 1900, p. 199.
[19] *NSW Arbitration Report* 2, 1903, p. 566, 3, 1904, pp. 321–2; for details, see G. J. R. Linge, *Industrial Awakening*, p. 565 and n. 93.
[20] Linge, *Industrial Awakening*, p. 567; *NSW PP*, 1905, vol. 3, pp. 1151–62; *Lithgow Mercury*, 3 May 1907; C of A,*RC on Bonuses (1903)—Evidence*, pp. 54–5 (1116–18); *AHM*, June 1902, p. 217, January 1908, p. 20.
[21] C of A, R*C on Bonuses (1904)*, pp. 1487, 1563–5; *SMH*, 14 May 1907; S. H. Prior, *Handbook of Australian Mines*, p. 33; *AI*, vol. 5, 1890, pp. 123, 233, 372, vol. 6, 1891, pp. 2, 65, vol. 12, 1897, pp. 66, 132, 391, vol. 13, 1898, p. 321; *Iron*, 13 February 1885, p. 136; C. Parker, *Mines and Minerals of New South Wales*, p. 170.
[22] *NSW PP*, 1905, vol. 3 pp. 1151–2.
[23] *SMH*, 29 April 1907; see *Australian Mining Standard*, 20 May 1907, for further details; also *AHM*, September 1906, pp. 268–70, June 1907, pp. 185–7.
[24] *SMH*, 14 May 1907; *AHM*, December 1907. Pennymore returned to England after the blast furnace was erected.

[25] *Lithgow Mercury*, 3 May 1907, published a long article giving biographical details and photographs of leading figures in the works.
[26] C. Hoskins, *The Hoskins Saga*, p. 97.
[27] *SMH*, 14 May 1907.
[28] Ibid.
[29] Sandford, *Australian Pig Iron*, p. 2.
[30] Ibid.
[31] *Hoskins Saga*, pp. 24–5.
[32] Ibid., pp. 31–2.
[33] Ibid., pp. 20–2, for details of the take-over; see also *SMH*, 4, 6, 7, 9, 10, 20 December 1907; *NSW PP, Debates*, vol. 28, pp. 1376, 1473–90 *passim*, 1629, 1878, 2366–7.
[34] *AHM*, January 1908, p. 22.
[35] *Hoskins Saga*, pp. 41–3; Sandford, *Australian Pig Iron*, contains another account of the take-over. Both were written by sons of the principals many years later.
[36] Sandford, *Australian Pig Iron*; *SMH*, 20 December 1907.
[37] *NSW Report of the RC of the Iron and Steel Industry (1911), Evidence*, p. 30.

## 5 TOWARDS A SOCIAL CONTRACT

[1] *C of A PP*, 1965, *Report of the Committee of Economic Enquiry* (Vernon Report), vol. 1, p. 64. See also G. Greenwood, *Australia A Social and Political History*, p. 428.
[2] R. Gollan in Greenwood, *Australia*, pp. 145–6.
[3] See P. O'Farrell, *The Irish in Australia*, especially pp. 16, 272, 299.
[4] Federation and the New Liberalism, pp. 4–5.
[5] N. B. Nairn, *Civilising Capitalism*, pp. 4, 50, 153, 181.
[6] B. Kennedy, *Silver, Sin and Sixpenny Ale*, pp. 55–6; A. W. Martin and P. Wardle, *Members of the Legislative Assembly of New South Wales 1856–1901*; G. Blainey, *The Rise of Broken Hill*, p. 59; B. Murphy, *Dictionary of Australian History*, pp. 257–8; A. Trengove, *'What's good for Australia...!'*, p. 51.
[7] Blainey, *Rise of Broken Hill*, pp. 60, 117.
[8] BHPA, S1/4, 8 March 1890, for Patton see Blainey, *Rise of Broken Hill*, p. 25; Kennedy, *Silver, Sin and Sixpenny Ale*, p. 32.
[9] See R. Gollan, *Radical and Working Class Politics*, pp. 172–5.
[10] P. G. Macarthy quoted in R. Murray and K. White, *The Ironworkers*, p. 3.
[11] Murray and White, *Ironworkers*, p. 4
[12] J. Hagan, *The ACTU*, p. 7.
[13] Kennedy, *Silver, Sin and Sixpenny Ale*, p. 99.
[14] R. Gollan, *The Coalminers of New South Wales*, p. 14.
[15] Blainey, *Rise of Broken Hill*, p. 59.
[16] Ibid., p. 60.
[17] Ibid., p. 62; Kennedy, *Silver, Sin and Sixpenny Ale*, p. 71. BHP's general manager, John Howell, declared that over 22 000 more tons of ore had been mined with 40% fewer men. Total number of men employed by BHP was 3203 in 1892 and 2938 in 1893.
[18] I. Turner, *Industrial Labour and Politics*, p. 28.
[19] C. Barnett, *The Collapse of British Power*, p. 45; *Lithgow Mercury*, 8 January 1908; Kennedy, *Silver, Sin and Sixpenny Ale*, pp. 51–61, 87–101, and especially p. 110.
[20] Blainey, *Rise of Broken Hill*, pp. 28, 164; Kennedy, *Silver, Sin and Sixpenny Ale*, pp. 45–8, 55–8.
[21] I.T.U.C. *Report* 1888, quoted in Gollan, *Radical and Working Class Politics*, p. 105; see also Nairn, *Civilising Capitalism*, pp. 32–4.
[22] Gollan, *Radical and Working Class Politics*, p. 209.
[23] See N. G. Butlin, A. Barnard and J. J. Pincers, *Government and Capitalism*, pp. 3, 11, 320.
[24] B. K. de Garis, '1890–1900', p. 243; R. Norris, *The Emergent Commonwealth*, p. 195.
[25] Quoted in C. Campbell, 'Liberalism in Australian History', p. 30.
[26] W. S. Robinson, *If I Remember Rightly*, p. 4.

## NOTES (CHAPTERS 5-6)

27 P. G. Macarthy, 'Justice Higgins and the Harvester Judgement', pp. 41-2, 45-6; see also M. Waters, *Strikes in Australia*, p. 110.
28 Quoted in C. M. H. Clark, *Select Documents in Australian History, 1851-1900*, p. 489.
29 *C of A PP Debates*, (Senate) IX, 1902, pp. 12499-50, XDXXX, 1904, pp. 947-53.
30 Ibid., XDXXX, pp. 957, 1295.
31 Gollan, *Coalminers*, pp. 11-12, 14ff.
32 I. Turner, *Labour in Eastern Australia*, pp. 40-1, 56-7, 61-2, 130. See *DNB* for an outline of Mann's career.
33 Kennedy, *Silver, Sin and Sixpenny Ale*, pp. 102-10; Blainey, *Rise of Broken Hill*, pp. 114-22; Trengove, *'What's good'*, p. 77. Delprat's relationship with the unions was complex—he could on occasions be called upon as a conciliator: see Kennedy, *Silver, Sin and Sixpenny Ale*, p. 120.

## 6 PROMETHEUS BOUND

1 *C of A PP, Report of the RC on Bonuses for Manufacture*, vol. II, pp. 1413-600.
2 Ibid., pp. 1415-16.
3 *Australian Mining Standard*, no. 81, 20 July 1891; A. Trengove, *'What's good for Australia . . . !'*, pp. 14-15; *C of A PP, Select Committee on Manufactures Encouragement Act*, 1904, vol. II, *Evidence*, pp. 32-41, min. 658-829. *PP*, Victoria.
4 *C of A PP, Select Committee on Manufactures Encouragement Act*, 1904, vol. II, *Evidence*, p. 55, min. 1131.
5 C. Hoskins, *The Hoskins Saga*, p. 84.
6 BHPA, S1/20, 19 May 1911: 'my position as director of both companies untenable'.
7 N. G. Butlin, A. Barnard and J. J. Pincers, *Government and Capitalism*, p. 62; H. Hughes, *The Australian Iron and Steel Industry*, p. 92.
8 C of A, *RC on Bonuses*, p. 33, min. 676 (Jamieson), pp. 54-5, min. 1117 (Sandford), p. 41, min. 827-9 (Jamieson).
9 *C of A PP, Report of the RC on Customs and Excise Tariffs*, 1906, vol. V, p. 14, and *Evidence*, pp. 2370ff.
10 *Lithgow Mercury*, 8 January 1908.
11 Hoskins, *Hoskins Saga*, pp. 50-66.
12 Ibid., pp. 47, 67.
13 *Lithgow Mercury*, 7 February 1908.
14 Ibid., 13 March 1908; Hoskins, *Hoskins Saga*, p. 71.
15 *Lithgow Mercury*, 7 February 1908.
16 Ibid., 20 January 1908.
17 Ibid., 13, 20 March 1908.
18 Ibid., 10 April, 26 October 1908; see also Hoskins, *Hoskins Saga*, p. 47. A subsequent revision of this rule allowed smoking so long as the cigarettes were rolled before coming to work.
19 *Lithgow Mercury*, 20 May 1908.
20 Ibid., 17 June 1908.
21 Ibid., 22 May 1908.
22 Ibid., 14 August 1908; Iron Trade (Lithgow) Wages Board, *Evidence of H. Bladon*.
23 *RC Bonuses (1903)—Evidence*, pp. 66-8, mins 1310-62; *Lithgow Mercury*, 12, 14 August 1908; see also Hoskins, *Hoskins Saga*, p. 48.
24 *Lithgow Mercury*, 6 July 1908.
25 *Amalgamated Miners Association*, vol. 24, no. 4, 1908, p. 113.
26 *Lithgow Mercury*, 6 July 1908.
27 They were born in London. Their father emigrated and died when they were aged 16 and 12. Before they established their engineering works in Sydney, their activities had included an unsuccessful period on the Victorian goldfields. D. G. Hoskins, *The Ironmaster: The Life of Charles Hoskins*, 1995, appeared after the completion of this manuscript.

[28] *Lithgow Mercury*, 6 July 1908.
[29] Ibid., 9, 17 July 1908.
[30] Ibid., 13, 15 July 1908.
[31] Ibid.
[32] Ibid., 5 August 1908; this report includes the union's table of wage claims.
[33] Ibid., 18 September 1908; *Government Gazette* (NSW), 12 March 1909; see also Hughes, *History*, p. 52.
[34] *Lithgow Mercury*, 21 December 1908; see N. R. Wills, *The Economic Development of the Australian Iron and Steel Industry*, p. 43: pig-iron £118 967; steel £14 339; puddled bar £4111 and galvanised sheets £674.
[35] R. Murray and K. White, *The Ironworkers*, pp. 17–18.
[36] *NSW PP (Ass.)*, vol. 2, *Annual Report of the Director of Labour*, 1909, pp. 650, 681, *Lithgow Agent's Report*, 1910, p. 39.

## 7 NATIONALISATION OR PRIVATE ENTERPRISE?

[1] *NSW PP*, 1911, vol. 2, *Annual Report of the Director of Labour* (1911), p. 609, *Lithgow Agent's Report*, p. 641; *Lithgow Mercury*, 20 Februry 1911.
[2] *Lithgow Mercury*, 22 February 1911; for Dooley, see *ADB*, vol. 8.
[3] *Lithgow Mercury*, 22, 27 February 1911.
[4] Ibid., 17 July 1911; *SMH*, 18 July 1911. Reports from the *Lithgow Mercury* were often reprinted in the *SMH*.
[5] *Lithgow Mercury*, 19 July 1911; *SMH*, 20 July 1911.
[6] *Lithgow Mercury*, 19, 26 July 1911; *SMH*, 22, 25 July 1911.
[7] *SMH*, 17 August 1911.
[8] Ibid., 21, 22 August 1911; *Lithgow Mercury*, 8 January 1912; see also R. Murray and K. White, *The Ironworkers*, p. 42. The rates were £1 per man, 10s for his wife and 2s 6d for each child. In some cases those with large families received more than their normal wage.
[9] *SMH*, 24, 25, 26 August 1911.
[10] Ibid., 29 August 1911.
[11] Ibid., 31 August 1911.
[12] Ibid.; C. Hoskins, *The Hoskins Saga*, p. 77.
[13] *SMH*, 1 September 1911.
[14] Ibid., 2, 4 September 1911.
[15] Ibid., 16 October 1911; see Murray and White, *Ironworkers*, p. 41, for a photograph of Cairns and Dixon.
[16] *NSW PP*, 1912, *RC on the Iron and Steel Industry* (Paul Report), p. v.
[17] Ibid., p. ix.
[18] Ibid., *Evidence*, p. 60.
[19] *Argus*, 28 October 1911, prints Hoskins's explanation: the money was a temporary loan to enable Burrow to visit his father in New Zealand, and Hoskins had informed the Minister of Works about the debt on 8 May 1911.
[20] *SMH*, 27, 30 October, 1, 22 November 1911; see also *NSW PP, Debates (Ass.)*, vol. 43, p. 1387, vol. 50, p. 286.
[21] Hoskins, *Hoskins Saga*, p. 108; *SMH*, 3 November 1911; *Argus*, 1 November 1911.
[22] *AHM*, January 1912.
[23] N. R. Wills, *Economic Development of the Australian Iron and Steel Industry*, pp. 70–1 and n. 1.
[24] C of A, *Interstate Commission—Tariff Investigation—Iron and Steel* (1916), *Evidence*.
[25] Hoskins, *Hoskins Saga*, p. 47, and see also BHPA, B193, N. Wills, Foundations of Steel, p. 14.
[26] Hoskins, *Hoskins Saga*, p. 69.
[27] Ibid., pp. 67–73, outlines the operation of the Lithgow works 1908–14.
[28] Ibid., p. 72.
[29] Ibid. The photographs following p. 74 show the increasing size of the ingots produced during the period 1908–15.

## NOTES (CHAPTERS 7-8)

30. H. Hughes, 'Industrial Relations in the Australian Iron and Steel Industry 1876–1962', p. 121.
31. Hoskins, *Hoskins Saga*, pp. 104–5; see also Murray and White, *Ironworkers*, pp. 44 and 39 for the Ironworkers Picnic, which survived the transfer to Port Kembla and remains a holiday to this day.
32. Hoskins, *Hoskins Saga*, p. 77.
33. Ibid, pp. 68–9, 75–6.

## 8 INTERSTATE AND INTERNATIONAL

1. *Official Report of Conference Proceedings*, 1912, pp. 29–30.
2. *NSW PP (Ass.)*, 1912, vol. 45, pp. 37–8ff., debates on State Iron and Steelworks Bill, 12 March 1912, especially the speeches of Fitzpatrick, Wood and Griffith.
3. Ibid.
4. *BHP Australia's International Resources Company*, p. 3.
5. G. Blainey, *The Rise of Broken Hill*, p. 31.
6. Ibid., pp. 44–5.
7. C of A, *RC on Bonuses (1903)—Evidence*, p. 41, min. 826.
8. BHPA, S1/10, 10 October 1895, S1/11, 28 September 1896; BHPA, A28/1, 'Notes on Iron deposits near Port Pirie', W. J. Koehler, 25 June 1895 (?1896).
9. BHPA, S1/10, 14 November 1895, 30 January, 12 March 1896; S1/11, 29, 29 September, 22 October 1896. For further discussion of the reasons for this move, see Blainey, *Rise of Broken Hill*, pp. 62–8.
10. The iron ore problem was frequently before the Board: e.g. BHPA, S1/10, 27 June, 22 August, 30 September, 3, 10, October, 14 November, 19 December 1895, 30 January, 25, 27 February, 5, 12, 20 March 1896. BHPA, S1/10, 12 March 1896, 27 February 1896, BHP had made enquiries about acquiring the 'old ironworks property Beaconsfield' but it was not available.
11. BHPA, S1/10, 28 September 1896.
12. For a discussion of the financial limitations of such a company, see W. G. Robinson, *If I Remember Rightly*, p. 85.
13. BHPA, S1/11, 1 April 1897. The area was referred to as Iron Monarch, although the site of the first development was called Iron Knob.
14. BHPA, S1/13, 9 June 1899. Bleeser's application was finally refused in June 1899.
15. BHPA, S1/11, 4, 11 February, 25 March 1897.
16. *SA PP*, 1900, vol. 3, *Select Committee—BHP Tramway Bill—Evidence*, W. Robinson (Port Pirie Manager), min. 163, 166; BHPA, S1/14, 5 October 1900, S1/12, 12 November, 2 December 1898, 13 January 1899; *South Australian Register*, 22 November 1900.
17. For biographical details of John and H. G. Darling (his son), see *ADB*, vols 4 and 8; A Trengove, *'What's good for Australia . . . !'*, pp. 59–60. Duncan also had BHP connections. Trengove describes Darling 'as dour and determined as any Scot'.
18. BHPA, A28/1, 13 November 1900.
19. *SA PP*, 1900, vol. 3, *Select Committee—BHP Tramway Bill—Report*, pp. v, vi.
20. BHP, *Chairman's Address*, 27 July 1900, 25 January 1901; BHP, *Directors' Report*, July 1900.
21. BHP, *Chairman's Address*, 31 January 1902.
22. BHPA, S1/9, 28 September, 6, 12 December 1894, 28 April 1895, S1/10, 25 July, 19 September 1895. See Trengove, *'What's good'*, p. 52, for a vignette of the shareholders' meeting of 31 January 1895.
23. See BHP, *Annual Report*, 1915, for the figures for silver, lead, copper and zinc 1885–1915.
24. BHPA, S1/12, 27 December 1897, 4 January, 6, 13, 20, 27 May 1898. Paquita Delprat, who became the wife of the Antarctic explorer, Sir Douglas Mawson, wrote a biography of her father, *Vision of Steel*. Blainey, *Rise of Broken Hill*, p. 25. In 1886 BHP had offered W. H. Patton, its first American manager, £4000 p.a., making him the best-paid mine manager in Australia.
25. BHPA, S1/13, 12 May 1899.

## NOTES (CHAPTER 8)

26. Trengove, '*What's good*', pp. 66–7. BHPA, PM/1854, Delprat's Diaries, 1902–20. The bust is in the Library of the Royal Blind Society in Melbourne.
27. BHPA, S1/13, 10 February 1899.
28. BHPA, S1/16, 7 July 1905, S1/18, 30 July 1908; see also *Australian Mining Standard*, 26 April 1905, p. 481. BHP in fact stopped mining at Broken Hill in 1939 and sold its interest there in 1943.
29. See Blainey, *Rise of Broken Hill*, pp. 68–77, for a discussion of the various solutions to the Broken Hill sulphide problem, the most notable of which was de Bavay's, see *ADB*, vol. 8; BHPA, M8/92, 29 April 1911; *NSW PP*, 1912, vol. 3, *Select Committee—Public Works 2nd Report*, p. xxii.
30. BHP, *Chairman's Address*, 26 August 1904, 22 February 1907, 27 August 1909; BHP, *Directors' Report*, 9 August 1907.
31. BHPA, PM/1854, Delprat's Diaries, 2 June 1911; BHP, *Chairman's Address*, 25 August 1911, 23 February 1912.
32. BHPA, PM/0862, G. D. Delprat Luncheon, 1920, typescript of speech.
33. BHPA, PM/1854, Delprat's Diaries, 8 January 1912.
34. D. Brody, *Steelworkers in America: the Nonunion Era*, p. 15.
35. For a short summary of Taylor's views, see D. S. Pugh, D. J. Hickson and C. R. Hinings, *Writers on Organizations*, pp. 133–7. See also D. S. Pugh, *Organization Theory*, for a general study of the subject.
36. Brody, *Steelworkers*, pp. 148–50, 152ff.; W. T. Hogan, *Economic History of the Iron and Steel Industry in the United States*, vol. 2, p. 533. The dinners attracted the scrutiny of the Stanley Committee, which investigated the activities of United Steel in relation to the anti-trust laws.
37. See Brody, *Steelworkers*, pp. 17–18.
38. BHPA, 45/1/10 January 1912; D. Baker, 'Reminiscences . . . of the Broken Hill Proprietary Company's Adventure in Steel', *BHP Review*, vol. 12, no. 5, October 1935, pp. 1–6.
39. *NSW PP (Ass.)*, 1912, vol. 3, p. 447, App. D, McGowan to Delprat, 22 May 1912, *Select Committee—Newcastle Iron and Steel Works Bill—Evidence*, p. 454, min. 154; BHPA, M8/92, p. 5.
40. *NSW PP (Ass.)*, 1912, vol. 3, p. 447, App. D.
41. BHPA, S1/20, 7 June 1912. The vote was 5 to 2 in favour.
42. BHPA, M8/92, Delprat to J. Darling, 7 June 1912.
43. Ibid., Baker's reports, and Delprat's reports and comments.
44. BHPA, B193, N. Wills, Foundations of Steel, ch. 4, p. 6, n. 2.
45. BHPA, S1/23, p. 59, 19 May 1916.
46. BHPA, M8/92, Baker Report, 29 June 1912.
47. Ibid., 30 May 1912.
48. BHPA, M8/92, Baker's reports and Delprat's reports and comments.
49. *NSW PP*, 1912, vol. 3, *Select Committee—Newcastle Iron and Steel Works Bill—Evidence*, p. 472, min. 589, see also App. D, p. 480.
50. BHPA, M8/92, Baker's Report, 30 May 1912.
51. *NSW PP*, 1912, vol. 3, *Select Committee—Newcastle Iron and Steel Works Bill—Evidence*, p. 472, min. 589, , see also App. D, pp. 477–8.
52. BHPA, S1/20, 28 June 1912.
53. *NSW PP (Ass.)*, 1912, vol. 3, pp. 477–8.
54. *NSW PP, Votes and Proceedings*, 1912, vol. vi, p. 121.
55. *NSW PP*, 1912, vol. 3, *Select Committee—Newcastle Iron and Steel Works Bill—Evidence*, p. 472, min. 586.
56. *NSW PP (Ass.), Debates*, 1913, vol. 50, p. 801.
57. *NSW PP (Ass.), Debates*, 1912, vol. 47, pp. 1705–8, 1988–92, vol. 48, pp. 2799–812, 1913, vol. 49, pp. 3230–42, 3803–6.
58. Ibid., 1913, vol. 49, p. 2051.
59. Ibid., 1913, vol. 49, pp. 2800–1, 3241, 3086.
60. Ibid., 1913, vol. 49, p. 3235.

61 *Lithgow Mercury*, 6 February 1914; Murray and White, *Ironworkers*, p. 48.
62 C of A, *Inter-State Tariff Investigation Report 1915—Evidence*, p. 104.
63 A. H. Smith, The Australian Wire Industry 1870–1959, p. 50.
64 Trengove, '*What's good*', pp. 44, 107–8; BHPA, B193, Wills, Foundations of Steel, ch. 4, p. 9, n. 2.
65 D. Dillard, *Economic Development of the North Atlantic Community*, p. 508.
66 Queensland PP, *RC on State Iron and Steel Works Report*, 1918, especially pp. xiv, xviii, xix; also *Evidence*, pp. 28–9.
67 H. Hughes, *The Australian Iron and Steel Industry*, p. 91. The *Queensland Royal Commission Report* was issued on 21 June 1918.

## 9 THE NEWCASTLE STEELWORKS

1 BHPA, M8/92, Delprat's final conclusions, 29 April 1912.
2 BHPA, B193, N. Wills, Foundations of Steel, ch. 3, pp. 21–4.
3 BHPA, S1/20, 19, 25, June 1912, 2, 5, 8, 9, 10, 12, 17, 19 July 1912; also S1/21/10, 19, 29, 13 December 1912, 3, 17 January 1913. Prospectus in 'Iron and Steel Industry: Details of Scheme' bound with *BHP Annual Reports*; *AHM*, vol. 28, no. 3, March 1913, p. 82; *Report of BHP's 55th Half-Yearly Ordinary General Meeting*, 28 February 1913; *Report of BHP's 56th Half-Yearly Ordinary General Meeting*, 29 August 1913. See also *Report of the Proceedings on the Extraordinary General Meeting*, 27 September and 14 October 1912.
4 *Argus*, 7 July 1914; see also *Age*, 7 July 1914. The other underwriters were Messrs Turner and Brownhill, Sydney (£275 000); Norris, Oakley Bros, London (£100 000); Tolhurst, Keats and Cumming, Melbourne (£50 000); John Goodhall & Co., Melbourne (£25 000). *BHP Review* (Jubilee no.), June 1935. BHP declared that it 'had provided for its £1,000,000 within two hours'.
5 *C of A PP, Debates* (Senate), 1914, vol. 74, pp. 2493–4.
6 BHPA, S1/24, 71, 78, 84, 106, 128; PM/0625, Baker's Diary, 25 October 1916. See also B193, Wills, Foundations of Steel, ch. 6, pp. 11–12; H. Hughes, *The Australian Iron and Steel Industry*, p. 79.
7 D. Baker, 'Reminiscences', October 1935, pp. 2–3.
8 Ibid., p. 5. The chart, now very faded, is still preserved at the Newcastle works.
9 BHP did not provide cars for its executives until after World War I, and then only after careful consideration.
10 Baker, 'Reminiscences', December 1935, p. 3.
11 BHPA, PM/0625, David Baker's Diary 1913–17, 28, 30 April, 1 May 1915.
12 See W. T. Hogan, *Economic History of the Iron and Steel Industry in the United States*, vol. 2, p. 400; K. Warren, 'Iron and Steel', p. 113.
13 The seating plan for the luncheon has been preserved at the Newcastle works.
14 Baker, 'Reminiscences', December 1935, p. 4; BHP, *Australians in Company*, p. 127; BHPA, PM/0625, Baker's Diary, 2 June 1915.
15 *NMS*, 3 June 1915, gives reports of the speeches.
16 BHPA, PM/1854, Delprat's Diaries, 23 May 1919, W5-2-1, Delprat to F. M. Dickenson, confidential report to the Board.
17 *NMH*, 3 June 1915.
18 Baker, 'Reminiscences', December 1935, p. 5.
19 BHPA, S1/22, pp. 434, 498, Bradford to Delprat, 19 January 1920.
20 Ibid., February 1936, p. 9.
21 BHPA, Bradford to Delprat, 19 January 1920; BHP, *Australians in Company*, p. 134; N. Crux, 'Centenary Portraits'; Baker, 'Reminiscences', December 1935, p. 5, February 1936, p. 9.
22 Baker, 'Reminiscences', December 1935, pp. 5, 6.
23 Ibid., October 1935, p. 4; see also BHPA, B193, Wills, Foundations of Steel, ch. 5, p. 11, ch. 8, p. 5.

## NOTES (CHAPTERS 9–10)

24. Baker, 'Reminiscences', December 1935, p. 5; BHPA, B193, Wills, Foundations of Steel, ch. 9, p. 1, n. 2.
25. BHPA, B193, Wills, Foundations of Steel, ch. 6, p. 6; Baker, 'Reminiscences', December 1935, p. 6.
26. Baker, 'Reminiscences', December 1935, p. 4; BHPA, PM/1854, Delprat's Diary, 16 May 1917; BHPA, Delprat to Baker, 'Confidential', 16 May 1917; B193, Wills, Foundations of Steel, ch. 6, p. 6.
27. Baker, 'Reminiscences', February 1936, p. 7.
28. C of A, *Inter-State Tariff Investigation Report (1915)*, p. 1.
29. Baker, 'Reminiscences', February 1936, p. 8.
30. C of A, *Inter-State Tariff Investigation Report (1915)—Iron and Steel—Evidence*, p. 92.
31. BHPA, M2/92, 25 June 1914, Delprat to Chairman, J. Darling.
32. C of A, *Inter-State Tariff Investigation Report (1915)—Iron and Steel—Evidence*, p. 92.
33. BHPA, A3/4, 29 July 1914.
34. Ibid.
35. L. F. Crisp, *Federation Prophets without Honour*, p. 11.
36. *Daily Telegraph*, 15 July 1898, quoted in ibid., p. 24.
37. C of A, *Inter-State Tariff Investigation Report (1915)—Iron and Steel—Evidence*, pp. 125, 127; see also C. R. Hall, *The Manufacturers*, pp. 292–5.
38. BHPA, B43, G. & C. Hoskins Ltd, *The Iron Industry: Iron and Steel Works Lithgow and Sydney*.
39. C of A, *Inter-State Tariff Investigation Report (1915)*, especially pp. 1, 5, 7–9, 11–12.
40. C. Forster, 'Australian Manufacturing and the War of 1914–18', p. 227; see also C. Bulbeck, 'State and Economy in Tariff Policy', p. 225.
41. Forster, 'Australian Manufacturing', especially pp. 216, 219; BHPA, B193, Wills, Foundations of Steel, chs 1, 2, p. 14; C. Hoskins, *The Hoskins Saga*, p. 74.

## 10 MANAGEMENT AND LABOUR

1. *Newcastle Morning Herald*, 3 June 1915.
2. S. Pollard, *The Genesis of Modern Management*, p. 255.
3. BHPA, Board Minutes, contain numerous references to these activities, e.g. S1/25/43, 177, 182, 207, 308, 327. Delprat was at various times against both ship-building and coal ownership, but he was open to argument—which makes it difficult to state his opinion conclusively on some points—and always very conscious of the need to convince the Board.
4. See W. S. Robinson, *If I Remember Rightly*, pp. 158–62, for improvements at Port Pirie and Broken Hill.
5. BHPA, S1/25, p. 168, 12 May 1920.
6. *Science and Industry*, vol. 2, no. 1, pp. 60–2; G. Blainey, *The Steel Master*, pp. 55–7.
7. P. Drucker, *Management*, p. 13.
8. Ibid., pp. 28–31; see Pollard, *Modern Management*, pp. 251–3. In early industrial Britain there had been entrepreneurs interested in developing theories of management, e.g. Boulton & Watt at their Soho Works, Robert Owen at Manchester and New Lanark, and the Dundee flax spinner William Brown. During the 1830s attempts were made to systematise managerial theory for various types of industry, e.g. Andrew Ure, *The Cotton Manufacture of Great Britain*, 2 vols, 1836.
9. BHPA, OS/0001, Overseas Reports 1, Delprat to Dickenson, Philadelphia, 11 April 1919. Delprat wrote progress report letters as his tour progressed. BHPA, S1/24, p. 550, 14 November 1919; S1/25/25 gives the details of the scheme. The cost per ton for the additional production stimulated by the bonus was: blooming mill, 4s 6d; 28-inch mill, 3s 6d; 18-inch mill, 8s 4d; 12-inch mill, 7s 2d; 8-inch mill, 6s; finishing mill 13s 7d, and open hearth, 5s 7d.
10. BHPA, OS/0001, Overseas Reports 1, Delprat to Dickenson, 2 February 1920, 'Confidential'. The memorandum outlines the higher executive structure of US Steel.

[11] For brief summaries of these theories in their historical context, see D. S. Pugh, D. J. Hickson and C. R. Hinings, *Writers on Organisations*, for Fayol, Taylor and Mayo; D. Brody, *Steelworkers in America*, for Carnegie, Taylor and Gary.
[12] See Introduction to H. P. von Stradmann, *Walther Rathenau*, pp. 20–3, 25; Rathenau's works included *Criticism of the Age* (1912), *The New Economy* (1918), *The New Society* (1919) and *The New State* (1919).
[13] D. Baker, 'Reminiscences', December 1935, p. 3.
[14] Ibid.; BHPA, S1/23, p. 26, 31 March 1916.
[15] BHPA, S1/24, p. 171, 31 May 1918, S1/24/78, 7 June 1918.
[16] BHPA, M8/92, Delprat's Report—Conclusions, 29 April 1912, p. 5.
[17] Quoted in R. Murray and K. White, *The Ironworkers*, p. 26; J. A. Merritt, A History of the Federated Ironworkers' Association of Australia 1909–1952, pp. 89–90.
[18] See I. Turner, *In Union is Strength*, pp. 64–5; I. Turner, *Industrial Labour and Politics*, pp. 232–4.
[19] BHPA, W005/002/001, H. A. Mitchell to G. D. Delprat, 21 November 1918.
[20] Ibid., another letter of the same date; BHPA, Delprat to Baker, 'Confidential', 23 November 1917.
[21] J. Hagan, *The ACTU*, pp. 18–19, Turner, *In Union is Strength*, p. 70.
[22] I. Turner, *Industrial Labour and Politics*, pp. 204–5; Merritt, History of the FIA, p. 92; Murray and White, *Ironworkers*, pp. 28–9.
[23] Murray and White, *Ironworkers*, pp. 26–7.
[24] Merritt, History of the FIA, p. 107.
[25] Baker, 'Reminiscences', February 1936, p. 6.
[26] There are no figures for Lithgow but the branch secretary reported a 3 to 1 majority for. The ballot was ruled illegal as only two branches had conducted it in accordance with FIA rules. See also Murray and White, *Ironworkers*, pp. 28–9.
[27] BHPA, S1/33, p. 168, 19 September 1916; Merritt, History of the FIA, pp. 76–7.
[28] BHPA, PM/1854, Delprat's Diary, 22–23 June 1916.
[29] Ibid., 12–14 September 1916.
[30] BHPA, S1/23, pp. 170, 178, 180, 182, 185, 191—BHP Board Minutes, 23 September to 13 October 1916.
[31] BHPA, PM/0471, D. Baker, Reminiscences, MS, p. 52.
[32] BHPA. The original Baker MS is abridged in the *BHP Review* articles, October 1935–April 1936, see Baker, 'Reminiscences', February 1936, p. 6.
[33] Merritt, History of the FIA, pp. 74–7; Murray and White, *Ironworkers*, p. 50.
[34] Murray and White, *Ironworkers*, p. 50; Baker, 'Reminiscences', February 1936, p. 6.
[35] BHPA, PM/0862, Delprat's Luncheon speech to the Millions Club.
[36] BHPA, PM/0471, Baker, Reminiscences, MS, p. 68.

## 11 A NEW WORLD

[1] BHPA, S1/23/304, 16 February 1917; D. Baker, 'Reminiscences', February 1936, p. 7; BHPA, PM/0625, Baker's Diary, 13 November 1917.
[2] See BHPA, B193, N. Wills, Foundations of Steel, ch. 7, pp. 1–6.
[3] BHPA, D. Wheeler, 'The Brains behind BHP'; A. Trengove, *'What's good for Australia ...!'*, p. 136. See also above p. 165. Knox had had reservations about BHP becoming a steel manufacturer and voted against the idea. He resigned from the Board of Directors in 1911, see *BHP 75 Years*.
[4] BHPA, Darling to Lewis, 12 December 1920.
[5] BHPA, W005/002/001, Delprat to Baker, 22 November 1918, 'Private & Confidential'; S1/24/224, 231 November–December 1917; Baker, 'Reminiscences', February 1936, p. 9.
[6] BHPA, PM/1854, Delprat's Diaries, 13 February 1919, S1/24/275, 14 February 1919. This may be connected with his being given the duties but not the title of assistant general manager.
[7] Quoted in Trengove, *'What's good'*, p. 121.

## NOTES (CHAPTER 11)

8. G. Blainey, *The Steel Master*, pp. 55–6.
9. BHPA, S1/23, p. 146, 1 September 1916, S1/24/119, 12 July 1918.
10. BHPA, PM/1854, Delprat's Diaries, 23 May 1919, memorandum, 2 February 1920.
11. BHPA, S1/24/10, 8 March 1918.
12. BHPA, S1/24, p. 10, 8 March 1918, S1/24/569, 22 November 1919. Delprat was obviously annoyed about this and brought it before the Board at some length on 22 and 23 November 1919, clearly indicating that Bradford felt slighted.
13. BHPA, S1/25/32, 12 December 1919. In 1920 Horwood was working at Head Office in Melbourne.
14. BHPA, S1/24/556, 17 November 1919, S1/25/571, S1/25/43, 231, PM/1854, Delprat's Diaries, 21 May 1920.
15. BHPA, S1/25/32, S1/25/6, 25 November 1919. 'Mr Delprat made a personal statement in regard to certain matters which was noted and consideration deferred': see BHPA, PM/1854, Delprat's Diaries, 25 November 1919.
16. BHPA, M009/001, L. Bradford to G. D. Delprat, 19 January 1920.
17. BHPA, PM/1854, Delprat's Diaries; S1/25/70, 6 February 1920, S1/25/74, 7 February 1920.
18. BHPA, Bradford to Delprat, 19 January 1920; S1/25/70, 74, 85, 106, 116, 6 February–20 March 1920.
19. BHPA, S1/23/522, 23 November 1917, S1/23/539, 12 December 1917.
20. See W. S. Robinson, *If I Remember Rightly*, pp. 88–9; J. Rickard, *H. B. Higgins*, p. 181. See also BHPA, S1/23, p. 95, 7 July 1916. Delprat cautioned the Board about allowing the London office to supply Robinson with information.
21. BHPA, H. G. Darling to Lewis.
22. Ibid.
23. Robert Hadfield, 'The World Hunger for Steel', *Iron and Coal Trades Review*, p. 1.
24. BHPA, S1/25/296, 16 September 1920, S1/25/304, 22 September 1920.
25. BHPA, M009/001, Darling to Lewis, 11 December 1920.
26. Ibid.
27. BHPA, OS/0001, Delprat to the Company Secretary (Dickenson), 23 July 1919, Delprat to the Company Secretary, 31 July 1919.
28. BHPA, S1/24/263, S1/25/280, 281, 432, January 1919–February 1922.
29. BHPA, S1/24/92, S1/25/331, 342, June 1918–October 1920. See also S1/24/106, 5 July 1918, when Baldwin's made enquiries about 'their putting in a plant at Newcastle for the manufacture of galvanised sheets'. BHP was willing to consider a proposition to supply them with material as 'Lysaght's had no monopoly'. But, S1/25/402, 22 December 1920, when Lysaght's suggested to Guest, Keen & Nettlefold that they should consider establishing a plant for nuts and bolts, H. V. McKay pointed out, S1/25/408, 7 January 1921, that such factories already existed and should any definite proposal be made Guest, Keen & Nettlefold should be put in touch with them.
30. BHPA, S1/24/18, 15 March 1918. BHP had been approached by H. O. Jones & Co., Hobart (jam manufacturers), about the need for tin plate.
31. See W. T. Hogan, *Economic History of the Iron and Steel Industry in the United States*, vol. 3, pp. 1055–6.
32. BHPA, A22/1, H. A. Gerney (Richard Thomas & Co.) to W. L. Raws (Elder Smith & Co.), 9 April 1918, Secretary to Prime Minister's Department to Managing Director, Elder, Smith & Co., 4 July 1918, Delprat to Ladd, 31 May 1918, Ladd to Delprat, 7 July 1918, Delprat to Ladd, 24 July 1918, Delprat to Ladd, 23 September 1918.
33. BHPA, A22/1, Delprat to Ladd, 23 September 1918, Delprat to Carr (London), 26 August 1918, Delprat to Ladd, 11 October 1918, Ladd to Delprat, 11 October 1918.
34. BHPA, A22/1, Ladd to Delprat, 11 December 1918, Report by Poppleton, 23 January 1919.
35. BHPA, S1/24, p. 437, Dickenson to Delprat, 27 June 1919, Ladd to Delprat, 30 June 1919, Baker to general manager, 8 August 1919, S1/25, p. 386, 3 December 1920.
36. BHPA, A22/1, Richard Thomas & Co. to BHP, 17, 25 February 1921, S1/25, p. 447, 18 February 1921, A22/1, Henry Bond (Richard Thomas & Co.) to BHP, 11 November 1924.

[11] For brief summaries of these theories in their historical context, see D. S. Pugh, D. J. Hickson and C. R. Hinings, *Writers on Organisations*, for Fayol, Taylor and Mayo; D. Brody, *Steelworkers in America*, for Carnegie, Taylor and Gary.
[12] See Introduction to H. P. von Stradmann, *Walther Rathenau*, pp. 20–3, 25; Rathenau's works included *Criticism of the Age* (1912), *The New Economy* (1918), *The New Society* (1919) and *The New State* (1919).
[13] D. Baker, 'Reminiscences', December 1935, p. 3.
[14] Ibid.; BHPA, S1/23, p. 26, 31 March 1916.
[15] BHPA, S1/24, p. 171, 31 May 1918, S1/24/78, 7 June 1918.
[16] BHPA, M8/92, Delprat's Report—Conclusions, 29 April 1912, p. 5.
[17] Quoted in R. Murray and K. White, *The Ironworkers*, p. 26; J. A. Merritt, A History of the Federated Ironworkers' Association of Australia 1909–1952, pp. 89–90.
[18] See I. Turner, *In Union is Strength*, pp. 64–5; I. Turner, *Industrial Labour and Politics*, pp. 232–4.
[19] BHPA, W005/002/001, H. A. Mitchell to G. D. Delprat, 21 November 1918.
[20] Ibid., another letter of the same date; BHPA, Delprat to Baker, 'Confidential', 23 November 1917.
[21] J. Hagan, *The ACTU*, pp. 18–19, Turner, *In Union is Strength*, p. 70.
[22] I. Turner, *Industrial Labour and Politics*, pp. 204–5; Merritt, History of the FIA, p. 92; Murray and White, *Ironworkers*, pp. 28–9.
[23] Murray and White, *Ironworkers*, pp. 26–7.
[24] Merritt, History of the FIA, p. 107.
[25] Baker, 'Reminiscences', February 1936, p. 6.
[26] There are no figures for Lithgow but the branch secretary reported a 3 to 1 majority for. The ballot was ruled illegal as only two branches had conducted it in accordance with FIA rules. See also Murray and White, *Ironworkers*, pp. 28–9.
[27] BHPA, S1/33, p. 168, 19 September 1916; Merritt, History of the FIA, pp. 76–7.
[28] BHPA, PM/1854, Delprat's Diary, 22–23 June 1916.
[29] Ibid., 12–14 September 1916.
[30] BHPA, S1/23, pp. 170, 178, 180, 182, 185, 191—BHP Board Minutes, 23 September to 13 October 1916.
[31] BHPA, PM/0471, D. Baker, Reminiscences, MS, p. 52.
[32] BHPA. The original Baker MS is abridged in the *BHP Review* articles, October 1935–April 1936, see Baker, 'Reminiscences', February 1936, p. 6.
[33] Merritt, History of the FIA, pp. 74–7; Murray and White, *Ironworkers*, p. 50.
[34] Murray and White, *Ironworkers*, p. 50; Baker, 'Reminiscences', February 1936, p. 6.
[35] BHPA, PM/0862, Delprat's Luncheon speech to the Millions Club.
[36] BHPA, PM/0471, Baker, Reminiscences, MS, p. 68.

## 11 A NEW WORLD

[1] BHPA, S1/23/304, 16 February 1917; D. Baker, 'Reminiscences', February 1936, p. 7; BHPA, PM/0625, Baker's Diary, 13 November 1917.
[2] See BHPA, B193, N. Wills, Foundations of Steel, ch. 7, pp. 1–6.
[3] BHPA, D. Wheeler, 'The Brains behind BHP'; A. Trengove, *'What's good for Australia ...!'*, p. 136. See also above p. 165. Knox had had reservations about BHP becoming a steel manufacturer and voted against the idea. He resigned from the Board of Directors in 1911, see *BHP 75 Years*.
[4] BHPA, Darling to Lewis, 12 December 1920.
[5] BHPA, W005/002/001, Delprat to Baker, 22 November 1918, 'Private & Confidential'; S1/24/224, 231 November–December 1917; Baker, 'Reminiscences', February 1936, p. 9.
[6] BHPA, PM/1854, Delprat's Diaries, 13 February 1919, S1/24/275, 14 February 1919. This may be connected with his being given the duties but not the title of assistant general manager.
[7] Quoted in Trengove, *'What's good'*, p. 121.

## NOTES (CHAPTER 11)

8. G. Blainey, *The Steel Master*, pp. 55–6.
9. BHPA, S1/23, p. 146, 1 September 1916, S1/24/119, 12 July 1918.
10. BHPA, PM/1854, Delprat's Diaries, 23 May 1919, memorandum, 2 February 1920.
11. BHPA, S1/24/10, 8 March 1918.
12. BHPA, S1/24, p. 10, 8 March 1918, S1/24/569, 22 November 1919. Delprat was obviously annoyed about this and brought it before the Board at some length on 22 and 23 November 1919, clearly indicating that Bradford felt slighted.
13. BHPA, S1/25/32, 12 December 1919. In 1920 Horwood was working at Head Office in Melbourne.
14. BHPA, S1/24/556, 17 November 1919, S1/25/571, S1/25/43, 231, PM/1854, Delprat's Diaries, 21 May 1920.
15. BHPA, S1/25/32, S1/25/6, 25 November 1919. 'Mr Delprat made a personal statement in regard to certain matters which was noted and consideration deferred': see BHPA, PM/1854, Delprat's Diaries, 25 November 1919.
16. BHPA, M009/001, L. Bradford to G. D. Delprat, 19 January 1920.
17. BHPA, PM/1854, Delprat's Diaries; S1/25/70, 6 February 1920, S1/25/74, 7 February 1920.
18. BHPA, Bradford to Delprat, 19 January 1920; S1/25/70, 74, 85, 106, 116, 6 February–20 March 1920.
19. BHPA, S1/23/522, 23 November 1917, S1/23/539, 12 December 1917.
20. See W. S. Robinson, *If I Remember Rightly*, pp. 88–9; J. Rickard, *H. B. Higgins*, p. 181. See also BHPA, S1/23, p. 95, 7 July 1916. Delprat cautioned the Board about allowing the London office to supply Robinson with information.
21. BHPA, H. G. Darling to Lewis.
22. Ibid.
23. Robert Hadfield, 'The World Hunger for Steel', *Iron and Coal Trades Review*, p. 1.
24. BHPA, S1/25/296, 16 September 1920, S1/25/304, 22 September 1920.
25. BHPA, M009/001, Darling to Lewis, 11 December 1920.
26. Ibid.
27. BHPA, OS/0001, Delprat to the Company Secretary (Dickenson), 23 July 1919, Delprat to the Company Secretary, 31 July 1919.
28. BHPA, S1/24/263, S1/25/280, 281, 432, January 1919–February 1922.
29. BHPA, S1/24/92, S1/25/331, 342, June 1918–October 1920. See also S1/24/106, 5 July 1918, when Baldwin's made enquiries about 'their putting in a plant at Newcastle for the manufacture of galvanised sheets'. BHP was willing to consider a proposition to supply them with material as 'Lysaght's had no monopoly'. But, S1/25/402, 22 December 1920, when Lysaght's suggested to Guest, Keen & Nettlefold that they should consider establishing a plant for nuts and bolts, H. V. McKay pointed out, S1/25/408, 7 January 1921, that such factories already existed and should any definite proposal be made Guest, Keen & Nettlefold should be put in touch with them.
30. BHPA, S1/24/18, 15 March 1918. BHP had been approached by H. O. Jones & Co., Hobart (jam manufacturers), about the need for tin plate.
31. See W. T. Hogan, *Economic History of the Iron and Steel Industry in the United States*, vol. 3, pp. 1055–6.
32. BHPA, A22/1, H. A. Gerney (Richard Thomas & Co.) to W. L. Raws (Elder Smith & Co.), 9 April 1918, Secretary to Prime Minister's Department to Managing Director, Elder, Smith & Co., 4 July 1918, Delprat to Ladd, 31 May 1918, Ladd to Delprat, 7 July 1918, Delprat to Ladd, 24 July 1918, Delprat to Ladd, 23 September 1918.
33. BHPA, A22/1, Delprat to Ladd, 23 September 1918, Delprat to Carr (London), 26 August 1918, Delprat to Ladd, 11 October 1918, Ladd to Delprat, 11 October 1918.
34. BHPA, A22/1, Ladd to Delprat, 11 December 1918, Report by Poppleton, 23 January 1919.
35. BHPA, S1/24, p. 437, Dickenson to Delprat, 27 June 1919, Ladd to Delprat, 30 June 1919, Baker to general manager, 8 August 1919, S1/25, p. 386, 3 December 1920.
36. BHPA, A22/1, Richard Thomas & Co. to BHP, 17, 25 February 1921, S1/25, p. 447, 18 February 1921, A22/1, Henry Bond (Richard Thomas & Co.) to BHP, 11 November 1924.

## NOTES (CHAPTERS 11–12)

37. BHPA, A22/1, Henry Bond (Richard Thomas & Co.) to BHP, 11 November 1924.
38. BHPA, A22/1, note by Lewis, 21 April 1933.
39. BHPA, A22/1, copy of address made by Firth to Iron and Steel Federation, 25 July 1933.
40. BHPA, S1/22/458, 15 October 1915. The figures for sulphate of ammonia and tar from the coke ovens, see *Souvenir*, p. 38, are a 'misprint'. See S1/22/506. A copy of the *Souvenir* was presented to King George V.
41. For projected markets, see BHPA, S1/23/366, 437, S1/24/119, 142, 181, 245, 255, 275 and also S1/23/292 for the town hall trade meeting. W. H. G. Armytage, *The Rise of the Technocrats*, pp. 219–37.
42. Baker, 'Reminiscences', February 1936, pp. 8–9. Construction started 10 March, test run 26 August and production began with 50 tons per shift on 2 September 1918.
43. BHPA, W5/2/1, Delprat to Baker, 2 June 1917.
44. BHPA, W5/2/1, Delprat to Baker, 8 March 1918. See also S1/24/10, 8 March 1918.
45. BHPA, S1/24/10, 8 March 1918, S1/24/206, 219.
46. BHPA, D. Wheeler, 'BHP's Quiet Achiever', *Centenary Portraits*.
47. BHPA, S1/24/245, PM/1854, Delprat's Diaries, 20 December 1918, 14 May 1919.
48. BHPA, S1/25/207, 280, 291, 3, 10 September 1920. There is obviously a mistake in the minutes, which state that the improvements reduced the time of the steel-making process by two-thirds. If true, this would have been a world record and would have made any consideration of the duplex operation unnecessary.
49. BHPA, S1/25/216, 2 July 1920.
50. BHPA, S1/25/231, 16 July 1920.
51. BHPA, S1/25/242, 21 July 1920.
52. BHPA, S1/25/244, 23 July 1920. The three reports are in the BHP Archives.
53. BHPA, S1/25/263, 13 August 1920, M009/001, Delprat to BHP Secretary, 16 August 1920.
54. BHPA, S1/25/299, 17 September 1920, S1/25/342, 22 October 1920, S1/25/337, 8 October 1920.
55. BHPA, S1/25/444, 446, 447, 453, 11–25 February 1921.

## 12 CRISIS AND SURVIVAL

1. BHPA, S1/25/402, 22 December 1920, S1/25/425, 27 January 1921, S1/25/474, 24 March 1921.
2. BHPA, M009/001, Darling to Lewis, 6 January 1922, Lewis to Darling, 7 January 1922, S1/26/493, 19 January 1923, S1/26/501, 26 January 1923.
3. D. Baker, 'Reminscences', December 1935, p. 3; also S1/26/170, 23 December 1921. Before coming to Australia, Saul had been the head roller at the blooming mill in the Dominion Iron and Steel Co. and mill superintendent with the American Tube and Stamping Co. of Bridgeport, Connecticutt. BHPA, S1/26/278, 28 April 1922, S1/26/430, 27 October 1922, S1/26/488, 12 January 1923, S1/25/402, 12 December 1920, S1/26/234, 10 March 1922.
4. BHPA, S1/26/106, 14 October 1921, also S1/26/131, 11 November 1921, S1/26/170, 12 December 1921.
5. BHPA, S1/26/430, 27 October 1922, S1/26/488, 12 January 1923, S1/26/493, 19 January 1923. Dickenson died 22 May 1923, see also S1/27/63, 20 July 1923. The remainder of the year's salary was paid to his estate.
6. BHPA, S1/26/517, 16 February 1923.
7. BHPA, S1/27/17, 1 June 1923.
8. BHPA, S1/27/17, 6 June 1923, S1/27/63, 20 July 1923, S1/27/104, 31 August 1923, S1/27/481, 27 March 1925, S1/27/554, 28 August 1925.
9. BHPA, S1/27/53, 13 July 1923, S1/27/63, 20 July 1923, S1/27/105, 7 September 1923.
10. BHPA. This statement was prepared for the committee probably in March or April 1921.
11. BHPA, S1/25/535, 13 May 1921. The Acting Premier of NSW was informed of the extent of these cuts and an indication of how seriously the company viewed the recent reduction in hours of labour.

## NOTES (CHAPTER 12)

12. BHPA, S1/25/522–30. The committee met at Newcastle on 28, 29, 30 April 1921. Its minutes were confirmed at the Board meeting on 6 May and entered into the Board Minute Book as a record, see S1/25/515.
13. BHPA, S1/26/82, 23 September 1921, S1/26/160, 9 December 1921, S1/26/170, 23 December 1921.
14. BHPA, M009/001, 8 December 1921, Baker to Lewis.
15. BHPA, S1/26/114, 21 October 1921, S1/26/196, 27 January 1922, S1/26/278, 28 April 1922, S1/26/357, 21 July 1922.
16. *Annual Report* of the Tariff Board, June 1925, quoted in N. R. Wills, *The Economic Development of the Australian Iron and Steel Industry*, p. 114.
17. Ibid.
18. Ibid.
19. BHPA, S1/26/80, 20 September 1921, S1/27/46, 6 July 1923, S1/27/53, 13 July 1923, S1/27/63, 20 July 1923, S1/27/310, 20 June 1924.
20. BHPA, W005/002/001, Lewis to Baker, 'Confidential', 18 April 1922, Baker to Lewis, 21 April 1922.
21. BHPA, W005/002/001, Lewis to Baker, 28 April, 6 May 1922, S1/26/312, 9 June 1922, S1/26/160, 9 December 1921.
22. BHPA, W005/002/001, 2 June 1922.
23. BHPA, S1/26/312, 9 June 1922. Morris was offered a three-year contract: £2000 for the first year to cover expenses, £1500 for subsequent years, but Morris demanded, and got, £1750 for these years. See also S1/26/336, 30 June 1922, S1/26/403, 15 September 1922, S1/26/454, 11 November 1922, S1/26/477, 22 December 1922. Coal samples were tested in the USA, see S1/26/369.
24. BHPA, S1/26/80, 20 September 1921, S1/27/46, 6 July 1923, S1/27/53, 13 July 1923, S1/27/63, 20 July 1923, S1/27/310, 20 June 1924, S1/27/437, 23 January 1925.
25. BHPA, S1/25/522–30, 28 April 1921, also S1/27/472, 20 March 1925, S1/26/526, 23 February 1923, S1/26/568, 20 April 1923, S1/26/572, 27 April 1923, S1/27/94, 24 August 1923.
26. BHPA, S1/25/535, 13 May 1921, S1/27/420, 19 December 1924, S1/26/125, 16 February 1923, S1/26/538, 9 March 1923, S1/27/292, 23 May 1924, S1/27/83, 10 August 1923, S1/27/464, 3 March 1925. The price was 27s per share; also S1/27/481, 27 March 1925, S1/27/505, 15 May 1925. It was estimated that Ryland's costs would be reduced by £30 000 p.a.
27. Quoted in A. Trengove, '*What's good for Australia ...!*', p. 130.
28. BHPA, S1/26/409, 29 September 1922, S1/26/415, 6 October 1922, S1/26/420, 13 October 1922, S1/26/425, 20 October 1922.
29. Address to shareholders, quoted in Trengove, '*What's good*', p. 133.
30. Quoted in ibid., p. 130.
31. BHPA, S1/26/508, 9 February 1923, S1/26/526, 23 February 1923, S1/26/533, 2 March 1923, S1/26/538, 9 March 1923, S1/26/551, 23 March 1923, S1/26/575, 4 May 1923.
32. See BHPA, B193, N. Wills, Foundations of Steel, ch. 7, pp. 22–6.
33. Quoted in G. Blainey, *The Steel Master*, p. 172.
34. *BHP Review*, Jubilee no., 1935, p. 92.
35. BHPA, OS/0020, Overseas Reports No. 20 (336), London, 12 June 1925.
36. BHPA, W005/002/001, Lewis to Baker, 6 May 1922: 'it is not possible for anyone to foretell how long the stoppage will be'.
37. BHPA, S1/27/189, 21 December 1923, see also S1/27/155, 166, November 1923; for Baker's opinion of the Wilputte coke ovens, see S1/27/184, 14 December 1923.
38. BHPA, S1/27/285, 16 May 1924. Baker was requested to review and to prepare a comprehensive report on all departments of the steelworks with any recommendations which he might like to make about them. See also S1/27/329, 25 July 1924, and S1/27/378, 17 October 1924. The report was prepared in three parts.
39. BHPA, S1/27/408, 5 December 1924, S1/27/443, 23 January 1925; see also S1/27/445, 30 January 1925.

40. Baker, 'Reminiscences', April 1936, p. 9; BHPA, S1/27/420, 19 December 1924, S1/27/437, 23 January 1925, S1/27/460, 27 February 1925.
41. BHPA, S1/27/472, 20 March 1925. The minutes list findings and decisions—the review was similar to that following the departure of Delprat; see also S1/27/472, 20 March 1925, S1/27/467, letter to Bradford indicating steps to be followed in the future. J. R. Young was appointed superintendent of the blast furnace, while Griffith succeeded Bradford as production superindendent and 'understudy'.
42. See J. C. Carr and W. Taplin, *History of the British Steel Industry*, pp. 371–3ff.; K. Warren, 'Iron and Steel', pp. 103–25.
43. Quoted in Carr and Taplin, *History of the British Steel Industry*, pp. 439–40.
44. BHPA, OS/0020, Overseas Reports No. 20 [E. Lewis 1925] (180), London, 6 October 1925.
45. BHPA, OS/0020, Overseas Reports No. 20 (110), 5 October 1925.
46. BHPA, OS/0020, Overseas Reports No. 20 (111), London, 9 June 1925.
47. BHPA, S1/27/525, 3 July 1925; see also S1/27/481, 27 March 1925.
48. BHPA, OS/0020, Overseas Reports No. 20 (111), London, 9 June 1925, and (114), London, 25 June 1925.

## 13 THE AUSTRALIAN IRON AND STEEL COMPANY

1. C. Hoskins, *The Hoskins Saga*, p. 78.
2. *BHP Review*, pp. 32, 52. In 1987 Don Hoskins recollected Miss Foskett's formidable abilities and loyalty with affection.
3. BHPA, B43, G. & C. Hoskins Ltd, *The Iron Industry: Iron and Steel Works Lithgow and Sydney*, 1915, M9/35.
4. BHPA, M9/35.
5. J. C. Carr and W. Taplin, *History of the British Steel Industry*, pp. 439–50, especially pp. 466–7; D. Burn, *The Economic History of Steelmaking, 1867–1939*, pp. 438–9ff.; K. Warren 'Iron and Steel', pp. 104–5.
6. Hoskins, *Hoskins Saga*, p. 89.
7. *Lithgow Mercury*, 5 January 1920.
8. Hoskins, *Hoskins Saga*, p. 90; *NSW PP*, vol. 3, 1923, p. 455.
9. Hoskins, *Hoskins Saga*, p. 100. The line was finished in 1932 during the depression and AIS was not able to freight the agreed minimum so the company had to pay the NSW government £25 000.
10. BHPA, PM/1320, *Hoskins Iron & Steel Company Ltd*.
11. BHPA, PM/0579, MSS.
12. Hoskins, *Hoskins Saga*, p. 73.
13. As seen by the authors on a visit to the Port Kembla works in February 1987.
14. *SMH*, 10 March 1930; Hoskins, *Hoskins Saga*, p. 97. BHPA, PA/94—the early development of the works is described, with illustrations, in The Growth and Development of Australian Iron & Steel Ltd., an address delivered by Mr A. S. Hoskins before the Institute of Engineers, Australia, Sydney Division, 10 July 1930.
15. *BHP Facts Sheet*, July 1986, Slab and Plate Products Division.
16. BHPA, PM/0578, AIS brochure, *New 800-Ton Blast Furnace Plant of Australian Iron and Steel Ltd., at Port Kembla, New South Wales, Australia*, 1928, p. 9. This illustrated brochure gives further details about the plant and its equipment as does BHPA, PA/94, A. S. Hoskins, The Growth and Development of Australian Iron & Steel.
17. Hoskins, *Hoskins Saga*, pp. 98–9.
18. *SMH*, 10 March 1930; T. Taylor, Australian Iron and Steel Limited 1928–39, pp. 43, 66.
19. *SMH*, 1 May 1929, Cecil Hoskins's address to Rotary Club.
20. *Iron and Coal Trades Review*, 11 January 1929.
21. Taylor, Australian Iron and Steel, pp. 16–17; N. R. Wills, *The Economic Development of the Australian Iron and Steel Industry*, p. 84. See also *SMH*, 9 March, 18 May 1928.

[22] BHPA, A24/38, Hoskins–Dorman Long negotiations, 24 August 1927.
[23] BHPA, W2/2/3, Wright to C. Hoskins, 5 October 1927, cables, 2, 3 February 1928, Hoskins to Wright, 13 February 1928.
[24] BHPA, S4/21 3/2/33, S4/22 2/2/34, S4/25 1/2/35, S24/25 3/2/35; Taylor, Australian Iron and Steel, p. 40.
[25] BHPA, W2/2/5, A. S. Hoskins's correspondence folder 2, 17 July 1935.
[26] Carr and Taplin, *History of the British Steel Industry*, p. 385.
[27] Ibid., p. 365.
[28] Ibid., pp. 384, 447, 490.
[29] British Steel Corporation Archives, Middlesborough, England, Dorman Long's Minute Book No. 6, p. 262; BHPA, A24/38, C. Hoskins to Bell, 12 December 1927.
[30] Hoskins, *Hoskins Saga*, p. 94.
[31] *SMH*, 12 January 1929.
[32] See *Iron and Coal Trades Review*, 14 October 1927, for an illustrated description of this mill. See also Hoskins, Growth and Development, p. 26. The Davy engine was still at Port Kembla in February 1987.
[33] See B. Schedvin, *Australia and the Great Depression*, p. 74, also pp. 3–10, 68–71.
[34] *SMH*, 9 April 1934, quoted in Taylor, Australian Iron and Steel, p. 40.
[35] Quoted in Schedvin, *Australia and the Great Depression*, p. 182.
[36] Ibid., p. 187; A Trengove, '*What's good for Australia ...!*', p. 147; G. Blainey, *The Steel Master*, pp. 108–9.
[37] See J. R. Robinson, '1930–39', p. 429.
[38] Wills, *Economic Development*, p. 124.
[39] *BHP Fact Sheet, Port Kembla*, 1986.
[40] *SMH*, 21 November 1931.
[41] D. Hoskins, *The Ironmaster*.
[42] *SMH*, 29 December 1929.
[43] *Lithgow Mercury*, 12 June 1931.
[44] J. A. Merritt, A History of the Federated Ironworkers' Association of Australia 1909–1952, p. 176.

## 14 A NATIONAL INDUSTRY

[1] BHPA, W2/2/3, Allen, Allen & Hemsley to Secretary HISC, 4 April 1928, A24/35, Lewis to HISC, 18 May 1928, notifying the HISC Board of the BHP Board's approval of the transfer of the contract to AIS.
[2] C. Hoskins, *The Hoskins Saga*, pp. 84–5.
[3] BHPA, S1/28/230, 21 January 1927, A24/35, notes of a meeting at Hoskins Sydney office, 14 January 1927, on the 10-year iron ore contract.
[4] Hoskins, *Hoskins Saga*, p. 85 (the amount paid for the leases was £33 000 not £27 000); BHPA, A24/46, August 1926, L. A. Westcott, Report to HISC on 'Yampi Sound Iron Ore Deposits'.
[5] BHPA, A24/35, Lewis to Hockey, 13 July 1927.
[6] T. Taylor, Australian Iron and Steel Limited 1928–39, p. 56.
[7] BHPA, A23/35, Lewis to C. Hoskins, 18 March 1932; see also memoranda BHP–Scott, Fell & Co. (shipping), 24 July 1928, Lewis, R. N. Kirk and C. Hoskins, 8 March 1932. Hoskins wanted both a reduction in freight charges (or to be allowed to make his own own arrangements) and a reduction in the price of ore delivered to Whyalla as a 'welfare gesture to help the industry'.
[8] *Daily Mail* (Brisbane), 28 May 1928.
[9] BHPA, W2/2/3, 11 May 1928.
[10] British Steel Corporation Archives, Middlesborough, England, Dorman Long Minute Book No. 7, p. 26—report of cablegrams from L. Ennis, Sydney to Board.
[11] British Steel Corporation Archives, 1066/5/6, L. Ennis to T. D. H. Stubbs, 23 July 1928.

# NOTES (CHAPTER 14)

[12] British Steel Corporation Archives, 1066/5/6, 12 June 1928.
[13] Ibid.; J. C. Carr and W. Taplin, *History of the British Steel Industry*, pp. 446–7. Both Dorman Long Ltd and Baldwins Ltd had contributed only plant and non-cash assests.
[14] D. Hoskins, *The Ironmaster*.
[15] Taylor, Australian Iron and Steel, pp. 66, 68–9, 120–1.
[16] BHPA, W2/1/10, Works Report 'C', 20 March 1935.
[17] BHPA, A24/35, Firth to Lewis, 29 April 1933, Lewis to Firth, 3 May 1933, Firth to Lewis, 4 May 1933.
[18] BHPA, A24/35, C. Hoskins to Lewis, 12 August 1935.
[19] British Steel Corporation Archives, 1066/5/6, Way to Ennis, 27 August 1935.
[20] Ibid., 24 September 1935.
[21] Ibid., F. M. Mitchell to C. Hoskins, 21 September 1935 (copy).
[22] Ibid., Way to Ennis, 21 October 1935.
[23] Ibid., 6 August 1935; see also 17, 24 September 1935.
[24] Ibid., 6, 27 August, 3 September 1935.
[25] *Argus*, 13 August 1935.
[26] British Steel Corporation Archives, 1066/5/6, Way to Ennis, 30 July 1935.
[27] See BHP, *Australians in Company*, p. 147, for a facsimile of the signatures.
[28] *BHP Report*, 1928.
[29] *BHP Facts Sheet, Newcastle*, 1986.
[30] BHPA, B193, N. Wills, Foundations of Steel, ch. 7, p. 27.
[31] *BHP Report* 1938; Taylor, Australian Iron and Steel, p. 85.
[32] Taylor, Australian Iron and Steel, pp. 83–5, 88.
[33] Ibid., p.65.
[34] Ibid., pp. 86–7; BHPA, B193, Wills, Foundations of Steel, ch. 7, p. 29.
[35] Taylor, Australian Iron and Steel, p. 93.
[36] BHPA, S4/26, Memorandum of a Conference held in the Managing Director's Office, Melbourne, on Tuesday 22nd October, 1935, at 2 p.m.'.
[37] C. R. Hall, *The Manufacturers*, pp. 434–6; Hoskins, *Hoskins Saga*, pp. 120–3.
[38] BHP, *Seventy-five years of BHP Development in Australia*, p. 28.

# BIBLIOGRAPHY

## NEWSPAPERS AND JOURNALS

*Argus*
*Australasian*
*Australasian Hardware and Machinery*
*Australasian Ironmonger*
*Australian Mining Standard*
*BHP Recreation Review*
*BHP Review*
*Cornwall Chronicle* (Launceston)
*Daily Mail* (Brisbane)
*Fortune*
*Illustrated Sydney News*
*International Socialist Review*
*Iron*
*Iron & Coal Trades Review* (London)
*Journal of the Iron and Steel Institute* (London)
*Launceston Examiner*
*Lithgow Mercury*
*Mercury*
*Newcastle Morning Herald*
*South Australian Gazette and Colonial Register*
*Sydney Morning Herald*

## OFFICIAL PUBLICATIONS

### Commonwealth of Australia

*Inter-State Commission—Tariff Investigation—Iron and Steel. Evidence.* 1916.
*Inter-State Tariff Investigation Report. Evidence.* 1915.

# BIBLIOGRAPHY

*Parliamentary Papers—Report of the Committee of Economic Enquiry* (Vernon Report). 1965.
*Parliamentary Papers—Report of the Royal Commission on Bonuses for Manufacture.* (1903). *Evidence.*
*Parliamentary Papers—Report of the Royal Commission on Customs and Excise Tariffs* (1906).
*Parliamentary Papers—Select Committee on Manufactures Encouragement Act* (1904), vol. II. *Evidence.*
*Parliamentary Papers—Senate* and *House of Representatives*
*Parliamentary Papers—Debates* (Senate) ix (1902).

## New South Wales

*Arbitration Report*, 2. 1903.
*Department of Mines Annual Report.* 1877.
*Government Gazette.*
*Parliamentary Papers*—1911, vol. 2. *Annual Report of the Director of Labour.* 1911.
*Parliamentary Papers*—1912, vol. 3. *Select Committee—Public Works 2nd Report.*
*Parliamentary Papers—(Ass.)*, 1912, vol. 3.
*Parliamentary Papers—(Ass.)*, 12 March 1912ff. (Debates on the State Iron and Steel Works Bill.)
*Parliamentary Papers—Royal Commission on the Iron and Steel Industry (Paul Report).* 1912.
*Parliamentary Papers—Select Committee Newcastle Iron and Steel Works Bill—Evidence.*
*Parliamentary Papers—Votes and Proceedings.*
*Report of the Royal Commission of the Iron and Steel Industry* (1911). *Evidence.*
*Report of the Royal Commission on Strikes. Evidence.* 1891.

## Queensland

*Parliamentary Papers—Royal Commission on State Iron and Steel Works Report.* 1918.

## South Australia

*Parliamentary Papers—Votes and Proceedings.*
*Parliamentary Papers*—(1900) vol. 3. *Select Committee Report and Evidence. BHP Tramway Bill.*

## Tasmania

*Tasmanian Legislative Council Journals.*

## Victoria

*Annual Report of the Victorian Secretary for Mines.*
*Parliamentary Papers.*
*Victorian Government Gazette.*

## Other

*Historical Records of Australia.*

# BIBLIOGRAPHY

## MANUSCRIPT SOURCES

### BHP Archives, Melbourne

BHP. *Annual Reports.*
——*Chairman's Addresses.*
——*Directors' Reports.*
*BHP Facts Sheets.*
Crux, N. 'Centenary Portraits'.
Wills, N. Foundations of Steel: the BHP Story.

### British Steel Corporation Archives, Middlesborough, UK

Dorman Long Minute Books

### Mitchell Library, State Library of New South Wales

Sandford MSS

### Public Record Office, Victoria

Defunct Company Papers

## BOOKS, ARTICLES AND THESES

Armytage, W. H. G. *The Rise of the Technocrats.* 1965.
Ashley, R. W. P. 'The Lal Lal Iron Tramway', *Light Railways 1970–1*, no. 34.
Baker, D. 'Reminiscences' in *BHP Review*, October 1935–April 1936.
Barnett, C. *The Collapse of British Power.* 1984.
Bauerman, J. *Treatise on the Metallurgy of Iron.* London, 1868.
BHP. *Australians in Company.* 1985.
——*Seventy-five years of BHP Development in Australia.* 1960.
Birch, A. *The Economic History of the British Iron and Steel Industry, 1784–1879.* 1967.
Blainey, G. *The Rise of Broken Hill.* 1968.
——*The Steel Master.* 1971.
——*The Tyranny of Distance.* 1980 edn.
Brody, D. *Steelworkers in America: the Nonunion Era.* 1969.
Brown, H. V. L. *A Record of the Mines of South Australia.* 1887.
Bulbeck, C. 'State and Economy in Tariff Policy' in B. W. Head (ed.), *State and Economy in Australia.* 1983, pp. 219–37.
Burn, D. *The Economic History of Steelmaking, 1867–1939.* 1940.
Butlin, N. G., A. Barnard and J. J. Pincers. *Government and Capitalism.* 1982.
Campbell, C. 'Liberalism in Australian History' in J. Roe (ed.), *Social Policy in Australia.*
Carr, J. C. and W. Taplin. *History of the British Steel Industry.* 1962.
Cash, D., E. M. Johnston-Liik, G. Liik and R. G. Ward. A Dream Unfulfilled: The Rise and Fall of Iron Smelting in Tasmania, 1872–78. Paper presented at ANZAAS, 1982.
Clark, C. M. H. (ed.). *Select Documents in Australian History, 1851–1900.*

Clegg, H. A., A. Fox and A. F. Thompson. *A History of the British Trade Unions from 1889.* 1964.
Conigrave, J. F. *South Australian Manufactures and Industries.* Adelaide, 1875.
Crisp, L. F. *Federation Prophets without Honour.*
de Garis, B. K. '1890–1900' in F. Crowley (ed.) *A New History of Australia*, 1974, pp. 216–59.
Deane, P. and W. A. Cole. *British Economic Growth, 1688–1959.* 1967.
Dillard, D. *Economic Development of the North Atlantic Community.* 1967.
Drucker, P. *Management.* 1979 edn.
Dutton, Francis. *South Australia and Its Mines.* 1846.
Else-Mitchell, R. 'Mittagong and District: Its Industrial Development', *Journal of the Royal Australian Historical Society*, vol. 26, 1940, pp. 418–78.
Forster, C. 'Australian Manufacturing and the War of 1914–18', *Economic Record*, vol. 29, 1953.
Gollan, R. *The Coalminers of New South Wales: A History of the Union 1860–1960.* 1963.
——*Radical and Working Class Politics.* 1960.
Greenwood, G. (ed.). *Australia A Social and Political History.* 1955.
Hagan, J. *The ACTU: A Short History on the Occasion of the 50th Anniversary 1927–1977.* 1977.
Hall, C. R. *The Manufacturers.* 1971.
Hogan, W. T. *Economic History of the Iron and Steel Industry in the United States.* 5 vols. 1971.
*Industrial Progress of New South Wales: Report of the Intercolonial Exhibition of 1870, at Sydney.* 1871.
Hoskins, Cecil. *The Hoskins Saga.* 1969.
Hoskins, D. G. *The Ironmaster: The Life of Charles Hoskins.* 1995.
Hughes, H. *The Australian Iron and Steel Industry 1848–1962.* 1964.
——'Industrial Relations in the Australian Iron and Steel Industry 1876–1962', *Journal of Industrial Relations*, vol. 4, 1962.
Jack, I. 'The Iron and Steel Industry' in J. Birmingham, I. Jack and D. Jeans (eds) *Australian Pioneer Technology*, 1979.
Jack, R. I. and A. Cremin. *Australia's Age of Iron: History and Archaeology.* 1994.
Jack, R. L. *The Iron Ore Resources of South Australia.* 1922.
Just, T. C. 'Iron deposits of the River Tamar District' in R. M. Johnston, *Tasmanian Official Record*, 1891.
——*The Official Handbook of Tasmania.* 1887.
Kennedy, Brian. *Silver, Sin and Sixpenny Ale: A Social History of Broken Hill 1883–1921.* 1978.
Linge, G. J. R. *Industrial Awakening: A Geography of Australian Manufacturing 1788 to 1890.* 1979.
Lyne, Charles. *The Industries of New South Wales.* 1882.
Macarthy, P. G. 'Justice Higgins and the Harvester Judgement' in J. Roe (ed.), *Social Policy in Australia*, pp. 41–59.
Martin, A. W. and P. Wardle. *Members of the Legislative Assembly of New South Wales 1856–1901.*
Mawson, Paquita. *Vision of Steel: The Life of G. D. Delprat.* 1958.

Merritt, J. A. A History of the Federated Ironworkers' Association of Australia 1909–1952. PhD thesis. Australian National University, 1967.
Murphy, B. *Dictionary of Australian History*. 1982.
Murray, R. and K. White. *The Ironworkers*. 1982.
Nairn, N. B. *Civilising Capitalism: The Labour Movement in New South Wales, 1870–1900*. 1973.
Niland, J. 'In search of shorter hours: the 1861 and 1874 Iron Trades Disputes', *Labour History*, May 1967, no. 12, pp. 13–15.
Norris, R. *The Emergent Commonwealth*. 1975.
O'Farrell, P. *The Irish in Australia*. 1986.
*Official Report of Proceedings*. Fifth Conference of the Australian Labor Party. 1912.
Parker, C. *Mines and Minerals of New South Wales*. 2nd edn. 1906.
Pike, Douglas. *Paradise of Dissent: South Australia 1829–1857*. London, 1957.
Pittman, E. F. *The Mineral Resources of New South Wales*. 1901.
Pollard, S. *The Genesis of Modern Management*. 1965.
——*Peaceful Conquest: The Industrialization of Europe, 1760–1970*. 1981.
Prior, S. H. *Handbook of Australian Mines*. Melbourne, 1890.
Pugh, D. S. *Organization Theory*. 2nd edn, 1984.
Pugh, D. S., D. J. Hickson and C. R. Hinings. *Writers on Organizations*. 3rd edn. Penguin, 1983.
Rickard, J. *J. B. Higgins*. 1987.
Riley, E. 'On Chromium Pig Iron produced by the Tasmanian Iron Company', *Journal of the Iron and Steel Institute*, 1887.
Robinson, J. R. '1930–1939' in F. Crowley (ed.), *A New History of Australia*, 1974, pp. 415–57.
Robinson, W. G. *If I Remember Rightly: The Memoirs of W. S. Robinson*, ed. G. Blainey. 1967.
Sandford, R. W. *Australian Pig Iron*. Premier Printers, n.d.
Schedvin, B. *Australia and the Great Depression*. 1970.
Smith, A. H. The Australian Wire Industry 1870–1959. M. Comm. thesis. University of Newcastle, 1981.
Staughton, P. S. and R. W. P. Ashley. *The Lal Lal Blast Furnace 1876*. Ballarat, 1976.
Taylor, T. Australian Iron and Steel Limited 1928–39: A Case-Study in the Theory of Merger. B.Ec. (Hons) thesis. University of Sydney, 1972.
Trengove, A. *'What's good for Australia . . .!': The Story of BHP*. 1973.
Turner, B. 'The Lithgow Furnace', *Proceedings of the University of Sydney Engineering Society*, 1900.
Turner, I. *In Union is Strength*. Rev. edn, rev. by L. Sandercock. 1983.
——*Industrial Labour and Politics. The Dynamics of the Labour Movement in Eastern Australia, 1900–21*. 1965.
——*Labour in Eastern Australia*. 1965.
Twelvetrees, W. H. and A. McI. Reid. *The Iron ore Deposits of Tasmania*. Tasmanian Department of Mines, Geological Survey, Mineral Resources. Hobart, 1919.

von Stradmann, H. P. *Walther Rathenau: Industrialist, Banker, Intellectual and Politician: Notes and Diaries 1907–22*. 1985.
Ward, J. M. Federation and the New Liberalism. ANZAAS History Section Presidential Address. 1982.
Warren, K. 'Iron and Steel' in N. K. Buxton and D. H. Aldcroft (eds), *British Industry between the Wars*, 1979, pp. 103–28.
Waters, M. *Strikes in Australia*. 1982.
Weickhart, C. G. T. 'The First Foundry', *Journal of the Royal Historical Society of Victoria*, September 1983.
Wheeler, D. 'BHP's Quiet Achiever' in *Centenary Portraits*.
Wilkinson, G. B. *South Australia: Its Advantages and Resources*. 1848.
Wills, N. R. *The Economic Development of the Australian Iron and Steel Industry*. 1948.

# INDEX

Adelaide, 52, 165, 227, 228
AIS, *see* Australian Iron and Steel Limited
Allard, Horace, 126
Allard, Way & Hardie (chartered accountants), 314–15
Allen, Allen & Hemsley (lawyers), 304
ALP, *see* Australian Labor Party
AMA, *see* Amalgamated Miners' Association
Amalgamated Ironworkers' Assistants' Union, 104
Amalgamated Miners' Association (AMA), 104
Amalgamated Society of Ironworkers' Assistants, 95, 104
American Iron and Steel Institute, 169, 232
American Society of Mining Engineers, 169
Anti-sweating League, 102
arbitration, 101; *see also* Conciliation and Arbitration
Ashton Gate Iron Rolling Mills, 69
Associated Smelters, 272
Atha, C. G., 283
Attunga (NSW), 194
Aubel, Mr, 214
Austral Nail Co. Ltd, 217, 241, 262
Australasian Iron and Steel Co. Ltd, 78
Australia: economy, 32, 92, 103, 110, 180, 292, 297; government, 35, 77, 91, 100, 174, 185, 244; iron and steel in, 32, 91, 180, 323; labour, 71, 90, 93, 109, 128, 215, 216, 217, 220, 277, *see also* unions; society, 35, 71, 91, 94, 99, 100, 103, 151, 203, 216, 266, 290, 324

Australian Club, 246, 275
Australian Iron and Steel Limited, 244, 285, 292, 294, 295, 297, 306, 307–8, 311, 312, 320, 321, 322; at Port Kembla, 9, 149, 150, 172–3, 190, 271, 279, 284, 287, 288, 290, 291, 292, 296, 299, 300, 301, 302, 303, 305, 309, 311, 320, 321, 323, 324; merger with BHP, 313, 321, 322, 324; *see also* Eskbank ironworks; Hoskins Iron & Steel Company Ltd
Australian Labor Party, 77, 92–3, 94, 104, 121, 129, 152, 215, 216, 218, 298
Australian Mutual Provident Society, 322
Australian Socialist League (NSW), 98
Australian Wire Rope Pty Ltd, 268
Australian Wire Rope Works Pty Ltd, 241
Australian Wiredrawing Company, 179
Australian Workers' Union (AWU), 94, 219

Babcock & Wilcox Ltd, 241
Baker, David, 5, 57, 166, 167, 168–73, 175, 179, 184, 186–7, 190, 191, 193, 194, 195–6, 198–9, 201, 209–14, 218–19, 221–2, 224–5, 227, 230–6, 238, 243, 245, 247–8, 250, 252, 256, 258–60, 261, 262, 265, 270, 274–5, 277, 285
Baker, David Jr, 214
Baker, John, 5
Baldwins Ltd, 292, 315; contributes Margam plant to AIS, 296
Ballarat, 48; foundries in, 52
Barclay & Sons (UK), 39
Barker, T., 216

350

# INDEX

Barossa Valley (SA), 180
Barter, Mr, 267
Bathurst, 56, 68, 135, 139
Battery Point (Tas.), 46
Bauerman, H., 52
BBH Bloomfield Iron Works, 14
Beale, Sir John, 274
Beale, O. C., 64
Beaudarick, Christie, 46, 49, 78
Beeby, G. S., 125, 129, 131, 132, 133, 269; decision on 44-hour week, 262
Bell, Sir Hugh, 292
Bell, Isaac Lothian, 28, 169
Bell Brothers Ltd, 294
Bellambi (NSW), 175
Belubula River (NSW), 272
Bessemer, Henry, 22, 24
Bessemer process, 22, 24, 29, 30, 39, 42, 75, 76, 142, 175, 196, 247, 248, 249
Bethlehem Steelworks (USA), 211
BHP (Broken Hill Proprietary Co. Ltd), 80, 94, 96–7, 107–9, 113, 153–65, 170, 171, 172–4, 175, 176–81, 183, 184–5, 186, 187, 188, 189, 190, 192, 193, 195–6, 198–200, 201, 202, 205, 209, 210, 212, 213, 214, 216, 218–19, 220, 221–2, 224, 226, 227, 228–9, 230, 231, 232, 236, 238, 239, 240–1, 242, 243–8, 251–3, 254, 256, 259–73 *passim*, 276–80, 283, 285, 293, 297, 304–5, 306, 308, 310–11, 313–14, 315, 316, 317–18, 320, 321–2, 322, 323, 324
BHP By-Products Ltd, 268
BHP Collieries Pty Ltd, 267
BHP Tramway Bill (SA), 157
Bice, J. G., 157
Blackwood, R. O., 236
Bladen & Co., 21, 22
Bladon, Herbert, 123
Blaenavon Co. Ltd (UK), 78
Bleeser, F., 156
Blythe River (Tas.), 111, 153
Blythe River Iron Mines Co. Ltd, 78, 111, 112
Bogolong Iron Mining Company, 52
Boilermakers' Society, 124
Bolckow, Vaughan & Co. Ltd, 294
Braddon, E., 111
Bradford, Kendall & Co., 256
Bradford, Leslie, 163, 183–4, 195–6, 210, 213, 228, 232, 233–5, 248–51, 256, 258, 259, 260, 270, 275, 321–2
Brassert, A., 233, 249
Brazenall, W., 6, 24

Britain, *see* United Kingdom
British and Tasmanian Charcoal Iron Company Ltd (BTCIC), 39, 40, 41, 42, 43, 44, 48, 78, 191
British Association, 28
British Commonwealth of Nations, 244
British Iron Trades Association, 77
Brodie, G. E., 85
Broken Hill, 107, 164, 183, 184; difficulties in development, 96, 97; unions at, 97, 98, 107, 108, 137, 215, 221
Broken Hill Associated Smelters Ltd, 321
Broken Hill Proprietary Co. Ltd, *see* BHP
Brown, Alexander, 33, 57
Brown–Boveri turbo-blower, 289
Brymbo Steel Works (UK), 111–12
BTCIC, *see* British and Tasmanian Charcoal Iron Company Ltd
Bulli (NSW), 41
Bullivants Ltd (UK), 241
Burgess, Arthur, 221, 270
Burnell, H. C., 18
Burns, R. J., 306, 321

Cadia (NSW), 146, 153
Cairns (Qld), 281
Cairns, James, 131, 132, 133, 139
Cairns & Amos, 14
Cameron, Donald, 47
Campbell, James, 258
Canada, 111, 167
Cann, J. H., 94, 170
Carboona (NSW), 196
Carcoar (NSW), 81, 86, 130, 146
Carleton Iron Company, 294
Carmichael, A. D., 163
Carnegie, Andrew, 167, 211–12, 276
Carnegie Steel Corporation (USA), 80, 214
Carruthers, J. H., 82, 86
Catalonia, 6
Chalder, Joseph, 12
Chapman Brothers, 33
Chillington and Springvale Iron Works, 14
China, 96
City Iron Works, 15, 33, 57
Cleveland (UK), 58, 79
Clyde Ironworks (UK), 16
coal industry, 53, 106, 173, 223
Cobb & Co., 56, 68
Cockatoo Island (WA), 182, 304, 306
Cohen, Mr, 177
Collaton, M., 217
Colonial Bank, 248

351

# INDEX

Coltness Ironworks (UK), 39
Commercial Banking Company, 87
Commonwealth, *see* British Commonwealth of Nations
Commonwealth Bank, 185
Commonwealth Scientific and Industrial Research Organisation, 210
Commonwealth Steel Products Co. Ltd, 217, 241, 268
Communist Party of Australia, 218
Conciliation and Arbitration, Court of, 101, 104, 222, 224
Condie, John, 16
Cooma (NSW), 272
Cooper, E. A., 139
Council for Scientific and Industrial Research, 210
Cowper regenerative stoves, 80
Cox's Creek (SA), 5
Cradock & Co., 79
Creusot (France), 27
CSIRO, *see* Commonwealth Scientific and Industrial Organisation
Curlewis, Judge H. R., 269
*Customs Tariff (Industries Preservation) Act*, 263

Darby, J. H., 111
Darling, H. G., 160, 228–9, 233–4, 236, 238–9, 243, 248, 252–3, 254, 256, 257–9, 261, 265, 269, 272–3, 298, 315, 318, 320–2
Darling, John, 33, 156–7, 159, 163–5, 171, 184, 196, 222–3, 228, 235–6, 237, 244, 249, 251, 253, 260–1, 267, 272, 321
Davey & Co. (UK), 75, 80, 119, 296
Davidson, Sir Walter, 262
Davison, L. A., 311
Dawson, Richard, 32
Dawson's Foundry, 32
de Burgh, E. M., 85, 321
de Largie, Hugh, 104
De Lavaud pipe process, 274, 277, 290; competition for patent, 278
De Merics Ltd, 258
Delprat, Guillaume, 107–8, 159–60, 161, 162–3, 164–6, 168, 169, 170–5, 177, 180–1, 183, 185, 186–7, 190, 193, 195–6, 199, 201–2, 204, 208, 209, 210, 211–15, 217, 218, 221, 222–3, 224, 225, 227, 228, 229–30, 231, 232–5, 236, 237–8, 239, 240–3, 245, 246, 247–53, 256, 261, 271, 279, 306, 311
Delprat, Paquita, *see* Mawson, Lady

depression (1890s), 71, 95; *see also* Australia, economy
Derwent Iron Works (Tas.), 46, 47, 78
Devonport, limestone quarries, 172
Dickenson, F. M., 170, 185, 212, 229, 257, 258, 261; resigns, 258
Disraeli, Benjamin, 31, 36
Dixon, J., 137, 139
Dominion Iron and Steel Company (Canada), 214
Dooley, James, 130, 131, 138
Dorman Long & Co. Ltd (UK), 292, 294, 296, 307, 313, 314, 315–16
Dowlais Iron Works (UK), 27, 75
Drinkfield Ironworks (UK), 66
du Cane, Charles, 38, 42
Duncan, K. W., 157
Duncan, W. D., 258
Dundyvan (UK), 40
duplex process, 232, 234, 246–7

Earp, Mr, 178
Ebbw Vale Iron, Coal and Steel Company, 16, 75
Edmunds, Mr Justice, 221, 269–70
Eilers, Karl, 166
Elder, Alexander Lang, 5
Elder Smith & Co., 242, 246
employment, 105
Engels, F., 107
England, *see* United Kingdom
English Steel Corporation Ltd, 294
Ennis, Laurence, 307, 314, 316
Eskbank coal-mines, 105–6
Eskbank ironworks, 25, 55, 57–9, 61–2, 64, 65, 66–80, 83, 84, 88, 105, 112, 115, 117, 118, 120, 121, 122, 124, 127, 136, 144, 146, 150, 174, 218, 303; *see also* Australian Iron and Steel Limited; Hoskins Ltd, G. & C.; Hoskins Iron and Steel Co. Ltd; Lithgow
Eskbank Ironworkers' Association of Mill and Forge Workers, 72, 104, 120, 121, 124, 128, 129
Essen (Germany), 27, 30

Fallins, Mr, 267
Farquharson, Mr, 270
Fayol, H., 211
Federal Basic Wage Commission, 239
Federal Iron Company, 78
Federal Munitions Committee, 198

# INDEX

Federated Engine-drivers and Firemen's Association, 130–1, 134, 222
Federated Ironworkers' Association (FIA), 105, 216, 217, 218, 219, 220, 224
Field, R. A., 214
Fifield (NSW), 194
Firth, Sir William, 244, 245, 312
Fitz Roy Iron and Coal Mining Company, 6, 11
Fitz Roy Iron Company, 6, 12–13, 14–20, 37, 57, 58
Fitz Roy Iron Mining Company, 6, 9
Fitz Roy Iron Works Ltd, 6, 14, 37, 41, 54, 58
Fitz Roy Ironworks, 6–7, 14
Fitzpatrick, J. C. L., 177
FitzRoy, Sir Charles, 7
Fitzroy Bessemer Steel, Hematite, Iron and Coal Co. Ltd, 6, 22, 33, 64
Flowers, Frederick, 134
Forbes, J. McGregor, *see* McGregor Forbes, J.
Forcett (Tas.), 46
Forest Iron Smelting and Steam Sawing Company, 5
Forrest, W. H., 85
Foskett, B., 281
France, 27, 30
Franki, J. P., 18
Frazer, J., 18, 22, 25
Fredrichs, B., 18
freight rates, 31, 61–2, 77, 207, 263, 284
Frodingham Iron and Steel Company, 80, 283
Fuller, Sir George, 266
furnaces: bell-and-hopper top, 20; Catalan, 6; cupola, 7

G. & C. Hoskins Ltd, *see* Hoskins Ltd, G. & C.
Garden, J. S., 298
Gary (Indiana), 168
Gary, Judge E. H., 168, 193, 212, 223, 232
Gayley, James, 166
Geological Society of the United States of America, 169
George, Henry, 94, 99
Germany, 16, 27, 29, 30, 151, 162, 179, 180, 204, 323
Gibson, Alexander, 213, 231, 256
Gilchrist, Percy, 24, 76
Gompers, Samuel, 169
Grahame, W. C., 177
Great Britain, *see* United Kingdom
Griffith, Arthur, 152, 175, 176, 177

Griffith, L. J., 258–9
Guest, Keen & Baldwins Ltd (UK), 294
Guest, Keen & Nettlefold (UK), 274, 292, 294
Gundagai, railway bridge, 18, 34

Hamilton, George, 5
Hampshire, J. K., 17
Hannan's North Mine, 272
Harbison-Walker Refactories Company (USA), 194
Hardware Association, 64
Harrison, J. H., 78
Harrison, William, 38–9, 78
Hart, John, 5
Harvey, Dr, 75
Hayes, William C., 139
Henderson, Mr, 233
Henley, Mr, 177
Heskett, J., 76
Heskett & Co., 76
Hibbard, Henry, 195, 247
Higgins, W. B., 102, 108, 203, 238
Hindmarsh Falls (SA), 52
Hirsh, Max, 99
HISC, *see* Hoskins Iron & Steel Company Ltd
Hockey, F. R., 265, 271
Holdsworth, P. R., 19
Hollis, R., 179
Holmes, Thomas, 6, 11
Horwood, E. J., 210, 231, 234
Hoskins, Arthur Sidney, 275, 281, 285, 287, 288, 293, 294, 302, 306, 307, 308, 312–13, 315, 316, 321–2
Hoskins, Cecil Harold, 87, 113, 137, 150–1, 275, 281, 285, 287, 292, 294–5, 297, 302, 306, 307, 308, 312–13, 314, 315, 316, 318, 321–2
Hoskins, Charles Henry, 84, 113, 115, 117, 119, 121–7, 130–9, 140–6 *passim*, 147–50, 153–4, 170, 179, 190, 200, 202–6, 277–8, 280–5 *passim*, 292, 293, 302, 304
Hoskins, Emily, 149, 289
Hoskins, George, 84, 116, 119, 124, 143, 146, 190, 280
Hoskins, Hilda, 150
Hoskins, Sid, *see* Hoskins, Arthur Sidney
Hoskins Iron & Steel Company Ltd, 241, 277–9, 280, 281, 282–94, 297, 302, 304–5, 306, 308, 309; *see also* Australian Iron and Steel Ltd; Hoskins Ltd, G. & C.

353

# INDEX

Hoskins Ltd, G. & C., 84–5, 87–8, 91, 113, 115, 117–28, 130–9, 140–51 *passim*, 153–4, 170, 171, 179, 189, 200, 202, 205, 247, 263, 277, 280; *see also* Hoskins Iron & Steel Company Ltd
Hotham Ironworks, 38
Howard Smith Ltd, 292, 307
Howe, J. H., 155
Howell, John, 159
Hughes, Enoch, 14–15, 16–17, 20–1, 33, 57–8, 60–1, 67
Hughes, W. M., 199, 206, 210, 217, 222, 240, 242, 246
Hummock Hill, *see* Whyalla
Huntsman, B., 22

Ilfracombe Iron Co., 44–6
Illawarra, 82, 285
Illawarra Syndicate, 78
Illinois Steel Co., 166, 214
*Industrial Disputes Act* (NSW), 130
industrial relations, 11, 150; *see also* Australia, labour; unions
Industrial Workers of the World, 106, 217, 218
*Industries Preservation Act, see Customs Tariff (Industries Preservation) Act*
inflation, post 1918, 248
Intercolonial Exhibition (1870), 32
Interstate Tariff Investigation Commission, 179, 199, 206, 207
iron and steel industry, 83, 180, 181, 253
Iron and Steel Institute (UK), 28, 31, 169
*Iron Baron*, 172
Iron Knob, 159, 160, 162, 164, 171, 172, 181, 187, 210, 228, 229, 262, 265, 268, 271, 305, 320
Iron Knob tramway, 228
Iron Monarch, 155, 156, 172; Quarry E, 271
iron ore, varieties, 9
*Iron Prince*, 172
Iron, Steel and Metals Manufacturing Company Ltd, 78
Iron Trades Protective Association, 95
Iron Trades (Lithgow) Arbitration and Conciliation Board, 102
Iron Trades (Lithgow) Wages Board, 123, 126, 128, 303
Iron Trades Union, 95
ironmasters, 28
ironworkers, 55, 71–2, 82, 123, 149, 210, 303
Ironworks Tunnel Colliery, 131
IWW, *see* Industrial Workers of the World

J. & W. Marshall (UK), *see* Marshall, J. & W. (UK)
James, Enoch, 77, 112
Jamieson, William, 78, 111, 114, 154, 233, 279
Jardine, Matheson & Co., 246
Joadja Creek shale mine, 25
John Lysaght & Co. Ltd (UK), 274; *see also* John Lysaght (Australia) Pty Ltd
John Lysaght (Australia) Pty Ltd, 69, 124, 217, 241, 259, 262, 275, 276, 292, 311, 320; *see also* Lysaght Brothers & Co. Pty Ltd
Johnson, H. W., 12
Jones, J. B., 75
Jones, John, 28–9
Jones, William, 214
Just, T. C., 42, 43

Keep, John, 18, 22, 64
Kelly, Bowes, 236, 248, 258, 269
Kelly, Syd, 130–1
Kendall, J. A., 233, 249, 256
Kendall, E. J., 235
Kennedy, Ross, 139
Kingston, C. C., 101, 110, 157
Kirk, Mr, 246
Knight, Robert, 36
Knox, William, 229
Koehler, W., 155
Koolan Island (WA), 306
Krupp, Alfred, 30

Labor Conference, 121; *see also* Australian Labor Party
Labor Party, *see* Australian Labor Party
labour, *see* Australia, labour; ironworkers; unions
Lackawanna Steel Co., 195, 214
Ladd, J. B., 186, 242, 243, 246, 268
Lal Lal (Vic.), 15, 48, 52, 64, 78
Lal Lal Iron Company, 49
Lane, William, 94, 95
Lang, J. T., 203, 298–9
Langlands Foundry, 75, 76, 95
Larke, Sir William, 244
Larkin, Mr, 25
Larkin, Hunter & Henshaw, 25
Lasseter, F., 18
Lattin, B. W., 13, 14, 17
Lee, C. A., 144, 177
Leonard, William, 38
Leonardsburgh (Tas.), 38
Levick, Thomas, 20, 41
Lewis, Essington, 157, 184, 196, 212, 227, 229, 233, 236, 238, 243, 249, 252–3, 254,

# INDEX

259, 262, 265, 271, 272, 274, 275, 276, 279, 282, 287, 306, 308, 310, 312–14, 315, 318, 321, 322
Lewis, John, 157, 228
Limestone Gully (Vic.), 52
Lindsay, Mr, 191, 234
Lippmann, J., 19
Lithgow, 9, 15, 25, 54–8, 60, 62–3, 65–9, 74–5, 77–84, 87–8, 91, 100, 105, 112, 116, 117, 119–20, 122, 124–5, 127–8, 130–5, 137, 138, 141–4, 146–7, 149–50, 152–4, 171–2, 179, 183, 189, 194, 198, 205, 206, 216, 220, 280, 282, 284, 285, 287, 288, 290, 296, 300, 302–3, 311, 318, 320; see also Eskbank ironworks
Lithgow, small arms factory, 208
Lithgow Iron Trades Wages Board, see Iron Trades (Lithgow) Wages Board
Loan Council, 298
Lockyer, Commissioner, 204
Lonsdale, Mr 177
Luhrmann, F., 80
Lyell & Allard (accountants), 126
Lyne, William, 65, 73
Lysaght, John, 69
Lysaght, John, & Co. Ltd, see John Lysaght & Co. Ltd (UK)
Lysaght, John, (Australia) Pty Ltd, see John Lysaght (Australia) Pty Ltd
Lysaght Brothers & Co. Pty Ltd, 268; see also John Lysaght (Australia) Pty Ltd

McBryde, D., 192, 236, 248, 258
McCrum, J., 258
McGann, J. C., 318
McGarry, Mr, 177, 178
McGowan, J. S. T., 87, 129, 170, 178
McGregor Forbes, J., 246
McKay, H. V., 236
McKee distributor, 291
MacKenzie, Mr, 195
McKenzie, Senior Sergeant, 135
McMeekan, J., 227, 229
Maitland, railway bridge, 34
Malaysia, 246
Mann, Thomas, 99, 107, 109
Manufacturers' Encouragement Bill, 84, 113, 144, 202
Marks, Mr, 14
Marshall, J. & W. (UK), 79
Martin, James, 19
Marulan (NSW), 285
Marx, Karl, 93, 107, 205

Marxists, 219
*Massey Greene Act*, 263
Mather, Joseph, 33
Mawson, Lady, 162
Mayo, Elton, 212
Meagher, R. D., 178
Meares, R. C., 318
Melbourne, 13–15, 21, 31, 37–8, 43, 47, 52, 61, 75, 84–5, 99, 108, 120, 122, 127, 153, 171, 179, 185, 216, 233–4, 260, 267, 271, 275, 285, 293, 313
Melbourne Trades Hall Council, 95
Menelaus, William, 27, 31
Merrett, F. T., 288
Metropolitan Water, Sewage and Drainage Board (Sydney), 84, 85, 88
Midvale steelworks (USA), 168, 211
Militant Minority Movement, 218
Miller, Denison, 185
Miller, William, 65, 66, 67, 70–1
mine managers' association (Broken Hill), 94
Mitchell, F. M., 78, 184, 229, 233–4, 256, 257, 258–61, 270, 314, 318, 321–2
Mitchell, H. A., 221
Mitchell, Joseph, 78
Mitsui Bussan Kaisha, 246
Mittagong, 6, 7, 9, 14, 15, 16, 17, 18, 24, 25, 69, 325
Montefiore, D., 100, 130
Montefiore, J. L., 22
Moore, J. J., 18
Moore–Heskett process, 78
Morgan, J. P., 167, 168
Morgan continuous rod mill, 201, 247
Morris, J. M., 266, 271
Mort, T. S., 54
Mount Barker (SA), 4
Mount Bischoff (Tas.), 37
Mount Jagged (SA), 52
Mount Lyell Company, 111
Mount Minden Mining Company, 155–6
Mountcastle, B., 19
Muecke, Hugo, 164–5, 180
Mushet, R. F., 24, 42

National Iron Corporation (Canada), 290
nationalisation, 129, 152
Neale, John, 6
Neilson, J. B., 16
New South Wales, 4, 6–9, 11, 12, 13–14, 18–19, 25, 34, 35, 53, 66, 67, 71, 78, 85, 104, 123, 125, 142, 176, 263, 285, 325

# INDEX

New South Wales Political Labour League, *see* Political Labour League
New South Wales State Iron and Steelworks Bill, 152, 176–9; *see also* Newcastle Iron and Steel Bill
New Zealand, 34, 60–1, 67
Newbold & Co., 194
Newcastle, 9, 173, 178, 210, 271; coalfields, 82, 173
Newcastle Coal and Copper Smelting Company, 9
Newcastle Iron and Steel Bill, 94; *see also* New South Wales Iron and Steelworks Bill
Niemeyer, Sir Otto, 298
North Eastern Steel Co. Ltd, 294
Noyes, H. F., 214, 232, 233, 234, 256, 257, 258

Oakey Park Coal and Coke Company, 120
Oakey Park Colliery, 82, 131
One Big Union (OBU), 217, 219
Onehunga Ironworks Co. (New Zealand), 60–1, 67
Ottawa Conference (1932), 244
Overall & McCray Ltd, 246

Page, Mr, 177
Parkes, Henry, 18–19, 99
Parry, George, 16
Pascoe, T., 157
Patterson, Harvey, 38, 158–9, 164, 236
Patton, W. H., 94
Paul Commission, *see* Royal Commission on the Iron and Steel Industry
Peaked Hill (Tas.), 45
Pennsylvania Steel Company, 166
Pennymore, P. G., 78
Penzer, E., 79
Perry, J., 177
Piddington, A. B., 202–4; *see also* Interstate Tariff Investigation Commission
pig-iron, costs, 71, 276
Pillans, Robert, 124, 133
Pittsburgh, 29, 38
Playford, Thomas, 104
Political Labour League (NSW), 111
Pope & Mather Ltd, 85
Poppleton, Clement, 236, 242, 243
Port Kembla, *see* Australian Iron and Steel Limited
Port Lempriere (Tas.), 41
Port Pirie, 271, 273; smelters, 155, 180, 238

Port Turton, 229
Port Victor (SA), 52
Port Waratah Stevedoring Co. Pty Ltd, 267–8
Potter–Delprat flotation process, 163
Povey, Mr, 11
Pring, Justice R. D., 139
Purchase Company Ltd, 43–4

Queanbeyan, rail contract, 146
Queensland, 100, 104, 180, 281

Railway Workers and General Labourers Association, 131
railways, 13, 18, 34, 35, 54, 61, 66–7, 68, 77, 146, 173, 174, 263, 285
Rathenau, W., 162, 213
Redbill Point (Tas.), 39, 41, 44
Reese, A. K., 283
Reid, Thomas, 55, 65, 66, 70, 73
Rhodes Pipe Works, 85, 285
Richard Thomas & Co. Ltd, 242, 243–4
Richardson & Wrench, 22
Robinson, W. S., 238
Rolin, Justice T., 269
Rossiter, Joseph Cartwright, 12
Rothery, F. J., 10, 12
Rowe, R. H. M., 246, 274
Royal Commission on Bonuses for Manufactures (Commonwealth), 18, 62, 70–1, 74, 78, 110, 115, 154
Royal Commission on Customs and Excise Tariffs (Commonwealth), 64
Royal Commission on the Iron and Steel Industry (NSW, Paul Commission), 89, 115, 129–30, 133, 136, 138, 139, 140–4, 152, 153, 172, 206
Royal Commission on the State Iron and Steel Works (Qld), 180–1
Rue, J., 286
Russell & Co., 33, 34
Russia, 217, 246
Rutherford, James, 55, 56, 57, 59, 60, 62, 63, 64, 65, 66, 67, 68, 70, 71, 72, 73, 78, 79, 81, 106, 117, 118, 302; *see also* Eskbank ironworks
Ryland Bros (Aust.) Ltd, 240, 268, 320

Samuelson & Co., 294
Sandford, J., 78
Sandford, Roy, 84
Sandford, William, 25, 62, 66–70, 71, 72–89, 112–13, 115, 117, 119–21, 125–6, 138, 143–4, 146–7, 153–4, 189–90, 202, 204,

# INDEX

225, 275, 285; *see also* Eskbank ironworks; Mittagong
Saul, Warren A., 214, 257
Scholes, Justice, 126, 133
Schwab, Charles, 212
Scotchman's Point (Tas.), 46
Scott, Robert, 39
Scott & Fell Ltd, 267
scrap iron, 73, 74
Scullin, J. H., 272, 299
Scully, B., 132, 139
See, J., 77
Semet–Solvay coke ovens, 186, 198, 274
Sheffield (UK), 22, 204
Sheffield Steel Works (Vic.), 76
Shield, Ripon, 47
Sibley, Mr, 268
Siekmann, E., 155–6
silver, 96, 159
Sleath, Richard, 94, 97, 98
Slee, Mr, 233, 234
Smith, Thomas Tipple, 6
Smith, William Tipple, 6
socialism, 98, 130
Socialist Sunday School Movement, 99
Socialist Labour Party, 100
Sorell Causeway (Tas.), 46
South Africa, 246
South Australia, 4, 5, 52, 82, 154, 173, 260, 325; *see also* Adelaide
South Australian Iron and Steel Company, 52
South Australian School of Mines, 196
Spooner, Mr, 131–2
Spooner, J. W., 122
Stanton Iron Company Ltd, 15, 277, 290
Steel Company of Scotland, 129
Steel Syndicate of New South Wales, 78
Stewart, Alexander, 156, 159, 160–1, 162, 240
Stewarts & Lloyd, 293
Storey, J., 217
strikes, 96, 217, 221–4; Lithgow (1911), 134; seamen's (1919), 263
*Sunday Observance Act*, 150
Sunshine Harvester Company, 102
Sutherland, H., 217
Sutherland, J., 56, 58, 59, 61, 62, 63, 66
Sweden, 9
Swift, A., 46–7
Swinburne, G., 204
Sydney Labour Council, 127
syndicalist movement, 217; *see also* One Big Union

Tallawang quarries, 146
Tamar Hematite Iron Company, 46, 47
*Tariff Act* (1906), 102
Tasmania, 4, 37, 47, 82
Tasmanian Charcoal Iron Company, 38; *see also* British and Tasmanian Charcoal Iron Company Ltd
Taylor, F. W., 168, 211
Terrey, William, 12
Tharsis Company (Spain), 161
Thomas, Mr, 270
Thomas, Sydney Gilchrist, 24, 76
Thompson & Co., 289
Thornley, William, 64, 71, 78
Thrower, T. H., 178
tin-plate industry, 241, 244, 293
Todhunter, W. J., 257
Tolpuddle martyrs, 36
trade unions, *see* unions
Transcontinental railway, 173–4
Truscott, Mr, 131–2

Ultimo (NSW), 85
unions, 35, 36, 94, 95, 99, 104, 216, 217, 219, 220, 223; *see also* Broken Hill, unions at
United States of America, 20, 29–31, 38, 67, 77, 94, 151, 162, 166–7, 168, 169, 172, 180, 186, 193–6, 204, 211, 221, 224, 249, 252, 259, 260, 268, 277, 290, 294
United States Steel Corporation, 166, 193, 216, 232
United Steel Companies Ltd, 294

van der Waals, J., 161
Vickery, E., 18, 19, 22
Victoria, 4, 14–15, 37, 43, 45, 47–8, 56–7, 74, 76, 96, 99, 101, 109, 153, 180, 220, 285; *see also* Melbourne
Victorian Iron Company, 52,
Victorian Iron Mines Syndicate, 78
Victorian Iron Rolling Mills, 14–15
Victorian Socialist Party, 108
Victorian Steel Foundry Company Ltd, 76

Wade, C. G., 86
Waratah (Tas.), 155
Wardang Island (SA), 172, 229, 271
Watkins, J. W., 18
Watkins process, 293
Way, F., 314, 315, 316
Webb, Beatrice, 99
Webb, Sydney, 94, 99
Weld, F. A., 42

# INDEX

Wellington (NSW), 272
Western Australia, 85, 272
Western Miners' Association, 131, 133
Whittington Iron Works (UK), 17
Whyalla (SA), 172, 187, 210, 229, 271
Wigham, F. H., 79
Wilkinson, John, 7
William Fairbairn and Sons (UK), 12
Williams, D., 56, 60, 67
Williams, E., 139
Williams, L. A., 246
Wilmot & Morgan, 84
Wilputte coke ovens, 198, 274
Wollongong, 285
Wongawilli (NSW), 285, 288, 300

Wood, W. H., 178
Wood, Walter, 277
workers, *see* Australia, labour; ironworkers; unions
World War I, 183, 197, 208
Wright, Sir Charles, 293

Yarwood, Mr, 316
Yates, Mr, 249
Young, Sir John, 18
Younghusband, William, 5

Zig-Zag railway (NSW), 54
Zollner, S., 18, 22, 33